MW01169319

EVIDENCE AND INNOVATION IN HOUSING LAW AND POLICY

No area of law and policy is more central to our well-being than housing, yet research on the topic is too often produced in disciplinary or methodological silos that fail to connect to policy on the ground. This pathbreaking book, which features leading scholars from a range of academic fields, cuts across disciplines to forge new connections in the discourse. In accessible prose filled with cutting-edge ideas, these scholars address topics ranging from the recent financial crisis to discrimination and gentrification and show how housing law and policy impacts household wealth, financial markets, urban landscapes, and local communities. Together, they harness evidence and theory to capture the "state of play" in housing, generating insights that will be relevant to academics and policy makers alike. This title is also available as Open Access on Cambridge Core at http://dx.doi.org/10.1017/9781316691335.

Lee Anne Fennell is Max Pam Professor of Law and the co-director of the Kreisman Initiative on Housing Law and Policy at the University of Chicago Law School. Her teaching and research interests include property, torts, land use, housing, social welfare law, state and local government law, and public finance. She is the author of *The Unbounded Home: Property Values Beyond Property Lines* (2009).

Benjamin J. Keys is an assistant professor of real estate at the Wharton School at the University of Pennsylvania and a Faculty Research Fellow of the National Bureau of Economic Research. He previously served as co-director of the Kreisman Initiative while an assistant professor at the Harris School of Public Policy at the University of Chicago. Keys's research interests include connections between mortgage finance, household finance, and macroeconomics. His work has been published in academic journals such as the *American Economic Review* and the *Quarterly Journal of Economics*.

Evidence and Innovation in Housing Law and Policy

Edited by

LEE ANNE FENNELL

University of Chicago Law School

BENJAMIN J. KEYS

Wharton School, University of Pennsylvania

CAMBRIDGE
UNIVERSITY PRESS

CAMBRIDGE
UNIVERSITY PRESS

University Printing House, Cambridge CB2 8BS, United Kingdom

One Liberty Plaza, 20th Floor, New York, NY 10006, USA

477 Williamstown Road, Port Melbourne, VIC 3207, Australia

4843/24, 2nd Floor, Ansari Road, Daryaganj, Delhi – 110002, India

79 Anson Road, #06–04/06, Singapore 079906

Cambridge University Press is part of the University of Cambridge.

It furthers the University's mission by disseminating knowledge in the pursuit of
education, learning, and research at the highest international levels of excellence.

www.cambridge.org
Information on this title: www.cambridge.org/9781107164925
DOI: 10.1017/9781316691335

© Cambridge University Press 2017

First published 2017

Printed in the United Kingdom by Clays, St Ives plc

A catalogue record for this publication is available from the British Library.

Library of Congress Cataloging-in-Publication Data
NAMES: Fennell, Lee Anne, editor. | Keys, Benjamin J., editor.
TITLE: Evidence and innovation in housing law and policy / edited by Lee Anne Fennell,
Benjamin J. Keys.
DESCRIPTION: Cambridge [UK] ; New York : Cambridge University Press, 2017.
IDENTIFIERS: LCCN 2017020504 | ISBN 9781107164925 (hardback)
SUBJECTS: LCSH: Housing – Law and legislation. | Housing policy. | BISAC: LAW / General.
CLASSIFICATION: LCC K3550 .E95 2017 | DDC 344/.063635–dc23
LC record available at https://lccn.loc.gov/2017020504

ISBN 978-1-107-16492-5 Hardback

Contents

Figures

Tables

Contributors

Ian Ayres is William K. Townsend Professor at Yale Law School, the Anne Urowsky Professorial Fellow in Law, and a professor at Yale's School of Management. Professor Ayres has been a columnist for *Forbes* magazine, a commentator on public radio's *Marketplace*, and a contributor to the *New York Times' Freakonomics* blog. He has published 11 books, including the *New York Times* best seller, *Super Crunchers*, and more than 100 articles on a wide range of topics. In 2006, he was elected to the American Academy of Arts and Sciences.

Raphael W. Bostic is Judith and John Bedrosian Chair in Governance and the Public Enterprise at the University of Southern California's Price School of Public Policy. For three years, he was the Obama administration's Assistant Secretary for Policy Development and Research at the U.S. Department of Housing and Urban Development (HUD). In that Senate-confirmed principal position, he advised HUD's secretary on policy and research to promote informed decisions on HUD policies, programs, and budget, and on legislative proposals.

Matthew Desmond is John L. Loeb Associate Professor of the Social Sciences at Harvard University and co-director of the Justice and Poverty Project. The author of four books, including *Evicted: Poverty and Profit in the American City* (2016), Desmond is a sociologist of poverty in America. His work has been supported by the Ford, Russell Sage, Gates, and National Science Foundations, and his writing has appeared in the *New York Times*, *The New Yorker*, and the *Chicago Tribune*. In 2015, Desmond was awarded a MacArthur "Genius" grant.

Ingrid Gould Ellen is Paulette Goddard Professor of Urban Policy and Planning at NYU's Robert F. Wagner Graduate School of Public Service and the faculty director of the NYU Furman Center. Her research centers on neighborhoods, housing, and residential segregation. Ellen is the author of *Sharing America's Neighborhoods: The Prospects for Stable Racial Integration* (2000) and the editor of *How to House the Homeless* (2010). She has published articles on housing and urban policy in a wide variety of academic journals and books.

Richard A. Epstein is Laurence A. Tisch Professor of Law at NYU Law School, Peter and Kirsten Bedford Senior Fellow at the Hoover Institution, and James Parker Hall Distinguished Service Professor Emeritus of Law and Senior Lecturer at the University of Chicago, where he was on the regular faculty from 1973 to 2010. His books include *Takings: Private Property and Eminent Domain* (1985), *Simple Rules for a Complex World* (1995), and *Skepticism and Freedom: A Modern Case for Classical Liberalism* (2003).

William A. Fischel is Professor of Economics and Hardy Professor of Legal Studies at Dartmouth College. He is the author of *Zoning Rules! The Economics of Land Use Regulation* (2015), which combines Fischel's scholarship, his students' insights, and his service on the Hanover Zoning Board to explain how zoning works and affects the American economy. Fischel's previous work on the economics of land use regulation includes *The Economics of Zoning Laws* (1985), *Regulatory Takings* (1995), and *The Homevoter Hypothesis* (2001).

Gary Klein is senior trial counsel in the Office of Massachusetts Attorney General Maura Healey, where he works on special projects in the Public Protection and Advocacy Bureau. Among other things, he has worked to investigate the availability of mortgage credit in the Commonwealth's low-income and minority communities. Mr. Klein has litigated groundbreaking cases against mortgage lenders and servicers, including class action cases challenging the predatory lending practices of Ameriquest Mortgage Corporation and Household Finance.

Christopher J. Mayer is Paul Milstein Professor of Real Estate and Finance and Economics at Columbia Business School, and CEO of Longbridge Financial, a start-up reverse mortgage lender. He serves as a research associate at the National Bureau of Economic Research, a director of the National Reverse Mortgage Lenders Association, and a member of the Academic Advisory Boards for Standard and Poor's and the Housing Policy Center at the Urban Institute. Mayer has also testified before congressional committees and wrote a commissioned paper for the Financial Crisis Inquiry Commission. His research has been funded by the National Science Foundation and the Pew Charitable Trusts.

Brian J. McCabe is an assistant professor of sociology at Georgetown University and a research affiliate at NYU's Furman Center for Real Estate and Urban Policy. His research focuses on housing, historic preservation, and social inequalities in American cities. McCabe is the author of *No Place Like Home: Wealth, Community and the Politics of Homeownership* (2016).

Patricia A. McCoy is Liberty Mutual Insurance Professor at Boston College Law School. In 2010–2011, she headed the Mortgage Markets group at the newly formed federal Consumer Financial Protection Bureau in Washington, DC. Previously a member of the Consumer Advisory Council of the Federal Reserve Board of

Governors and of the board of directors of the Insurance Marketplace Standards Association, McCoy now sits on the Advisory Committee on Economic Inclusion of the Federal Deposit Insurance Corporation. Professor McCoy's latest book, *The Subprime Virus* (written with Kathleen C. Engel), was published in 2011.

Atif Mian is Theodore A. Wells '29 Professor of Economics and Public Affairs at Princeton University and director of the Julis-Rabinowitz Center for Public Policy and Finance at the Woodrow Wilson School. His latest book, *House of Debt* (2014), with Amir Sufi, builds on powerful new data to describe how debt precipitated the Great Recession. Mian's research has appeared in top academic journals, including the *American Economic Review*, *Econometrica*, *Quarterly Journal of Economics*, *Journal of Finance*, *Review of Financial Studies*, and *Journal of Financial Economics*.

Anthony W. Orlando is a PhD student in public policy and management at the Sol Price School of Public Policy at the University of Southern California. He is a lecturer in the College of Business and Economics at California State University, Los Angeles, an op-ed columnist for the *Huffington Post*, and the managing partner of the Orlando Investment Group. His latest book, *Letter to the One Percent*, was published in November 2013.

Georgette Chapman Phillips is Kevin and Lisa Clayton Dean of the College of Business and Economics and a faculty member in the Perella Department of Finance at Lehigh University. Additionally, she holds an appointment in the Africana Studies Program in the College of Arts and Sciences. Dean Phillips's teaching and research focuses on the intersection of law, economics, and public policy within the context of the built environment. She publishes in the areas of urban/regional planning and local government law.

David Schleicher is an associate professor of law at Yale Law School and is an expert in election law, land use, local government law, and urban development. His work has been published widely in academic journals as well as in popular outlets. His scholarship focuses on state and local elections, the relationship between local government law and agglomeration economics, and pathologies in land use politics and procedure. Schleicher was previously an associate professor of law at George Mason University School of Law, where he won the university's Teaching Excellence Award.

Stephanie M. Stern is a professor of law at the IIT Chicago-Kent College of Law specializing in property and environmental law. Professor Stern's research addresses housing policy, land use, and applications of behavioral law and economics to property law. Her past work has studied the psychology of homeownership and its implications for property law and the consequences of fostering social capital through land use law.

Lior Jacob Strahilevitz is Sidley Austin Professor of Law at the University of Chicago, where he has taught since 2002. He teaches and writes in the areas of property and land use law, privacy law, intellectual property, contract law, and law and technology. Strahilevitz is the author of *Information and Exclusion* (2011) and numerous law review articles, and he is also a coauthor of the leading property law textbook in the United States with Jesse Dukeminier, James Krier, Greg Alexander, and Mike Schill.

Amir Sufi is Bruce Lindsay Professor of Economics and Public Policy at the University of Chicago Booth School of Business. He is also a research associate at the National Bureau of Economic Research. His recent research on household debt and the economy was profiled in major media outlets and presented to policy makers at the Federal Reserve, the Senate Committee on Banking, Housing, Urban Affairs, and the White House Council of Economic Advisors. This research forms the basis for his book with Atif Mian, *House of Debt* (2014).

Susan Wachter is Albert Sussman Professor of Real Estate, a professor of finance at The Wharton School, and the co-director of Penn Institute of Urban Research at the University of Pennsylvania. From 1998 to 2001, Wachter served as Assistant Secretary for Policy Development and Research, U.S. Department of Housing and Urban Development. At the Wharton School, she was Chairperson of the Real Estate Department and Professor of Real Estate and Finance from July 1997 until her 1998 appointment to HUD. She founded and currently serves as Director of Wharton's Geographical Information Systems Lab. Wachter was the editor of *Real Estate Economics* from 1997 to 1999 and currently serves on multiple editorial boards. She is the author of more than 200 scholarly publications. Wachter currently serves on the Financial Research Advisory Committee for the Office of Financial Research, in the U.S. Department of the Treasury.

Jeffrey West is an independent economic consultant in Arlington, Virginia, who frequently works with other economists from academia and consulting firms such as Precision Economics and Navigant. Mr. West has served as a consultant in dozens of litigation matters involving the origination and servicing of mortgages. Through his work on these matters, Mr. West has analyzed the loan pricing, product placement, loan modification, and foreclosure practices of many of the largest lenders and secondary market participants in the mortgage industry.

Acknowledgments

This book grew out of a conference that the Kreisman Initiative on Housing Law and Policy convened in June 2016 in downtown Chicago at the University of Chicago's Gleacher Center. The impetus behind the conference – and the animating vision for this book – was to break down barriers in what is often a fragmented academic discussion around housing issues, and to generate new policy-relevant ideas as well as a springboard for further discussion. We could not have realized that vision without the engaged, thoughtful, and spirited participation of all of the conference participants, and we are grateful to all who attended. In particular, we thank the discussants who provided commentary on the chapters included here: Vicki Been, Brian Brooks, Kate Cagney, Nestor Davidson, Nicole Garnett, Daniel Kay Hertz, William Hubbard, Damon Jones, John Mangin, Eduardo Peñalver, Karen Pence, and Luigi Zingales. We are also indebted to our conference moderators, whose expert syntheses and guidance of the discussion made the event unusually generative: Daniel Biss, David Dana, Jeff Leslie, Paul Shadle, Geoff Smith, and Janet Smith.

We also thank Thomas J. Miles, dean of the University of Chicago Law School, and Daniel Diermeier, provost of the University of Chicago (and former dean of the Harris School of Public Policy) for their support of the event and resulting book project, as well as Michael Schill, former dean of the University of Chicago Law School, for encouraging us at the crucial early stages of this project. We are indebted to many people who have provided support behind the scenes, but most especially Curtrice Scott, who orchestrated every aspect of the conference's execution and played a key role in ensuring that this book came together as planned.

Finally, we extend our deep gratitude to David and Susan Kreisman, whose generosity through the Kreisman Initiative on Housing Law and Policy at the University of Chicago Law School made the conference and this book possible. We are honored to have the opportunity to advance a truly Chicago-style spirit of rigorous interdisciplinary dialogue around the crucial issue of housing through this project, and we look forward to continuing the conversation in the future.

Introduction

Lee Anne Fennell and Benjamin J. Keys

No area of law and policy presents more important and pressing questions, or ones more central to human well-being, than that of housing. Yet academic discourse around housing is too often siloed into separate topical areas and disciplinary approaches, while remaining distanced from the contentious housing policy debates unfolding in communities across the nation. In June 2016, the Kreisman Initiative on Housing Law and Policy at the University of Chicago Law School convened a conference in downtown Chicago with the goal of breaking down these barriers and forging new connections – between different facets of housing law and policy, between different disciplinary approaches to housing issues, between academic inquiry and applied policy, and between the lessons of the past and adaptations for the future.

This volume is the product of that conference and the dialogue it provoked among academics, practitioners, and policy makers. Its baker's dozen of contributions comprises cutting-edge interdisciplinary work on housing and housing finance from leading scholars in law, economics, and policy. The pieces individually and collectively showcase how research and policy can come together in the housing arena. We hope the end result will have lasting relevance in setting the course – and identifying the obstacles – for housing law and policy going forward.

This book is organized around two interlocking roles that housing serves: as a vehicle for building community, and as a vehicle for building wealth. These facets of housing carry implications both for the households who consume residential services and for the larger economic, political, and spatial domains in which housing plays such a primary and contentious role. Cumulatively, the pieces here confront, and respond innovatively to, the dilemmas that these two facets of housing create for law and policy at different scales of analysis.

Part I takes a wide-lensed look at how housing fits into the larger metropolis and the communities and spatial structures contained within it. The contributions in this part consider the ways in which decisions about land use controls, transportation, and housing affordability shape where and how people live. Zoning regulations heavily influence the quantity and location of different kinds of housing stock throughout the urban landscape, and their restrictiveness plays a key role in inflating home prices. William Fischel's chapter pushes beyond these well-documented findings to interrogate the causal mechanisms at play. Restrictive zoning policies are not just the *cause* of rising home prices, he posits; they are also the *result* of rising home prices. In his view, escalating home prices in the 1970s turned homeowners, who had previously seen the home as just a place to live, into a powerful interest group – "homevoters" – bent on employing local politics to protect the value of what they now saw as a growth stock.

Homeowners thus became intensely motivated to mobilize against development, which they perceived as a threat to the value of the household's single largest asset, the home. One way they did so, Fischel explains, was by allying themselves with the then-nascent environmental movement, which provided protective cover for their less-than-selfless goals. This account underscores the connections between different land use agendas and interest groups, as well as between different elements of housing policy. Fischel argues that tax breaks for homeownership help fuel a cycle of overinvestment in housing that contributes to overprotective land use policies and higher housing prices, which in turn reinforce a vision of the home as a household's primary growth asset. His analysis also emphasizes path dependence, as home-owners sort into communities that feature the restrictive land use policies that they favor, further entrenching the political will to preserve or tighten those restrictions. In this way, housing policy begets housing policy, and breaking the cycle requires rethinking the forces – including tax policy – that contribute to this entrenchment.

Interconnectedness and path dependence also feature heavily in David Schleicher's contribution, which examines interactions between land use controls and transportation innovations – from the now-familiar GPS systems for cars, to popular ride-hailing services like Uber and Lyft, to emerging developments in autonomous vehicles. These and other transportation innovations might make one's existing commute easier, but, as Schleicher explains, their real power lies in their capacity to transform where housing can be located relative to workplaces and other points of interest. Schleicher argues that innovative shifts in transit could make useful new forms of "distributed density" possible. But if the real estate development that would produce these patterns is prohibited by existing land use controls and cannot be readily changed – and Fischel's analysis suggests some reasons why this might be the case – transportation technologies may be unable to fulfill their potential in contributing to more functional urban agglomerations. In fact, Schleicher suggests, we might see new transit technologies used in the service of increased sprawl as autonomous vehicles and similar innovations enable longer commutes by rendering them less tedious and unproductive.

Whether one urban pattern is to be preferred over another is of course a normative question, one that raises broader questions of what makes for a good city or a good way of life. While land use controls can thwart the realization of preferences, they can also at times solve collective action problems and address costly externalities.

What is certain is that the future placement of housing stock within the metropolis will depend not just on the possibilities that transportation innovations open up, but also on the avenues that land use controls shut down – for better or worse. Schleicher's work prompts thoughtful attention to transportation policy as an element in housing policy (and vice versa), and highlights land use law as foundational to both.

The third chapter in Part I examines another facet of land use policy as it relates to housing: "inclusionary zoning" laws that require housing developers to set aside a certain percentage of units in their projects for affordable housing. Although the details of these laws vary widely, they have in common the goal of enhancing housing affordability in areas that are undergoing new residential development, typically by requiring the in-kind provision of affordable units or the payment of an "in lieu of" fee for the development of affordable housing offsite. Using the recent California Supreme Court case *California Building Industry Association v. City of San Jose* (2015) as a springboard, Richard Epstein argues that such laws are counterproductive as a matter of economics, and should be impermissible as a matter of constitutional law.

Epstein's economic argument is straightforward. If the business of residential development is made more expensive by a requirement to provide affordable units, we would expect to see less residential development – something that would reduce supply and be bad for housing affordability. What complicates the picture, however, is the fact that these inclusionary zoning mandates are enacted against a backdrop of pervasive regulation of housing stock – the zoning restrictions that were the subject of Fischel's chapter and that featured prominently in Schleicher's. Under a typical inclusionary zoning ordinance, developers are permitted to build more housing or build it at higher densities than would otherwise be allowed if they provide the required number of affordable units. What, then, is the appropriate baseline when assessing the impact of such an ordinance on housing supply: a world without any other restrictions on developing housing, or the already heavily restricted world in which developers seek to build?

Answering this question leads us to Epstein's legal analysis. His interpretation of the takings clause eschews the distinctions that the Supreme Court uses to determine when a regulation is so invasive or confiscatory as to require just compensation. In Epstein's view, *every* diminution in the value of property is a taking that must be accompanied by just compensation, whether in cash or in kind. Thus, although Epstein focuses his critique in this chapter on affordable housing mandates, his legal and economic critiques extend broadly to a range of land use controls that constrain owners and restrict housing supply – including those that provide the backdrop against which affordable housing mandates operate. Given the capacity of the government to set these background conditions, the deal extended to developers through inclusionary zoning ordinances is, in Epstein's view, an impermissible land use exaction. Epstein's chapter thus prompts readers not only to investigate when well-intentioned laws might have unintended consequences, but also to consider how the burdens associated with achieving housing policy goals should be distributed among members of society.

Part II zooms in to consider how community identity and resident perceptions shape the housing consumption experience. A recurring theme is the interplay between stability and change in residential neighborhoods. One tool for managing these tensions is through historical preservation initiatives, through which individual landmarks or entire neighborhoods are protected from redevelopment. In their chapter, Ingrid Gould Ellen and Brian McCabe argue for more explicit and balanced assessments of the costs and benefits of historic preservation. They offer a compelling approach to estimating development constraints imposed by preservation initiatives in historic districts. By estimating the amount of unbuilt floor area within a district, and comparing the density of historic districts to their undesignated but nearby counterparts, Ellen and McCabe provide a clear methodology for measuring the direct costs of preservation.

Their evidence from New York City suggests that supply restrictions in historic districts reduce density, increase prices and rents, and likely exacerbate economic segregation. Ellen and McCabe conclude by recommending a restructuring of the preservation decision-making process in New York City, highlighting the need for independent assessments beyond the Landmarks Preservation Commission, a formal comment from the City Planning Commission, an "as of right" framework for construction on vacant and non-contributing sites, and a direct estimated impact on housing supply. Their analysis highlights the fact that historic preservation is at its core land use regulation, with development-suppressing effects that echo those identified by Fischel, Schleicher, and Epstein in Part I. While the countervailing benefits of neighborhood stability and landmark preservation are acutely difficult to measure, this chapter provides a necessary rethinking of the costs of historic district designation.

Historical preservation is, of course, a central way in which communities construct and preserve their identities – and, in so doing, influence the composition of their populations. Lior Strahilevitz's chapter raises pointed questions about this process by focusing on a setting where history is literally manufactured out of thin air. The Villages, a set of retirement communities in Florida, seeds its walkable and golf-cartable "downtown" areas with dozens of plaques recounting fictitious historical events, and pairs them with suitably themed and distressed buildings featuring peeling signs from a nonexistent past. While this overlay of artifice strikes some observers as rather creepy on its own terms, more troubling is the uncanny degree of racial homogeneity that exists in The Villages – despite its location in a diverse region, its residents are overwhelmingly white. Strahilevitz raises the possibility that contrived history could serve as a kind of "exclusionary amenity" that induces residential sorting along racial lines. But he does much more than this: he provocatively suggests that "real" history is nearly as inauthentic, and fully capable of operating in an equally exclusionary fashion.

The kind of history that gets preserved through land use law, Strahilevitz observes, is always highly selective. If preservationists were serious about preserving the past, he suggests, choosing random buildings from particular eras would do a better job, and at less social cost. Recognizing that all history is consciously constructed and curated should weaken any reflexive normative deference to preserving the past in setting land use policy. Strahilevitz's contribution pushes us not only to examine carefully the sorts of costs that Ellen and McCabe explore, but also to question the benefit side of the equation as well. Counterintuitively, false histories may serve just as well – or just as poorly – as anchors for community identity. And if historical truth is not necessary for establishing a community's identity, neither is it sufficient, as Strahilevitz's randomization thought experiment emphasizes.

Ultimately, the case for preserving or redeveloping the past must turn on its impacts on the residents – present and potential – who stand to gain or lose. That community change brings losers as well as winners comes through clearly in Georgette Phillips's contribution, which examines the repurposing of churches for secular ends, including upscale condominiums and lofts. Church conversions typically follow dramatic attrition in church membership in particular areas and offer the potential both to generate funds for the church (through the sale of valuable, well-positioned real estate) and to inject new development into a foundering area. But because churches serve as more than worship centers and play a crucial role in delivering services to the communities in which they are located, the conversion process may have ripple effects that undermine the viability of the remaining community and accelerate community change. Phillips considers a variety of approaches to this dilemma, which is sharpened by the fact that land use restrictions may often limit the introduction of stand-alone community service providers, and suggests the use of impact fees to induce decision makers – whether developers or churches – to internalize the effects of their choices on the community.

Church conversions to condominiums may be largely a symptom rather than a cause of the decline in the community for which the church served as anchor and mainstay, and could even be a marker of a shift to a more diverse community that is no longer centered around a single faith tradition. Nonetheless, the phenomenon could exacerbate a trend toward gentrification in the area, spurring fears of involuntary displacement or a diminished neighborhood experience. Even though housing is being added to the mix, a fact that should advance housing affordability, there may be concerns that the new housing stock will be configured and priced in a way that would place it out of reach for the original residents who are simultaneously losing services.

Some of the more subtle and pernicious effects of involuntary displacement from one's home are explored in Matthew Desmond's chapter. Desmond finds that renters who arrived in their neighborhood through "forced moves" (via eviction, foreclosure, or building condemnation) were half as likely to trust their neighbors relative to other renters, and far more likely to perceive suffering in their neighborhood. Such perceptions of the neighborhood will have a key impact on residents' willingness to strengthen neighborhood ties, improve local public goods like schools and parks, and participate in local government. Desmond explores the role of housing dynamics and neighborhood perceptions using data from a survey of renters in Milwaukee, Wisconsin. The survey both measured the degree to which renters trusted their neighbors, and asked a series of questions regarding the perception of social problems in the neighborhood.

Crucially, the analysis accounts for neighborhood quality and housing characteristics, so this comparison isolates a difference in perceptions about their current neighborhood between renters with and without a forced relocation. Renters who found their housing through government or nonprofit agencies also held a more negative view of their neighborhood. Desmond's work raises new questions regarding the importance of housing dynamics in determining a resident's outlook on her community. The results from this timely and ambitious study should encourage policy makers to revisit the eviction process, temporary housing alternatives, and source-of-income discrimination laws to help low-income families improve their level of trust in community. It also carries implications for the ways in which housing policy assists homeseekers.

Housing is not only central to residents' sense of community, it is also critical to their financial well-being. Part III thus turns to the wealth-building facet of housing policy, considered from the perspective of the housing consumer. Homeownership is often viewed as virtually the only viable path to significant wealth building for most Americans. It offers both a highly leveraged stake in a large asset and an automatic vehicle for regular savings, while at the same time controlling housing expenditures over time. There are some problems with this vision of homeownership, however. Not only is the home an undiversified asset that is highly vulnerable to risks that lie out of the homeowner's control, as the recent foreclosure crisis dramatically demonstrated, it may also prompt the sorts of risk-averse defensive behaviors that Fischel identifies, which raise the costs of housing by limiting development. Moreover, discrimination in housing finance can derail a household's wealth-building plans and produce devastating setbacks by making mortgages unnecessarily expensive and risky. The chapters in this part take on these challenges from a number of perspectives.

Variations on homeownership that would reduce the amount of housing market risk that households must bear have received some attention, but the potential for a variation on the rental model to deliver some of the wealth-building benefits of homeownership has been almost entirely ignored. Stephanie Stern takes up this topic in her chapter by examining some emerging models of "renter equity" that enable tenants to build up savings for undertaking particular behaviors. While these models do not extend a true equity stake to renters, they do provide an automatic savings vehicle with vesting rules that encourage staying put in one's residence – and leaving the money in place to grow – as well as an incentive structure that rewards the kinds of behaviors, including maintenance and upkeep, in which homeowners often engage. Selection effects make evaluating this form of tenancy tricky, however, and the fact that existing models bundle multiple features together makes tracing causal mechanisms difficult. Stern's contribution highlights the importance of parsing these effects and queues up a set of empirically testable questions for future researchers to pursue. It also emphasizes the importance of taking into account the findings of behavioral law and economics about human cognition, willpower, and precommitment in setting housing policy.

Homeownership has traditionally enabled wealth accumulation through self-amortizing mortgages that represent a form of automatic or forced savings. As the baby boomers reach retirement, a crucial source of wealth and opportunity is tied up in their homes. More than 75 percent of retirees own (and have substantial equity in) their homes. In his chapter, Christopher Mayer explores the relationship between homeownership and retirement stability, connecting a number of disparate datasets and measures of financial health. Mayer documents that over the past two decades mortgage debt has increased substantially among older cohorts, especially those nearing retirement age. Furthermore, more households are entering retirement without fully paying off their mortgages. Thus, mortgage debt will serve as a greater burden on consumption in retirement years. Mayer also finds that few households pay down debt by selling their homes, keeping much of their equity in their homes until very late in life. The results suggest that baby boomers' decisions on how and when to extract equity from their homes, either through downsizing or reverse mortgages, will determine much of their financial health during their retirement years. This analysis carries important legal and policy implications, as it bears on the choice sets and protections that will be most useful to housing consumers over the life cycle.

The capacity of households to build wealth through homeownership can be thoroughly undermined by invidious discrimination, as the contribution of Ian Ayres, Gary Klein, and Jeffrey West demonstrates. Ayres and his coauthors show how discretion granted to mortgage brokers led to higher-cost mortgages for African American and Hispanic borrowers for reasons unrelated to the substantive measures of creditworthiness built into lenders' underwriting algorithms. Not only do these more costly mortgages undercut efforts to accumulate equity, they also increase the risk of foreclosure. Moreover, because of entrenched residential segregation, the prevalence of high-cost loans in communities of color – "reverse redlining" – produces a negative synergy of heightened risk as proximate foreclosures cause property values to fall, making further foreclosures more likely. The resulting involuntary moves can be personally as well as financially devastating for households.

Disparate impact analysis might seem to provide a promising avenue for redress, especially in the wake of the Supreme Court's recent decision in *Texas Department of Housing & Community Affairs v. The Inclusive Communities Project* (2015), which recognized the validity of the disparate impact cause of action under the Fair Housing Act. But as Ayres and his coauthors show, there are significant legal road-blocks in the path. In *Inclusive Communities* itself, the Supreme Court articulated tight causation requirements that may be difficult for litigants to meet. Another hurdle is found in another Supreme Court decision, *Wal-Mart Stores v. Dukes* (2011), that suggests individual discretion of the type exercised by mortgage brokers might not constitute the sort of unified policy that could be subject to legal attack through a class action lawsuit. As a result, Ayres, Klein, and West suggest that meaningful relief may depend on the choices of government actors such as the Consumer Financial Protection Bureau. The evidence that this chapter marshals showing the costs to minority households from inappropriate and excessively expensive mortgage products provides an important input for future legal and policy initiatives.

Part IV examines housing finance's role from a broader economic perspective. In a series of influential papers, Atif Mian and Amir Sufi have investigated the relationship between credit supply and the recent housing bubble. In their chapter in this volume, the authors provide additional new evidence that supports the "credit supply view" of the boom and bust. Their chapter establishes four key facts about the boom and bust. First, mortgage credit grew independently from economic conditions. Second, this credit growth directly increased house prices. Third, home equity extraction was a common response to house price growth. Fourth and finally, the default of homeowners with lower credit scores precipitated the broader default crisis.

Using a range of data sources, Mian and Sufi carefully document these four facts, and conclude that the financial sector played a crucial role in explaining the boom and bust. The centrality of the financial sector suggests a role for macro-prudential regulation, such as countercyclical loan-to-value restrictions. The credit supply view also supports the need for innovation in mortgage contracts to spread risk more broadly, reduce leverage, and infuse more equity into a highly levered system that amplifies housing cycles.

A key element of the modern mortgage system is the transformation of mortgage debt from an asset on the originator's balance sheet to a tradable security through securitization. However, securitization passes nearly all mortgage risk from the originator to the securities market. Contractual obligations, such as legal representations and warranties regarding the quality of the mortgage loans being sold, are supposed to assure investors that underwriting standards are kept at a high level.

In their chapter, Patricia McCoy and Susan Wachter examine why representations and warranties failed to protect the securitization system. They argue that, prior to 2008, the representations gave investors false assurance, which led to overinvestment in mortgage-backed securities (MBS). However, after the bust and massive losses on these securities, the securitization system has been hampered by excessively restrictive representations and warranties, and the enforcement of those provisions, leading to underinvestment in MBS and an underprovision of mortgage credit. McCoy and Wachter conclude that lenders should have been required to build up reserves to cover representation and warranty enforcement; they propose stricter capital standards to ensure that lenders have more ability to withstand the inevitable housing cycles of the future.

In this book's final chapter, Raphael Bostic and Anthony Orlando examine three causes of the housing crisis that have received little scrutiny from regulators thus far. First, the authors argue that nothing has been done to prevent firm owners and managers from "looting" their firms at the expense of long-run profitability for shareholders. This disconnect between short-run and long-run incentives may be best addressed by reforms in executive compensation and increased penalties for over-weighting the short-run financial gains over the long-run viability of the firm. Next, the authors examine why the credit ratings agencies failed to impose market discipline on mortgage lending. They outline the problematic agency–investor conflicts of interest inherent in the "issuer pays" model of credit ratings, and propose a structure to mitigate these issues. Third and finally, the authors shed new light on the tradeoff between access to credit and risk exposure in consumer credit markets. They emphasize the potential for greater financial literacy, as well as the possibility of creating subsidies for lending to creditworthy low-income borrowers.

With a colorful set of historical examples, Bostic and Orlando's chapter creatively charts out a series of reform proposals for making the financial system smarter and safer. Although it is not possible to anticipate the novel problems that the future will bring, some of the long-standing tensions and incentive mismatches that emerged in the recent crisis had deep roots in the past, and deserve continued attention going forward. There are recurring tensions between access to credit and vulnerability to risk, and between financial innovation and concerns for stability. And, as other chapters in this book emphasize in a variety of ways, the stakes could not be higher. People's lives are deeply bound up in the places that they live, both financially and experientially. Housing policy also carries repercussions for, and is impacted by, everything that affects the spatial structure of our urban areas and the soundness of our financial systems.

In all, this book's broad-ranging scope and mix of methodologies provide an unprecedented, holistic look at how these facets of the housing puzzle interact. At the same time, the contributions we bring together here are only the start of a series of important and necessary conversations around housing. We look forward to continuing the dialogue.

PART I

Housing and the Metropolis: Law and Policy Perspectives

The Rise of the Homevoters: How the Growth Machine Was Subverted by OPEC and Earth Day

William A. Fischel

1.1 INTRODUCTION

In the 1970s, unprecedented peacetime inflation, touched off by the oil cartel OPEC, combined with long-standing federal tax privileges to transform owner-occupied homes into growth stocks in the eyes of their owners. The inability to insure their homes' newfound value converted homeowners into "homevoters," whose local political behavior focused on preventing development that might hinder the rise in their home values. Homevoters seized on the nascent national environmental movement, epitomized by Earth Day, and modified its agenda to serve local demands. The coalition of homeowners and environmentalists thereby eroded the power of the pro-development coalition called the "growth machine," which had formerly moderated zoning. As this chapter shows, these changes in the meaning of homeownership and in the political behavior of homeowners explain why local zoning has become so restrictive.

Zoning is not a new institution. Housing in the United States has been the subject of comprehensive local government regulation since 1916, when New York adopted the nation's first zoning laws. Zoning spread rapidly to other cities, and now almost all cities and towns in urban areas have zoning and a host of related land use regulations (Fischel 2015). It is now well established that in certain areas of the nation – the Northeast and West Coast especially – local land use regulation is associated with unusually high housing prices. The excessive housing prices retard mobility of labor, reduce national productivity, and worsen income inequality (Ganong and Shoag 2013). Some have also argued that the inelastic supply of housing contributed to the 2000s housing bubble and the financial crisis that resulted when it burst (Jansen and Mills 2013).

This chapter seeks to establish that the restrictive zoning policies that contributed to the housing crisis arose at a particular time – the 1970s – in conjunction with worldwide inflation and American political movements that undermined the transactional relationship between local governments and developers. Evidence presented here establishes that the 1970s represented a sharp break with the past. It is important to understand both the history and probable causes of growth controls in order to shape reasonable responses to excessive land use regulation.

My empirical contribution in this chapter is something called Ngrams. Not shown are some other trends that are important but hardly novel. The first is that the time trend of real housing prices (that is, adjusted for inflation) in the post–World War II era was flat or gradually falling up to about 1970 (Shiller 2015, 20). In the early 1970s, real housing prices rose rapidly for several years, fell during the recessions of 1981 and 1991, and then rose at an accelerated rate until the financial crash of 2007. Up to about 1970, owning a house was not a good investment relative to stocks and bonds. After 1970, it became a major portion of middle-class financial portfolios and thus subject to macroeconomic and local risks (Skinner 1994, 191).

My major thesis is that homeowners once looked on their houses as places to live, but now look at them as growth stocks. This is not a new claim. In *Irrational Exuberance*, Robert Shiller wrote, "Life was simpler once; one saved and then bought a home when the time was right. One expected to buy a home as part of normal living and didn't think to worry what would happen to the price of homes. The increasingly large role of speculative markets for homes, as well as of other markets, has fundamentally changed our lives" (2015, 35). My contribution is to point out that one of the fundamental changes has been to make homeowners acutely defensive about new developments that might possibly affect their homes' value. My theory inverts, or at least complicates, the claim that growth controls cause higher housing prices. It is possible that growth controls themselves are caused by inflating housing prices, which goad homeowners to organize more effectively against developers. It might be better for all concerned if homeowners could again see their homes as steady investments and good places to live rather than a way to get rich.

1.2 NGRAMS AND THE ORIGINS OF GROWTH CONTROLS

Google has a free on-line feature called the Ngram Viewer. It graphs the annual frequency of uses of a word or phrase in Google's digitized collection of millions of books, scanned mostly from university libraries. (It does not include newspapers or periodicals.) The word or phrase can be used in any context, and simply being mentioned more or less frequently can be a measure of its salience in public discourse.

Ngrams may offer clues about why zoning was adopted in the United States. I had written an article that argued that zoning's rapid rise and spread in the 1910 to 1930 era was caused by the spread of low-cost automobiles and, more particularly, their adaptations as freight trucks and inexpensive passenger buses, the latter popularly called *jitneys* (Fischel 2004). Motorized trucks and jitneys enabled industry and apartment houses to relocate from ports, railheads, and central cities to the suburbs.

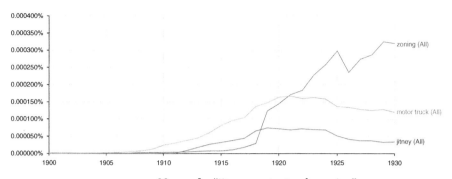

FIGURE 1.1 Ngram for "jitney, motor truck, zoning"
Source: Author's Ngram. Courtesy of http:books.google.com/ngrams

In an early planning publication, a zoning advocate complained, "The motor-truck has enabled the indifferent or the blackmailing industrial concern to threaten to locate its factory in the heart of the loveliest of lawn-decorated suburbs. Formerly a factory had to be near a railroad, but that is no longer necessary. It is, indeed, more desirable for a factory to locate near a labor supply – that is, near a district where labor lives – than to be near a railroad" (L. Purdy et al. 1920, 6). Homebuyers' reluctance to commit to a large purchase that might be devalued by subsequent development was the main reason responsible developer organizations sought to promote zoning (Weiss 1987).

In Figure 1.1, an Ngram for the terms "jitney," "motor truck," and "zoning" illustrates a rapid take-off of their use in books during the 1910s. (Both "jitney" and "motor truck" decline after 1925 as the jitney was replaced by the conventional bus and the motor truck became so common as to just be called a *truck*.) The jitney's booming popularity caused concerns among real estate developers, who had formerly depended on managing the location of streetcar lines to keep apartment developers out of single-family home areas (Cappel 1991). An article in the *New York Times Magazine* (1915) noted that opposition to the free-wheeling service was not just from streetcar interests: "Realty associations are backing up the protests of the traction [streetcar] people on the ground that the prosperity and extension of the streetcar service go hand in hand with the development of real estate, which is not fostered by these jitney men."

But it appears that land use regulation became notably more restrictive during the 1970s. This is suggested by the Ngrams for terms related to those restrictions: "growth management," "NIMBY," and "exclusionary zoning" (Figure 1.2). ("Growth management" is used in the Ngram rather than "growth control" because the latter phrase includes many scientific applications.)

These terms were statistically nonexistent before 1970. The late-century decline in mentions of the pejorative "exclusionary zoning" seems to be roughly offset by the more acceptable means of exclusion embodied by the terms illustrated in Figure 1.3:

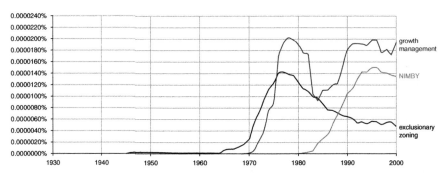

FIGURE 1.2 Ngram for "growth management, NIMBY, exclusionary zoning"
Source: Author's Ngram. Courtesy of http:books.google.com/ngrams

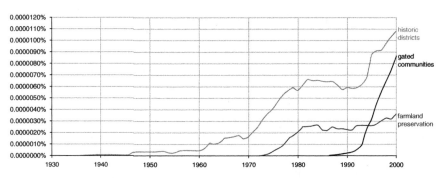

FIGURE 1.3 Ngram for "farmland preservation, gated communities, historic districts"
Source: Author's Ngram. Courtesy of http:books.google.com/ngrams

"farmland preservation," "gated communities," and "historic districts," the last being
the subject of Chapter 4 in the present volume by Ellen and McCabe. Similar
Ngram patterns, not shown here, can be seen for terms such as "wetland protection,"
"downzoning," "regulatory takings," and "urban growth boundary." Land use regulation after 1970 involved a major change from the immediate past, a change that
invoked a new vocabulary that is now so pervasive that we may have forgotten that
mid-century planners and scholars were unfamiliar with it.

The Ngram that encapsulates the thesis I advance in this chapter is Figure 1.4,
which juxtaposes "stock market prices" with "housing prices." Before the 1970s,
mentions in the general literature of housing prices were few relative to stock market
prices. People talked and wrote about the stock market, but not much about housing
prices. In the early 1970s (the data are smoothed by three-year shoulder intervals),
discussion of housing prices zoomed both in an absolute sense and relative to stock
market prices. (The Ngram for the more general term "stock prices" is so large as to
dwarf the frequency of "housing prices." Generally speaking, Ngram analysis is most

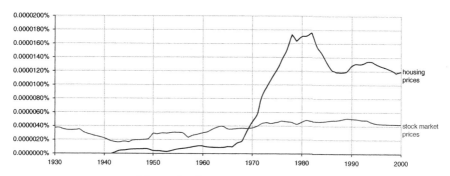

FIGURE 1.4 Ngram for "housing prices, stock market prices"
Source: Author's Ngram. Courtesy of http:books.google.com/ngrams

revealing with phrases of comparable frequency, and "stock prices" can refer to cattle and inventories as well as equities.)

A similar story is told by the quantitative data on the growth of housing prices and capital gains from homeownership. According to my colleague Jon Skinner, "Between 1955 and 1970, the share of owner occupied housing in total household net wealth hovered around 21 percent. In the nine years between 1970 and 1979, housing wealth climbed to 30 percent of net wealth" (1994, 191). This shift in the composition of wealth portfolios corresponds closely with a fundamental shift in land use regulation. (The rise from 21 percent to 30 percent may not sound enormous, but it should be understood that, as with housing prices, capital gains from home values were much larger in the urban areas of the Northeast and West Coast, as discussed presently.)

My theory holds that inflation in the 1970s, driven initially by the rise in world oil prices by OPEC, made owner-occupied housing a highly desirable asset. The benefit of the tax-favored status of homeownership rises relative to other assets during inflation (Poterba 1984). But this asset has a large downside that was the fundamental premise of my 2001 book, *The Homevoter Hypothesis*: as an asset, an owner-occupied home is almost impossible to diversify and is subject to risk from changes in the neighborhood and the community in which it is located. Unlike fire and theft, adverse community and neighborhood effects cannot be insured against by homeowners. Homeowners had since the 1910s cared about keeping footloose industry and apartment houses separate from their neighborhoods, but they lacked the organizational ability to forestall community and regional growth that would threaten the upward growth of their home values in the 1970s. The unprecedented rise in housing prices gave homeowners additional reasons to care about public land use decisions (Taylor 2013).

1.3 THE "GROWTH MACHINE" PREVAILED BEFORE 1970

Yet homeowners who wanted to control the development process were at a political disadvantage. Conventional public choice theory predicts that organized interest groups will tend to capture the regulatory authority, and housing should be no different. Housing developers had the advantage of being well organized and strongly motivated to control the development process. Sociologist Harvey Molotch (1976) invented a term for this political control, "the growth machine." Developers in the early twentieth century were originally in favor of zoning because it served as a kind of insurance policy for prospective homebuyers (Fogelson 2005; Weiss 1987). With zoning in place, homebuyers could be assured that subsequent neighborhood changes would be less likely to adversely affect their large investment.

Developers did not promote zoning with a starry-eyed faith in regulation. They knew that letting this particular genie out of the bottle could be hazardous. J. C. Nichols, a pioneer in developing (privately) planned suburban communities in Kansas City, also advocated zoning, but, as his biographer points out, "Real estate operatives slowly came to realize that by accepting zoning *and getting themselves appointed to zoning boards and commissions,* they could influence governmental and public decisions in their favor to an even greater degree than before" (Worley 1990, 90 [my emphasis]). Marina Moskowitz describes how 1920s land use commissions were dominated by a pro-development "professional-managerial class" (1998, 311). Developers were willing to cater to homeowners' desire to avoid localized external costs, but they did not want established homeowners to control zoning.

In the pre-1970 era, established homeowners sometimes did oppose development, but they were usually unsuccessful. In his lengthy history of the planning profession, Mel Scott describes two instances of suburban homeowners opposing apartment developments (1969, 458) and public housing (p. 418), but the mentions are surprisingly few, and the opposition did not halt all development. Growth controls and similar constraints are not mentioned at all, even though Scott was influential in the movement to preserve San Francisco Bay. His history laments that planners had little to do with zoning, and his wide-ranging examples could have been taken by Molotch as evidence in support of the dominance of the developer-dominated growth machine. (Molotch in his original paper was more concerned with exploring the implications of his idea than testing it against alternative hypotheses. A later elaboration of the theory with John Logan did discuss some contrary evidence about the effect of growth controls, but Logan and Molotch [1987] dismiss it as a minor issue, a conclusion they reaffirmed in the preface of the 2007 reissue of their book.)

There is little doubt that zoning regulations were relatively permissive before the 1970s. This is not to say that developer interests always got what they wanted. But they were able to manage opposition through negotiation with local authorities. A well-known example was the development of the original Levittown (as it became known) housing tract in Hempstead, Long Island (Kelly 1993). The Levitt company acquired experience building wartime housing for workers and adapted its mass production techniques for suburban houses. The company needed Hempstead to change its zoning laws to accommodate its construction methods, particularly the town's requirement that units have basements rather than the concrete slab foundations that Levitt wanted to use. There was some opposition to the project from neighbors, but the town council and planning authorities gave the builders almost all of the changes they requested. Levitt packed one town hearing with recent World War II veterans who were looking for housing. The fledgling suburban newspaper *Newsday* was eager to expand its subscriber base and wrote numerous articles and editorials in support of Levitt. The newspaper's occasional screeds against unnamed "elitists" in nearby communities who opposed expansion of Levittown indicate both that there was opposition and that it was ineffective.

1.4 HOMEVOTERS JOINED AND SUSTAINED THE ENVIRONMENTAL MOVEMENT

After 1970s inflation caused homeowners to demand more protection of their assets, they needed to break the hold of the pro-development forces on zoning regulation. The increasing value of their homes created a common interest among homeowners, but they needed access to institutions to control growth. Part of the access came from the local political process. In smaller governments, such as those of the suburbs, homeowners simply elected officials who were more attuned to their interests. In a series of nuanced histories of regulation by suburbs in the Boston area, Alex von Hoffman found that in the 1970s, developer-friendly zoning was displaced by procedures that reduced total homebuilding. One long-time developer whose family had been local farmers lamented the unexpected popular opposition to further development, "Paradoxically, I sell to people who become my enemies" (von Hoffman 2010, 17).

Where the "growth machine" was better entrenched, homeowners needed to adopt devices that could do an end run around zoning or add layers of review so that the local government's decision to rezone or otherwise accommodate new development would not be the final word. In political affairs, homeowners became an interest group that I have labeled "homevoters." They use their local votes and other political activities to protect and promote the value of their owner-occupied homes.

The environmental movement in 1970 provided the main vehicle for homeowners to add the layers of regulatory review to gum up the growth machine. The environmental laws themselves were not obviously designed for this purpose. They were largely motivated by concerns that were either nonurban – wilderness preservation and public lands management – or were applicable to urban development only in an indirect way, such as water quality and air pollution (Sax and Conner 1972).

Environmental organizations had always been at a disadvantage when they were opposed by development organizations. Even with new laws that offered them more leverage, they suffered from the fact that what they were seeking was the provision of a widely shared public good that represented a small fraction of the public's consumption budget. But they did have institutions organized around outdoor activities, and this offered a mutually advantageous merger of interests with home-voters. Homeowners had a rising demand to control development in their neighborhoods, but not an effective antigrowth organization. Environmental groups provided the organization, and they were willing, even eager, to extend their goals to include protection of suburban open space as well as that of non-farming rural areas. Bernard Frieden (1979) was one of the first to systematically describe the new use of environmental standards to retard housing development in the San Francisco Bay Area.

This deal – largely unconsciously entered into – created an offset to the growth machine. Membership and contributions grew as environmental organizations allied themselves with homeowner interests. (Adam Rome [1994] describes the early history of this alliance, and Richard Walker [2007] offers a largely admiring view of its early evolution in Northern California.) The new antigrowth machine passed state laws mandating second review of local zoning decisions (Bosselman and Callies 1971), expanded the legal standing of objectors to growth both within the community and to outsiders (Sterk 2011), and, somewhat paradoxically, embraced preservation of farmland on the edges of urban areas. (Paradoxical because in truly rural areas, environmental interests in water quality especially have often been at odds with the interests of commercial farmers and ranchers.)

One might ask whether the newfound power of homevoters was simply an extension of previous trends, amplified by a new environmental consciousness of the 1970s. It is difficult to prove a negative, but histories of environmental thought indicate that the tension between industrialization and the pastoral ideal began in the early nineteenth century (L. Marx 1964). It was if anything disdainful of things urban. As a political movement, what became environmentalism was often the domain of patrician elites, who often as not expressed a general contempt for the lower classes through a sometimes painful-to-read eugenics argument (J. Purdy 2015). Environmentalism for the first two-thirds of the twentieth century was concerned mainly with nonurban areas.

Christopher Sellers argues that populist environmentalism took root in the suburbs in the 1960s, and that provided an opportunity for new directions: "As national conservation groups watched the many local and regional groups singling out pollution and other suburban issues, they realized that this new environmental agenda had recruitment potential" (2012, 272). The Sierra Club's membership grew from about 113,000 in 1970 to almost a million by 2000. In 1969, its former director, David Brower, founded a more activist organization, Friends of the Earth, whose motto brilliantly summarized the merger of environmental and homeowner interests: "Think globally, act locally" (Walker 2007, ix). Other organizations formed specifically to "act locally" included San Francisco's People for Open Space (now the Greenbelt Alliance), and they have been quite successful. By 2006, the nine Bay Area counties had more than a million acres (of about 4.4 million total) perpetually protected from development, an area that exceeded the existing urban and suburban land area (Walker 2007, 108).

One reason for the success of the marriage of environmentalism and suburban concerns was that environmentalism offered a unifying ideology that allowed home-voters to avoid talking about home values directly. Growth controls are the product of collective action at the local level, and establishing collective action requires a unifying public discourse (Ellickson 1991). Declaring that the goal of preserving local open space is to maximize voters' property values is actually somewhat divisive. It also seems selfish in a public setting. It invites invidious comparisons among residents. ("Oh, your home is so much more important than mine?") Environmental justification for policies that just happen to increase existing home values is a shield against outside criticism of exclusion and a source of unification among home-owners with otherwise unequal interest in the policies. It serves the same function as the "hearth and home" ideology that brought homeowners together to support zoning in the early twentieth century (Fischler 1998; Lees 1994).

1.5 SOURCES OF NATIONAL VARIATION: SHIFTS IN INDUSTRY AND DIFFERENCES IN LOCAL GOVERNMENT

My explanation for the rise of growth controls, then, is that they were the interaction of a shift in demand for home value protection in the 1970s and an increase in the supply of regulatory devices that operated outside the traditional growth-machine framework. These political and social forces displaced pro-development forces in local governments. But this deals with only one part of the puzzle. The now-conventional wisdom among urban economists is that stringent land use regulations account for the excessively high housing prices in Northeast and West Coast urban areas compared to those in the rest of the United States.

Peter Ganong and Daniel Shoag (2013) have shown that states that now have the highest housing prices and the most land use litigation (an indicator of land use regulation) had not, before 1970, led in either of those categories. Their model demonstrates that the regional regulations have had important effects on internal migration, significantly reducing the ability of Americans in poor states to better their lot by moving to richer areas. Numerous other studies confirm the unusual differential between housing prices on the coasts and elsewhere in the nation. As Karl Case observed, "Prior to 1970, house prices moved slowly at about the rate of inflation or slightly below, and regional differences, while they existed, were relatively modest by current standards" (1994, 29).

But what caused land use regulations to ramp up so much more in those states after 1970? My answer is that exogenous forces shifted the national demand for labor in ways that made the metropolitan areas of the West Coast and, soon after, the Northeast more attractive to high-income, college-educated people. I approach this explanation by introducing the dog that did not bark. The energy crisis of the 1970s

induced a substantial relocation of manufacturing employment from the Rust Belt –
the cities of the Great Lakes and the Ohio Valley – to the Sun Belt. States of the
South and Southwest experienced substantial population growth from internal
migration. But this migration did not result in an unusual increase in housing
prices. Developers responded to the higher immigration by building more housing,
which kept new and existing home prices from rising unduly (Glaeser and Tobio
2008). Demand for housing shifted out, and supply responded fairly quickly.

Another internal industrial shift occurred at almost the same time. The largest
cities of the West Coast and (a decade later) the Northeast were at the forefront of the
shift from manufacturing to high-tech-driven services (Glaeser and Gottlieb 2009).
The introduction of computer technology reduced the demand for lower-skilled
manufacturing jobs. Manufacturing was replaced in cities by high-skilled service
jobs such as finance and computer software development. Global forces such as the
reduction in trade barriers and the rise of Asian manufacturing capacity further
accelerated the American shift from manufacturing to knowledge-based services,
which played to the historical advantages of the large, trade-oriented cities on the
West Coast and in the Northeast. Such shifts in regional advantage have long been
a part of American economic growth, as historical geographer Daniel Meinig (1995)
has shown.

The growth of West Coast computer industries, for example, increased their
demand for highly educated workers in the 1970s and 1980s. The workers bought
housing at a time when national inflation fueled the demand for owner-occupied
housing. As its value rose, homeowners on the West Coast demanded even more
protection. As described previously, organizations such as the Sierra Club and
People for Open Space were available to offset growth-machine politics.
The judiciary in California and later Oregon and Washington became more hospitable to growth controls (DiMento et al. 1980; Galvan 2005).

In the Northeast, the fragmented structure of local government and traditions of
local democracy made it possible for local homevoters to take the reins of zoning and
planning. The knowledge classes of workers started in the suburbs to adopt growth
control, and their state representatives and the judges they appointed soon undermined the growth machine (von Hoffman 2010). Towns formerly hospitable to
apartment house development reversed course, largely in response to local voters'
demands (Schuetz 2008). Even larger central cities such as Washington, DC and
New York have turned from their formerly enthusiastic embrace of development as
they have become repopulated with affluent homeowners (Schleicher 2013).
The supply reduction in the metropolitan West Coast and Northeast was further
facilitated by the fact that the new workers were high income and highly educated,
just the stratum most eager to protect the value of their owner-occupied homes.
In contrast, the migrants from the Rust Belt to the Sun Belt were typically lower
income. Both political participation and demand for environmental quality tend to
rise with personal income.

The Sun Belt had another historical quality that made it less hospitable to growth controls. Local government in the old South was historically weak compared to the North. The reason, I have argued, is because of slavery and its legacy, racial discrimination (Fischel 2009, chap. 5). Blacks and whites were not evenly distributed across the South, and so there would inevitably be localities where a large majority would be African American. Despite voter disfranchisement efforts, some blacks could vote, and they could thus influence the outcomes of local elections. This would not just create pressure for integrated schools. It would, even in the absence of integration, divert resources from white institutions. Thus Southern state legislatures were loath to grant localities much leeway to provide schools and other local public goods (Bond 1934; Key 1949).

The county, with its largely state-appointed officials, was the primary unit of local government in the old South. The county was maintained as the primary unit for school districts and thus the focus of other local government after the civil rights laws undermined racial segregation. Subsequent local demand to create smaller units in the South was largely frustrated by the Voting Rights Act of 1965, which required the approval – rarely given – of the U.S. Justice Department for local government reorganizations (Motomura 1983). Thus both racial segregation and desegregation made the county the default unit of government in the South. Exurban counties tend to be more pro-development in their politics (Anderson 2012), and this appears to apply especially to the South.

The other institution that the South generally lacks is the voter initiative (www.iandrinstitute.org). The larger units of government in the West, where counties rather than cities often governed the exurban land, might be dominated by developer interests. But county and city land use policies are hemmed in by the use of the voter initiative. Homeowners and environmental organizations can thus bypass the influence of the growth machine with ballot initiatives to create open space and even stop individual projects. The county governments of the old South remain in the grip of the growth machine because their voters lack the initiative. Even where land use issues are resolved by sub-county governments, as in Texas, the use of the initiative in land use issues in highly constrained by the state's courts (Callies, Neuffer, and Caliboso 1991, 75).

1.6 THE IMPORTANCE OF IRREVERSIBILITY AND A NOTE ON RENTERS

The catalytic event in my account of the rise of the homevoters and growth controls is unprecedented peacetime inflation in the 1970s. Inflation has since dropped, and it might reasonably be asked why this has not led to a reversion to the growth-machine model of zoning that prevailed before the 1970s. The growth-control model has weathered disinflation and three serious recessions in which housing values declined, especially in 2008, but also in 1981 and 1991. What processes keep the growth-control regime afloat when home values are actually declining and inflation is moot?

One was the deliberate attempt to make growth controls irreversible. From an economic point of view, irreversibility makes a lot of sense for homevoters. They need to convince buyers that the rules that make their homes valuable – the rules that create future scarcity – will not be easily changed. (The classic article on the need to create irreversible commitments to establish monopolies over durable assets is Ronald Coase [1972].) Ordinary zoning laws from the start were intended not to be easily changed. Minor exceptions administered by zoning and planning boards are subject to rules of procedure such as written notice to neighbors and demanding criteria about unique characteristics of the property in question (Reynolds 1999). Major rezonings are likewise subject to more rules than most other changes in police-power regulations. One example is the "twenty percent protest clause," which empowers nearby property owners to demand that changes in zoning be adopted by a supermajority of the governing body (Bartley 1953, 370).

These forces of stability have been supplemented since 1970 by both procedural and substantive changes in land use law. In some states (New York and California), rezoning often involves a state-required environmental impact statement, whose adequacy can be challenged by citizen groups (Sterk 2011). In other states, like Vermont, a state or regional review body can review and veto pro-development decisions. Some states have taken more seriously the requirement for conformity with the master plan (although this can also protect developers from downzonings), and hostility to small-scale rezonings is embodied in the pejorative term "spot zoning."

A more innovative device is the use of conservation easements. These convey the right to develop unused land to a conservation organization, which promises to prevent development, usually in perpetuity. This resolves the anxiety of prospective buyers that the nearby cornfield or stand of trees might someday be rezoned and used for more homes to compete with the existing homes or at least sully their view. Conservation easements have been made financially attractive to donors in many states through the use of tax deductions and even tax credits (Pidot 2005). Some local governments have seized on them as a way of tying the hands of future officials (Serkin 2010). Conservation easements have been widely used in farmland preserva-tion near cities. Historic districts (rather than just single monuments) have also added to the transaction costs of redeveloping older areas for more intensive "infill development."

The persistence of growth controls is also due to evolving community values. Once open space and large-lot zoning districts are established, the homebuyers who most care about them are apt to end up in communities that establish them. This sorting by preference is part of the well-known model of Charles Tiebout (1956). Even if the original growth controls were created solely to protect home values (and not from preference for open space), the later homebuyers who bought with the expectation of open space as part of their purchase are more likely to want existing land uses to persist. An implication of the institutionalization of growth control devices is that the regulatory framework becomes easier to use by citizens who do not have as intense an interest as homeowners. The transformation of land use regulation was undertaken, I submit, by homeowners, but, once transformed, land use regulation became more accessible to all.

Vicki Been, who is a professor at NYU Law School and Commissioner of Housing Preservation and Development in New York City, emphasized in her comments on this chapter the need to account for what in her experience is the homevoter-like behavior of urban renters. New York's renters seem as active in policing neighborhood change as suburban homeowners. In the homevoter model, renters should have less interest in land use change because they cannot capitalize on the benefits of neighborhood quality. If local conditions get better and the tenants move away, their landlord gets the benefit of neighborhood improvement in the form of higher rents. Even if the leaseholder does not move, higher rents would offset to a large extent the benefits of neighborhood improvement.

Both of these mechanisms are attenuated by the existence of rent control (Fischel 1991). Improved neighborhood conditions do not result in higher rents under rent control, and renters protected from rent increases are less likely to move and thus can enjoy the improved neighborhood quality. In these conditions, renters should behave much like homeowners in the political realm, even though they cannot fully capitalize on the benefits of neighborhood improvements. New York City renters are also an especially well-organized group – they regularly battle landlords in the political realm – and should benefit from the wide availability of growth controls.

It is important to understand, however, that New York City's conditions are relatively rare. Two-thirds of the city's housing is renter occupied, among the highest in the nation, and it should not be surprising that renters rather than homeowners get the most political attention. It is one of the few cities that has had rent control and related tenant protections for almost a century. When economists make models of local government, they usually want to capture the experience of a majority. Outliers like New York are always interesting to test the limits of the homevoter model (as Been, Madar, and McDonnell [2014] have done), but confirmations of the homevoter theory in the nation's second-largest city, Los Angeles (Gabbe 2016; Morrow 2013), as well as smaller cities such San Jose (Holian 2011) and various municipalities in Canada (McGregor and Spicer 2016), suggest that projecting the political influence of New York's renters to other places may not be warranted.

1.7 ALTERNATIVE EXPLANATIONS FOR THE 1970S GROWTH CONTROLS

The two alternative – or supplemental – explanations for the rise of growth controls in the 1970s are (a) the rapid completion of the interstate highway system and the suburbanization it facilitated and (b) the civil rights movement and the accompanying unrest in central cities and the political response to it. Both of these surely contributed to some of the demand for growth controls.

The interstate highway system was an enormous undertaking and was special in two important ways (Swift 2011). One is that it was built within a relatively short period of time, between 1956 and 1972. The other was that it was almost entirely financed and directed by the federal government. Limited-access highways are highly disruptive to the cities and neighborhoods through which they are built. Locations immediately adjacent to them have their neighbors displaced or effectively cut off from everyday commercial and personal connections. Railroad construction did that in the nineteenth century, too, but they were different in several ways. Grade crossings were more feasible for railroads, and the location of their routes was subject to some degree of local control because the railroads needed local facilities (terminals and stations) to be integrated with the through lines. The railroad builders could be high-handed bullies, but their need for continuing local cooperation in the indefinite future stayed some of their excesses.

The builders of the interstate highway were almost entirely federal and state agencies. Their need for local input and cooperation was much less than that of the railroad builders. As an engineering-based group, the highway designers were short of models of behavioral response. The designers expected that the highways would promote urban growth, but they did not anticipate the suburbanization that it caused. The decision to run many of them through central cities was based on the belief that doing so would reduce traffic congestion in those places. Federal planners had contemplated – and rejected – using tolls to finance the system, but no thought was given to using tolls to manage the inevitable congestion that an urban freeway is subject to.

The heavy-handed tactics of the highway builders generated a species of protest in the 1960s called *freeway revolts* (Mohl 2004). These ad hoc organizations were precursors to the antigrowth coalitions of the 1970s, and many of them continued their lives long after the highways were built – or not built, if the organization was successful. They are important for my argument that growth controls were a bottom-up movement because they did overcome the torpor of local residents – what economists call the free rider problem – in combatting local change that threatens their home values. A proposed new highway was large enough and adverse enough that it got homeowners out from in front of their TV sets to attend hearings and protest meetings.

Thus the interstate highway system could have contributed to the growth-control movement in two distinct ways. One was by increasing suburbanization by making it easier to live farther from the city (Baum-Snow 2007), and the other was by generating opposition groups that became part of the nucleus of antigrowth organizations in the 1970s. The difficulty with the suburbanization argument is that most of the evidence does not point to any special increase in the measured rate of suburbanization in this period (Mieszkowski and Mills 1993). The way that most economists measure suburbanization is through population density and price gradients, the rate at which density of population or price of housing declines as one moves away from the center of the city. These measures began to decline (in absolute value) in the late nineteenth century with the invention of electric-powered street railroads, and they have kept declining more or less continuously ever since. Suburbanization does not seem to have accelerated during the period 1956 to 1972, when the interstate highways were built.

Local resistance to major highway development was indeed an occasion for citizen action, but its underlying concern was home values. Louise Dyble details the galvanizing effect on local politics of proposals to build new bridges and freeways in Marin County, north of San Francisco, in the 1960s. This antigrowth coalition was successful in stopping most new highway development and making Marin County a pioneer in the growth-control movement. Dyble concluded, "A close look at the dynamics of regime change in Marin reveals that power in the county shifted only when the real value of exclusivity, open space, and natural beauty became clear to property owners. Marin's celebrated environmentalism was founded on the value of real estate" (2007, 59).

The other phenomenon that may have made the 1970s land use policies different was the product of the civil rights movement. Desegregation of central city schools often pushed middle-class whites to the suburbs (Boustan 2010; 2012). Even if the rate of suburbanization was not much changed by that, it is possible that the nature of suburban zoning was altered by it. A population increase in a developing suburb in the 1950s was not difficult to accommodate with new public facilities. More families meant towns had to build more schools, but the expanded tax base more or less covered the cost. An important offshoot of the civil rights movement, however, insisted that suburbs had to accommodate low-income people and minorities along with market-rate development (Downs 1973; Sager 1969).

In the past, allowing more growth brought more of the same sort of people to the suburbs. After political and legal pressure began to be applied to accommodate a variety of housing, general population growth looked less attractive to suburban voters. The thinking by homevoters might have been, if we have to take blacks and the poor along with everyone else, maybe we would prefer to have no growth at all. Of course, public expressions of such ideas was unacceptable, so an alternative rationale for stopping growth was necessary. Preservation of the environment by preserving open space – even environmentally problematical open space like commercial farmland – began to be especially popular (Schmidt and Paulsen 2009).

As evidence for this, I would note that the two states that have imposed a long-standing obligation on communities to accommodate the construction of low-income housing, Massachusetts and New Jersey, are also the states with by far the largest number of local initiatives to preserve farmland and other open space (Banzhaf et al. 2006). The primary means by which communities discharge their state-imposed obligations is a tax on developers of market-rate housing, called "inclusionary zoning." Such a tax depends on making market-rate housing scarce, which is what growth controls do (Schuetz, Meltzer, and Been 2011).

On the whole, however, it seems difficult to pin too much on the civil rights backlash as a cause of growth controls. Real pressure to accommodate low- and moderate-income housing exists in only a few states. Politically liberal communities, which one would expect to be sympathetic to civil rights concerns, seem actually more inclined to limit housing growth than others (Kahn 2011). And I have argued that a suburban majority is not all that opposed to them even there (Fischel 2015, chap. 4). A Massachusetts initiative that would have eliminated the obligation to accommodate low-income housing was easily defeated in 2010. Substantial majorities opposed it in all but one of the suburban counties of Boston, which faced the most pressure from the state law that required inclusionary zoning.

1.8 REFLECTIONS ON REFORM: REGIONALISM AND TAKINGS

A substantial number of economists now believe that regional housing supply in productive areas has been adversely affected by growth controls and that the excessively high housing prices have reduced American productivity and promoted inequality (Ganong and Shoag 2013; Hsieh and Moretti 2015). Relatively few of these studies have addressed what to do about it. The usual idea is that some higher-level government – the federal or state governments, sometimes a regional body – should intervene to override unreasonable local behavior. Economists typically commend devices such as "a simple system of fees, much like congestion tolls, that cover whatever social costs there are from taller buildings and other consequences of increasing urban density" (Glaeser 2011, 161). Developers willing to pay for their social cost should not be stopped by local governments or NIMBY forces. The higher government, able to internalize both the political benefits as well as the costs of development, would override parochial interests.

Bob Ellickson suggested a different approach to the problem (1977). He presciently identified the burgeoning growth-control movement as at least partly a legal problem. Voters in local government who wanted to control growth by downzoning available land could do so without having to face much of an opportunity cost. Police-power regulations are generally not compensable, and rational governments – a concept embraced by the "median voter" model in public economics – are apt to respond to the low cost by doing too much regulation. Ellickson advocated using the regulatory takings doctrine to make local officials (and presumably local voters) raise taxes to compensate development-minded landowners if the local government wanted to unreasonably downzone land to prevent development.

Neither of these approaches has worked. Land use policies of the state and federal governments have more often worked against development than for it (Fischel 2015, chap. 2). The multiple layers of review have generally been of the double veto variety: only in rare instances do they allow developers to go from a local "no" to a state or regional "yes." The expansion of legal entitlements and their wide and indefinite distribution has greatly extended the time that development takes, when it can be done at all.

The underlying reason for state governments' reinforcement of local preferences is the geographic basis for representation in state legislatures. Americans do not select their legislatures from statewide party lists, as parliamentary systems do. Americans elect legislators from local districts whose boundaries usually correspond to some set or subset of municipalities. The saying "all politics is local" is an Americanism – Ngram frequency three times that of British English – because it really is local in the United States. State legislatures remain amalgams of local governments even after the 1960s reapportionment decisions declared that they must be selected according to the principle of one person, one vote. It is possible that the reason American judges feel the need to declare that localities are formally "creatures of the state" is that so many other institutional arrangements work to make the state the creature of localities.

The viability of the takings doctrine is confounded by the numerous parties, most of them not a government that could incur constitutional liability, that contribute to stalling development. James Krier and Stewart Sterk (2016) find that the modern takings litigation has had remarkably little success for complaining landowners and developers. Moreover, local land use regulation is so popular that court efforts to rein it in have led to state constitutional amendments and threatened supreme court reappointments. New Jersey voters adopted a state constitutional amendment in 1927 to authorize zoning after its courts had struck it down (National Municipal Review 1927).

The economic-historical account of the rise of growth controls suggests a different approach to reform. It is surely true that growth controls cause housing prices to rise. But it is equally true, I argue, that growing housing prices cause homeowners to demand more regulation to protect their asset. They don't care whether the additional regulation is more stringent zoning, private covenants, or environmental lawsuits. Home value inflation begets a demand for more regulation, which begets more home value inflation.

The large metropolitan areas of the Northeast and the West Coast are historically unusual in that the demand for housing in these regions increased at a time – the 1970s and 1980s – when the balance of power in land use regulation shifted away from development-minded parties toward seated homeowners who wanted to protect the value of their largest and largely uninsurable asset. I point this out again to suggest that growth control policies are not usefully parsed by region. The states and cities of the Northeast and West Coast do not have fundamentally different legal frameworks from those in other states. Land use laws are sufficiently similar that law professors can put together casebooks and courses that can realistically prepare students to practice (after bar exam study) land use in any state. This suggests that if economic shifts occur that make Chicago and St. Louis the favorite destinations of high-skilled, college-educated workers, the cities of the Midwest will become the centers of growth controls and rising housing prices.

1.9 DEMAND-DAMPENING POLICIES TO MITIGATE GROWTH CONTROLS

The purpose of this exercise in recent economic history is to understand what types of policies might work to make housing supply more elastic in regions that are now repelling firms and lower-income immigrants by their high housing prices. Accommodating growth in the Boston-to-Washington corridor and in the larger cities of the West Coast is important for national economic growth and for reducing the level of income inequality in the United States. It is clear from experience that the courts are not able or inclined to protect the interests of development-minded landowners. Federal and state policies that attempt to increase supply or lower local barriers are inevitably frustrated by the political power of the locals and the NIMBY alliance with high-minded environmental goals.

I have argued here that the primary reason people participate in stopping development is their concern with their home values. The policies that I mention next are designed to undercut excessive concerns, but it might reasonably be asked at the outset whether institutional change is actually possible even if homeowners were no longer excessively touchy about nearby development. I mentioned earlier that one reason for the persistence of growth controls in the absence of home value inflation is that the original institutions were designed to be difficult to undo. There is a built-in hysteresis to growth controls that may warrant just leaving them alone.

The evidence that we have about the growth of growth controls suggests that voters make them more stringent as their home values rise (Lutz 2015). Surveys in California show that voters are less inclined to adopt growth controls when home values are no longer rising (Baldassare and Wilson 1996). My own informal evidence is consistent with this. During the housing boom of 2001 to 2007, a new layer of local regulation was developed to provide additional protection for urban neighborhoods. They are called "neighborhood conservation districts," which give neighborhoods the right to review local development independent of citywide zoning (Fischel 2013; Lovelady 2008).

What is conserved by the "conservation districts" is the value of existing homes, especially in high-demand areas where city authorities might be inclined to shoe-horn some unwelcome development or where existing zoning is not tight enough to prevent an unlovely renovation next door. They differ from historic districts in that the neighborhood does not have to be historic, and they differ from private covenants in that consent of all property owners is not necessary to establish the district. I undertook an online survey of neighborhood conservation districts to see what they were doing, but I noticed an interesting break. After the housing crash of 2007, almost no new districts were formed. Once housing values stopped rising, I infer, residents became less interested in going to the trouble of forming districts.

So perhaps the best that can be expected from demand-dampening policies is to slow down the growth of growth controls, not reverse them. This may be too pessimistic, however. There are signs that the centers of large cities are no longer repelling middle- and high-income people. Indeed, one of the manifestations of the back-to-the-city movement is that the affluent newcomers demand neighborhood growth controls to protect their investments. Unlike the suburbs, though, big cities have an array of other interest groups to offset the growth of the homevoter population. If the homevoter population in the bigger cities can be made less frantic about its assets, it is possible that creative reforms supported by developers, planners, and other stakeholders would have a chance (Hills and Schleicher 2014).

The demand-dampening reforms themselves are mainly to reduce the tax advantages of homeownership. The two big advantages of owning this asset as opposed to most others is the lack of taxation of the implicit rent that owners "pay" to themselves and the explicit exemption of the first $500,000 of realized capital gains for homes of a married couple (Follain and Melamed 1998). The first advantage – the lack of recognition of imputed rent – would largely be undermined by eliminating the mortgage interest deduction from federal and most state income taxes. This is an imperfect way to tax implicit rent, since it leaves untaxed all the implicit rent for people who have no mortgage – usually the elderly and the very rich. But actually taxing implicit net rent is administratively daunting. Doing so would require all homeowners to file their taxes as if they were small business owners, listing an invisible-to-them hypothetical annual rent and keeping track of maintenance and depreciation costs as well as local taxes and mortgage payments.

The mortgage deduction is sometimes regarded as inconsequential because only a small fraction of taxpayers – those in high brackets – find it worthwhile to itemize their deductions. If you don't itemize and instead take the standard deduction, goes the story, you don't get any benefit from the mortgage deduction. This is probably wrong. The standard deduction was conceived as a device to save administrative hassle on the part of taxpayers. The amount of the standard deduction is based on what typical taxpayers in that income bracket could have deducted (Brooks 2011). Reducing one of the usual itemized deductions – mortgage interest paid – should in principle result in a similarly reduced standard deduction. Whether Congress would actually do this is not clear, but doing so would be consistent with the original function of the standard deduction.

More important in my mind is to equalize the tax treatment of capital gains from housing with that of other assets. This is probably a larger source of political distortion than the mortgage subsidy. Homeowners through the 1970s enjoyed the mortgage deduction, but faced a heavily constrained capital gains exemption in that a home of equal or greater value had to be purchased. Homeowners' excessive attention to the value of their home began, I submit, when they started to think of their homes as a growth stock rather than a steady investment.

A modest, income-contingent subsidy to homeownership in the form of a mortgage deduction (or a tax credit) would serve the national interest in promoting a homeowner society (Glaeser and Shapiro 2002). The more reasonable and practical reform would be to treat capital gains on homes the same as capital gains on other assets. It may be that we want to tax capital gains more lightly than ordinary income, but equalizing the tax rates among all assets would have both economic and political advantages. Land use regulation could proceed more rationally and humanely if homeowners were encouraged to hold other assets besides their homes.

Practical people may argue that the tax subsidies to homeownership are too well entrenched to be modified significantly. Homebuilder organizations and the multitude of homeowners themselves create a formidable political barrier to reform. This may be too pessimistic. Homeowners are powerful at the local level, but their interests are too diffuse at the national level to form a strong lobby. Homebuilders are well organized and formidable at the national level, but perhaps they would support some moderate reforms if they were persuaded by the arguments of this chapter. The subsidies to homeownership stimulate the demand for housing – good for homebuilders – but cause a political response – growth controls – that restrict supply. Homebuilders might have fewer regulatory problems, of which they complain often, if homes were not regarded as a major source of capital gains for their owners.

AUTHOR'S NOTE

I thank without implicating Vicki Been, Lee Anne Fennell, John Logan, and Harvey Molotch for helpful comments.

REFERENCES

Anderson, Michelle W. 2012. "Sprawl's Shepherd: The Rural County." *California Law Review* 100: 365–80.

Baldassare, Mark and Georgeanna Wilson. 1996. "Changing Sources of Suburban Support for Growth Controls." *Urban Studies* 33: 459–71.

Banzhaf, H. Spencer, Wallace Oates, James N. Sanchirico, David Simpson, and Randall Walsh. 2006. "Voting for Conservation: What Is the American Electorate Revealing?" *Resources* (Winter): 7–12.

Bartley, Ernest R. 1953. "Legal Problems in Florida Municipal Zoning." *University of Florida Law Review* 6: 355–84.

Baum-Snow, Nathaniel. 2007. "Did Highways Cause Suburbanization?" *Quarterly Journal of Economics* 122: 775–805.

Been, Vicki, Josiah Madar, and Simon McDonnell. 2014. "Urban Land-Use Regulation: Are Homevoters Overtaking the Growth Machine?" *Journal of Empirical Legal Studies* 11: 227–65.

Bond, Horace Mann. 1966. *The Education of the Negro in the American Social Order*. New York: Octagon Books. (Orig. pub. 1934.)

Bosselman, Fred P. and David Callies. 1971. *The Quiet Revolution in Land Use Control*. Washington, DC: Council on Environmental Quality.

Boustan, Leah Platt. 2012. "School Desegregation and Urban Change: Evidence from City Boundaries." *American Economic Journal: Applied Economics* 4: 85–108.

2010. "Was Postwar Suburbanization 'White Flight'? Evidence from the Black Migration." *Quarterly Journal of Economics* 125: 417–43.

Brooks, John R. 2011. "Doing Too Much: The Standard Deduction and the Conflict Between Progressivity and Simplification." *Columbia Journal of Tax Law* 2: 203–46.

Callies, David L., Nancy C. Neuffer, and Carlito P. Caliboso. 1991. "Ballot Box Zoning: Initiative, Referendum and the Law." *Washington University Journal of Urban and Contemporary Law* 39: 53–98.

Cappel, Andrew J. 1991. "A Walk along Willow: Patterns of Land Use Coordination in Pre-zoning New Haven (1870–1926)." *Yale Law Journal* 101: 617–42.

Case, Karl E. 1994. "Land Prices and House Prices in the United States." In *Housing Markets in the United States and Japan*, Yukio Noguchi and James M. Poterba, eds. Chicago: University of Chicago Press.

Coase, Ronald H. 1972. "Durability and Monopoly." *Journal of Law and Economics* 15: 143–49.

DiMento, Joseph F., Michael D. Dozier, Steven L. Emmons, Donald G. Hagman, Christopher Kim, Karen Greenfield-Sanders, Paul F. Waldau, and Jay A. Woollacott. 1980. "Land Development and Environmental Control in the California Supreme Court: The Deferential, the Preservationist, and the Preservationist-Erratic Eras." *UCLA Law Review* 27: 859–1066.

Downs, Anthony. 1973. *Opening Up the Suburbs: An Urban Strategy for America*. New Haven, CT: Yale University Press.

Dyble, Louise N. 2007. "Revolt against Sprawl: Transportation and the Origins of the Marin County Growth-Control Regime." *Journal of Urban History* 34: 38–66.

Ellickson, Robert C. 1991. *Order Without Law*. Cambridge, MA: Harvard University Press.

1977. "Suburban Growth Controls: An Economic and Legal Analysis." *Yale Law Journal* 86: 385–511.

Fischel, William A. 2015. *Zoning Rules! The Economics of Land Use Regulation*. Cambridge, MA: Lincoln Institute of Land Policy.

2013. "Neighborhood Conservation Districts: The New Belt and Suspenders of Municipal Zoning." *Brooklyn Law Review* 78: 339–53.

2009. *Making the Grade: The Economic Evolution of American School Districts*. Chicago: University of Chicago Press.

William A. Fischel

2004. "An Economic History of Zoning and a Cure for Its Exclusionary Effects." *Urban Studies* 41: 317–40.

2001. *The Homevoter Hypothesis*. Cambridge, MA: Harvard University Press.

1991. "Exploring the Kozinski Paradox: Why Is More Efficient Regulation a Taking of Property?" *Chicago-Kent Law Review* 67: 865–912.

Fischler, Raphael. 1998. "Health, Safety, and the General Welfare – Markets, Politics, and Social Science in Early Land-Use Regulation and Community Design." *Journal of Urban History* 24: 675–719.

Fogelson, Robert M. 2005. *Bourgeois Nightmares: Suburbia 1870–1930*. New Haven, CT: Yale University Press.

Follain, James R. and Lisa Sturman Melamed. 1998. "The False Messiah of Tax Policy: What Elimination of the Home Mortgage Interest Deduction Promises and a Careful Look at What It Delivers." *Journal of Housing Research* 9: 179–200.

Frieden, Bernard J. 1979. *The Environmental Protection Hustle*. Cambridge, MA: MIT Press.

Gabbe, Charles J. 2016. Do Land Use Regulations Matter? Why and How? PhD dissertation, Urban Planning, UCLA.

Galvan, Sara C. 2005. "Gone too Far: Oregon's Measure 37 and the Perils of Over-regulating Land Use." *Yale Law and Policy Review* 23: 587–600.

Ganong, Peter and Daniel Shoag. 2013. "Why Has Regional Income Convergence in the US Declined?" Harvard Kennedy School Working Paper No. RWP12-028.

Glaeser, Edward L. 2011. *Triumph of the City: How Our Greatest Invention Makes Us Richer, Smarter, Greener, Healthier, and Happier*. New York: Penguin Press.

Glaeser, Edward L. and Joshua D. Gottlieb. 2009. "The Wealth of Cities: Agglomeration Economies and Spatial Equilibrium in the United States." *Journal of Economic Literature* 47: 983–1028.

Glaeser, Edward L. and Jesse M. Shapiro. 2002. "The Benefits of the Home Mortgage Interest Deduction." National Bureau of Economic Research Working Paper no. w9284.

Glaeser, Edward L. and Kristina Tobio. 2008. "The Rise of the Sunbelt." *Southern Economic Journal* 74: 610–43.

Hills Roderick M., Jr., and David Schleicher. 2014. "City Replanning." George Mason Law and Economics Research Paper 14–32.

Holian, Matthew J. 2011. "Homeownership, Dissatisfaction and Voting." *Journal of Housing Economics* 20: 267–75.

Hsieh, Chang-Tai and Enrico Moretti. 2015. "Why Do Cities Matter? Local Growth and Aggregate Growth." National Bureau of Economic Research Working Paper no. w21154.

Jansen, Brian N. and Edwin S. Mills. 2013. "Distortions Resulting from Residential Land Use Controls in Metropolitan Areas." *Journal of Real Estate Finance and Economics* 46: 193–202.

Kahn, Matthew E. 2011. "Do Liberal Cities Limit New Housing Development? Evidence from California." *Journal of Urban Economics* 69: 223–28.

Kelly, Barbara M. 1993. *Expanding the American Dream: Building and Rebuilding Levittown*. Albany: State University of New York Press.

Key, V. O. *Southern Politics in State and Nation*. New York: Vintage Books, 1949.

Krier, James E. and Stewart E. Sterk. 2016. "An Empirical Study of Implicit Takings." *William and Mary Law Review* 58: 35–95.

Lees, Martha A. 1994. "Preserving Property Values – Preserving Proper Homes – Preserving Privilege – The Pre-Euclid Debate over Zoning for Exclusively Private Residential Areas, 1916–1926." *University of Pittsburgh Law Review* 56: 367–439.

Logan, John and Harvey Molotch. 1987. *Urban Fortunes: The Political Economy of Place*. Berkeley: University of California Press.

Lovelady, Adam. 2008. "Broadened Notions of Historic Preservation and the Role of Neighborhood Conservation Districts." *Urban Lawyer* 40: 147–83.

Lutz, Byron. 2015. "Quasi-experimental Evidence on the Connection between Property Taxes and Residential Capital Investment." *American Economic Journal: Economic Policy* 7: 300–30.

Marx, Leo. 1964. *The Machine in the Garden: Technology and the Pastoral Ideal in America*. New York: Oxford University Press.

McGregor, Michael and Zachary Spicer. 2016. "The Canadian Homevoter: Property Values and Municipal Politics in Canada." *Journal of Urban Affairs* 38: 123–39.

Meinig, Daniel W. 1995. *The Shaping of America: A Geographical Perspective on 500 Years of History*. New Haven, CT: Yale University Press.

Mieszkowski, Peter and Edwin S. Mills. 1993. "The Causes of Metropolitan Suburbanization." *Journal of Economic Perspectives* 7: 135–47.

Mohl, Raymond A. 2004. "Stop the Road: Freeway Revolts in American Cities." *Journal of Urban History* 30: 674–706.

Molotch, Harvey. 1976. "The City as a Growth Machine: Toward a Political Economy of Place." *American Journal of Sociology* 82: 309–32.

Morrow, Greg. 2013. The Homeowner Revolution: Democracy, Land Use and the Los Angeles Slow-Growth Movement, 1965–1992. PhD dissertation, Urban Planning, UCLA.

Moskowitz, Marina. 1998. "Zoning the Industrial City: Planners, Commissioners, and Boosters in the 1920s." *Business and Economics History* 27: 307–17.

Motomura, Hiroshi. 1983. "Preclearance under Section Five of the Voting Rights Act." *North Carolina Law Review* 61: 189–246.

National Municipal Review. 1927. "Editorial Comment." *National Municipal Review* 16 (June): 353.

New York Times. 1915. "Jitney Bus Wins Favor Quickly." *New York Times Magazine*, March 21.

Pidot, Jeff. 2005. *Reinventing Conservation Easements*. Cambridge, MA: Lincoln Institute of Land Policy.

Poterba, James M. 1984. "Tax Subsidies to Owner-Occupied Housing: An Asset-Market Approach." *Quarterly Journal of Economics* 99: 729–52.

Purdy, Jedediah. 2015. "Environmentalism's Racist History." *The New Yorker*, August 13.

Purdy, Lawson, Harland Bartholomew, Edward M. Bassett, Andrew W. Crawford, and Herbert S. Swan. 1920. *Zoning as an Element in City Planning, and for Protection of Property Values, Public Safety, and Public Health*. Washington, DC: American Civic Association.

Reynolds, Osborne M. 1999. "The 'Unique Circumstances' Rule in Zoning Variances – An Aid in Achieving Greater Prudence and Less Leniency." *The Urban Lawyer* 31: 127–48.

Rome, Adam. 1994. "Building on the Land: Toward an Environmental History of Residential Development in American Cities and Suburbs, 1870–1990." *Journal of Urban History* 19: 407–34.

Sager, Lawrence G. 1969. "Tight Little Islands: Exclusionary Zoning, Equal Protection, and the Indigent." *Stanford Law Review* 21: 767–800.

Sax, Joseph L. and Roger L. Conner. 1972. "Michigan's Environmental Protection Act of 1970: A Progress Report." *Michigan Law Review* 70: 1003–1106.

Schleicher, David. 2013. "City Unplanning." *Yale Law Journal* 122: 1670–1737.

Schmidt, Stephan and Kurt Paulsen. 2009. "Is Open-Space Preservation a Form of Exclusionary Zoning? The Evolution of Municipal Open-Space Policies in New Jersey." *Urban Affairs Review* 4: 92–118.

Schuetz, Jenny. 2008. "Guarding the Town Walls: Mechanisms and Motives for Restricting Multifamily Housing in Massachusetts." *Real Estate Economics* 36: 555–86.

Schuetz, Jenny, Rachel Meltzer, and Vicki Been. 2011. "Silver Bullet or Trojan Horse? The Effects of Inclusionary Zoning on Local Housing Markets." *Urban Studies* 48: 297–329.

Scott, Mel. 1969. *American City Planning Since 1890*. Berkeley: University of California Press.

Sellers, Christopher C. 2012. *Crabgrass Crucible: Suburban Nature and the Rise of Environmentalism in Twentieth-Century America*. Chapel Hill: University of North Carolina Press.

Serkin, Christopher 2010. "Entrenching Environmentalism: Private Conservation Easements over Public Land." *University of Chicago Law Review* 77: 341–66.

Shiller, R. J. 2015. *Irrational Exuberance*. Princeton, NJ: Princeton University Press.

Skinner, Jonathan S. 1994. "Housing and Saving in the United States." In *Housing Markets in the U.S. and Japan*, Yukio Noguchi and James Poterba, eds. Chicago: University of Chicago Press.

Sterk, Stewart E. 2011. "Structural Obstacles to Settlement of Land Use Disputes." *Boston University Law Review* 91: 227–72.

Swift, Earl. 2011. *The Big Roads: The Untold Story of the Engineers, Visionaries, and Trailblazers Who Created the American Superhighways*. Boston: Houghton Mifflin Harcourt.

Taylor, Elizabeth Jean. 2013. "Do House Values Influence Resistance to Development? – A Spatial Analysis of Planning Objection and Appeals in Melbourne." *Urban Policy and Research* 31: 5–26.

Tiebout, Charles M. 1956. "A Pure Theory of Local Expenditures." *Journal of Political Economy* 64: 416–24.

Von Hoffman, Alexander. 2010. *Wrestling with Growth in Acton, Massachusetts: The Possibilities and Limits of Progressive Planning*. Cambridge, MA: Rappaport Institute for Greater Boston.

Walker, Richard. 2007. *The Country in the City: The Greening of the San Francisco Bay Area*. Seattle: University of Washington Press.

Weiss, Marc A. 1987. *The Rise of the Community Builders: The American Real Estate Industry and Urban Land Planning*. New York: Columbia University Press.

Worley, William S. 1990. *J. C. Nichols and the Shaping of Kansas City: Innovation in Planned Residential Communities*. Columbia: University of Missouri Press.

2

How Land Use Law Impedes Transportation Innovation

David Schleicher

Necessity, it is said, is the mother of invention.[1] This wonderful volume studies innovation in housing policy. This chapter asks why we *need* innovation in our housing policy, or rather what is changing to make our current housing policy inappropriate, to the extent that it made sense in the first place. I argue that changing transportation technologies have created opportunities for economic growth, but that land use regulations and other housing policies reduce the gains from these technological improvements. In order to capture the gains from new transportation technologies, and to help reverse the slow economic growth we have seen in the United States in most of the period since 1970, we need a housing policy that matches our current (and future) transportation system.

* * *

In discussions of the American economy, the transportation industry and transportation innovation plays a central role. Politicians regularly point to the health of the transportation industry as an indicator of the economy's broader well-being. Think of Charles Wilson's famous (mis)quote that "what's good for General Motors is good for the United States." Or of President Obama's argument that, as a result of a federal bailout, the auto industry is now "leading the way" toward a type of economic growth that benefits middle-class Americans (Miller 2015; Patterson 2013).

Similarly, scholars attempting to project economic growth often focus on transportation innovation. Techno-optimists like Erik Brynjolfsson and Andrew McAfee point to innovations like self-driving cars and drones and predict rates of growth on par with the Industrial Revolution (Brynjolfsson and McAfee 2014, 1–12). Skeptics like Robert Gordon argue that growth has been slow since 1970 and will continue to be so based on their assessment of the likely effects of the same technologies (Gordon 2014).

But transportation innovation does not create economic growth in the same way as innovation in other sectors.[2] For the most part, people do not directly consume the benefits of innovative transportation technology, nor is its direct use a major factor in determining whether businesses can produce goods more cheaply or more efficiently. Most of the benefits of transportation innovation do not come from faster and easier travel to existing homes, offices, and businesses.

Instead, transportation innovations allow us to *move* our homes, offices, factories, and stores into more pleasing and efficient patterns. Early automobiles, for example, were not much more effective than streetcars or even horses at navigating the crowded and pockmarked streets of dense, urban cores (Foster 1981, 9–24; Norton 2011). But cars allowed people and firms to spread outward across a region, creating new opportunities for suburban life, particularly following substantial public investment in roads designed for automobiles (Mohl and Biles 2012, 204–06). Likewise, the elevator, on its own, would not have provided many benefits to residents of cities; elevators are not *that* much better than stairs in existing low-rise buildings.[3] But elevators make the use of taller buildings possible, increasing a city's capacity for density. While transportation innovations provide some benefits to people making their existing commutes, the bulk of the economic gains from transportation innovations comes from changes in patterns of land use.

Transportation scholars have long known that infrastructure investments both depend on current land use patterns and spur changes in those patterns. There is a massive literature built around what are known as Land Use Transport Interaction (LUTI) models, which analyze the complex interrelationship between infrastructure investments, land use, and transportation developments (Van Wee 2015; Wegener 2014).

But the scholars and practitioners in the field (and their increasingly complex software) almost entirely ignore the ubiquity of *legal* limitations on land use. In comprehensively planned cities, market forces do not, on their own, determine the flow of benefits to the broader economy from transportation innovations or investments. If one wants to know how a road or light rail line will affect land uses in a comprehensively regulated city or region, one must understand both the content of zoning and other regulations – rules governing what can be built, where, and how it can be used – and the politics of changing these regulations. New housing, for instance, will not simply emerge around new highways or rail lines. Governments must allow the market to work by revising zoning and subdivision ordinances that accommodate construction.

The same logic applies to new transportation technologies. The kinds and amounts of gains from advances in transportation technology depend heavily on how land use law reacts (or, sometimes, overreacts) to their presence.

This chapter will assess how well modern land use law has or might accommodate three major recent or soon-to-arrive transportation innovations: (1) global positioning systems (GPS), mobile mapping, and real-time traffic information services (like Google Maps, Apple Maps, TomTom, Garmin, and Waze); (2) e-hailing apps for taxis, shared rides, and shuttles (like Uber, Lyft, and their competitors);[4] and (3) still-developing self-driving autonomous cars.

These technological innovations should allow two separate types of changes to land use patterns.

First, they will allow what I will call "distributed density" within urban areas. Each technology should allow for more overall density in cities. To varying degrees, they make travel through dense areas easier, allow for more efficient use of existing infrastructure, and reduce the costs of congestion (and need for parking spaces) for a given density of people and businesses. Further, the advantages of these developments do not depend on extreme density. Nodes of heavy density (e.g., stores along a high street, or apartments within a quarter of a mile of a train station) may spread a bit further outward without losing the gains of agglomeration. Regions will maximize the economic gains from these technologies if they allow dense and diverse development – if buyers can choose townhouses *or* apartments in towers.

Second, the innovations will allow development to spread around cities, as they – particularly GPS and potentially autonomous cars – reduce the costs of traveling substantial distances, both in time and in effort (Anderson et al. 2014).

But modern land use law does not equally allow both of these types of development. Land use law and politics are particularly ill-equipped to produce distributed density. Its deep procedural rules and the multiple ways current residents can block new construction make incremental housing growth particularly difficult (Hills and Schleicher 2011, 81–89). While massive new projects sometimes can run the gauntlet of the zoning amendment process, environmental review and Not In My Backyard (NIMBY) political opposition, developers and homeowners proposing incremental changes in existing neighborhoods often cannot afford the lawyers and lobbyists necessary to do so (Platt 2004, 317–20).

These limitations on "distributed density" precede transportation innovations like Uber and GPS. Housing advocates have started discussing the "missing middle" of the housing market – townhouses, two-tops, triple deckers, etc. – that flourished before modern zoning rules, but that are now almost impossible to construct (Hurley 2016; Schleicher 2013). Similarly, U.S. land use regulations excessively keep retail out of residential zones, separating land uses more than any other advanced economy (Hirt 2013). Finally, and most pressingly, land use regulations substantially harm the regional and national economies by limiting overall density in many rich regions and cities, a trend that really took off in the 1970s and 1980s, as Bill Fischel details in Chapter 1 of this volume (Hsieh and Moretti 2015; Schleicher 2013). In contrast, the fringes of metropolitan areas are less regulated, so these transportation innovations should allow our metropolitan areas to spread further.

This leads to two basic predictions. In downtowns and heavily zoned metropolitan areas, the land usages that zoning regulations allow will fall even shorter of what is economically ideal. Today's urban and inner-ring suburban zoning politics will undercut future opportunities to restructure housing and retail. Innovations in transportation will increase the cost of our dysfunctional land use law regime. Further, land use law will hinder further transportation innovation. The incentive to develop, say, autonomous taxis will be lower in less dense cities. If we hope to maximize the gains from transportation innovation and avoid biasing future technology innovations,[5] we must reform land use regimes, particularly in the richest metropolitan areas.

2.1 AN INTRODUCTION TO TRANSPORTATION AND AGGLOMERATION ECONOMIES

To discuss new transportation technologies, I lay out a simple model of how transportation technologies interact with land usage generally. This section will discuss (a) the interaction between transportation technology and urban economic activity, and (b) how the study of the economic effect of zoning on regional economies can tell us how to study the economic impact of transportation technologies.

2.1.A Transportation Technologies and Agglomeration Economies

All analyses of urban economies start with the same basic question: why do people and firms move to cities? (Glaeser 2008a). Economists usually describe three basic types of "agglomeration economies," or gains from density (Marshall 1890; Schleicher 2010, 1517–28).

The first kind of agglomeration economies deal with shipping costs for goods. Intermediate goods manufacturers can save on shipping costs by moving closer to one another. Much of the history of American urban development turns on decisions by firms to reduce shipping costs by moving to cities (Glaeser and Kohlhase 2004, 198–99; Glaeser and Ponzetto 2007). Almost every major urban center in the United States developed around a major port or rail transport hub. As innovative transportation technologies (like the combustion engine or the shipping container) have driven transportation costs downward, though, manufacturing firms have less and less reason to move to urban areas (Schleicher 2013, 1551–52). Other factors better explain modern urbanization.

The second major category of agglomeration economies includes the benefits of deep markets. Workers in a particular metropolitan region can often participate in a deeper labor market (Rodriguez and Schleicher 2012, 640–47). Think of actors moving to Los Angeles. They can specialize (perhaps becoming an expert in one type of role), match more easily (find a studio that needs their specialty), invest in human capital development (acting school or private lessons), and insure themselves against firm-specific risk. These benefits do not accrue to similarly talented workers in rural areas or regions with less labor market depth.

Further, transportation technologies and infrastructure define the depth of a given labor market. Workers must be able to reach employers in order to work for them, a point clear to those who advocate that we give cars to the poor to increase their labor market opportunities (Logan and Molotch 1987, 262).

Depth matters in markets besides labor and in areas smaller than metropolitan ones, too. Retail markets benefit from market depth. Perhaps the most traditional form of retail development is the "high street," where various stores cluster along a single strip. By locating along one strip instead of spreading out through a neighborhood, stores can specialize (Schleicher 2010, 1522). Consider, for example, a stretch of restaurants and bars. They form "restaurant rows" because consumers can go to the street knowing that there will be lots of different options and that, if one place is too crowded, another place will have seats (Rodriguez and Schleicher 2012).

The third big category of agglomeration benefits is information spillovers. People learn from others, and so population density leads to more productive workers. As Alfred Marshall famously noted, in cities, "the mysteries of the trade become no mystery but are, as it were, in the air" (1890). Software developers and entrepreneurs move to Silicon Valley for more than just the deep labor markets and the California sun; they move to learn from other tech people over coffee or drinks (Rodriguez and Schleicher 2012, 651). Indeed, those who move to urban areas see faster wage growth as a result of learning (Glaeser and Mare 2001; Rodriguez and Schleicher 2012). Patent applications are much more likely to cite other research done in the same place (Jaffee 1993). Chance interactions between residents provide such substantial benefits that firms sometimes design their office space to generate "random" encounters. When Steve Jobs was at Pixar, he placed bathrooms in a central location in order to get different kinds of people to run into one another (Silverman 2013).

The key insight for this chapter is that people move to cities because being close to other people provides economic and social benefits that offset the higher costs for property (and congestion) in cities.[6] As Edward Glaeser notes, "conceptually, a city is just the absence of space between people and firms" (2008b, 4). This "absence of space between people" is not mere physical space, but rather the ease of communal interaction, either intentionally or by chance. Two people on different sides of a wall are physically proximate, but will find it difficult to interact.[7] Similarly, cultural differences can make even physically proximate people quite distant.

The central factors that translate proximity into interactions are the ease of travel and information. Before the invention of the automobile, people living in what are now suburbs of major cities could not participate in regional labor markets. Land that was quite physically proximate to downtown was used for low-intensity purposes like farming because there was no easy way to commute (Mohl and Biles 2012, 204–05). Only those places attached to downtown by omnibuses and streetcars developed into suburbs, because they made commuting and thus participation in urban labor markets possible (Mohl and Biles 2012, 87–88). Information plays a similar role. On high streets, for example, stores benefit from colocation because shoppers can easily see nearby retailers. A physically close shop on a side street would not capture agglomeration benefits from being part of a deep market, since shoppers would never see it or know about it.

Urban economic models have always relied heavily on transportation costs to explain land use patterns. Starting with Von Thunen and going through Alonso and Mills in the 1970s, economists developed "mono-centric models" assuming that business would be done in the city center (Glaeser 2008a, 15–17; Schleicher 2010, 1516–17). Distance from the city center predicted the kind of economic activity of the land, be it farmland or housing; the longer it took to travel downtown, the less intense the land usage. Trade theorists like Masahira Fujita, Paul Krugman, and Tony Venables use shipping costs to predict where firms will locate (Fujita, Krugman, and Venables 1999; Krugman 1995). Transportation technologies determine urban fates.

This is true across types of agglomeration economies. The depth and quality of urban labor markets turn on the quality of urban transportation networks. Alain Bertaud writes: "The potential economic advantages of large cities are reaped only if workers, consumers, and suppliers are able to exchange labor, goods, and ideas with minimum friction and to multiply face-to-face contacts with minimum time commitments and cost. The productivity of a city with a growing population can increase only if travel between residential areas and firms and among firms' locations remains fast and cheap" (Bertaud 2014, 7; 2004). Studies across countries show that worker productivity correlates with the number of jobs reachable within 20 minutes and 60 minutes (Bertaud 2014, 10). Labor market depth depends on both housing density and ease of transportation.

Further, patterns of development are highly dependent on transportation technologies. As mentioned previously, suburbs developed first around horse-drawn omnibus stops, then near electric streetcar stops; most of these developments were within walking distance from the commuter stops (Foster 1981, 18–20; McShane and Tarr 2007). Cities, for good and ill, invested heavily in remaking streets for automobile traffic. These investments created much more distributed development across metropolitan regions (Foster 1981, 10). The automobile now allows suburban residents to participate in regional labor markets without paying for expensive urban real estate.

Of course, many people want to live in urban areas and are willing to make tradeoffs against housing prices (per square foot) to do so. And labor markets are not purely regional. People who work heavy-hour, high-pay jobs in finance, law, and technology frequently want to live in cities and do not want to commute, meaning firms have incentives to do so (Edlund, Machado, and Syiatschi 2015). And cities retain many agglomerative advantages due to information spillovers and market depth in other areas, from retail to dating markets. But the rise of the car is associated with spreading out in all directions around urban areas.

Implicit in this well-known insight that the car enabled "sprawl" lies an important concept. Descriptive accounts of transportation innovation must integrate land use.

The importance of a new road or rail line depends on how this new infrastructure will change demand for homes and offices, and how, in turn, those changes will affect the use of the infrastructure.

All (good) modern transportation planning focuses on the endogeneity of land uses and transportation. Land Use Transport Interaction (LUTI) models study the effect of new transportation infrastructure on traffic and land usage (Aditjandra 2013; Wegener 2013). These studies recognize that causality points in all directions. To address these difficulties, these models have become unbelievably sophisticated, built around "activity-based and agent-based or microsimulation models working with high-resolution parcel or grid-cell data" and individualized to particular urban areas, making them costly and requiring lots of data and computing power (Wegener 2013).

Their basic idea, however, applies to transportation innovation. All transportation technologies decrease the transaction costs of travel and therefore interaction, allowing firms and people to better capture agglomeration economies. Elevators make possible taller buildings, allowing more firms to be closer together, and commuter rails allow more people to access the regional labor market.

But people cannot just relocate wherever new transportation makes it possible. First, transportation decisions themselves largely depend on state investment in roads, railroads, traffic controls, etc. Second, and more importantly for our purposes here, *land use law* constrains relocation choice.

Modern LUTI models do little to acknowledge that law and politics – not just market forces – determine land uses. In contemporary American cities, local governments restrict the height, place, and uses of buildings through zoning, subdivision laws, parking requirements, building codes, historic preservation laws, and more. U.S. urban development has been caused not only by the car, but also by regulations that limited denser development and therefore made sprawl necessary (Barron 2003). Compared to Europe, U.S. policies encourage (and even require) more sprawl, and both Europe and the United States encourage more sprawl than technological change alone would (Lewyn 2008). It is law and not just the market that determines how transportation technologies affect land usage.

While LUTI models and software have grown ever more sophisticated, they fail to take into consideration the content (and the pathologies) of land use law. As Michael Wegener has found, the most popular LUTI models are "are not prepared to model policies" (2013).

This failure bakes in a particular (and wrongheaded) assumption about politics. Burt van Wee reports that there is a saying among LUTI scholars that "in the long term, every light rail line is located correctly. That is, the new light rail line, and in particular its stations, will fuel land-use changes in the vicinity of stations" (2015). This assumes that land use planners will permit denser land use near train stations. There is no reason to believe that this will always be the case, at least in the United States. Just look at the lack of density around stations on one of the oldest (and the second busiest) commuter rail lines in the United States, the Metro-North that runs through Westchester and Connecticut. Even in the long run, density does not necessarily follow train construction. By ignoring politics, LUTI models effectively assume that land use regulation will not bias development. This is deeply wrong.

2.1.B How Should We Think about Land Use Law and New Transportation Technologies?

Over the past 30 or so years, there has been a rise of restrictive zoning in the richest metropolitan regions in the United States, as Bill Fischel shows forcefully in Chapter 1. Starting in the 1970s and 1980s, zoning restrictions (along with other land use regulations, like the historic preservation zones Lior Strahelivitz discusses in Chapter 5) began substantially limiting the construction of housing at the regional level (Fischel 2015; Ganong and Shoag 2014; Schleicher 2013). These land use restrictions have become increasingly strict and inefficient. Edward Glaeser, Joseph Gyourko, and Raven Saks have shown that land use regimes in major American urban areas have caused housing costs to rise far higher than the cost of constructing housing (2005).

These local inefficiencies harm the *national* economy. Enrico Moretti and Chang-Tai Hsieh, for example, analyze how local land use inefficiencies affect the national labor market. They use regional demand for labor, as expressed by the price of labor, to determine how many people would move to rich regions if they were not barred by restrictive land use regimes. They find that lifting land use restrictions and thus allowing labor to move to its optimal location would increase GDP by 13.5 percent (Hsieh and Moretti 2015, 3)!

Peter Ganong and Daniel Shoag have shown that a long-term trend of convergence in average wages and per-capita GDP between states slowed in the 1980s and then stopped entirely. The reason is that a number of rich states and regions made it harder for people to move there (Ganong and Shoag 2014). People *want* to move to San Francisco or southern Connecticut, but can't; land use regimes make housing construction difficult and thus drive up costs. When people move to less-rich places with cheaper housing, they indirectly harm the economy. As Glaeser notes: "[I]t's a bad thing for the country that so much growth is heading to Houston and Sunbelt sister cities Dallas and Atlanta. These places aren't as economically vibrant or as nourishing of human capital as New York or Silicon Valley. When Americans move from New York to Houston, the national economy simply becomes less productive" (2008c).[8]

The same idea applies within regions. People badly want to live in Silicon Valley towns like Cupertino or Mountain View, since they house the richest companies in the country. But limits on housing construction in these towns mean that people move to less desirable but cheaper locales.[9] This displacement creates losses. As Daniel Rodriguez and I have argued, the micro-displacements created by excessive or inapt zoning generate deadweight losses as people are forced to move from the locations where their labor or leisure would be most valuable (Rodriguez and Schleicher 2012, 638). This is true even if there is, in aggregate, enough housing in a region. A lobbyist forced to move from Capitol Hill to Shirlington, VA, will learn less through information spillovers during chance dinners where legislative procedure is discussed. She will network and learn less, even if she keeps the same job.[10]

We can use a similar concept to understand the degree to which economies take advantage of transportation technologies. New transportation innovations will affect optimal land use patterns. But laws might not allow the changes that would maximize these gains. The difference between what is allowed and what should follow from the technology should be understood as lost potential output.

This is the basic strategy this chapter will employ. It will first ask what types of land use changes new technologies will encourage. It will then ask whether our land use law system is likely to allow such changes.

One caveat is worth mentioning: while land use regimes can undermine the potential of transportation technologies, the opposite is true as well. If our goal is to have certain types of land uses, we need to engineer (or limit) transportation systems to support them. Governments can use zoning to permit substantial density, but if there is no mass transit, it can be hard to support. Or governments can legislate for spread-out country living through regulations requiring large minimum-lot sizes and other zoning tools, but if locations are attractive enough because of access to transportation, people will cheat, moving more people into a house than are legally allowed, or secretly subdividing lots. For the purposes of this chapter, I will analyze land use policies for their effect on potential economic output created by transportation technologies. But to the extent that the goal of policy is not output or economic growth, but rather something else – the maintenance of traditional modes of living or some such – the question would be whether we should ban transportation technologies that undermine the land use regime, rather than the reverse.

2.2 TODAY'S TRANSPORTATION INNOVATION AND DISTRIBUTED DENSITY

This section will look at three major advances in transportation technology and ask what effects they should have on land use and why we might imagine that they have not.

2.2.A *Mapping and Location Technologies and Land Use: Where Should Retail Locate in a World with GPS, Mobile Maps, Mobile Phones, and Waze?*

While satellite-based vehicle tracking dates back to the late 1950s, the military developed the Global Positioning System (GPS) in the 1970s and 1980s (Brownell 2014; Pace 1995). In the mid-1980s, the federal government made GPS technology available for civilian use. In 1989, the Magellan Company developed a handheld navigation device, and in 1995, General Motors began including GPS devices in new cars. But these early devices were expensive and not particularly accurate. When President Clinton signed an order making "precision GPS" data available, the modern GPS was born. Standalone GPS devices from companies like Garmin, Mio, Navigon, Magellan, and TomTom flooded the market. Today, cell phones combine GPS technology with advanced mapping software, making it unbelievably easy to navigate a city or search for local shops.

There are three central interactions between these technologies and land uses. First, they alter traffic patterns. Services like Google Maps make finding shortcuts that circumvent traditional highways or through-roads much easier. Traffic on nontraditional roads therefore increases. Technologies like Waze (now owned by Google) enhance this effect. Waze incorporates traffic reports from drivers on the road into its mapping software, redirecting drivers away from delayed highways and onto side streets. Both ordinary mapping and social directions have disrupted the quiet lives of homeowners on residential streets (Vanderbilt n.d.). For instance, in fancy neighborhoods off the 405 in LA (like Brentwood), residents have falsely reported accidents on Waze to prevent the program from directing drivers to their streets (Wallace-Wells 2015).

From a broader perspective, the problem with mapping technologies sending people down residential streets is not that this disrupts existing patterns of land use. The problem is that zoning regulations distort the way the property market should respond to new technologies. For example, right now, retail locates along highways and major thoroughfares (think strip malls) because of the high amount of traffic. If new technologies spread traffic out,[11] then the demand for retail should increase along the now-residential streets that serve as the alternative routes Google Maps or Waze prescribe. The highest value use of property along these streets would change from low-intensity uses like single-family homes into higher-intensity uses like retail and multifamily developments.

Thus, mapping and location technologies open more locations to more intense land uses. This constitutes a real economic gain. More properties can provide retail and hence lower costs for consumers. Mapping and location technologies ought to increase the density of retail in a given shopping area, but also distribute that density along more roads. But it can only produce these gains if land use law allows retail to emerge on these once-residential streets.

The second way mapping technologies can change retail locations is by reducing search costs for consumers. Recall the discussion about high streets. Retail frequently locates along an avenue, often for many blocks, but not on side streets. Why? In order for stores to be part of the same market, and thus benefit from market depth, consumers must be able to find one store from another. Stores arrayed along an avenue present shoppers with *information* – which stores sell what, how deep the market is, etc. Stores on side streets provide no such information.

Enter mobile maps. Today, to find a shop or bar, consumers pull out a phone and look at Google Maps. Stores need not locate within sight of one another. In a world with mobile maps and searches, stores should locate in a neighborhood – not just along an avenue – effectively increasing the size of the "high street." Again, this is an economic gain. More properties participate in the agglomeration gains. Overall, retail density should increase, but the density should be more distributed along now-residential side streets.

But Euclidean zoning is famously protective of residential zones. Zoning for retail is permitted along avenues, but largely barred on residential streets, even right next to major thoroughfares. The blocks between 5th Avenue and Madison Avenue in the 60s, for example, are almost entirely zoned residential.[12] Similarly, while retail might emerge on the roads in Brentwood that have seen Waze-induced traffic increases, zoning laws do not allow it.[13]

Third, GPS, mobile mapping and Waze make finding and getting to far-flung places much easier. Shortcuts to avoid traffic matter more the further you travel. These technologies should make living further away from work or stores more attractive, as they reduce travel time by providing better directions. Again, the effect is twofold. Mapping technologies should increase the overall size of metropolitan regions, as more people can commute to jobs, but also should spread that development out.

2.2.B *Transportation Network Companies and Residential Density*

Perhaps the most debated current innovation in transportation in recent years has been the rise of so-called transportation network companies (TNCs), or ride-hailing services, like Uber and Lyft (Rauch and Schleicher 2015). These companies create a two-sided market. On one side are riders, who press a button on their cell phones and hail a ride. On the other are drivers, either professionals or just people with cars, who agree through the service to drive a rider somewhere. The TNCs provide the mechanism for payment, reputational ranking of drivers and riders, and the technological backbone through which these transactions take place.

These services are both a technological advance and a regulatory "hack." The services use mobile technology to track the location of both parties, to connect them, and get one where she wants to go and the other some cash. This is an important technological innovation.

But the success of TNCs is also due to their capacity to overcome outdated regulation. Governments have traditionally limited taxi supply with something like a "medallion" system, and then regulated prices too (Wyman 2013). The result was undersupply and prices that were usually too high and sometimes too low (during periods of high demand). Uber and Lyft overcame local regulations by simply not complying with them, then using their political influence and vast customer base to push cities to normalize and legalize their product (Rauch and

Schleicher 2015). Backed by incumbent taxi drivers, cities and states across the United States attempted to limit the entry of these firms. But they largely failed. With few exceptions, Uber and Lyft services are available in every major metropolitan area.

Uber and Lyft both provide new drivers with access to the taxi market and create variable "surge" pricing when there are fewer drivers than riders. Because Uber/Lyft drivers are not limited by traditional regulations, they can provide surge services. Many drivers *only* work during peak demand hours – like early morning or late afternoon, for example – because Uber is for them a part-time job (Hall and Krueger 2015). Drivers also provide specialized services like child seats or oversized cars for added prices in ways that traditional cabs could not (Uber 2016). Most importantly, they increase supply generally by making cars more available.

The effect of Uber and Lyft on the cab market has been profound. In a comparison between April and June in 2014 and 2015, Uber rides in New York City increased by 6 million and the number of yellow cab rides decreased by 4 million. The price of New York City taxi medallions has fallen from $1.32 million to $600,000. In San Francisco, since the introduction of Uber and Lyft, the number of taxi rides has fallen by more than half. Both Uber and Lyft now have extremely high market valuations – $62.5 billion for Uber and $5.5 billion for Lyft (Barro 2014; Newcomer 2016).

Along with a number of other firms like Via and Bridj, Uber and Lyft have moved into the jitney business as well. UberPool and LyftLine combine riders into cars, driving down prices further. Uber and Lyft say that their real goal is allowing people to live in cities without owning cars (Manjoo 2014). Travis Kalanick, the CEO of Uber, recently said, "Every car should be Uber" (Wagner 2015).

Despite these changes, few cities or regional planning agencies has taken TNCs into account when creating long-run transportation and land use plans (Dupuis, Martin, and Rainwater 2015). This is a mistake.

To start, consider transit-oriented development. Cities frequently (and reasonably) seek to promote development next to new subway or light-rail locations, for both economic and environmental reasons. They want people to take the train and not drive. But valuable land right next to a given train station frequently gets turned into a parking lot since people have to get to the station somehow. This transforms some of the most valuable land – land right next to a station – into low-value parking spaces, where cars sit useless for the day.

TNCs can ameliorate this problem. Around 25 percent of Uber and Lyft rides are to and from mass transit stops (Higgs 2015; Holmes 2014). There have always been taxis at train stations, but the increased supply at peak hours and the ease of finding a driver make it much easier to get a cab to the station. Thus, TNCs mean more people can get to a train station without driving and parking a car. Further, these companies have increasingly partnered with the agencies that run rail lines to provide an integrated commuting product (Jaffe 2015).

TNCs should allow greater density near train stations. More people living in more properties can use the station without driving there. Properties right next to stations will not need to be as tall; developers can build lower-rise but still-dense housing units, rather than parking lots, nearby. These can be transit-oriented since residents will not have to drive their own car to the train. Of course, the limiting factor is the cost of a taxi traveling a substantial distance, but TNCs should mean that for every train station, there are more carless developments – or rather, fewer cars per property.

This is somewhat generalizable. TNCs decrease the cost of trips longer than walking distance. Where buildings in cities used to have to be very dense if people were meant to travel between them without driving (or taking mass transit), now they can spread a bit further. This should produce the kind of "distributed density" that I mentioned earlier.

People writing about TNCs frequently ask whether they reduce car trips (Bialek, Fischer-Baum, and Mehta 2015). Surely they have both increased trips (when people take an Uber instead of walking or taking mass transit) and decreased trips (because people who use them for some trips instead of owning cars make fewer other trips). More important for land use purposes, though, is their effect on demand for parking and dense land uses.

TNCs should reduce demand for parking and increase demand for density generally.[14] TNC cars – like taxis – are either constantly in motion, and thus not parked, or are largely parked outside dense areas. As parking needs decrease, repurposing parking lots and garages could be a tremendous economic gain.

A shocking amount of urban land is devoted to parking; in many cities, surface parking and garages constitute more than 20 percent of all property (Gardner 2011), but *not* just because the market demands it. Zoning and subdivision laws require parking in unbelievable ways. New housing, for example, frequently has to provide *at least* one parking space per bedroom, which is substantially more than developers who do not have to comply with minimums provide (McDonnell 2011, Shoup 2005 130–50). These requirements can have huge effects. Donald Shoup has shown they add 18 percent to the cost of construction and reduce land value by 33 percent of the cost of apartments in Oakland. For other uses, the effects are even greater. For instance, the "Golden Rule" for local zoning ordinances for office buildings is four spaces per 1,000 square feet of rentable office space. As long as such rules exist, the country will not see all of the economic gains from TNCs.

Similarly, TNC should increase demand for urban property generally, as it makes it easier to get around in cities. But to the extent land use laws limit urban density, the benefits of TNCs are wasted.

2.2.C *Autonomous Cars*

Technologists are getting closer and closer to developing autonomous, or self-driving, cars.[15] The idea is intoxicatingly futuristic. Riders will input an address, and a car without a driver will take them there far more safely than any human driver could. Google has developed and road tested autonomous cars in several cities, logging a combined 1 million miles. Google claims that such cars will be generally available by 2020 (Korosec 2016; Lee 2015b). Similarly, Uber has spent millions and partnered with Carnegie Mellon University's robotics department to develop autonomous cars (and ultimately hired away most of CMU's team) (Thompson 2015). Not to be outdone, Tesla has invested in self-driving cars, and CEO Elon Musk declared that fully autonomous cars are only a "few years away" (Hollister 2015). In its last year, the Obama administration proposed spending $4 billion over the next 10 years to study autonomous cars, and promised to develop regulations to enable their use (Spector and Ramsey 2016). Even traditional automakers have gotten in on the action, although most of their activity has been in developing partially autonomous driving features. But General Motors invested $500 million in Lyft as part of a joint project to build autonomous cars. Toyota, Nissan, Ford, and others are investing heavily in fully autonomous vehicles, some targeting as early as 2020 for commercial availability (Vanian 2016).

Obviously, challenges to the technology remain. In particular, these cars do not yet react well to other drivers or to changing weather conditions (Lee 2015b). But if they can overcome these challenges, autonomous cars will revolutionize transportation. They should reduce car crashes, the twelfth leading cause of death of Americans, and make travel easier (National Highway Traffic Safety Administration 2015). The potential change to the economy presented by autonomous cars is on a different scale from the innovations discussed earlier – it might be truly transformative.

Thus far, governments seem confused about how to regulate them. California is considering regulations that will require a licensed driver available to take over for the machine, for instance (Vekshin 2016). More pressing for our purposes here, states and localities are not sure how to think about the effect of autonomous cars on land use planning. Although the arrival of autonomous cars seems somewhat imminent, only 6 percent of long-term regional transit and land use plans mention them, and government officials around the country have expressed doubts about how they will respond to developments (Dupuis et al. 2015; Guerra 2015).

This lack of planning follows from two factors: first, uncertainty about *when* these cars will be available; second, and more interesting, *how* they will be used. Scholars and technologists have suggested two possible models.

The first possibility is that autonomous cars will be used like taxis (Fagnant, Kockelman, and Bansal 2015; Lee 2015a; Neil 2015). The cars would be constantly in motion, waiting to be summoned by a rider. If this happens, they will drive down the cost of taking a cab significantly. Some models suggest that costs could fall by as much as 80 percent, though other models suggest more modest savings – around 33 percent (Burns, Jordan, and Scarborough 2013; Fagnant et al. 2015). Either way, many urban dwellers will choose to buy minutes of mobility rather than own their own cars. The need for parking would go down massively, as many fewer cars could provide the same or more rides (Anderson et al. 2014).

This suggests that autonomous cars will have the same type of effect on land uses, then, as TNCs, but on a far, far greater scale. Autonomous cars will contribute meaningfully to urban density by making it easier to get around dense areas and by reducing the space wasted on parked cars. Further, they will expand the area that can be described as "downtown," allowing urban density to spread a bit even as it increases.[16]

Another possibility exists (Ohnsman 2014; Smith 2015). Autonomous cars may simply replace driver-operated ones. If this occurs, most people will own an autonomous car and leave it parked when they stop to get to their home, office, or stores. Autonomous cars will surely make regions more spread out. People will be willing to have longer commutes as they will not need to drive themselves, making commuting time more productive (or more fun) (Anderson et al. 2014). Under this model, self-driving cars will result in more sprawling metropolitan areas.

Which model will win out? Perhaps some combination of both. The cost of producing self-driving cars and the path technological innovation takes will both be factors. But so too will land use law. Taxis make sense in dense places, where most rides are short. In spread-out exurbs, however, taxi services make less sense. If people are spread out, cars cannot be nearby when requested. While self-driving cars will permit greater (but distributed) densities, they also need such densities to be useful as taxis. If such density is not permitted, there will be little incentive to build cars to fit that use. That is, land use laws will partially drive technological development.

2.3 THE PROBLEM OF CREATING DISTRIBUTED DENSITY WITH EXISTING LAND USE PROCEDURES AND POLITICS

If we hope to maximize the economic gains from transportation technologies that techno-optimists predict, we must overcome certain pathologies in our land use policy and politics. These pathologies persist most strongly in urban cores, so those areas will see the most limited economic growth from transportation innovation. In this section, I plan to outline these pathologies and their effects on economic growth.

To start, American law confines land to certain uses quite stringently. As Sonia Hirt argues, the central goal of the creation of American zoning law was the protection of exclusively residential neighborhoods (2013). Today, we restrict land to residential uses – and particularly, detached single-family homes – to a far greater degree than any other country. Even on blocks right next to commercial high streets, it is common to find exclusively residential zones. This prevents stores from locating on side streets that intersect a given high street. American land use law's emphasis on separation frustrates the potential benefits of GPS and mobile mapping for broadening the potential places in which retail exists.

Further, modern land use law prevents "distributed density" in many of our biggest, richest cities. For instance, Glaeser, Gyourko, and Saks estimate the "zoning tax" – the difference between the price of housing and the cost of building housing – to be more than 50 percent in Manhattan (2005).

Regulations that disfavor the "missing middle" of housing account for much of this loss (Hurley 2016; Missing Middle 2016). While older cities have lots of midsized housing, newer-built cities depend largely on *either* single-family homes *or* multi-unit apartment buildings (Badger and Ingraham 2015). For instance, the most common form of housing in Boston is the "triple-decker," a three-unit, small apartment building. But almost none of them have been built in the past 50 years (Cloutier 2015). This is not because of a lack of demand – prices are soaring on units in triple-deckers in much of the Boston area – but rather because it is illegal to build them in many places.

This is a product of deeply embedded aspects of land use procedure and law, as I have outlined in a series of articles that I will summarize here (Hills and Schleicher 2011, 2015; Schleicher 2013). Most zoning changes happen through neighborhood-specific amendments, rather than as the product of citywide deals. In currently low-rise areas, this often leads to zoning amendments – "downzonings" in the parlance – that prevent any or much as-of-right development. In the absence of citywide partisan competition (something most big cities lack), city councils frequently give members "councilmanic privilege" – the exclusive capacity to make decisions about land use changes in their district. Downzonings succeed because there are no real opponents (no developer has yet made an investment), and nearby homeowners support them as tools to cartelize the housing stock and to avoid externalities from new construction. Even cities with political leaders publicly committed to housing growth, like New York City under Mayor Michael Bloomberg, approve many such downzonings.

As a result, in desirable areas in many cities, there is little or no as-of-right development. Of course, this does not mean that there is no new development. Cities can and do approve new zoning amendments to allow growth. But they only do so either when they can charge high fees – through impact fees, affordable housing requirements, or indirectly through things like community benefits agreements – or when a big developer has the political wherewithal to push a project through the difficult land use review process and subsequent litigation. Or both.

Because of this political, administrative, and legal thicket, the only types of amendments that will succeed are those that provide massive gains to their proponents. Repeat-player developers proposing big new buildings may have the resources and political sophistication to overcome NIMBY opposition and convince the city to approve a zoning amendment. But incremental housing growth becomes nearly impossible. While big developers in theory could develop lots of mid-rise housing (and sometimes do), the problems of lot assembly are severe. The result is the "missing middle" – towers but not triple-deckers.

But there is much less regulation on the urban fringe. There, underdeveloped local governments generally allow growth. Further, many Southern and Sun Belt cities – like Atlanta and Houston – have much less strict land use restrictions. Transportation technologies therefore will create the most economic gains on the urban fringe and in less regulated urban areas. In the richest and most productive parts of the country, in contrast, these gains will be largely squandered.

2.4 CONCLUSION: FIXING LAND USE TO GET THE MOST OUT OF TRANSPORTATION INNOVATION

The simplest answer to the question of what can be done is to change our zoning laws. Allow retail in residential areas. Allow more density generally and more mid-rise construction specifically. And so forth. But many people *like* our land use laws, so they are hard to dislodge. As Richard Babcock noted, "No one is enthusiastic about zoning except the people" (1966, 17). Rather than simply advocating for change, reformers should focus on changing the political structure of decision making or the incentives for homeowners.

First, transit innovators should push for changes in land use procedure. In the past, I have proposed that cities adopt "zoning budgets" (Hills and Schleicher 2011; Schleicher 2013). Local government would set a target for the number of new houses that should be built over a period of time. Until that target is met, no "downzonings" are allowed; after the target is hit, all downzonings would have to be matched by comparable rezonings for greater capacity. Nothing about adopting a budget would directly cause housing growth – a city could choose zero or a negative number. But if cities decide the amount of growth at the outset, neighborhoods will not shut off development out of fear that they will become dumping grounds.

"Zoning budgets" offer another benefit. If land use decisions regularly took place at the citywide level, employers and transportation companies would become interested in the issue. Currently, no individual zoning amendment affects the housing supply enough to attract lobbying by general business interests. But employers *should* want more supply. Lower housing prices mean greater real value for the wages they offer.

The same goes for TNCs, since greater density should lead to greater profits for them. If decisions were made citywide, employers would have a strong incentive to lobby for housing growth against the narrower interests of particular communities. Adopting zoning budgets or like procedures would allow transportation companies to become players in land use.

Second, advocates could use transportation benefits to bribe NIMBYs. Developers have long paid opponents to allow them to build, usually through exactions or community benefits agreements (Been 2010). These bribes increase the cost of housing, of course, but transportation companies might be able to limit this increase. For example, developers often bribe NIMBYs with parking spaces, so that new neighbors do not take up existing parking. But some cities have allowed or required developers to replace these parking-space bribes with car-sharing contracts, substituting a ZipCar for a few parking spaces (Rauch and Schleicher 2015). Since these benefits are cheaper than parking spaces, the transportation company can reduce the "tax" on new housing. The next step might be doing the same thing with TNCs. Cities could require that developers provide residents with annual Uber or Lyft gift certificates instead of building parking. If TNCs played along (with discounts), you might see greater density instead of more parking (and more demand for TNC use).

These are just a few possible reform ideas. If these technologies are to succeed, firms like Uber and Lyft, Google and Tesla must begin to fight for these important land use reforms. Otherwise, the economic benefits of these incredible, innovative transportation technologies will be squandered.

AUTHOR'S NOTE

I would like to thank Christine Kwon and Garrett West for providing terrific research assistance. I would also like to thank Deven Bunten, Anika Singh Lemar, and Matthew Yglesias for insightful comments. All errors are my own, of course.

REFERENCES

Aditjandra, Paulus Teguh. 2013. "The Impact of Urban Development Patterns on Travel Behavior: Lessons Learned from a British Metropolitan Region Using Macro-analysis and Micro-analysis in Addressing the Sustainability Agenda." *Research in Transportation Business & Management* 7 (July): 69–80.

Aldana, Karen. 2013. "U.S. Department of Transportation Releases Policy on Automated Vehicle Development." National Highway Traffic Safety Administration (press release). May 30. www.nhtsa.gov/About+NHTSA/Press +Releases/U.S.+Department+of+Transportation+Releases+Policy+on +Automated+Vehicle+Development.

Anderson, James M., Nidhi Kalra, Karlyn D. Stanley, Paul Sorenson, Constantine Samaras, and Oluwatobi A. Oluwatola. 2014. *Autonomous Vehicle Technology: A Guide for Policy Makers*. Santa Monica, CA: RAND Corporation. www.rand.org/content/dam/rand/pubs/research_re ports/RR400/RR443-1/RAND_RR443-1.pdf.

Babcock, Richard F. 1966. *The Zoning Game: Municipal Practices and Policies*. Madison: University of Wisconsin Press.

Badger, Emily and Christopher Ingraham. 2015. "The Most Popular Type of Home in Every Major American City, Charted." *Washington Post*. September 21. www.washingtonpost.com/news/wonk/wp/2015/09/21/the-most-popular-type-of -home-in-every-major-american-city-charted/.

Barro, Josh. 2014. "Under Pressure from Uber, Taxi Medallion Prices are Plummeting." *New York Times*. November 14. www.nytimes.com/2014/11/28 /upshot/under-pressure-from-uber-taxi-medallion-prices-are-plummeting.html.

Barron, David J. 2003. "Reclaiming Home Rule." *Harvard Law Review* 116(8): 2255–2386.

Been, Vicki. 2010. "Community Benefit Agreements: A New Local Government Tool or Another Variation on the Exactions Theme?" *The University of Chicago Law Review* 77(1): 5–35.

Bertaud, Alain. 2014. "Cities as Labor Markets." Working Paper #2, Marron Institute of Urban Management, New York University, New York, NY. http://marronin stitute.nyu.edu/uploads/content/Cities_as_Labor_Markets.pdf.

    2004. "The Spatial Organization of Cities: Deliberate Outcome or Unforeseen Consequence?" Working Paper 2004–01, Institute of Urban and Regional Development, University of California, Berkeley, Berkeley, CA. http://escholar ship.org/uc/item/5vb4w9wb.

Bialek, Carl, Reuben Fischer-Baum, and Dhrumil Mehta. 2015. "Is Uber Making NYC Rush-Hour Traffic Worse?" *FiveThirtyEight*. December 9. http://fivethir tyeight.com/features/is-uber-making-nyc-rush-hour-traffic-worse/.

Brownell, Brett. 2014. "The 2000-Year History of GPS Tracking." *Mother Jones*. April 15, www.motherjones.com/mixed-media/2014/04/you-are-here-book-hiawatha -bray-gps-navigation.

Brynjolfsson, Erik and Andrew McAfee. 2014. *The Second Machine Age: Work, Progress, and Prosperity in a Time of Brilliant Technologies*. New York: W. W. Norton.

Brynjolfsson, Erik and Paul Milgrom. 2013 "Complementarity in Organizations." In *The Handbook for Organization Economics*, Robert Gibbons and John Roberts, eds. Princeton, NJ: Princeton University Press.

Burns, Lawrence D., William C. Jordan, and Bonnie A. Scarborough. 2013. "Transforming Personal Mobility." Working Paper, Earth Institute, Columbia University, New York, NY, January 27. http://sustainablemobility.ei.columbia .edu/files/2012/12/Transforming-Personal-Mobility-Jan-27-20132.pdf.

Cloutier, Catherine. 2015. "Boston's Triple-Deckers in Demand, Families Getting Pushed Out." *Boston Globe*. October 8. www.bostonglobe.com/metro/2015/10 /08/boston-three-deckers-remain-mainstay-but-bigger-buildings-are-rise /s15Oc6pXMXHe8sB2wLoUZK/story.html.

DuPuis, Nicole, Cooper Martin, and Brooks Rainwater. 2015. *City of the Future: Technology and Mobility*. Washington, DC: National League of Cities. www .nlc.org/Documents/Find%20City%20Solutions/Research%20Innovation/City %20of%20the%20Future/City%20of%20the%20Future%20FINAL% 20WEB.pdf.

Edlund, Lena, Cecilia Machado, and Maria Micaela Syiatschi. 2015. "Bright Minds, Big Rent: Gentrification and the Rising Returns to Skill." NBER Working Paper No. 21729, National Bureau of Economic Research, November. www.nber.org /papers/w21729.

Fagnant, Daniel J., Kara M. Kockelman, and Prateek Bansal. 2015. "Operations of a Shared Autonomous Vehicle Fleet for the Austin, Texas Market." Presentation,

94th Annual Meeting of the Transportation Research Board, Washington, DC, January. www.caee.utexas.edu/prof/kockelman/public_html/TRB15SAVsin Austin.pdf.

Fischel, William A. 2015. *Zoning Rules!: The Economics of Land Use Regulation*. Cambridge: Lincoln Institute of Land Policy.

Foster, Mark S. 1981. *From Streetcar to Superhighway: American City Planners and Urban Transportation, 1900–1940*. Philadelphia, PA: Temple University Press.

Fujita, Masahisa, Paul Krugman, and Anthony J. Venables. 1999. *The Spatial Economy: Cities Regions, and International Trade*. Cambridge, MA: MIT Press.

Ganong, Peter and Daniel Shoag. 2014. "Why Has Regional Income Convergence in the U.S. Declined?" HKS Working Paper No. RWP12-028, Harvard Kennedy School, Cambridge, MA, March 28. http://papers.ssrn.com/sol3/papers.cfm?abstract_id=2081216##.

Gardner, Charlie. 2011. "We Are the 25%: Looking at Street Area Percentages and Surface Parking." *Old Urbanist*. December 12. http://oldurbanist.blogspot.com/2011/12/we-are-25-looking-at-street-area.html.

Glaeser, Edward L. 2010. "Cities Do It Better." *Economix. New York Times.* April 27. http://economix.blogs.nytimes.com/2010/04/27/cities-do-it-better/?_r=0.

2008a. *Cities, Agglomeration, and Spatial Equilibrium*. Oxford: Oxford University Press.

2008b. "The Economic Approach to Cities." Discussion Paper No. 2149, Harvard Institute of Economic Research, January. ftp://ftp.repec.org/RePEc/fth/harver/hier2149.pdf.

2008c. "Houston, New York has a Problem." *City Journal.* www.city-journal.org/2008/18_3_houston.html.

Glaeser, Edward L. and Janet Kohlhase. 2004. "Cities, Regions and The Decline of Transport Costs." *Regional Science* 83 (January): 197–228.

Glaeser, Edward L. and David C. Mare. 2001. "Cities and Skills." *Journal of Labor Economics* 19(2): 316–42.

Glaeser, Edward L. and Giacomo A. M. Ponzetto. 2007. "Did the Death of Distance Hurt Detroit and Help New York?" Working Paper No. 13710, National Bureau of Economic Research, December. www.nber.org/papers/w13710.pdf.

Glaeser, Edward L., Joseph Gyourko, and Raven Saks. 2005. "Why Is Manhattan so Expensive? Regulation and the Rise in Housing Prices." *Journal of Law and Economics* 48 (October): 331–69.

Gordon, Robert J. 2014. "The Demise of U.S. Economic Growth: Restatement, Rebuttal, and Reflections." NBER Working Paper No. 19895, National Bureau of Economic Research, January 20. http://content.csbs.utah.edu/~mli/Economics%207004/Gordon_NBER%20P383F%20Sequel_140126.pdf.

Guerra, Erik. 2015. "Planning for Cars That Drive Themselves: Metropolitan Planning Organizations, Regional Transportation Plans, and Autonomous Vehicles." *Journal of Planning Education and Research* (November 2): 1–15. http://jpe.sagepub.com/content/early/2015/10/29/0739456X15613591.abstract.

Hall, Jonathan V. and Alan B. Krueger. 2015. "An Analysis of the Labor Market for Uber's Driving-Partners in the United States." Working Paper # 587, Industrial Relations Section, Princeton University, Princeton, NJ, January. http://data space.princeton.edu/jspui/handle/88435/dsp010z708z67d.

Higgs, Larry. 2015. "Uber Took 300 K N.J. Commuters to the Bus or Train Last Month." *NJ.com: True Jersey.* October 27. www.nj.com/traffic/index.ssf/2015/10/uber_took_300k_nj_commuters_to_the_bus_or_train_last_month.html.

Hills, Roderick M., Jr., and David N. Schleicher. 2015. "Planning an Affordable City." *Iowa Law Review* 101(1): 91–136. http://ilr.law.uiowa.edu/files/ilr.law.uiowa.edu/files/ILR_101–1_Hills%26Schleicher.pdf.

2011. "Balancing the Zoning Budget." *Case Western Law Review* 62(1): 81–134. http://heinonline.org/HOL/Page?handle=hein.journals/cwrlrv62&g_sent=1&id=84.

Hirt, Sonia. 2013. "Form Follows Function? How America Zones." *Planning, Practice & Research* 28(2): 204–30. http://dx.doi.org/10.1080/02697459.2012.704736.

Hollister, Sean. 2015. "Elon Musk Describes the Future of Self-Driving Cars." *Gizmodo.* March 18. http://gizmodo.com/elon-musk-describes-the-future-of-self-driving-cars-1692076449.

Holmes, Jeremy. 2014. "Uber, Lyft May Add Convenience ... And Traffic Jams." *Mobility Lab.* September 24. http://mobilitylab.org/2014/09/24/uber-lyft-may-add-convenience-and-traffic-jams/.

Hsieh, Chang-Tai and Enrico Moretti. 2015. "Why Do Cities Matter? Local Growth and Aggregate Growth." NBER Working Paper No. 21154, National Bureau of Economic Research, May. www.nber.org/papers/w21154.pdf.

Hurley, Amanda Kolson. 2016. "Will U.S. Cities Design Their Way Out of the Affordable Housing Crisis?" *Next City.* https://nextcity.org/features/view/cities-affordable-housing-design-solution-missing-middle.

Jaffe, Eric. 2015. "Uber and Public Transit Are Trying to Get Along." *CityLab,* August 3. www.citylab.com/cityfixer/2015/08/uber-and-public-transit-are-trying-to-get-along/400283/.

Jaffee, Adam B. et al. 1993. "Geographic Localization of Knowledge Spillovers as Evidenced by Patent Citations." *Quarterly Journal of Economics,* 108: 577.

Korosec, Kirsten. 2016. "Google Preparing to Expand Self-Driving Car Program to Four More Cities." *Fortune.* January 29. http://fortune.com/2016/01/29/google-self-driving-cars-cities/.

Krugman, Paul. 1995. *Development, Geography, and Economic Theory.* Cambridge, MA: MIT Press.

Lee, Timothy B. 2015a. "Driverless Cars Will Mean the End of Mass Car Ownership." *Vox.* January 31. www.vox.com/2014/5/28/5758560/driverless-cars-will-mean-the-end-of-car-ownership.

2015b. "Self-Driving Cars Have Logged a Million Miles on the Roads. Here's Their Safety Record." *Vox.* October 30. www.vox.com/technology/2015/10/30/9640230/self-driving-car-crashes.

Lewyn, Michael. 2008. "Sprawl in Europe and America." Working Paper. http://papers.ssrn.com/sol3/papers.cfm?abstract_id=1194862.

Logan, John R. and Harvey L. Molotch. 1987. *Urban Fortunes: The Political Economy of Place.* Berkeley: University of California Press.

Manjoo, Farhad. 2014. "With Uber, Less Reason to Own a Car." *New York Times.* June 11. www.nytimes.com/2014/06/12/technology/personaltech/with-ubers-cars-maybe-we-dont-need-our-own.html?_r=0.

Marshall, Alfred. 1890. *Principles of Economics.* London: Macmillan.

McDonnell, Simon, et al. 2011. "Minimum Parking Requirements and Housing Affordability in New York City." *Housing Policy Debate*, 21(1).

McShane, Clay and Joel Tarr. 2007. *The Horse in the City: Living Machines in the Nineteenth Century.* Baltimore, MD: Johns Hopkins University Press.

Miller, Jake. 2015. "Obama: Auto Industry 'Leading the Way' in America's Comeback." *CBS News.* January 7. www.cbsnews.com/news/obama-auto-industry-leading-the-way-for-americas-comeback/.

Missing Middle. 2016. "Missing Middle: Responding to the Demand for Walkable Urban Living." http://missingmiddlehousing.com/.

Mohl, Raymond A. and Roger Biles. 2012. *The Making of Urban America.* Plymouth: Rowman & Littlefield Publishers.

Mueller, Benjamin. 2014. "In Connecticut, Breaking Barrier Between a Suburb and Public Housing." *New York Times.* July 11. www.nytimes.com/2014/07/12/nyregion/in-connecticut-breaking-barrier-between-a-suburb-and-public-housing.html?_r=0.

National Highway Traffic Safety Administration. 2015. *Traffic Safety Facts: Research Note.* DOT-HS-812–203. Washington, DC. October. www-nrd.nhtsa.dot.gov/Pubs/812203.pdf.

Neil, Dan. 2015. "Could Self-Driving Cars Spell the End of Ownership?" *Wall Street Journal.* December 1. www.wsj.com/articles/could-self-driving-cars-spell-the-end-of-ownership-1448986572.

Newcomer, Eric. 2016. "G.M. Invests $500 Million in Lyft." Bloomber, January 4. https://www.bloomberg.com/news/articles/2016-01-04/gm-invests-500-million-in-lyft-to-bolster-alliance-against-uber

Norton, Peter D. 2011. *Fighting Traffic: The Dawn of the Motor Age in the American City.* Cambridge, MA: MIT Press.

Ohnsman, Alan. 2014. "Automated Cars May Boost Fuel Use, Toyota Scientist Says." *Bloomberg.* July 16. www.bloomberg.com/news/articles/2014-07-16/automated-cars-may-boost-fuel-use-toyota-scientist-says.

Pace, Scott, et al. 1995. *The Global Positioning System: Assessing National Policies,* Washington, DC: RAND Corporation Press.

Patterson, Robert W. 2013. "What's Good for America … " *National Review.* July 1. www.nationalreview.com/article/352429/whats-good-america-robert-w-patterson.

Plato. 1931. *The Republic.* In *The Dialogues of Plato* (3rd edition). Translated by B. Jowett. Oxford: Oxford University Press.

Platt, Rutherford H. 2004. *Land Use and Society, Revised Edition: Geography, Law, and Public Policy.* Washington, DC: Island Press.

Rauch, Daniel E. and David Schleicher. 2015. "Like Uber, but for Local Government Law: The Future of Local Regulation of the Sharing Economy." *Ohio State Law Journal* 76: 901–63.

Rodriguez, Daniel B. and David Schleicher. 2012. "The Location Market." *George Mason Law Review* 19(3): 637–64.

Schleicher, David. 2013. "City Unplanning." *Yale Law Journal* 122(7): 1670–1737.

2010. "The City as a Law and Economic Subject." *University of Illinois Law Review* 2010: 1507–63.

Shoup, Donald. 2005. *The High Cost of Free Parking*. 130–50. Chicago: American Planning Association Planners Press.

Silverman, Rachel Emma. 2013. "The Science of Serendipity in the Workplace." *Wall Street Journal*. April 30. www.wsj.com/articles/SB10001424127887323798104578455081218505870.

Smith, Bryant Walker. 2013. "Managing Autonomous Transportation Demand." 52 *Santa Clara Law Review* 52 (4) 1401–1422.

Smith, Noah. 2015. "Like the Suburbs? You'll Love Driverless Cars." *BloombergView*. November 4. www.bloombergview.com/articles/2015-11-04/like-the-suburbs-you-ll-love-driverless-cars-.

Spector, Mike and Mike Ramsey. 2016. "U.S. Proposes Spending $4 Billion to Encourage Driverless Cars." *Wall Street Journal*. January 14. www.wsj.com/articles/obama-administration-proposes-spending-4-billion-on-driverless-car-guidelines-1452798787.

Thompson, Clive. 2015. "Uber Would Like to Buy Your Robotics Department." *New York Times Magazine*. September 11. www.nytimes.com/2015/09/13/magazine/uber-would-like-to-buy-your-robotics-department.html.

Uber. 2016. "UberFAMILY: For Parents on the Go." *UberNewsroom*. https://newsroom.uber.com/us-new-york/uberfamilyfor-parents-on-the-go/.

2015. "Driving Solutions to Build Smarter Cities." *UberNewsroom*. https://newsroom.uber.com/us-massachusetts/driving-solutions-to-build-smarter-cities/.

Van Wee, Bert. 2015. "Viewpoint: Toward a New Generation of Land Use Transport Interaction Models." *Journal of Transport and Land Use* 8(3): 1–10, www.jtlu.org/index.php/jtlu/article/viewFile/611/710.

Vanderbilt, Tom. N.d. "Waze: The App That Changed Driving." *Gear Lab. Men's Journal*. www.mensjournal.com/gear/cars/waze-the-app-that-changed-driving-20160208.

Vanian, Jonathan. 2016. "Toyota Hires Artificial Intelligence Gurus for Self-Driving Cars." *Fortune*. January 5. http://fortune.com/2016/01/05/toyota-hires-artifical-intelligence-expert/.

Vekshin, Alison. 2016. "Self-Driving Cars Would Need a Driver in California." *Bloomberg*. January 28. www.bloomberg.com/news/articles/2016-01-28/self-driving-cars-would-need-a-driver-under-california-rules.

Wagner, Davis. 2015. "Uber CEO Travis Kalanick: Every Car Should Be Ours." *InformationWeek*. September 16. www.informationweek.com/cloud/uber-ceo-travis-kalanick-every-car-should-be-ours/d/d-id/1322212.

Wallace-Wells, Benjamin. 2015. "Waze and the Politics of Public Spaces." *New York Magazine*. January 30. http://nymag.com/daily/intelligencer/2015/01/waze-and-the-politics-of-public-spaces.html.

Wegener, Michael. 2014. "Land-Use Transport Interaction Models." In *Handbook of Regional Science*, Manfred M. Fischer and Peter Nijkamp, eds. Berlin: Springer-Verlag. http://link.springer.com/referenceworkentry/10.1007/978–3 -642–23430-9_41.

    2013. "The Future of Mobility in Cities: Challenges for Urban Modelling." *Transport Policy* 29 (September): 275–82.

"Why Autonomous and Self-Driving Cars are Not the Same." 2015. *Economist.* July 1. www.economist.com/blogs/economist-explains/2015/07/economist-explains.

Wyman, Katrina. 2013. "Problematic Private Property: The Case of the New York Taxicab Medallion." *Yale Journal on Regulation* 30: 125–88.

Yglesias, Matthew. 2012. *The Rent Is too Damn High: What to Do about It, and Why It Matters More Than You Think.* New York: Simon & Schuster.

Notes

1. First by Plato and then by others (Plato 1931).
2. It is worth asking whether transportation innovation is really *distinct* in this respect. Some have argued, for instance, that information technology innovations will have a greater effect on growth in the future as we change things like the internal organization of firms (Brynjolfsson and Milgrom 2013). Not much turns on this for this chapter, as transportation more than other innovations turns on changes in land use.
3. In manufacturing, elevators play a crucial but distinct role.
4. As I will discuss later, a similar logic applies to "car sharing" or short-term car rental services like ZipCar and Car2Go.
5. I should be careful here. That technological development responds to a regulatory universe does not mean that it is suboptimal. Regulations may make things better, after all. But in this case, it seems likely that allowing these technologies to work well in far-flung areas but not in denser ones will make existing pathologies (against density, environmental problems) worse.
6. Congestion in this literature consists of the higher rents in urban areas, the negative externalities of density (traffic, dirt, easily passed germs), and what I have called in the past "negative agglomerations," or activities that see agglomeration gains but that are socially costly, like crime (Schleicher 2010).
7. Lest you think this is a metaphor, the town of Hamden, CT, built a chain-link fence that separated it and the public housing projects in New Haven and kept it up from the 1950s through 2014 (Mueller 2014).
8. A few commentators at the conference associated with this volume asked whether, contrary to the arguments made by me, Hsieh and Moretti, and Glaeser, it might be better to use public policy to spread people out to urban centers that they would not otherwise choose, as different people will be exposed to those individuals' agglomeration externalities. This critique, which is brought up frequently enough, is not *theoretically* wrong. Agglomeration economies are by their very nature, externalities, and therefore it is theoretically possible to use policy to fix market failures. But, as Daniel Rodriguez and I have argued

(Rodriguez and Schleicher 2012), the critique is premised on both a deep distrust of the ability of property markets to function well and a high degree of faith in the ability of governments to measure and dole out agglomeration externalities optimally. There is no reason to believe that a real national governmental social planner can outperform the property market in allocating people across regions, and even less to reason to believe that the self-interested behavior of hundreds of local governments will. The optimal land use policy, Rodriguez and I contend, is to be as neutral as possible about locational choices at the neighborhood or regional level absent some very strong specific justification. The technological innovations discussed here expand the choice set for individuals about where to move, but do not require much forethought by local officials about which locational choices are best for specific people.

9. The same force also causes gentrification – if construction in rich areas is impossible, people who want to live in those areas have to move to other areas, increasing prices elsewhere (Yglesias 2012).

10. Sorry, Shirlington!

11. They not only spread out existing cars, but they surely increase the number of cars on the road. This is a product of what transit planners call "induced demand." In short, new roads create traffic by reducing the cost of driving, thus encouraging people to drive more. Usually, people who talk about induced demand use it as an argument against building new roads, on the grounds that these new roads are sure to become congested. In extremis, this argument doesn't make a whole lot of sense – it applies equally to the first road built as to the last one. The point of roads is to make it easy to drive places, and we should judge their utility by whether the increased capacity is worth the costs (including externalities like carbon emissions). What is true is that new roads are not likely to get rid of traffic because of induced demand (solving traffic would require addressing the externality created by your car for all others behind it, something that can really be addressed only with congestion charges). So too with Waze. It is not likely to reduce traffic – it will and does induce demand – but it may allow more cars to use the same number of roads.

12. See ZOLA, New York City's terrific zoning web application. The zoning along these streets is largely R8B, or roughly for tall, brownstone houses. www.nyc.gov /html/dcp/html/zone/zh_r8b.shtml.

13. The reader should search ZIMAS, Los Angeles' zoning map application: http:// zimas.lacity.org. While there are existing commercial strips on San Vicente in Brentwood, no new strip could emerge – and those are already totally full.

14. The same point also applies to short-term car rentals like ZipCar and Car2Go. These services are useful only in relatively dense areas, as the rentals have to be returned to a permissible parking place. And as they are used by many rather than individually, they cut down on overall parking used.

15. To be a bit more technical, the National Highway Traffic Safety Administration has announced five categories of "automation" – Level 0 (fully driver-operated); Level 1 ("function-specific automation" like electronic stability control); Level 2 ("combined function automation" like adaptive cruise control combined with

lane centering); Level 3 ("limited self-driving" or mixed driver control and autonomous driving); and Level 4 ("fully autonomous") (Aldana 2013; "Why Autonomous and Self-Driving Cars Are Not the Same" 2015). For the purposes here, I am talking about Level 4.

16. Unlike TNCs, it is pretty clear they will increase vehicle miles traveled (Smith 2013).

3

The Unassailable Case against Affordable
Housing Mandates

Richard A. Epstein

Current disquiet about the shape of housing markets in the United States has brought forth systematic proposals for their reform. Some of these move in a pro-market direction. These include removing zoning restrictions on new construction in order to increase supply. They also include direct public subsidies for specific classes of housing paid from general public revenues, such as Section 8 Housing, which offers rental housing assistance to private landlords on behalf of low-income tenants (Housing Act of 1937, 42 U.S.C. § 1437f). As between these two, I prefer the market liberalization because only it can produce the double benefit of lower administrative costs and the expansion of supply. In contrast, direct public subsidies require higher taxes of unknown incidence and severity that generate political controversy and deadweight social losses. This chapter, however, bypasses both these programs to exclusively critique affordable housing mandates for "inclusionary zoning." These mandates have gained in popularity in recent years, precisely because they do not require any direct appropriation of public funds. In June 2015, a unanimous California Supreme Court, speaking through Chief Justice Tani Cantil-Sakauye in *California Building Industry Association v. City of San Jose* (61 Cal. 4th. 435 (2015)) (*CBIA*), rebuffed constitutional challenges to the San Jose affordable housing program that "requires all new residential development projects of 20 or more units to sell at least 15 percent of the for-sale units at a price that is affordable to low-or moderate-income households" (*CBIA* at 442). Those programs are now operative in more than 170 municipalities in California alone (*CBIA* at 441).

Inclusionary zoning is defended as a way to combat:

> within the urban and rural areas of the state a serious shortage of decent, safe, and sanitary housing which persons and families of low or moderate income . . . can afford. This situation creates an absolute present and future shortage of supply in relation to demand . . . and also creates inflation in the cost of housing, by reason of its scarcity, which tends to decrease the relative affordability of the state's housing supply for all its residents. (Cal. Health and Safety Code section 5003, subdivision (a))

The statutory finding, however, does not explain why competitive markets are in permanent disequilibrium. Nonetheless, the California Supreme Court upheld the statute against a takings challenge that treated this mandate as an unconstitutional exaction against developers, without explaining how the inclusionary zoning mandate could achieve its intended result. More recently, New York City in March 2016 adopted an aggressive affordable housing mandate that requires the developers of new housing to include, on a negotiated basis, two tiers of affordable housing: one for low-income persons earning between 40 percent and 80 percent of the median income, and a second for people earning about 115 percent of the median income. Only developers who comply with both mandates will receive the benefit of rezonings offering them either greater height or density. The combined number of units under both programs constitutes about 20 percent of the total units in any project.

In this chapter, I will examine these programs through both an economic and legal perspective. In so doing, note the vivid contrast between bundled cross-subsidies on the one hand, and explicit cash subsidies on the other. The difference is that conditional permits keep these expenditures off the balance sheet, and thus further away from political scrutiny and public deliberation. If these programs are desirable, let the state rent or purchase the units at market value, and then re-let or resell them at below-market prices. As the late Justice Scalia wrote in *Pennell v. City of San Jose* (458 U.S. 1 (1988)):

> The traditional manner in which American government has met the problem of those who cannot pay reasonable prices for privately sold necessities – a problem caused by the society at large – has been the distribution to such persons of funds raised from the public at large through taxes, either in cash (welfare payments) or in goods (public housing, publicly subsidized housing, and food stamps). Unless we are to abandon the guiding principle of the Takings Clause that "public burdens . . . should be borne by the public as a whole," *Armstrong* [*v. United States*, 364 U.S. 40, 49 (1960),] this is the only manner that our Constitution permits.

Ignoring this principle leads to a broad set of unfortunate consequences. In order to explain why, I shall proceed as follows. Part 3.1 addresses the means-ends question of whether these programs are capable of achieving their stated goals, or whether, as seems likely, they exacerbate the current housing shortages, given that any restriction on new entry into housing markets should both constrict supply and raise prices at all rent levels. But in these cases, it would be a mistake to concentrate attention solely on the particulars of a program, given its interaction with other housing market regulations. Thus, in New York City, it seems likely that its strict rent stabilization law will further reduce effective supply, putting greater stress on affordable housing programs to make up the slack. The combination of higher costs and lower benefits can hardly be expected to improve the overall situation in housing markets.

Once the economic analysis is complete, I shall turn to the constitutional question of whether the effort to force the costs of new housing onto the developers of future housing projects violates the Takings Clause by imposing an unconstitutional condition on new real estate development. That position is widely rejected today on grounds articulated in *CBIA*, which are that the doctrine of unconstitutional exactions only applies in those cases where the government attaches conditions on the physical occupation and use of land, as in *Nollan v. South Carolina Coastal Council* (483 U.S. 825 (1987)), in which the state demanded that a homeowner yield a lateral easement to the public across his beachfront property in order to obtain a building permit to build a new and large house on his property; or in *Dolan v. City of Tigard* (512 U.S. 374 (1994)), which involved a bike path over and a flowage easement across the Dolan parking lot. The requirement that some undesignated fraction of units be reserved for low- and middle-class affordable housing was held not to burden the occupation of land in *CBIA*, and thus did not qualify as a per se taking under the rule in *Loretto v. Teleprompter* (458 U.S. 419 (1982)). Accordingly, the court upheld its constitutionality under the far-lower standard of rational basis review articulated in *Penn Central Transportation Co. v. City of New York* (438 U.S. 104 (1978)), which sustained New York City's landmark preservation ordinance. But this classification is incorrect even under existing law. Without question, the *Loretto* rule applies when the state directs a private owner to allow a private person to occupy a specific property. In principle, it continues to apply even when the property owner is allowed to decide which unit will be so assigned to an eligible tenant against his will.

3.1 THE ECONOMICS OF AFFORDABLE HOUSING PROGRAMS

The initial inquiry for inclusionary zoning asks why the law of supply and demand fails in an unregulated housing market. One claim is that such housing is impacted by "public actions involving highways, public facilities, and urban renewal projects" (Cal. Health and Safety Code section 5003, subdivision (a)). Two replies should be decisive. First, these commonplace actions have not stopped housing markets from clearing in thousands of settings that do not involve inclusionary zoning. Second, to the extent that intrusive urban renewal projects do distort housing markets, the first-best solution is to curtail those innovations, not to heap a second imperfection atop the first. Less, rather than more, state intervention is required.

Nonetheless, California moves sharply in the opposite direction by creating a complex regime of positive rights in which "the provision of a decent home and a suitable living environment for every American family," is said, without proof, to depend on inclusionary zoning to create a strong state economy with low levels of unemployment (Cal. Health and Safety Code section 5001). That system is most definitely not one "in which the housing consumer may effectively choose within the free marketplace" (Cal. Health and Safety Code section 5001). Recall that in normal market settings, supply and demand tend to come into equilibrium through entry and exit. Shortages induce new entry until anticipated rates of return are reduced to a risk-adjusted competitive level. Conversely, market gluts lead the least efficient suppliers to exit until the market is once again in equilibrium. To be sure, entry and exit are never costless, even in an unregulated economy, so we can always expect some deviations from optimal housing levels. But these problems are only aggravated by stringent zoning and excessive permitting restrictions that hamper both entry and exit – who can leave if there is no clear place to go? In contrast, open markets allow individual players to rely on their specialized knowledge to decide on entry and exit strategies. The presence of queues in price-regulated markets, as happens with inclusionary housing, is an unmistakable sign of market disequilibrium. Affordable housing is in fact a form of rent control that always creates systematic shortages.

To see the exit point, note that one reason why developers will commit to new construction of housing is if they know that they (or their buyers) can switch their end uses if the original plan does not work. This one insight condemns statutes like the San Francisco Residential Hotel Unit Conversion and Demolition (Ordinance (S. F. Admin. Code) ch. 41), which requires that any property owner who wants to replace long-term resident units with short-term units in a tourist hotel must either supply substitute units of similar housing, or pay an "in lieu" fee to the City in order to construct new units of low- and moderate-income housing. In sustaining the ordinance, the California Supreme Court stressed that the legislation reverted to a rational basis to argue that the City had wide latitude in choice of means to address the perceived shortage of affordable housing within the City, especially for its most vulnerable populations (*San Remo Hotel v. San Francisco City & Cty*, 41 P.3d 87 (2002)).

The Court acknowledged that the San Francisco ordinance recognized both tourism and housing were essential to the welfare of the City, but then missed the central point. The Court did not explain how any planning agency could know which use is more valuable in what location, which owners do best. In addition, the Court in *San Remo* thought, incorrectly, that displaced residents had some vested right to secure substitute housing within the City. That analysis misfires on two grounds. First, it requires double benefits from a single move, for in addition to the benefit of the new operations coming in, it becomes critical to supply workable substitutes for the displaced operations elsewhere. Why burden unregulated transactions that produce net social benefit? Second, these communities might easily supply residential facilities even if their locational disadvantages make it virtually impossible to supply short-term rental space for the tourist trade. Needless to say, *San Remo* did not exhibit a glimmer of recognition that restraints on exit rights will necessarily reduce the willingness of developers to engage in new construction.

A similar logic applies to the inclusionary zoning programs that the California Supreme Court blessed in *CBIA*. But how these increase housing supply for the most vulnerable populations is left unclear. On the supply side, any affordable housing mandate necessarily increases the administrative costs of running every aspect of the development process. For starters, inclusionary zoning proposals say nothing about required quality standards for the various private units and the public spaces. In practice, it is difficult to find the right level of amenities that meet the budget and preferences for individuals with gross disparities in income levels and personal tastes. To close that gap, developers traditionally catered each project to individuals who shared the same taste in public amenities, which cannot be done under inclusionary zoning.

A similar dilemma arises in designing the individual units. To build units of equally low quality will guarantee a sharp decline in the rents for the market-rate units. To use high-class materials, appliances, and finishes for the affordable units would increase the loss per unit. Thus it is necessary to figure out three different classes of appliances, finishes, and designs, for low-, middle-, and market-rate units, thereby raising costs for all units. Costs further increase when regulations require that the different types of units be evenly dispersed throughout the larger structure. Different brokerage teams, marketing strategies, and credit reviews are needed for the three different types of units, driving up staff size and costs. Qualifying particular applicants for the low- and middle-income units is a constant headache, given annual fluctuations in family composition and income. Higher-income or -net worth individuals cannot be allowed to gobble up the subsidies targeted to lower-income people. But determining annual eligibility is costly and error ridden when current tenants and future applicants change jobs from time to time, often work off the books, or fraudulently conceal income sources. None of these external standards applies to market leases, where tenants are always free to spend less on housing than they can afford. Yet what property owner wants to force out tenants who become better risks when their incomes improve? Much-needed public audits drive costs still higher.

The situation looks no better from the demand side. This entire edifice rests on the vagaries of non-quantified cross subsidies. The basic conceit is that the ability to charge high rents on the market-rate units will offset the mandated losses on the low- and moderate-rate units, thus allowing the developers to secure a reasonable rate of return on the overall investment. But new entrants offer a far better way to constrain developer returns at all market levels. In contrast, this regulatory system is fraught with risk that tenant resistance in the market-rate units not offset the losses in regulated units, thus pushing any comprehensive project into negative territory. The off-book accounting means that increasing the fraction of affordable units magnifies a future risk, which is subject to changes in future regulations. No regulator has any a priori way to determine the level of the net profits needed from the market-rate units or the prospects of their realization. Traditional rate making for public utilities knew of this risk and required a reasonable rate of return on each separate project for each annual period.[1]

The situation is made even more difficult because unit values are not just a function of their location, size, and quality, but also of their immediate neighborhoods. A *New York Times* story by Nelson Schwartz (2016), ominously titled "In an Age of Privilege, Not Everyone Is in the Same Boat,"[2] attacked the Norwegian Line for outfitting its luxury cruise ships with a safe "Haven" reserved for premium passengers who wanted superior accommodations and priority access to common facilities. The separation improved matters for both groups, by increasing total revenues available to cover common costs (e.g., the engine room) without driving away customers in either service tier. Opportunity for gains arises in all forms of housing. A luxury building with large and small units can work if both groups want the same kind of public amenities, but it will fail if one group wants doormen and the other does not. It is just these pressures that drive residential developers to target discrete groups, not the whole population. They internalize all the soft externalities and thus tend to get the optimal mix of tenants along multiple dimensions that outsiders find difficult to identify.

These rules influence the strategic responses of developers to forced inclusion of different social and economic groups. When forced to include tenants with wildly different tastes, developers add a "poor door" to separate their customers along class lines, just as many large, swanky buildings have service elevators to separate maintenance and delivery functions. It is easy to denounce this practice by insisting, as does Manhattan Borough President Gale Brewer, that "[b]uildings that segregate entrances for lower-income and middle-class tenants are an affront to our values" (Keil and Danika 2015). And it is equally easy to pass legislation that provides that "affordable units shall share the same common entrances and common areas as market rate units."[3] But it is far harder to get people to invest money in buildings under rules that reduce anticipated returns from marketplace units. Constraints of this sort will make it far harder for Mayor de Blasio to reach his target of 200,000 affordable units in New York.

The California rules in *San Remo* are less restrictive because they allow developers to make "in lieu" payments to an affordable housing fund. But money is fungible, so the question from *Pennell* arises anew: why not use an explicit allocation of general revenues instead of non-monetized cross-subsidies with serious negative impacts? Under that regime, San Francisco can insist on its SRO replacement program only if it pays developers cash equal to the lost revenue from having to include affordable units – including both reduced revenues and higher costs. The absence of these programs is good evidence that they will fail at the local level.

The effect of this novel regime of price controls through inclusionary zoning is to contract overall supply – thereby driving out residents and raising rents. Thus in evaluating San Jose's affordable housing ordinance in *CBIA*, Chief Justice Cantil-Sakauye never addressed Benjamin Powell and Edward Stringham's findings on the impact of affordable housing restrictions on housing supply in San Jose (2005). That information was supplied to the California Supreme Court in explicit form by the

Amicus Curiae National Association of Homebuilders, which illustrated the negative effects of the inclusionary zoning system: "A $1,000 increase in home price leads to about 232,447 households priced out of the market for a median-priced new home. . . . The priced-out effect is exacerbated through government regulations and constraints on housing development. Already, regulations imposed by government at all levels account for 25 percent of the final price of a new single family home built for sale." These numbers suggest that at least in the sales market, the parties subject to affordable housing mandates cannot recover the revenue lost from the legal mandates. Clearly, the loss in supply hurts first-time homebuyers, as well as those who sell one home in order to buy another.

The Powell and Stringham study also demonstrated that the San Jose affordable housing program fell far short of expectations (2005). In the seven years before the program's passage, 28,000 new homes were built in San Jose. In the seven years afterward, only 11,000 new units were built, of which some 770 were affordable. The tradeoff could not be clearer: is the community better off with 770 affordable units at the price of 17,000 fewer aggregate units? This looks like a terrible tradeoff, given that any supply increase lowers home prices and expands housing stock for all homebuyers, not just a select few. Fewer homes meant a smaller tax base, which in turn compromised the ability of San Jose to maintain essential services, while meeting its onerous pension obligations.[4] A stronger tax base could have reduced these pressures.

The adverse effects of inclusionary zoning programs are compounded by their interactions with other land use regulations that further erode the tax base. In this regard, note that the highest rates for unregulated rental housing occur in cities like New York and San Francisco (City and County of San Francisco: Residential Rent Stabilization and Arbitration Board 2015). Current rent stabilization programs privilege sitting tenants, who are locked into a unit, often with ample rights of inheritance, for indefinite renewals at stabilized prices until the current tenant on the lease dies or moves.[5] Rent stabilization creates a two-tier rental structure without any pretense of incorporating egalitarian values. It also contributes to the shortage in affordable housing units.

Thus in New York City at this time, rent stabilization covers about 1 million of the 2 million total rental units (Furman Center Fact Brief, Profile of Rent-Stabilized Units and Tenants in New York City 2014).[6] This statistic is incomplete because it does not separate out the many stabilized units in New York City that currently rent for prices below the allowable maximums, so that the price constraint does not bind. However, that proposition is decidedly not true in key areas of Manhattan and Brooklyn, where the maximum allowable rates fall far below the market rate. In Manhattan, in 2002, the gap was between $2,285 per month for market-rate housing and $878 for stabilized or controlled units. By 2011, the respective numbers in Manhattan were $2,600 for the market-rate units and $1,283 for the stabilized units. These numbers do not set out apples-to-apples comparisons, because they do not try even in Manhattan and Brooklyn to isolate the rent-stabilized units in the high-rent areas from those elsewhere in Manhattan and Brooklyn. However, in 2015, the Rent Stabilization Board authorized a zero percent rate increase for the area. It is likely the gap between market rents and stabilized rents has increased under the influence of progressive politics in the past five or so years. In these settings, the rent differential will in all likelihood reduce the effective carrying capacity of the current usable space. An elderly widow or couple who lives in a large, rent-stabilized unit in one of the premium areas will not move voluntarily, for it is cheaper to hold on to a large unit than to rent a smaller, unregulated one elsewhere. Under a market-rate system, that person would think seriously of downsizing in order to save rent, allowing large families or groups to occupy the larger unit at market rates. The result is an effective increase in the size of usable housing stock. Opening up only 100,000 currently stabilized units could increase total occupancy by perhaps 200,000 people, just as if new stock had been built for that purpose. Rent stabilization does more than give huge windfalls to lucky tenants. It also reduces the available spots for occupation. Phasing out rent stabilization, say by allowing a 10 percent rent increase every year, will allow a smooth transition to a market-based system that will increase total supply. This in turn will exert downward pressure on rents throughout the entire system, at zero cost. Cases like *CBIA* block this development, but do so under an unsound theory of unconstitutional conditions, even under current law. The second half of this chapter analyzes the current legal situation, using *CBIA* as a template.

3.2 THE UNCONSTITUTIONALITY OF AFFORDABLE HOUSING PROGRAMS

CBIA sustained the constitutionality of the San Jose affordable housing program by insisting that it had a legitimate police power justification for its restriction on both economic liberties and private property. Its opinion marked a reversal of the victory below for CBIA when the superior court (trial court) held that even if the affordable housing program was for a public use, nonetheless it "determined that the city had failed to show that there was evidence in the record 'demonstrating the constitutionally required reasonable relationships between the deleterious impacts of new residential developments and the new requirements to build and dedicate the affordable housing or pay the fees in lieu of such property conveyances'" (61 Cal. 4th 454 (2002)).

The *CBIA* court relied on *San Remo Hotel, LP v. City and County of San Francisco* (27 Cal. 4th 643 (2002)), for the proposition that:

> The controlling state and federal constitutional standards governing such exactions and conditions of development approval, and the requirements applicable to such housing exactions [and] the conditions imposed by the city's inclusionary housing

ordinance would be valid only if the city produced evidence demonstrating that the requirements were reasonably related to the adverse impact on the city's affordable housing problem *that was caused by or attributable to the proposed new developments that are subject to the ordinance's requirements,* and that the materials relied on by the city in enacting the ordinance did not demonstrate such a relationship.

Under that standard, its argument was that new housing did not displace any preexisting units, so the exaction was illegal. That argument was rejected in the Court of Appeal, which was affirmed by the California Supreme Court:

> The appropriate legal standard by which the validity of the ordinance is to be judged is the ordinary standard that past California decisions have uniformly applied in evaluating claims that an ordinance regulating the use of land exceeds a municipality's police power authority, namely, whether the ordinance bears a real and substantial relationship to a legitimate public interest. (61 Cal. 4th 443 (2002))

The California Supreme Court then explained that the traditional test survived because the doctrine of unconstitutional conditions developed in *Nollan v. California Coastal Commission* (483 U.S. 825 (1987)) and *Dolan v. City of Tigard* (512 U.S. 374 (1994)) only applied to cases of "physical takings," where a property owner was required to dedicate some portion of his property to public use. It did not apply to a mere regulation under the lax *Penn Central* test. The restriction of *Nollan* and *Dolan* to possessory interests flowed easily from the Supreme Court's earlier decision in *Loretto v. Teleprompter* (458 U.S. 419 (1982)), which involved the permanent occupation of a small space on the roof of Loretto's apartment house on which Teleprompter located its cable box. Justice Marshall announced: "We conclude that a permanent physical occupation authorized by government is a taking without regard to the public interests that it may serve" (*Loretto* at 426 (1982)). In *CBIA*, the California Supreme Court refused to apply *Loretto* because, in its view, "the unconstitutional conditions doctrine under *Nollan* and *Dolan* [does not] apply where the government simply restricts the use of property without demanding the conveyance of some identifiable protected property interest (a dedication of property or the payment of money) as a condition of approval."

In essence, the same distinction that applies generally applies to cases of permit application. That extension is incorrect on both grounds. First, the purported line between physical and regulatory takings cannot withstand analysis. The two areas must be treated under a single unified conceptual frame. Second, even if that is accepted, the inclusionary zoning mandates fall on the possessory side of the line.

3.2.A *The Unity of Physical and Regulatory Takings*

The great conceptual challenge in takings laws is to deal with partial takings, that is, those situations where the original owner is stripped of only some, but not all the rights associated with normal outright ownership. Just that happened in both *Nollan* and *Dolan.* In *Nollan,* the physical taking came from the requirement that the Nollans dedicate a lateral public easement across their property in order to receive in exchange an ordinary building permit. In *Dolan,* the physical taking took place when the city required the Dolans to allow both a bike path and a flowage easement across the Dolans' property in exchange for their building permit. Assume for the sake of argument that this distinction can be drawn, so that physical takings involve situations where the government either enters into the possession of private property or authorizes private individuals to do so. The question is whether the distinction matters here.

To see why it does not, it is critical to note why the unconstitutional conditions doctrine applies to physical takings cases in the first place – a point on which *CBIA* is silent. The explanation is that it is intended to prevent against widespread government abuse, akin to the situation where one private individual takes something of value from its owner and agrees to return it only upon payment of ransom money. The second transaction looked at in isolation leaves both parties better off. I prefer to regain custody of my child or my keepsake. The kidnapper or the thief prefers to keep the ransom money. But the full analysis notes that allowing the second transaction in either case will necessarily increase the likelihood of the initial kidnapping or theft – with adverse social consequences.

The same dynamic is at work in permit situations. The government could first announce that no one could build without a permit, and then agree to sell back that right to build in exchange for some fraction of the property or some easement over the whole. That process leads to widespread abuse because if the two transactions are stepped together, the government now acquires the possessory interest for itself or for some preferred private party at zero cost, a massive circumvention of the prohibition against takings without just compensation. The social distortion arises because the government now has an antisocial incentive to take private property for public use even when its value is greater in private hands.[7] Thus assume that the permit to build is worth $100,000 to the landowner, while surrendering the easement will cause the owner only $20,000 worth of loss. The temptation to surrender is overwhelming, given the potential gain of $80,000 to the landowner. Yet if the easement in the hands of its recipient is only $10,000, the transaction generates a social loss of $10,000, which could be avoided if the two transactions were unbundled, so that the case for a permit had to stand on its own, separate from the condemnation of the easement.

At this point, it is critical to note the two key limitations on the permit power are "nexus" and "rough proportionality" – the public law analogs to the private law requirements of legitimate ends and appropriate means. On the first point, the state must show some justification for the restriction it imposes, for which its own benefit is never sufficient. In practice, there are only two ends that justify this state use of its monopoly permit power. The first is to prevent the commission of a nuisance or other tort. At this point, the state only asserts the same powers available to private parties who likewise can enjoin the commission of the nuisance, typically without paying compensation. This line of argument folds into the traditional police-power justification for the protection of health and safety. Alternatively, the state can impose the restriction if it can demonstrate that it has compensated the owner in kind for the loss that it has imposed, at which point the social losses that arise from bundling do not occur. In neither of these two cases is there the risk of the types of abuse that can flow from the power to improperly reduce the returns to investment in new housing.

For all public acquisitions that do not fall into these two classes, the government has to pay for them out of general revenues. Thus it is one thing to require a landowner to take precautions to prevent pollution run-off from his own lands. It is quite another to insist, as in *Dolan*, that he grant the easement to control the run-off from the land of some independent third party, where the state action is no more legitimate than a revised tort rule that makes A pay for the wrongs of an unrelated B. Indeed, just this distinction is routinely developed and applied under state law cases that allow for impact fees to control potential nuisances, but not to fund various activities like new schools that should be paid for out of general revenues.[8]

Once the legitimate ends are specified for takings cases, the next inquiry asks whether there is "rough proportionality" between the means and the ends, in order to ensure that common improvements are paid for from common funds. Thus in *Koontz*, it was improper for the state to condition its permit on the willingness of *Koontz* to either fix or pay for fixing a broken culvert located upstream along the river. Those expenditures belong on the public books to ensure public officials properly weigh all the relevant benefits and burdens to prevent the overproduction of asserted public goods by an implicit in-kind subsidy levied on one party.

The political risks with implicit subsidies are not confined to possessory interests, but apply to any and all land use restrictions. Thus the same set of considerations applies with equal force to height or setback restrictions. They also apply to the various in lieu fees used in *San Remo* and in *Koontz*. Covering all forms of exactions by the same two-part test eliminates the gamesmanship that arises when the government attempts to circumvent important restrictions by using one technique instead of another.[9] The endless fragmentation of government strategies to evade this mandate opens the door to massive political abuse. Is there any meaningful difference between the government asking for the lateral easement or for $20,000 that it turns around to buy that easement? Or in using that money to condemn a restrictive covenant that restricts the height of the Nollans' new house to 10 feet? The private law has long regarded both easements and restrictive covenants as part of the unified branch of servitudes, and there is no reason to deny them like protection under the takings law. Paying cash is an important revelation device that establishes that the easement, or the restrictive covenant, is worth more to the state than to its private owner. Unbundling the easement or restrictive covenant from the permit stops the potential government abuse cold, because the property interest will only be taken if its perceived value is greater than its cost.[10]

Accordingly, it is easy to see the danger from any switch to the laxer standard that asks about "the real and substantial relations to the public welfare." Historically, this standard draws on *Nebbia v. New York* (291 U.S. 502, 539 (1934)), which enshrined the rational basis test in cases of economic liberty. Under that test, San Jose's preexisting conditions do not matter at all. So long as the legislature thinks it has taken steps to expand the supply of some class of affordable housing, it has met the constitutional standard. Under *CBIA*, the simple observation that the chosen standard is likely to prove counterproductive is irrelevant to the current system of constitutional law. It is for the legislature to decide on the merits of the means–ends connections, so it is perfectly proper for the Court to bypass without so much as a single word of comment the earlier study by Powell and Stringham, because there is no constitutional issue to which the demonstration of major economic dislocation is directed.

A closer analysis shows how using the lower level of judicial scrutiny led the California Supreme Court badly astray in both *San Remo* and *CBIA*. In *San Remo*, the Court used this test to uphold the requirement that the developer either build similar units at some other (undetermined) location within the city, or alternatively, that he contribute money into an "in lieu" fund that the City thereafter would use exclusively for the purpose of developing long-term housing. The new requirement was regarded as "reasonably related to mitigating the impact that the landowner's proposed conversion would have on the preservation of long-term rental housing in the city" (*San Remo Hotel* at 87 (2002)). The use of the term "mitigating" says it all. Where is the wrong that needs to be mitigated? Normally mitigation is required to offset some prior wrong. But here the tenant has no property interest that is violated by any action of the landlord, for the refusal to renew any short-term lease is not a wrong to the tenant, but the exercise of the retained right of the landlord, who may exercise its common law right to regain possession of the property at the end of the lease, on the ground that the holdover tenant is a trespasser who gains no rights by his wrong against the landlord, as holder of the reversion.[11] The attitude toward displacement thus explains all forms of rent stabilization and rent control laws, whether they operate on the wholesale or retail basis. In order to close that gap, New York law, consistent with the California approach, requires that all new projects consider "the potential displacement of local residents and businesses, [which count] as an effect on population patterns and neighborhood character."[12]

This huge expansion in the definition of harm has literally zero connection to the nuisance prevention rationale applied under the traditional police-power justifications. Under this definition, the question is never whether there are externalities justifying the triggering of public force. It is a virtual certainty that any reduction in existing stock will produce some changes in quantity and price that count as a deleterious effect. Accordingly, the *San Remo* ordinance is necessarily valid, because the displacement of any long-term resident counts as an adverse effect sufficient to trigger administrative relief, at least if the state is prepared to supply it. There is no way that this requirement satisfies either the "nexus" or "rough proportionality" tests of the *Nollan/Dolan* line of cases, which is why resort to the *Penn Central* test is so critical.

At this point, the element of choice between the replacement units and the in lieu fee is quite irrelevant. As Justice Holmes said long ago: "It always is for the interest of a party under duress to choose the lesser of two evils. But the fact that a choice was made according to interest does not exclude duress. It is the characteristic of duress properly so called" (*Union Pac. R.R. Co. v. Pub. Serv. Comm'n of Mo.*, 248 U.S. 67, 70 (1918)). Of course the in lieu fee is, *ceteris paribus*, likely to be far more attractive to the developer than requirement of new construction, which requires the developer to run the gauntlet of the many zoning and other ordinances that stand in the path of new construction throughout San Francisco. No wonder the developer in San Remo first paid a $567,000 in lieu fee, which he properly sought to recover as a payment made under duress.

From a social point of view, moreover, the San Remo ordinance does not produce any social gains that justify its massive administrative costs. In *San Remo*, no one doubted that the increase in available short-term housing for tourists was essential for the continued growth of one of San Francisco's key industries. So this is not a case of property going from a higher- to a lower-value use. Quite the contrary, the set of suitable locations for tourists is much more restricted than the space for long-term housing. Wholly apart from any long-term tenant protection, the shift in land use should generate net social gains.

It is equally clear, however, that this change will not generate a Pareto improvement because the displacement of sitting tenants produces large losses for multiple reasons. First, these tenants have locational benefits that are difficult to duplicate elsewhere, including a wide array of support services and social relationships that are location-bound. Second, finding accommodations in other neighborhoods is no easy feat when housing markets are uncommonly tight because San Francisco's baroque land use regulations block the new construction that could ease the loss, not only for tenants who are displaced by tourist housing, but also to any and all tenants who are displaced at all. So the *San Remo* standard compounds the blunder by blocking the landlord's right to reclaim premises at the end of any lease. In so doing, it takes the law in the wrong direction. The only structural solution to the problem of displaced tenants requires San Francisco to remove the restrictions on supply by allowing freer entry of new housing, including the conversion of other kinds of units, if appropriate, into rental housing. The sad truth is that dislocation losses are compounded by giving inordinate protection to sitting tenants elsewhere. Yet this added round of restrictions will in the end lead to the decline of tourist housing and a shortage of new rental units, accounting in part for the sky-high rentals found throughout San Francisco. No effort to constrain housing supply will produce distributional gains sufficient to offset the allocative losses.

With this said, the superior court was probably right in holding that the San Jose ordinance went too far under the *San Remo* test. That standard was tailored to meet the situation at hand, i.e., one in which individual tenants had been displaced. The San Jose ordinance did not apply to existing tenants, but only to new housing, removing the displacement of existing tenants from the equation. Filling in of vacant land presents an easier social problem than displacing tenants. So the ordinance in *CBIA* went beyond what was decided in *San Remo* by requiring affordable housing concessions from developers undertaking the construction of new units even when no old ones were removed from the marketplace. That rule applies even for projects that only increase, as noted, the long-term supply of housing that is so critical to improving the overall situation.

3.2.B *The Higher Scrutiny of* Nollan *and* Dolan

At this point, the only challenge left to the California Supreme Court in *CBIA* was to justify its unwillingness to apply *Nollan* and *Dolan*. In my view, ignoring those two cases was improper because its overall analysis depended on it giving an indefensibly narrow reading of the *Loretto* test that requires per se compensation when there is a permanent loss of possession. According to *CBIA*, that test does not apply whenever the state "simply restricts the use of property without demanding the conveyance of some identifiable protected property interest (a dedication of property or the payment of money) as a condition of approval."

The key mistake here is that the court misdefines a land use restriction as that term was used in *Penn Central*. Correctly understood, the government in those cases does not change the party in possession but only limits the way in which that party can use what he possesses. Hence the restriction of new construction in *Penn Central*. But the inclusionary zoning cases are not just restrictions on how the property is used. They are also explicit restrictions on who can use the property. In the *Loretto* situation, the government told Loretto that she had to allow Teleprompter onto its premises. In the inclusionary housing cases, the government does not identify who shall go into any affordable housing unit. And it does not indicate which units shall be open to some member of the protected class. But it does make very clear that it authorizes some individuals to enter some units at below-market rates. The fact that the government gives the developer the option to decide which unit shall be turned over to a particular tenant does not convert that mandated occupation into a simple restriction on land use. It is still the possessory taking of a particular unit that will be specified not at the time the project starts, but when it is completed. The additional element of choice does not convert a physical taking into a regulatory one. It only allows the landowner to mitigate losses, and thus to reduce the level of compensation owed by the state.

The key mistake in *CBIA* derives from the confused concurring opinion of Justice Kennedy in *Eastern Enterprises v. Apfel* (524 U.S. 498, 540 (1998)), which insisted that the Takings Clause does not apply because the Coal Act "does not appropriate, transfer, or encumber an estate in land (e.g., a lien on a particular piece of property). [It] simply imposes an obligation to perform an act, the payment of benefits." He therefore concluded that the retroactive imposition of huge taxes to fund health care benefits for retirees in the coal industry "must be invalidated as contrary to essential due process principles, without regard to the Takings Clause of the Fifth Amendment" (*Eastern Enterprises* at 539 (1998)). Note that the word "property" is not used in this capsule summary of the due process claim, because Justice Kennedy believed a general charge on the revenues of certain energy companies called for a higher level of due process scrutiny, because it singled out unpopular groups or individuals. The conclusion is sound. The argument is not.

First, the Due Process Clause requires that the claimant be asked to surrender "life, liberty or property." It follows therefore that the absence of any property interest removes the protection of the Due Process Clause. But if the want of an identifiable interest does not block the application of the Due Process Clause, it cannot block the application of the Takings Clause either. The retroactivity concern applies equally to both, which in turn requires asking the two questions about the police power and implicit-in-kind compensation relevant in all takings cases. The former does not apply in *Eastern Enterprises* given that the forced contributions to the black lung disease programs were imposed on firms that had long been out of the coal business. Yet while they were in business, they had complied with all their legal obligations. Similarly, that program generated no return benefit to these firms. Hence we have the pure net loss that the Takings Clause prohibits. General revenues, not special assessments, should cover these expenses if they are to be covered at all. The prohibition against retroactive liability blocks the impermissible burdens on private firms for public benefits. The analysis is identical under both the Takings and Due Process Clauses.

Second, as a matter of private law, the want of identifiable property interests is no obstacle to the protection of property interests. Many businesses commonly use floating liens that allow the borrower to use property freely, especially inventory, until some default occurs, after which the lien attaches to the assets that remain in the possession of the debtor up to the amount of the lien.[13] This device increases the value of the business and thereby reduces the likelihood of default – a win/win situation. But on default that lien is possessory and should be fully protected under *Loretto*.

A similar strategy is involved with taxation. The government identifies the total tax base and then lets the taxpayer pick whatever assets it wants to satisfy the bill – a floating lien. But once the taxes are not paid, the government can attach its tax lien to whatever property it chooses in order to discharge the debt. Taxes and takings do not fall into different worlds, for there is no conceptual gap between them.[14] The key difference comes in on the *benefit side*, where the taxes are justified by the in-kind benefits in the form of public goods.

Indeed, the logic of *Loretto* also covers any case where government forces the owner off the land that it then declines to occupy, which is what it did in *Penn Central* when it kept the owner from using the air rights, without using them itself. It is incomprehensible that the government should be allowed to avoid paying any compensation at all if it chooses to leave the air space empty, but must pay full compensation if it develops it in some modest way. Conservation easements often leave land undeveloped. In this case, the difference, if any, goes to the issue of valuation, where the loss to the owner is somewhat smaller (because of the preservation of view and light) if the government leaves the air rights empty than if it builds (Epstein 2013). But there is no on-off switch that tracks the requirement of compensation, or not in such a minute difference.

As has been hinted before, *Loretto* also applies with full force to all rent control and rent stabilization statutes. In the majority opinion in *Yee v. Village of Escondido* (503 U.S. 519 (1992)), Justice O'Connor claimed that the typical rent control statute involved only a regulatory taking, not a physical taking under the *Loretto* rule. Her argument was: "On their face, the state and local laws at issue here merely regulate petitioners' *use* of their land by regulating the relationship between landlord and tenant" (*Yee* at 528 (1992)). But her logic is a transparent misuse of the word "use." She thus manages in a single sentence to upend 1,000 years of property law. Clearly the tenant in *Yee* has possession of the premises, and his entry was authorized by the government under *Loretto*: after all, the basic rent control law found it "is necessary that the owners of mobile homes occupied within mobile home parks be provided with the unique protection from actual or constructive eviction afforded by the provisions of this chapter" (Mobilehome Residency Law, Cal. Civ. Code Ann. § 798 (West 1982 and Supp. 1991), § 798.55(a)). Justice O'Connor cannot deny that a rent control tenant, any more than an affordable housing tenant, is in possession, so she shifts grounds to insist that landlords "voluntarily rented their land to mobile home owners" (*Yee* at 527 (1992)). But the lease was for a year, not in perpetuity, so that the tenant is, as noted earlier, a holdover tenant who can be evicted as of right. It follows therefore that the affordable housing program, by forcing landowners to set aside given property for tenants or buyers, results in a possessory taking as that term was used in *Loretto*. The huge loss in capital value is not compensated in kind by the supposed right to evict a tenant, so long as the landlord is prepared to convert the property to some lower-valued use when the applicable constitutional standard under *Monongahela Nav. Co. v. United States*, 148 U.S. 312, 325 (1893) requires "a full and just equivalent" for the property surrendered. The simple point is that the rent control statutes and the affordable housing legislation are both possessory takings, and hence out from under the *Penn Central* rule.

CONCLUSION

In this chapter, I have explored both the economic and constitutional rationales for inclusionary zoning programs. The economics of this area show that the perverse incentives created by the various set-aside programs have a negative effect on overall welfare. For the gain of a few affordable units, the entire housing system is thrown into major forms of disarray that result in fewer housing units available at all levels of income. The takings analysis starts with an abstract commitment to the protection of private property against expropriation, but it too marches off in the same direction.

Once the Takings Clause is understood to cover all takings of partial interests, the inquiry then turns to sensible justifications for takings, of which the control of nuisances is the major one in land use contexts. Nothing of this sort is at issue in the affordable housing set-asides. The next question is whether compensation is provided for the losses in question, to which the answer is always negative. Once these connections are established, the inability to find either cash or in-kind compensation in affordable housing cases should be their constitutional death knell. Why allow any program to go forward that promises losses in excess of gains? But if the economic analysis is clear, the constitutional analysis in both federal and state courts is a hopeless tangle of transient distinctions and pained rationalizations of confiscatory programs that give little help to their intended beneficiaries but cause much social dislocation for everyone else. They are strictly dominated by a program that either removes entry barriers to new housing, or uses direct subsidies to support it. The popularity of these programs proves that their political salience is inversely correlated with their social welfare. They should be terminated forthwith.

AUTHOR'S NOTE

My thanks to Connor Haynes, NYU School of Law, Class of 2017 and Mala Chatterjee, NYU School of Law, Class of 2018 for their excellent research assistance.

REFERENCES

Epstein, Richard A. 2016. "The Hidden Virtues of Income Inequality, Defining Ideas." May 2, available at www.hoover.org/research/hidden-virtues-income-inequality.

2015a. "The Bundling Problem in Takings Law: Where the Exaction Process Goes Off the Rails." *Brigham-Kanner Property Rights Conference Journal* 4: 133–49.

2015b. "The Upside-Down Law of Property and Contract: Of Fannie Mae, Freddie Mac, and San Jose." *Nebraska Law Review* 93: 869–900.

2014. *The Classical Liberal Constitution.* Cambridge, MA: Harvard University Press.

2013. "The Takings Clause and Partial Interests in Land: On Sharp Boundaries and Continuous Distributions." *Brook. Law Review* 78: 589–623.

1995. "The Harms and Benefits of *Nollan* and *Dolan*." *Northern Illinois University Law Review* 15: 479–92.

1985. *Takings: Private Property and the Power of Eminent Domain.* Cambridge, MA: Harvard University Press.

Harrington, Arthur J. 1980. "Insecurity for Secured Creditors: The Floating Lien, and Section 547 of the Bankruptcy Act." *Marquette Law Review* 63: 447–88.

Keil, Jennifer Gould and Danika Fears, 2015. "'Poor Doors' Are No More Thanks to Rent-Regulation Bill." *New York Post*. June 28.

Powell, Benjamin and Edward Stringham. 2005. "The Economics of Inclusionary Zoning Reclaimed: How Effective Are Price Controls?" *Florida State University Law Review* 33: 471–99.

Schwartz, Nelson. 2016. "In an Age of Privilege, Not Everyone Is in the Same Boat." *New York Times Magazine*. April 24.

Thompson on Real Property. Vol. 3. 1959.

Cases

Board of Public Utility Commissioners v. New York Telephone Co., 271 U.S. 23 (1926)

Brooks-Scanlon Co. v. Railroad Commission, 251 U.S. 396 (1920)

California Building Industry Association v. City of San Jose, 61 Cal. 4th. 435, 351 P.3d 974 (2015).

Crechale & Polles, Inc. v. Smith, 295 So. 2d 275 (Miss. 1974)

Daniels v. Borough of Point Pleasant, 129 A.2d 265 (N.J. 1957)

Dolan v. City of Tigard, 512 U.S. 374 (1994)

Drees Company v. Hamilton Township, 970 N.E.2d 916 (Ohio 2012)

Eastern Enterprises v. Apfel, 524 U.S. 498 (1998)

Katz v. United States, 389 U.S. 347 (1967)

Kern v. City of Long Beach, 179 P.2d 799, 801 (Cal 1947)

Koontz v. St. Johns River Water Mgmt. Dist., 133 S. Ct. 2586, 570 U.S. [] (2013)

Loretto v. Teleprompter, 458 U.S. 419 (1982)

Monongahela Nav. Co. v. United States, 148 U.S. 312, 325 (1893)

Nebbia v. New York, 291 U.S. 502, 539 (1934)

New York Times v. Sullivan, 376 U.S. 254 (1964)

Nollan v. California Coastal Commission, 483 U.S. 825 (1987)

Penn Central Transportation Co. v. City of New York, 438 U.S. 104 (1978)

Pumpelly v. Green Bay Co., 80 U.S. 166 (1872)

San Jose Police Officers' Association v. City of San Jose, No. 1–12-CV 225926 (Consolidated with Nos. 1–12-CV 225928, 1–12, CV-226570, 1–12-CV 226574, 1–12-CV 227864 & 1–12-CV-233660) (Super. Ct. Santa Clara Cnty. Dec. 20, 2013) (unreported tentative decision)

San Remo Hotel, LP v. City and County of San Francisco, 41 P.3d 87, 117 Cal. Rptr. 2d 269, 27 Cal. 4th 643 (2002), aff'd on unrelated procedural grounds, 545 U.S. 323 (2005).

State ex rel. Petroleum Underground Storage Tank Release Comp. Bd. v. Withrow, 579 N.E.2d 705 (Ohio 1991)

Union Pac. R.R. Co. v. Pub. Serv. Comm'n of Mo., 248 U.S. 67, 70 (1918)

Yee v. Village of Escondido, 503 U.S. 519 (1992)

Statutes

California Health and Safety Code sections 5001, 5003
Housing Act of 1937, 42 U.S.C. § 1437f
Mobilehome Residency Law, Cal. Civ. Code Ann. § 798 (West 1982 and Supp. 1991), § 798.55(a)
N.Y. Envtl. Conserv. Law §8–0105
N.Y. Real Property Tax Law Section 421-a, amended by Chapter 20 of the Laws of 2015, available at www1.nyc.gov/site/hpd/developers/tax-incentives-421a -main.page
Ordinance (S. F. Admin. Code) ch. 41

Miscellaneous

City and County of San Francisco: Residential Rent Stabilization and Arbitration Board, Allowable Annual Rent Increases (December 4, 2015), available at http://sfrb.org/sites/default/files/Document/Form/571%20Allowable%20Annual %20Increases%2016–17%20FINAL_0.pdf
Furman Center Fact Brief, *Profile of Rent-Stabilized Units and Tenants in New York City*, Table C for various areas, available at http://furmancenter.org/files /FurmanCenter_FactBrief_RentStabilization_June2014.pdf
Investopedia, www.investopedia.com/terms/f/floating-lien.asp#ixzz48CXoKlnC
NYC Rent Guidelines Board, Succession Rights FAX, available at www.nycrgb.org /html/resources/faq/succession.html

Notes

1. *See Brooks-Scanlon Co. v. Railroad Commission*, 251 U.S. 396 (1920) (holding that gains from nonregulated activities cannot be used to offset shortfalls from regulated businesses); *Board of Public Utility Commissioners v. New York Telephone Co*, 271 U.S. 23 (1926) (holding it impermissible to allow losses in the current period to be offset by the promise of future profits).
2. I have critiqued this article in Epstein (2016).
3. Chapter 20 of the Laws of 2015, amending New York Real Property Tax Law Section 421-a, www1.nyc.gov/site/hpd/developers/tax-incentives-421a-main.page.
4. Note that San Jose's sensible pension reform ordinance was struck down in *San Jose Police Officers' Association v. City of San Jose*, No. 1–12-CV 225926 (Consolidated with Nos. 1–12-CV 225928, 1–12, CV-226570, 1–12-CV 226574, 1–12-CV 227864 & 1–12-CV-233660) (Super. Ct. Santa Clara Cnty. Dec. 20, 2013) (unreported tentative decision), under a rule whereby "the right to a pension vests upon acceptance of employment." *Kern v. City of Long Beach*, 179 P.2d 799, 801 (Cal 1947) For my critique, see Epstein (2015a, 888–900).
5. See NYC Rent Guidelines Board, Succession Rights FAX, available at www .nycrgb.org/html/resources/faq/succession.html.

6. Furman Center Fact Brief, Profile of Rent-Stabilized Units and Tenants in New York City, Table C for various areas, available at http://furmancenter .org/files/FurmanCenter_FactBrief_RentStabilization_June2014.pdf.
7. For more detailed discussions, see Epstein (1995, 2015a).
8. See, e.g., *Drees Company v. Hamilton Township*, 970 N.E.2d 916 (Ohio 2012) (rejecting as disproportionate an impact fee from developers for roads, parks, and fire and police protection); *Daniels v. Borough of Point Pleasant*, 129 A.2d 265 (N.J. 1957) (same). In contrast, see *State ex rel. Petroleum Underground Storage Tank Release Comp. Bd. v. Withrow*, 579 N.E.2d 705 (Ohio 1991) (allowing special fees to counter the risk of petroleum releases from underground storage facilities).
9. For discussion, see Epstein (2014). The principal applies to takings *Pumpelly v. Green Bay Co.*, 80 U.S. 166 (1872); searches and seizures, see, e.g., *Katz v. United States*, 389 U.S. 347 (1967); and the first amendment, see, e.g., *New York Times v. Sullivan*, 376 U.S. 254 (1964).
10. For fuller expositions, see Epstein (1995, 2015a).
11. "As a general rule, a tenancy from year to year is created by the tenant's holding over after the expiration of a term for years and the continued payment of the yearly rent reserved. … By remaining in possession of leased premises after the expiration of his lease, a tenant gives the landlord the option of treating him as a trespasser or as a tenant for another year." Thompson on Real Property § 1024, at 65–66 (1959). See also *Crechale & Polles, Inc. v. Smith*, 295 So. 2d 275 (Miss. 1974).
12. For a similarly broad law, see N.Y. Envtl. Conserv. Law §8–0105.
13. "A legal claim placed on a set of assets rather than on a single asset," such as accounts receivable that fluctuate over time. Investopedia, www.investopedia .com/terms/f/floating-lien.asp#ixzz48CXoKlnC. For a general discussion, see Harrington (1980).
14. For discussion, see Epstein (1985).

PART II

Housing as Community: Stability, Change, and Perceptions

4

Balancing the Costs and Benefits of Historic Preservation

Ingrid Gould Ellen and Brian J. McCabe

4.1 INTRODUCTION

Historic preservation efforts typically invite controversy, especially in high-cost cities. Advocates of preservation loudly trumpet the benefits of protecting the historic assets of a city, while critics charge that preservation freezes city neighborhoods and constrains their vital growth and development. Few observers have provided a balanced and thorough assessment of these costs and benefits, yet such an assessment is critical as city leaders make choices about which properties and neighborhoods to protect and preserve.

On the one hand, historic preservation clearly delivers benefits. The creation of historic districts may help to strengthen neighborhood identity, encourage social cohesion, and increase property values by providing certainty about future development. As Strahilevitz (Chapter 5, this volume) notes, preserving history – even a "fake" history created artificially to commemorate nonevents – has the power to generate feelings of community through a shared narrative of place-making. More fundamentally, preservation protects critical architectural and historical assets for future generations and provides a tangible link to our past. In New York City, preservation efforts have protected such architectural treasures as Grand Central Terminal and such classic nineteenth-century brownstone neighborhoods as Brooklyn Heights. We can still see the Greenwich Village townhouses where Edith Wharton, Hart Crane, and Malcolm Cowley were inspired to write and the Harlem brownstones where W. E. B. Du Bois, Paul Robeson, Count Basie, and other artists and intellectuals of the Harlem Renaissance brought to life twentieth-century African American culture. These historic assets are enjoyed not only by local residents, but also by visitors who travel to experience these historic buildings and neighborhoods.

On the other hand, historic preservation places constraints on a city's ability to grow and develop by limiting the opportunity to construct new buildings or increase density on protected sites. Like other land use regulations, historic preservation rules impose new constraints that often halt the demolition of older buildings and limit the size and density of any newer ones. By imposing supply restrictions, the preservation process is likely to lead to higher housing prices and rents, both citywide and, quite possibly, within individual districts. By limiting the supply of rental housing through restrictions on new construction activity, it may drive overall prices up across the city. The requirements for higher-cost building materials in historic districts may translate into higher rents, creating obstacles for low- and moderate-income households to live in these neighborhoods. In the long run, these restrictions could limit the growth and economic development of cities as businesses seek out other places with lower housing costs and wages.

Decisions about which properties and neighborhoods to preserve are often politically charged, pitting preservation advocates against real estate developers. Developers lament the onerous restrictions the preservation process imposes while preservation advocates charge that the development process undervalues characteristics of the city that cannot be easily monetized in property transactions. Without a preservation process that explicitly values the historical character of neighborhoods and buildings outside of the market, these advocates worry that many places that contribute to the rich history and cultural fabric of the city will be lost to new development.

In this chapter, we argue for a more explicit and balanced assessment of the costs and benefits of preservation efforts in New York City. We focus on the establishment of historic districts, rather than individual landmarks, because these districts cover far more properties than individual landmark designations and, as a result, tend to invite more controversy. In calling for a balanced analysis of the costs and benefits, we acknowledge that many of the benefits of preservation are hard to quantify. After all, how do we put a dollar value on the existence of Grand Central Terminal or quantify the enjoyment of the streetscape of Greenwich Village by residents and visitors? But the difficulty in quantifying the full set of benefits does not mean we should avoid quantifying the costs.

To offer a balanced perspective on historic preservation, we offer new evidence on the development constraints imposed by historic preservation. We do so by calculating the amount of unbuilt floor area within historic districts and comparing the density and development of lots inside historic districts and lots in the neighborhoods immediately outside of them. In brief, we find that historic districts are built to a similar density level as the neighborhoods surrounding them, a finding that appears to suggest minimal constraints. However, we report that less new construction takes place in historic districts and that residential soft sites, defined as lots that are built to less than half of their zoned capacity, are less likely to experience redevelopment when they are located in historic districts. To create a more balanced approach to historic preservation, we argue that the planning process in New York City should consider these costs of preservation alongside the important, but less tangible benefits that preservation creates for the city. We conclude with a set of procedural suggestions for how the city can better make decisions about historic preservation in ways that balance their benefits against other planning goals.

4.2 THE LANDSCAPE OF PRESERVATION IN NEW YORK CITY

Established in 1965, the New York City Landmarks Preservation Commission (LPC) designates historic neighborhoods, properties, and scenic landmarks for protection under the Charter and the Administrative Code of the City of New York (Allison 1996; Wood 2007). In this capacity, the LPC is empowered to preserve historic districts that contain buildings with a unique historic or aesthetic appeal, represent one or more architectural styles in the city, and create a distinct body of urban history. While designated historic districts may include properties that do not contribute to the unique character of the neighborhood, a large majority of properties included in a historic district are supposed to contribute to the architectural, cultural, or historic character of a designated neighborhood.

Since the establishment of Brooklyn Heights as the city's first historic district in 1965, the LPC has designated more than 100 districts across the five boroughs of New York City. By the end of 2014, with the designation of the Chester Court Historic District, the LPC had created 114 unique historic districts.[1] Although these designations have occurred in communities throughout the city, they are largely concentrated in only a handful of areas. In Manhattan, historic districts are located disproportionately on the Upper East Side, the Upper West Side, and portions of the borough south of 14th Street, as shown in Figure 4.1. In Brooklyn, historic districts are concentrated largely in downtown Brooklyn and the neighborhoods surrounding Prospect Park.

As the number of historic districts has grown over the past five decades, so too has the amount of land regulated by the Landmarks Preservation Commission. Figure 4.2 shows the growth in the number of lots included in historic districts over time, highlighting this growth across different mayoral administrations. The figure reveals a relatively steady pace of designation since the 1960s. By the end of 2014, there were more than 27,700 lots in historic districts in New York City. On average, district designations added 557 lots each year, though the pace of growth has varied across mayoral administrations. Mayor Wagner's single year saw the designation of 1,279 lots, while Mayor Beame's administration added an average of only 172 lots annually over his four years in office. While Figure 4.2 suggests a steady increase in the number of lots protected through the preservation process, it is worth noting that only 3.3 percent of lots were located in a historic district at the end of 2014. If preservation were to continue at the same pace going forward, it would take more than 700 years before the majority of the city's lots were in designated historic districts. In Manhattan, however, it would take only another 50 years.

Because lots in New York City are not uniformly sized, it is also useful to examine the proportion of total lot *area* included in historic districts. We report the

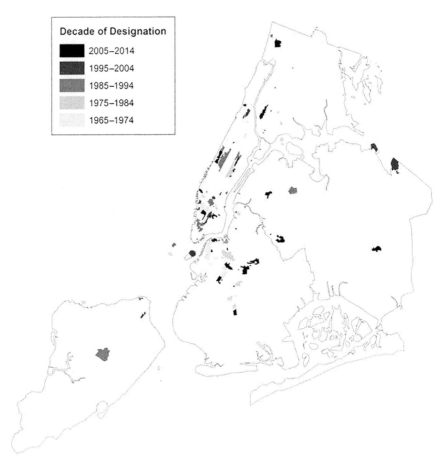

FIGURE 4.1 New York City Historic Districts and Extensions Added, by Decade
Sources: New York City Landmarks Preservation Commission, NYU Furman Center

comparisons between lots and lot area in Table 4.1. By 2014, about 3.3 percent of the lots in the city were regulated as part of a historic district. Historic districts covered about 3 percent of lot area, or slightly more than 125 million square feet of land, across New York City. These aggregate measures for New York City mask substantial variation across the five boroughs. In Manhattan, more than 25 percent of *lots* and nearly 15 percent of *lot area* were located in historic districts by 2014. These totals amounted to more than 50 million square feet of land on 10,762 lots. For critics of historic preservation worried about the impact of preservation policies on construction and development, the square footage of land regulated by the LPC in Manhattan is a worrying indication of excessive regulation in the city's densest borough.

However, in the other boroughs, the LPC regulates a substantially smaller share of lots.[2] Table 4.1 highlights this variation across boroughs. In Brooklyn, for example,

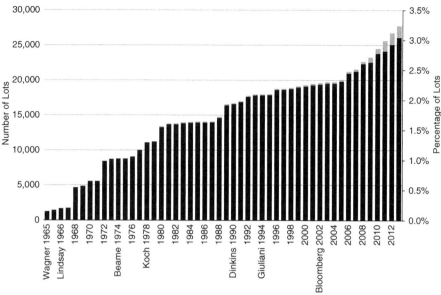

Light shading at the ends of the bars reflects extensions to existing districts

FIGURE 4.2 Count and Percent of City Lots in Historic District, by Year
Sources: New York City Landmarks Preservation Commission, MapPLUTO, NYU
Furman Center

TABLE 4.1: *Percent of Borough and New York City Lots and Lot Area Regulated by the*
Landmarks Preservation Commission, 2014

	Metric	NYC	Brooklyn	Bronx	Manhattan	Queens	Staten Island
Historic Districts	Lots	3.3%	4.4%	1.0%	25.4%	1.1%	0.2%
	Lot Area	3.0%	3.4%	1.3%	14.7%	1.5%	1.8%
Individual + Interior Designations*	Lots	0.1%	0.1%	0.1%	1.6%	0.0%	0.1%
	Lot Area	1.4%	1.8%	1.9%	5.2%	0.1%	1.3%
LPC Designated	Lots	3.4%	4.5%	1.0%	27.0%	1.2%	0.3%
	Lot Area	4.4%	5.2%	3.2%	19.9%	1.6%	3.1%

Note: * The individual + interior designation row includes only designations not within historic districts.
While the table shows that 1.4 percent of lot area for New York City is covered by a lot containing an
individual or interior landmark, the percentage drops to 0.6 if we restrict to the building footprint of
individually designated landmark structures.
Sources: New York City Landmarks Preservation Commission, MapPLUTO, NYU Furman Center

only 4.4 percent of lots – and 3.4 percent of lot area – were regulated through historic districts by 2014. This includes approximately 37 million square feet of land located on 12,276 individual lots in the borough. In Queens, only 1.1 percent of lots and 1.5 percent of lot area were included in historic districts at the end of 2014.

4.3 THEORY AND PAST LITERATURE: BENEFITS AND COSTS OF HISTORIC DISTRICTS

The preservation of historic neighborhoods is likely to generate costs and benefits both for the residents of designated neighborhoods and for the city as a whole. To date, much of the research studying the impact of historic districts examines the net benefits property owners enjoy within districts, focusing specifically on housing price impacts following historic designation. Studies relying on longitudinal data to examine price changes in the wake of designation generally find that historic preservation has a negligible or even negative effect on property values (Asabere, Huffman, and Mehdian 1994; Coulson and Leichenko 2001; Heintzelman and Altieri 2013; Noonan and Krupka 2011).[3]

Been and colleagues (2016) offer a model showing that the net effect of historic designation on the value of properties within the district is theoretically ambiguous. On the one hand, designation restricts the changes property owners can make to their buildings and largely prohibits demolition and redevelopment. As such, designation should reduce land and property values. On the other hand, designation minimizes the risk that new investments in neighborhoods will undermine the distinctive character of a historic community. As such, designation should boost property values to the extent that it preserves the historic character and architectural fabric of a neighborhood.

This model suggests that these relative costs and benefits will vary across neighborhoods. In neighborhoods where buildings are initially built to the allowable zoning cap or demand for the location is low, preservation should increase property values because owners are not giving up much in terms of development rights. However, in neighborhoods where demand is high and heights are far below the allowable zoning cap, the lost option value will be large. In those neighborhoods, we would expect property values to increase less, or even to fall, following the designation of a historic neighborhood. In addition, preservation should provide more benefit to owners if the neighboring historic homes preserved by the district rules are more aesthetically attractive.

Studying New York City, Been and colleagues (2016) undertake empirical work that largely confirms the predictions of their theoretical model. Designation appears to raise property values within historic districts, but only in the lower-valued boroughs outside Manhattan. Further, designation has a more positive impact on prices in neighborhoods that score higher on a measure of aesthetic appeal. Notably, properties located in the immediate neighborhood surrounding the historic district, defined by a 250-foot buffer, also experience a boost in property values following designation. These nearby homes enjoy many of the benefits of preservation, including neighborhood continuity and minimal risk of new development, without the restrictions imposed on individual property owners. Although the boundaries of existing districts are modified only occasionally to include additional lots, property owners in buffer zones may anticipate opportunities for future inclusion in an expanded historic district.

In addition to the changes to property values, historic preservation is likely to bring other long-term changes to designated neighborhoods. McCabe and Ellen (2016) report that the socioeconomic status of a neighborhood rises and the poverty rate declines after designation by the Landmarks Preservation Commission. While this process of community "upgrading" likely benefits many neighborhood residents, it may also create obstacles for low- and moderate-income renters looking for affordable housing in designated historic neighborhoods. As Phillips (Chapter 6, this volume) reminds us, physical preservation of architectural treasures, like churches, may do little to preserve the social capital in a community. In their conversion to residential units, these buildings often lose the role they played as key community institutions.

Beyond the impacts within individual neighborhoods, historic preservation efforts create benefits and costs for much broader populations, many of whom do not live in the neighborhoods protected by the preservation process. City residents and tourists alike often visit, enjoy, and learn from the architectural examples and cultural landscapes preserved through historic designation. These districts contribute to the creation of a distinctive identity for the city, promoting tourism and contributing to economic development. A set of comparative case studies argues that historic preservation has helped to fuel the economic revitalization of downtown office and retail districts and thereby helped to further broader economic development (Ryberg-Webster and Kinahan 2014; Wojno 1991), although these studies tend to focus on National Historic Trust designation, rather than local designations. Designation through the National Historic Trust often comes with accompanying financial benefits that are likely to contribute to this process of economic development.

While preservation efforts may support tourism and contribute to economic growth, such benefits may come at the cost of restricting the supply of housing citywide. Critics contend that widespread historic preservation puts pressure on cities already grappling with challenges to building a sufficient supply of affordable housing (Glaeser 2010). Yet, there has been little effort to quantify the impact of preservation on the citywide supply of housing, or to identify the number of housing units that could have been built absent historic preservation efforts. To the extent that historic designation restricts the supply of housing within districts, it will also restrict the overall supply of housing in a city unless other areas outside of the district are upzoned to compensate for the lost development capacity. Although regulating a small number of lots through the historic preservation process is unlikely to dramatically reduce the overall supply, as the number of lots included in historic districts increases, concerns about supply restrictions become more valid. In cities with both a robust preservation process and a tight housing market, restrictions imposed by historic designation could put upward pressure on housing prices and rents, ultimately limiting economic growth, heightening economic segregation, and contributing to concerns about housing affordability.

4.4 HISTORIC PRESERVATION, GROWTH, AND DEVELOPMENT

Critics of historic preservation policies often express concern about the regulatory burdens imposed by efforts to protect historic neighborhoods. In protecting historically significant neighborhoods from changes to the historic character of a community, the preservation process may also limit opportunities for continued growth and development across the city. Critics contend that preservation policies restrict the buildable capacity of neighborhoods, eliminate opportunities for new construction, and inhibit the redevelopment of residential soft sites. If so, then historic preservation policies may contribute to the crisis of affordable housing by constraining opportunities to increase density or build additional housing.

There has been little empirical research to formally analyze the degree to which historic districts constrain development. Given that designation is clearly not random, estimating the impact of historic districts is challenging. For example, historic districts are more likely to be established in areas with older homes. It is possible that historic districts are proposed in neighborhoods that don't already have other zoning constraints, or that these zoning constraints are more likely to be adopted in areas without historic buildings. Even though we do not claim to precisely identify the impact of historic districts, we seek to better understand the relationship between preservation and development by comparing the density levels, buildable capacity, and construction activity on lots inside and outside of historic districts in New York City.

We begin by comparing the built density of lots located inside these districts with lots located outside of them, including the fraction of allowable density used. Next, we consider new construction and alteration activity on individual lots. By comparing lots located in historic districts to other nearby lots in the community, we quantify the extent to which these lots attract less new construction activity. Finally, we examine whether residential soft sites, or lots built to *less than half of their zoned capacity*, are less likely to be redeveloped inside of historic districts. Soft sites create a unique opportunity for residential redevelopment, and our analysis investigates whether historic preservation affects the likelihood of this redevelopment.

Because historic districts tend to be concentrated in particular neighborhoods in the city, simple comparisons of density and development intensity between lots located inside of historic districts and those outside of them are likely to be misleading. These comparisons may simply capture differences between the high-density neighborhoods in lower Manhattan and downtown Brooklyn, where historic districts are concentrated, and other parts of the city. To provide a more accurate comparison, we instead compare lots inside historic districts to those lots outside of the district that are still located in the same general neighborhood, as measured by community districts. Community districts are sub-borough areas that include between 50,000 and 250,000 residents. By the end of 2014, 32 of the city's 59 community districts housed at least one historic district. Each of these community districts also contained many unregulated parcels.[4]

Throughout the analysis, we estimate regressions for several measures, including lot density and development ratios. We include a dummy variable that identifies whether a parcel is located in a historic district, as well as community district fixed effects. With these fixed effects, the coefficient on the historic district indicator identifies whether, on average, the characteristics of lots located inside historic districts differ from those of lots located outside those districts, but still in the same general neighborhood.

4.4.A Sample

Throughout the analysis, we rely on shape-files provided by the New York City Landmark Preservation Commission. As of March 2015, these files identify the lots located within historic districts. We overlay MapPLUTO shape-files from the New York City Department of City Planning with the historic district maps to determine the land area of each lot covered by a historic district. Lots with less than 100 square feet of coverage by a historic district were not included within a historic district for purposes of our analysis. We exclude lots with a land use category of "09," known as "Open Space and Outdoor Recreation," as well as other lots classified as parks. We also exclude Ellis Island, Liberty Island, airports, large underwater lots, and lots with no calculated lot area.

We use the Zoning Resolution of the City of New York and the primary zoning district information on MapPLUTO 2007 to assign maximum residential and non-residential floor area ratios (FAR) to each lot (and assigned FAR based on majority lot area coverage in the instances of a split zoning lot) as of 2007. Adjustments are made to the maximum floor area to account for special district regulations and as-of-right zoning bonuses (e.g., Inclusionary Housing Program and plaza bonuses).

For the regression analyses summarized in Table 4.2, we begin with a sample of 851,059 lots.[5] From there, we exclude 1,154 New York City Housing Authority (NYCHA) lots, 1,272 lots located in transfer districts, and 1,164 lots with individual or exterior landmarks. For the analysis of permitted floor area ratio, the final sample is 847,469 lots. For the remaining analyses in Table 4.2, we exclude lots designated as a historic district after 2004 because we are testing for differences in development patterns between 2004 and 2014 for parcels within and outside of historic districts as of 2004. This brings our sample to 838,963 lots. The sample used for the analysis of residential soft sites, which we report in Table 4.3, starts with lots as of 2007, makes the same exclusions, and is then restricted to 194,360 residential lots classified as soft sites in 2007.

TABLE 4.2: *Differences between a Historic District Lot and a Non-historic District Lot*

	In New York City	In the Same Community District
In the Share of Permitted Floor Area Used (2014)	12.30 percentage points	7.15 percentage points
In the Share of Lots with New Construction Activity (2004–2014)	– 3.28 percentage points	– 2.91 percentage points
In the Share of Lots with an Alt 1 Permit (2004–2014)	4.03 percentage points	0.48 percentage points (not significant)

Sources for Floor Area Use: Landmarks Preservation Commission, MapPLUTO, NYC Zoning Resolution, NYU Furman Center.
Sources for New Construction: Landmarks Preservation Commission, MapPLUTO, NYU Furman Center. Lots designated as part of a historic district between 2004 and 2014 are excluded.
Sources for Alt 1 Permits: New York City Department of Buildings, Landmarks Preservation Commission, MapPLUTO, NYU Furman Center. Lots designated as part of a historic district between 2004 and 2014 are excluded.

TABLE 4.3: *Probability of 2007 Residential Soft Site Receiving a New Building, 2008–2014*

	(1)	(2)
Lot Characteristics, as of 2007	New Building, 2008–2014	New Building, 2008–14
In Historic District	-0.0357^{***}	-0.0303^{***}
	(0.00498)	(0.00559)
Building Age		$7.65e-05^{*}$
		(4.20e-05)
Vacant Lot		0.0489^{***}
		(0.00821)
Built FAR		-0.0260^{***}
		(0.00344)
% Allowable Residential Area Used		-0.0468^{***}
		(0.00433)
Constant	0.0339^{***}	0.0479^{***}
	(0.0000991)	(0.00494)
Observations	194,360	194,360
R-squared	0.009	0.043
Community District Fixed Effects	X	X

Robust standard errors in parentheses.
*** p < 0.01, ** p < 0.05, * p < 0.1

4.4.B Allowable and Built Density

We begin by simply comparing the built density levels of lots inside and outside of historic districts. As of 2014, we find that lots within historic districts were built to the same density as lots that were outside of these districts, but located in the same community district. Our first pass, then, suggests that historic districts might not do much to constrain density levels.

Rather than considering the built density of lots, however, an arguably better test is whether properties located in historic districts use less of their allowable zoning capacity than other nearby properties. Although this finding would not prove that lots in historic districts would be built to higher density absent their designation, it would suggest a constraint on the development process resulting from historic preservation. To identify the proportion of development capacity used on a lot, we divide the built floor area by the maximum floor area allowed on the lot.

The first row of Table 4.2 shows the difference in the share of permitted floor area used by lots inside and outside of historic districts. On average, we find that lots located inside historic districts utilize 12 percentage points more of their permitted floor area than other lots around the city. Citywide, the average lot within a historic district uses 59 percent of the permitted floor area. By comparison, the average lot outside of a historic district uses only 47 percent of permitted floor area. When we estimate our regressions with community district fixed effects, we find that this basic difference holds within community districts, but that the gap between lots located in historic districts and those outside of them shrinks: the initial gap of 12 percentage points from the citywide comparisons shrinks to just 7 percentage points when we make comparisons within the same community district. Both differences are statistically significant at the 5 percent level.

In short, as of 2014, our analysis reveals that owners of parcels in historic districts used *more* of their formal development rights than owners of other properties.[6] In part, this is because historic districts are protecting properties that were built prior to the 1961 Zoning Resolution, which reduced allowable density levels throughout the city (New York City Department of City Planning). In historic districts, 98 percent of buildings were built before 1961 and nearly 9 percent of those pre-1961 parcels were built to density levels that current zoning would not allow. But going forward, the more relevant questions concern the likelihood that lots will be redeveloped in the future and that the development rights that technically exist in historic districts will be used. Thus, analyzing actual development activity within historic districts arguably offers a better test of the constraints imposed by historic preservation.

4.4.C New Construction and Alteration Activity

To analyze new construction, we examine whether lots located in historic districts by the start of 2004 were less likely to see new construction activity between 2004 and 2014 than other lots. The second row of Table 4.2 shows that lots in historic districts were, on average, just over three percentage points less likely to see new construction than other lots around the city. When we estimate a regression of new construction activity including community district fixed effects, we see that lots located inside historic districts were slightly less than three percentage points less likely to experience new construction compared to lots outside those districts but located in the same community district. These differences are both statistically significant. There are some notable outliers to this citywide average. For example, in the Tribeca North Historic District, 10 percent of lots saw new construction activity during this 10-year period. On the other hand, more than half of districts – 52 in total – reported no new construction activity between 2004 and 2014.

Finally, the third row of Table 4.2 shows differences in the share of lots that received alteration permits approving building renovations. We focus on *Alteration 1* permits, which include a change in the Certificate of Occupancy. When we compare citywide differences, the results show that lots in historic districts were more likely to receive alteration permits than lots not regulated by the LPC. However, this difference goes away (or loses statistical significance) when we estimate a regression to account for differences across community districts. In other words, historic districts were no more or less likely to receive alteration permits than other nearby lots.

While these analyses show that lots inside of historic districts are less likely to see new construction than other nearby lots, these findings do not control for the likelihood of redevelopment or new construction *before* historic district designation. It is possible that historic districts are designated in areas where little new construction would take place even absent the designation. In previous research, we find that although new construction is less common on sites within historic areas than on other sites, even before they are designated as districts, the district designation widens the gap (Been et al. 2016). In other words, following designation, sites within historic districts are significantly less likely to see new construction than they were before designation, even after controlling for development trends in the surrounding neighborhood.

4.4.D The Development of Residential Soft Sites

Finally, we consider the development of residential soft sites, or lots built to less than *half* of their permitted development capacity under current zoning regulations.[7] Because these sites are substantially underbuilt relative to the allowable density under existing zoning regulations, they are prime locations for redevelopment. In this section, we explore whether such residential soft sites are less likely to be redeveloped when they are located within historic districts.

Across New York City, 19 percent of lots located in historic districts were soft sites in 2007 compared to 22 percent of lots located outside of those districts.[8] To test whether these sites are less likely to be redeveloped when they are located in historic districts, we estimate a regression of the probability that a 2007 soft site was redeveloped, or a new building was constructed on it, between 2008 and 2014.[9] We control for several features of the lot, including whether the site is vacant, the share of allowable density used, and the age and size of any existing building. With these controls, we can test whether buildings of a similar size, age, and allowable zoning capacity were less likely to be redeveloped when they were located in a historic district. We also include community district fixed effects to control for the local neighborhood.[10] Our key independent variable is whether the parcel is located in a historic district as of 2007.[11] Our analysis is reported in Table 4.3.

Consistent with our expectations, we find that vacant lots are substantially more likely to be redeveloped than lots with existing buildings. Lots with structures built more recently, as well as those with larger buildings and buildings that use up more of their allowable development rights, are less likely see new construction. Critical for our analysis, we find that after controlling for these factors, soft sites located inside a historic district are significantly less likely to experience new construction than those located outside of a historic district. The owners of soft sites are less likely to redevelop their lots when they are located in historic districts.

While in the short run, these differences are not likely to radically alter the course of development, in the longer run, they might. Historic districts have locked up quite a bit of floor area in New York City, or at least made it more difficult to develop. In 2014, we estimate, roughly 119 million square feet of allowable residential floor space was unused on privately owned lots in historic districts, based on built density and currently allowable floor area ratios. This translates into roughly 119,000 housing units. To be sure, these units would not immediately (or necessarily) be built absent historic district designation, and there may be other zoning constraints present that make it impossible to build to the maximum allowable floor area ratio. Historic districts constrain density only to the extent that development is unconstrained by other regulatory tools. However, our results show that this "allowable" residential square footage would be more likely to be built in the absence of designation.

4.4.E The Cost of Supply Restrictions

Our analysis reveals that while lots in historic districts are not built less densely than other lots today, they are likely to see less new construction, and therefore add less density, in the future. Such supply restrictions have several implications. First, we expect these restrictions to increase prices and rents. In neighborhoods designated as historic districts, Been and colleagues (2016) report localized property value increases following the designation of historic districts. These price changes are concentrated in neighborhoods in the outer boroughs where the lost option to redevelop is high. However, the establishment of historic districts is also likely to constrain overall development in the city, especially as additional districts are added.

It is difficult to quantify this more generalized impact of preservation on citywide prices. Identifying a citywide counterfactual – for example, a similarly high-cost city without preservation efforts – is impossible. And while we expect preservation efforts to contribute to skyrocketing prices by restricting the supply of housing, we expect these supply constraints are *not* among the most important explanation for rising prices and rent inflation across New York City. Many other factors contribute to rising prices and rents in the city, including the strong economy of the city, the enduring popularity of New York as a place to do business, the limited supply of land, and the many other restrictions on building activity in the city (Salama et al. 2005). Beyond concerns about increasing prices and rents, it is possible that these supply restrictions could limit overall economic growth in the city. Workers may demand higher wages to afford the cost of living in the city, and businesses untethered to the economy of New York City may choose to leave the city for places with cheaper housing and an ample supply of workers.

Finally, supply restrictions that result from historic preservation are likely to exacerbate patterns of economic segregation in urban neighborhoods. In the decades following historic designation, neighborhoods experience increased polarization as poverty rates decline and neighborhood incomes climb within districts (McCabe and Ellen 2016). It appears that the supply restrictions imposed by historic preservation are attracting high-income households who value the amenities of historic neighborhoods and are willing to pay a premium to live in these aesthetically appealing, high-status neighborhoods.

These patterns of economic segregation are increasingly evident in neighborhoods regulated through the historic preservation process. By 2012, the composition of neighborhood residents living in New York's historic districts was substantially different than the composition of residents outside of them. In Figure 4.3, we compare the average household income in census tracts with at least half of their lots located in a historic district to tracts with fewer than half of their lots in historic districts and tracts located completely outside of those districts. The average household income in census tracts comprised mostly of lots within a historic district was $160,192 – more than twice the income of neighborhoods entirely outside of districts.[12] These differences, which are driven by Manhattan and Brooklyn, result from both initial differences between neighborhoods and the actual impact of historic preservation.

Beyond these variations in average income, we find other substantial differences between the population living within historic districts and the comparable population living within the same community but outside the district boundaries. The poverty rates in census tracts made up mostly of historic districts are significantly lower than the rates in nearby tracts within the same community district, and the share of the population with college degrees is substantially higher.

4.5 POLICY RESPONSES

By offering a more nuanced account of the costs and benefits of historic preservation, this chapter invites a rethinking of the preservation process in New York City. To be clear, we are not questioning the designation of any existing historic districts, nor are

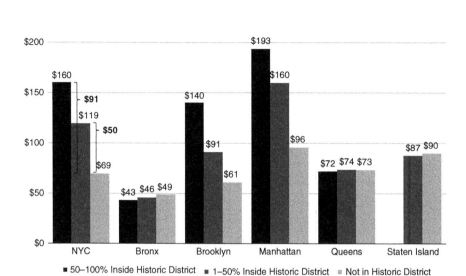

FIGURE 4.3 Average Household Income (in Thousands) for Census Tracts by Historic
District Coverage, 2012
Sources: U.S. Census Bureau, New York City Landmarks Preservation Commission,
MapPLUTO, NYU Furman Center

we advocating for the active preservation community in New York City to curtail their efforts to protect the historic fabric of the city. The Landmarks Preservation Commission, in collaboration with countless advocates and allies, has preserved many historically important buildings and neighborhoods, contributing to the richness of the city that attracts visitors and residents alike. Instead, our analyses are intended to highlight that historic preservation does not come without costs. Preservation limits opportunities for redevelopment and, in doing so, constrains the supply of housing in the city.

Currently, the process for designating historic districts in New York City does not allow for deliberate consideration of the full range of costs associated with designation. Because the Landmarks Preservation Commission is tasked with preserving the rich historic assets of the city, it does so with limited consultation from other agencies. The Department of City Planning and the City Council are formally brought into the process only after approval from the Landmarks Preservation Commission. As such, the current process does not allow for a rigorous balancing of the goals of preservation against other planning goals, including efforts to develop affordable housing. Although officials from the Landmarks Preservation Commission present the district at a public hearing at the City Planning Commission following LPC approval, the City Planning Commission has no power to amend the proposal before it goes to the City Council. Indeed, although the Commission can recommend modifications to the proposal (e.g., the removal of particular properties), in practice, it typically just forwards the approved district along to the City Council.

Similarly, the City Council reviews LPC designations, but the process is an administrative rather than a legislative action. As a result, the Council is constrained in its ability to reject or modify historic designations, as it can only make decisions based on the administrative record and cannot take other considerations into account. In practice, the City Council has approved all proposed districts with only minimal changes.

Several reforms could allow policy makers to weigh a broader set of benefits and costs. First, New York City's preservation decision-making process could be restructured. In some cities, like Baltimore and Chicago, historic preservation officials sit within the city planning agency, allowing for greater coordination and consideration of broader planning goals in historic preservation decisions. Similarly, in Washington, DC, the Historic Preservation Review Board (HPRB) – the city's comparable agency to New York City's Landmarks Preservation Commission – is incorporated into the Office of Planning, ensuring that the goals of historic preservation are considered within the planning process. The mayor of Washington, DC, also appoints a special agent for historic preservation to help adjudicate conflicts about development in historic districts, including conflicts about whether the demolition of buildings within historic districts can be permissible on a case-by-case basis to strengthen other goals of the planning process. The agent can decide if the city should issue a building permit for projects deemed of "special merit," or if the failure to do so would result in "unreasonable economic hardship to the owner." This process creates the opportunity for an independent assessment that weighs the benefits of preservation against other goals of the city-planning process. While there is no guarantee that such an agent will be balanced in his or her assessment, this process at least offers the potential for an additional independent voice in this politically charged process.

While it is hard to imagine adopting these approaches in New York City, given the size and history of the Landmarks Preservation Commission, it is worth considering other ways for the designation process to meaningfully consider potential adverse impacts. One alternative would be to create a process that requires formal comment from the City Planning Commission prior to an LPC vote of designation. This would bring the City Planning Commission's expertise on zoning, development patterns, and broader planning goals into the designation process. Indeed, city law could require that the Department of City Planning issue a report describing the effects of historic designation on residential development. These reports could include a "Housing Impact Statement" that would estimate the number of potential housing units (or residential square footage) that could no longer be built *as-of-right* following the designation of a proposed district. This calculation is surely imperfect; for example, it merely suggests the amount of residential square footage that is locked in or hindered given current zoning. Still, with this information, the City Council could be better armed to weigh the benefits of preserving historic assets against a more complete assessment of the costs of preservation. Public disclosure of the supply restrictions that the preservation process imposes would create a more balanced process that considers the costs of historic designation alongside the many benefits.

Once the debate surrounding a historic district designation includes consideration of the impact on housing supply, there might be greater pressure for the City Council to seek mitigation measures for the adverse impact. A mitigation could include an effort to upzone nearby areas to preserve the total amount of residential capacity. City officials might also consider supporting the creation of affordable housing in newly designated historic districts to mitigate the potential effects on localized housing prices and rents.

In addition, New York City's historic district regulatory framework could permit *as-of-right* development activity on vacant sites and noncontributing buildings within historic districts. While anecdotally, the LPC attempts to keep such sites outside of historic districts when sites are on the periphery of a proposed district, there are many instances where vacant and noncontributing structures are included. The uncertainty regarding development on those lots increases the risk and cost associated with investing in new housing within historic districts.

The city might also reconsider the review process for noncontributing buildings within historic districts. New York City could follow Washington, DC, and Philadelphia's example and specifically identify which structures are noncontributing in order to provide greater certainty regarding redevelopment opportunities of noncontributing sites. While the owner of a vacant lot knows that her lot can be developed within a historic district pending design review by the LPC, an owner of what appears to be a noncontributing building does not currently have certainty that the LPC will permit redevelopment.[13] Policy could be modified so that designation reports explicitly identify noncontributing structures and permit owners to demolish such structures without any further LPC review. While the design of a new building would still be subject to LPC review through the Certificate of Appropriateness approval process, owners would have greater certainty about the potential for redevelopment. This might facilitate increased investment in new construction within historic districts.

To go one step further, New York City law could be amended to provide for an *as-of-right* framework for new construction on vacant and noncontributing sites. While the Certificate of Appropriateness approval process for new construction currently requires public review and a Commission-level review, one could imagine a designation report detailing design guidelines for new construction on developable sites. As long as a developer met clear design guidelines as certified through a ministerial LPC staff-level review, the Department of Buildings would issue permits for new construction. If a developer sought to construct a building with an alternative design, the developer would still have the ability to go through the typical Certificate of Appropriateness review process.

4.6 CONCLUSIONS

In New York City, the Landmarks Preservation Commission plays a critical role in preserving the unique history of the city through the designation of historic neighborhoods and individual landmarks. Protecting the architectural integrity and cultural significance of urban neighborhoods offers an array of benefits to residents of designated neighborhoods and the city as a whole. The iconic buildings of New York help to attract millions of tourists each year, and the streetscapes of neighborhoods like Harlem, Greenwich Village, and Brooklyn Heights attract highly skilled workers who contribute to the economy of New York City. The designation process keeps alive the unique and rich history of the city. Although many of these benefits are difficult to quantify, they should not be undervalued in any assessment of the place of preservation.

But while affirming the benefits of preservation, this chapter serves as a reminder that historic preservation, like other land use regulations, imposes costs by restricting development. To be sure, historic preservation is just one of many regulations that limits opportunities for redevelopment and new construction. Indeed, our findings suggest that lots in historic districts are built at comparable densities to those of others nearby, in part because historic districts generally protect buildings that were developed at a time when the city's zoning code was more lenient.

However, our analysis suggests that the creation of historic districts is likely to constrain the development and supply of housing in the future. Residential soft sites located in historic districts are *less* likely to see redevelopment activity compared to nearby soft sites outside of the district. More generally, lots located in historic districts experience less new construction relative to nearby lots that are not regulated by the Landmarks Preservation Commission. And significantly, this gap in construction activity is heightened after historic districts are designated. These findings suggest that historic preservation is likely to restrict the supply of housing going forward. These costs of preservation must be balanced against the benefits of preserving the historic assets of the city. An integrated process that incorporates preservation goals into the broader planning process would ensure that the costs and benefits of historic preservation are more adequately assessed in New York City.

AUTHORS' NOTE

We would like to thank Eric Stern for his excellent research assistance with this chapter.

REFERENCES

Ahlfeldt, Gabriel M., Nancy Holman, and Nicolai Wendland. 2012. "An Assessment of the Effects of Conservation Areas on Value." English Heritage, London, United Kingdom. Available at www.english-heritage.org.uk/content/imported -docs/a-e/assessment-ca-value.pdf.

Allison, Eric. 1996. "Historic Preservation in a Development-Dominated City: The Passage of New York City's Landmark Preservation Legislation." *Journal of Urban History* 22: 350–76.

Asabere, Paul K., Forrest Huffman, and Seyed Mehdian. 1994. "The Adverse Impacts of Local Historic Districts: The Case of Small Apartment Buildings in Philadelphia." *Journal of Real Estate Finance and Economics* 8: 225–34.

Been, Vicki, Ingrid Gould Ellen, Michael Gedal, Edward Glaeser, and Brian J. McCabe. 2016. "Preserving History or Restricting Development? The Heterogeneous Effects of Historic Districts on Local Housing Markets in New York City." *Journal of Urban Economics* 92: 16–30.

Birch, Eugenie Ladner and Douglass Roby. 1984. "The Planner and the Preservationist: An Uneasy Alliance." *Journal of the American Planning Association* 50(2): 194–207.

Coulson, N. Edward and Robin M. Leichenko. 2001. "The Internal and External Impact of Historical Designation on Property Values." *The Journal of Real Estate Finance and Economics* 23(1): 113–24.

Glaeser, Edward L. 2010. "Preservation Follies." *City Journal* 20(2): 62–67.

Heintzelman, Martin D. and Jason A. Altieri. 2013. "Historic Preservation: Preserving Value?" *Journal of Real Estate Finance and Economics* 46: 543–63.

McCabe, Brian J. and Ingrid Gould Ellen. 2016. "Does Preservation Accelerate Neighborhood Change? Examining the Impact of Historic Preservation in New York City." *Journal of the American Planning Association* 82(2): 134–46.

Minner, Jennifer. 2016. "Revealing Synergies, Tensions, and Silences between Preservation and Planning." *Journal of the American Planning Association* 82 (2): 72–87.

New York City Department of City Planning. "New York City Zoning History." Accessed July 30, 2016. www1.nyc.gov/site/planning/about/city-planning-history .page?tab=2.

Noonan, Douglas S. and Douglass Krupka. 2011. "Making – or Picking – Winners: Evidence of Internal and External Price Effects in Historic Preservation Policies." *Real Estate Economics* 39(2): 379–407.

NYU Furman Center for Real Estate and Urban Policy. 2014. "Unlocking the Right to Build: Designing a More Flexible System for Transferring Development Rights." Available at: http://furmancenter.org/files/FurmanCenter _UnlockingtheRighttoBuild.pdf.

Ryberg-Webster, Stephanie and Kelly L. Kinahan. 2014. "Historic Preservation and Urban Revitalization in the Twenty-first Century." *Journal of Planning Literature* 29(2): 119–39.

Salama, Jerry J., Michael H. Schill, and Jonathan D. Springer. 2005. "Reducing the Cost of New Housing Construction in New York City: 2005 Update." Available at http://furmancenter.org/files/publications/NYCHousingCost2005.pdf.

Sohmer, Rebecca and Robert E. Lang. 1998. "Beyond *This Old House*: Historic Preservation in Community Development." *Housing Policy Debate* 9(3): 425–30.

Wojno, Christopher T. 1991. "Historic Preservation and Economic Development." *Journal of Planning Literature* 5(3): 296–306.

Wood, Anthony C. 2007. *Preserving New York: Winning the Right to Protect a City's Landmarks*. New York: Routledge.

Notes

1. Through 2014, the LPC also approved 17 extensions to existing designated historic districts.
2. In Manhattan, 29.3 percent of properties built before 1939 are included within a historic district. Citywide, only 5.6 percent of properties constructed before 1939 are regulated through a historic district designation. Although the majority of lots built before 1939 are not included in a historic district, we anticipate that a high percentage of lots with architectural or historical significance *are* regulated by the LPC.
3. Although our review of previous research focuses primarily on cities in the United States, a few studies estimate the relationship between preservation and property values in other places, including England (Ahlfeldt, Holman, and Wendland 2012).
4. For example, community district 3 in Brooklyn includes three historic districts: the Stuyvesant Heights Historic District, the Alice and Agate Courts Historic District, and the recently designated Bedford Historic District.
5. We initially cut 5,024 lots because they are not buildable (e.g., cemeteries, parks, and airports) and 1,430 lots because they are recorded as having zero lot area or are missing the maximum allowable square footage.
6. This comparison may be misleading because some historic districts may be downzoned following designation (to preserve the existing scale of a neighborhood), and the city may have upzoned nearby non-historic district areas to facilitate new construction. As a result, the development ratio may understate the degree to which property owners have given up development rights as a result of the historic district.
7. For a lot to be classified as a residential soft site, we required that two conditions be met. First, more than 50 percent of permitted residential floor area must be unused. Second, more than 50 percent of total floor area must be unused. We require both conditions to avoid classifying certain lots as soft sites that are not likely to be redeveloped into new residential buildings. For instance, we would not want to consider a commercial building built to 10 FAR on a lot that permits 10 FAR of commercial or 10 FAR of residential a soft site for residential redevelopment even though it has zero built residential floor area.

8. When we limit the analysis to residential zoning districts, which exclude commercial and manufacturing zones, we find that 17.1 percent of lots in historic districts were soft sites compared to 23.3 percent of lots outside of historic districts.

9. To determine if a 2007 residential soft site had a new building constructed between 2008 and 2014, we see whether the centroid of a 2007 residential soft site intersects with the area of a newly constructed building. We identify newly constructed buildings by selecting lots in MapPLUTO from 2014 where variable Year Built fell between 2008 and 2014.

10. We run an additional set of models that includes census tract fixed effects, rather than community district fixed effects. The results are substantively similar to those reported in Table 4.3.

11. The regression sample excludes 1,233 NYCHA lots, 1,211 lots located in transfer districts, and 6,877 lots designated as part of a historic district between 2008 and 2014. It excludes 2,517 lots with age of more than 400 years and 832 lots that are individual or interior landmarks. The final sample is 194,360.

12. For the demographic analysis, we use the census tract as the unit of analysis. We categorize three types of tracts – tracts with more than 50 percent of lots located in a historic district; tracts with at least one lot, but less than half of lots located in a district; and tracts located entirely outside of historic districts.

13. All new buildings constructed within a historic district are required to receive a Certificate of Appropriateness from the LPC.

5

Historic Preservation and Its Even Less Authentic Alternative

Lior Jacob Strahilevitz

Land's permanence is also what makes land unique. Every spot on earth has a past and an enduring future, and those attributes spark human curiosity about any given spot's significance. This dynamic plays out when people are considering where to live, where to shop, where to work, or where to spend their leisure time. And history is frequently a selling point.

For example, at a picturesque country club in Sterling, Virginia, a solemn stone marker commemorates the scores of Civil War soldiers who died at a Potomac River crossing. A lovely plaque, installed on a riverside boulder, reminds golfers and passersby that "Many great American soldiers, both of the North and South, died at this spot. ... The casualties were so great that the water would turn red and thus became known as 'The River of Blood.'"

There is one small problem with the River of Blood monument. There is no historical evidence suggesting that any soldiers were killed at the spot in question. The closest known Civil War battle occurred 11 miles away. The River of Blood tale appears to have been concocted by the country club's namesake, who insisted that "numerous historians" had told either him or his people (accounts varied during a single conversation with a reporter) that the golf course was built at the site of a river-crossing conflict. So the dubious plaque remains, near the fifteenth tee at the Trump National Golf Club (Fandos 2015).

A natural first instinct upon hearing of this apparent fabrication is recoil. There is something troublesome about an inauthentic stone marker and the tale underlying it. Perhaps a false marker like this one leaves people confused about history they ought to understand or makes people mistrust the historical memorials at sites of genuine bloodshed. What motive would someone have to lie about such a thing? It isn't obvious that consumers demand golfing opportunities where the players must avoid the river in order to spare themselves guilt over desecrating a battlefield, to say nothing of a one-stroke penalty.

And yet, of all the lies Donald Trump has told, this seems a rather harmless one. There were certainly plenty of Civil War soldiers who did die near the Potomac, even if none of them fell anywhere close to the fourteenth green. Perhaps the stone marker piques the curiosity of some caddies, and sparks their own research into the war. Or it causes a golfer to reflect on the life of a great, great grandfather, who really did die during America's bloodiest conflict.

This story about the River of Blood implicates a broader question. Is authentic history, in the hands of imperfect human institutions, superior to the kind of fake history commemorated at the Trump National Golf Club? With reluctance, the author has tentatively concluded that the answer is "not by much." When society presents authentic historical facts to present generations, especially in a manner tied to historical markers in physical space, it often does so in a manner that is so selective, so simplified, or so beholden to contemporary preferences that its value over contrived history appears to be marginal. At the same time, the costs of historical preservation can be quite significant. Societies that prompt private property owners to preserve their property in a particular way either substantially constrain what owners can do or devote substantial financial resources (via tax incentives, typically) to inducing forms of past-preservation in which many owners would not otherwise engage. Contrived history is cheap and voluntary. "Genuine" history is expensive and often needs to be compelled. Against that backdrop, this chapter will reconsider an implicit premise in American constitutional law that is now decades old – the idea that there is a strong state interest to compel the preservation of historic property.

Along the way, this chapter will also examine previously ignored aspects of fake history and historic preservation. Real estate developers who embrace contrived history can send powerful signals to would-be residents about who is welcome in a particular community. Choices about how to construct a community's mythology may influence who decides to settle there. A new community in Florida has embraced Trump-style fake history with gusto, albeit with an occasional admission of the narrative's fictitious nature. That same community also happens to be one of the most racially segregated places in the United States. This correlation is perhaps not coincidental. And to the extent that the segregation arises by design, the success of that strategy in Florida should alert us to the possibility that more traditional forms of historic preservation, which selectively highlight some aspects of a built environment's past while ignoring other parts of a community's history, can also promote residential homogeneity.

Comparing the phenomenon of fake history to traditional historical preservation efforts in cities may help us understand previously underemphasized implications of historic preservation regulation and fair housing laws. Part 1 of this chapter begins with a case study of The Villages, the Florida community in question. Drawing on scholarship from geography and other fields, it shows how the tendency to concoct, embellish, or distort a community's history is widespread and exists in a great many cultures. Part 2 then examines the costs and benefits of historic preservation requirements in the United States, and Part 3 reviews the Supreme Court's landmark decisions in *Berman v. Parker* and *Penn Central Transportation Co. v. New York City.*

5.1 FAKE HISTORY IN THE VILLAGES AND ELSEWHERE

The Villages, Florida, is an interesting residential community from a social scientific perspective. Four things stand out about The Villages. First, in percentage terms, it is the fastest-growing metropolitan area in the United States (Fishleder et al. 2016). Second, it is evidently the largest age-restricted community in the United States (Ness 2013). Third, The Villages is strikingly homogenous with respect not only to age but to other demographic dimensions as well. Although it is located in a very diverse state, less than one percent of its residents are African American and barely more than one percent of its residents are Latino (Fishleder et al. 2016; U.S. Census Bureau Villages CPD 2016). The nearest large city, Orlando, is an hour's drive from The Villages, and its population was 28 percent African American and 25 percent Latino in the 2010 census (U.S. Census Bureau Orlando City CPD). The Villages is therefore one of the whitest parts of the United States. Several other large retirement communities in the United States are also overwhelmingly Caucasian, but not to the extent of The Villages.[1] Finally, The Villages sports thousands of clubs for residents and an abundance of social capital.

The Villages is a collection of numerous gated communities, each with its own swimming pool and community center. Nearly all of the homes in The Villages are single-story, with a collection of ranch-style, single-family homes and townhouses. Home prices typically range from the $200,000s to the $600,000s. The Villages population in 2010 had an adult labor force participation rate of just 15 percent, according to the Census Bureau, suggesting nearly universal retirement. Economic life in The Villages is organized around three pedestrian- and golf-cart-friendly "downtowns," each of which has its own movie theater, bars, restaurants, and shops, all catering to the community's elderly residents. These downtowns are not gated and attract some residents from outside the development. Restaurants tend to be very busy at 5:30 P.M. and largely empty by 7:30. Music is piped into the downtowns from omnipresent speakers, occasionally interrupted by news bulletins from Fox News. Republican presidential candidates run very well ahead of their Democratic counterparts.

The Villages began, rather ignominiously, in 1982, when Harold Schwartz purchased a mobile home park in a rural part of Florida between Orlando and Ocala (Bartling 2008). During the 1990s, Schwartz took advantage of a Florida-specific institution called the Community Development District, which permitted large-scale real estate developers to form their own quasi-municipal governments that could levy taxes and issue tax-favored bonds to raise money for community infrastructure (Bartling 2007). Schwartz and his son, Gary Morse, then acquired large swaths of land surrounding his mobile home park, land previously occupied by watermelon farmers and ranchers, with plans to quickly grow the population from nothing to 100,000 people by 2020. The Villages' development proceeded ahead of schedule; its population actually reached 110,000 people by 2014 (Olorunnipa 2014).

Given its very recent formation, the extreme racial homogeneity found among The Villages' population is stunning. Some municipalities that are similarly overwhelmingly Caucasian, like Mentor, Ohio, have been in existence since the eighteenth century. Over generations, patterns of racial segregation can persist and can affect the residential location choices of subsequent potential homebuyers. Neighborhoods known to be overwhelmingly white signal African American buyers to exclude themselves (Boddie 2010). But The Villages was founded in a very diverse part of the country during an era in which the Fair Housing Act was already on the books. So the mechanisms by which this extreme racial homogeneity arose are less blatant.

The Villages is largely a company town. The Morse family initially owned all the residential and commercial real estate, as well as all 42(!) of the golf courses, and other recreational amenities. The development generated $9.9 billion in revenue from 1986 to 2014, enabling the Morses to amass a $2.9 billion family fortune (Olorunnipa 2014). Morse-owned entities contracted with one another, often obligating The Villages homeowners to pay assessments that covered the costs of the golf courses and other amenities (Bartling 2007).

A visitor to any of The Villages' three downtowns will quickly notice their distinctive retro theming. Mediterranean architecture pervades Spanish Springs, Lake Sumter Landing is designed to look like a Florida beach town set alongside a large, manmade lake, and Brownwood brings to mind an Old West cattle town out of West Texas or Arizona. No structures in any of the downtowns clash with the towns' respective themes, and the developers went to great lengths to evoke a particular era, mood, and place in each of the downtowns. There is not a single example of modern architecture to be found, and yet all the downtowns are essentially new. Nor are there any residences in the downtowns. Those single-story homes are all a car or golf-cart ride away, providing residents with the sorts of low-density residential suburban sprawl that they became accustomed to before moving to Florida and the sorts of walkable commercial spaces that new urbanists favor (Rybczynski 2010).

Fake history is omnipresent throughout The Villages' downtowns. The Villages' developer "hired a design firm [Forrec] with experience working for Universal Studios to invent this make-believe town, including its history, customs, and traditions" (Blechman 2008). Newly constructed buildings sport fake "Established 1792" signs. There are phony disused railroad tracks with an old caboose in the Lake Sumter Landing town center, and faded (but not too faded) "ghost advertisements" for old movies or for the saddle sellers of yore who purportedly occupied a building now occupied by a different commercial tenant. Plaques in front of numerous downtown buildings weave complex tales of adventure, successes, setbacks, and betrayals, introducing numerous fictitious town founders and other characters. There are 56 fake history plaques scattered through the three downtowns, with 16 in Brownwood, 8 in Spanish Springs, and 32 in Lake Sumter Landing.[2] The widely read local newspaper has featured quizzes that test residents about the community's fake history (*The Villages Daily Sun* 2016).

Perhaps the developers' most self-referential bit of fake history is a recently installed text at "Paddock Square," the social hub of the newest downtown in Brownwood, where music is performed nightly. An impressive bronze plaque tells the story of the place:

> The central plaza of Brownwood is now known as Paddock Square. Once slated for demolition, its historic value was championed by a group of visionary citizens in the 1950s. Today it contains remnants of the earliest roots of the town from its days as a cow camp used by legendary Cracker K. O. Atlas. The original Atlas dog-trot cabin has been relocated here, within the perimeter of what was once the original corral of the Atlas Ranch. Numerous buildings from the earliest days of the settlement, including K. O. Atlas's barn and bunkhouse, still surround Paddock Square.
>
> The grandstands were built in the 1880s to accommodate crowds who came to Paddock Square to attend rodeos staged by William G. Brown after he purchased the Atlas Ranch in 1879. Subsequent city leaders found these raucous gatherings too disruptive to downtown business and later moved the popular events downwind of the town center. The grandstands were left intact and used as seating for civic and theatrical events well into the next century.

Brownwood and Paddock Square opened to the public in 2012 (Gonzalez 2013). The land on which Paddock Square was built was most likely a watermelon farm in the 1880s and the 1950s (Blechman 2008). Another noteworthy plaque refers to an Ebenezer Matthews, whose "dislike of young people was a well-known fact in the community" and who became the target of various practical jokes by local high school students as a consequence. Although Matthews is in that sense the patron saint of a community with no resident children, the historical origins of The Villages' prohibition of child residents is explained on none of the downtowns' 56 plaques.

Notwithstanding the developers' efforts to erase and replace it, the "real" history of the land The Villages now occupies is interesting. As Amanda Brian points out, there was indeed a cattle industry in nineteenth-century Florida (2014). At the conclusion of the Seminole Wars, native tribes were forcibly removed from their ancestral lands to make way for white cattlemen. The bloody Seminole Wars raged on for decades, and these wars would have provided an interesting backdrop for an alternative fake history of the Villages. Yet the Seminoles and other indigenous Floridians go completely unmentioned in all of the 56 fake history plaques that grace Spanish Springs, Lake Sumter Landing, and Brownwood.[3] Indeed, among all of these plaques, two plaques reference possibly Latino residents[4] – both of these involve the same nuclear family (the Sanchez family) – and no plaques feature apparent references to any other individuals who weren't of European ancestry.[5] The fictitious story told in The Villages is therefore an overwhelmingly European American narrative, and it would not be surprising if stories about The Villages' past function as "exclusionary vibes" that influence the residential composition of The Villages' present (Strahilevitz 2011). Under this strategy, The Villages' architecture, fake history, marketing choices, and initial population uses language and imagery to establish a focal point that attracts white homeowners and repels nonwhite home-buyers. It quickly becomes known as a place where homeowners seeking racial homogeneity can find one another. Traces of African Americans' historic presence in The Villages have been wiped out too. Included within The Villages is an African American Baptist cemetery that predates the community's status as an age-restricted community. Strategically placed hedges and bamboo plantings render it invisible from the neighboring homes (Brian 2014).

There are plausibly larger factors at play too. Older Americans are whiter than younger Americans, and among seniors whites are more likely to be able to afford homes in retirement communities that are beyond the reach of seniors without substantial savings. Beyond that, dozens of golf clubs are part of The Villages, and all homeowners pay for access to most of these clubs via their monthly assessments. (Residents wishing to play on a handful of "champion-ship" courses have to pay an additional membership fee.) Given that for much of The Villages' residents' lives golf was the most racially segregated mass participation sport in the United States, one would expect that The Villages would be particularly appealing to Caucasians and particularly unappealing to African American and Latino retirees. Prospective Caucasian homeowners would be more likely to purchase homes in The Villages than African Americans, and even Caucasian buyers who play no golf might be willing to play a premium to live among the overwhelmingly white residents who are attracted to mandatory membership golf communities. "Exclusionary ame-nities," like exclusionary vibes, thus seem pervasive in The Villages, and they may well trigger the same segregation-promoting dynamics. An exclusionary amenity is a costly club good that is embedded in a residential community where all residents must pay for it. Willingness to pay for that amenity becomes a proxy for race or other demographic factors (Strahilevitz 2011). It is plausible that The Villages' exclusionary vibes and exclusionary amenities reinforce each other, though identifying the causal relationships and magnitudes is a tall order.

That said, something else important seems pervasive in The Villages too: happi-ness. In a health survey sent by academic researchers to all identified residents of the community, one that generated a very high 37.4 percent response rate, residents of The Villages expressed extraordinary satisfaction with their lives in the community. Fully 90.8 percent of The Villages' residents surveyed rated their satisfaction with life in The Villages as an 8, 9, or 10 on a 10-point scale (Fishleder et al. 2016). Although any comparison to a baseline will raise problems about representative income levels, senior citizens nationally are much less likely to report such high levels of satisfaction (Strine et al. 2008).

While residents' high satisfaction in a racially homogenous community is in many respects unfortunate, racial segregation among seniors is probably less harmful to society than racial segregation among younger Americans.[6] Residents of The Villages lack school-aged children, so segregation there isn't contributing to school segregation. And residents are mostly involved in economic life only as consumers, so the segregated nature of their local social networks probably does not prevent people of color from enjoying access to employment-related economic opportunities. The racial segregation of Americans in their twenties, thirties, forties, and fifties is more pernicious.

To be sure, The Villages' fake history itself is unlikely to play a large role in explaining why its residents express such high levels of satisfaction with their surroundings. At least in the short term, the racial homogeneity of The Villages could be itself an alternative explanation for aspects of the community like its high levels of generalized trust and social cohesion (Putnam 2007). Yet the available data are hard to square with the proposition that presenting community residents with a contrived and phony version of the history of a place significantly undermines residents' subjective well-being. And data from other researchers suggest that some survey respondents prefer fake historical architecture to modernist contemporary architecture, though there are legitimate questions about the external validity of this data (Levi 2005).

Given this satisfaction, it is worth asking why The Villages' model has not been replicated more widely. Indeed, perhaps it is only a matter of time until residential life modeled on theme park visits becomes the norm. Given the success and consumer appeal of The Villages, it is easy to imagine real estate developers embracing fictitious, built-environment narratives in a manner that is more expensive (because of licensing fees) but has ready-made cultural resonance. Millennial retirees might want to live in a retirement community that looks precisely like Hogsmeade or King's Landing. In such a community, the residents are likely to know the built environment's "historical" narrative well, to care about it, and to view it as central to the community's identity. Can Lancaster, Pennsylvania's, or Akron, Ohio's residents say the same thing?

The discussion so far has taken Villagers' preferences for granted, but it is worth noting, at least in passing, that audiences where this chapter has been presented inevitably want to understand or critique their embrace of fake history. These audiences regard what is happening in The Villages as creepy, though the basis for their intuitions vary widely. Perhaps the concern is that fiction has so thoroughly and self-consciously displaced fact – maybe residents embrace this concocted history to assuage subconscious guilt about their having left communities in which they were rooted as adults. Alternatively, maybe what's jarring is that the community seems to be one where "play" has become a full-time pursuit for the residents, crowding out other important values associated with ordinary life (Hurka and Tasioulas 2007). It could be instead that by trying to create a planned version of a community that grew and changed organically the community is subtly but power-fully missing important aspects that make it human (Jacobs 1961). Or maybe the clear racial and evident political homogeneity in The Villages produces a kind of echo chamber among residents that may adversely affect political discourse among a population who vote in very large numbers. Finally, the strategies used in The Villages resemble those employed by authoritarian regimes, which sometimes go to great lengths to present their citizens with a narrative about the built environ-ment's past that serves the contemporary aims of the leadership class (Johnson 2016).

On the other hand, to Villages residents, the ability to play in a community that caters to their needs, that is designed specifically for people like them (with golf cart paths, ample public restrooms downtown, easily readable signs, and restaurants that open early for dinner), that doesn't regard their aging as embarrassing, and that provides them the opportunity to focus on consumption after a lifetime of working, parenting, and saving seems appealing. Residents might pointedly ask what gives us the right to judge them and the way they have chosen to retire. They have paid their dues, and perhaps when we reach their life stage, we will want something similar.

All of this discussion raises some hard questions that will be pursued in the remainder of this chapter. First, is there inevitably such a thing as "genuine history" that we can contrast with The Villages' contrived history? And relatedly, do we have reason to believe that fake history is more likely to promote the troubling forms of segregation that have arisen in The Villages? Finally, and subversively, what if Villages-style fake history is a perfectly adequate (but much more affordable) sub-stitute for "genuine" history? That is, if satisfying some abstract preference for authenticity entails limiting how current owners can use and modify their property by requiring owners to comply ex ante with a zoning or covenants scheme that requires conformity with a broadly applicable theme, are the limits justifiable? Preserving old buildings can be a very costly endeavor, particularly when hazardous substances like lead paint or asbestos were used in its initial construction. In some extreme cases, governments force building owners to maintain structures that are not economically viable (J. C. & Associates 2001). Is the game worth the candle?

5.2 IS ALL HISTORY FAKE HISTORY?

There is a school of thought that questions whether the presentation of a commu-nity's genuine history is a realistic possibility in human society. David Lowenthal is most famous for the claim that "the past is a foreign country." In Lowenthal's view, so many of the objects contemporary society preserves represent a distorted picture of life in the past. Worse, the story is often distorted in the present precisely so that the narrative can be placed in the service of contemporary needs and wants (1999). Ada Louise Huxtable called historic preservation a "semantic trap," something different only in degree from fantastical communities like Disneyland or Seaside, Florida (1997). Ethnographic studies of revitalization efforts, such as Jeremy Wells' assessment of historic preservation efforts on Anderson, South Carolina's Main Street, identify a common theme of local stakeholders embracing efforts to create a kind of "spontaneous fantasy," with the local architecture reflecting an aspirational account of what life on the main thoroughfare should have been like during the town's earlier days (2010).

As we survey the way that historical sites and buildings are preserved, the arbitrariness of what successor generations decide to emphasize, ignore, embellish, and conceal stands in sharp relief (Lowenthal 1998a). Nineteenth-century Americans bemoaned the fact that the precise spot where the Pilgrims disembarked in 1620 was lost to time, so they found a rock that looked like it could have been "Plymouth Rock" and moved it to the harbor under a classical canopy commemorating its importance (Lowenthal 1998a). Tourists wishing to see the Alamo between 1960 and 2010 might have stopped at the original in downtown San Antonio, Texas, or they may have preferred the reproduction, built in Brackettville, Texas, as the set for a John Wayne movie about the Alamo and maintained as a tourist site for the next five decades (Huxtable 1997). Sam Houston's Greek revival home in Texas has been transformed by subsequent generations into a "rough-hewn log cabin which Houston himself would have disdained," but which tourists deem more consistent with their mind's-eye vision of Houston's home (Lowenthal 1998a). Hannibal, Missouri, has state historical markers commemorating not only spots where the real Mark Twain lived, but also locations where the fake characters from his books supposedly had their adventures (Daly 2010). Similar "landmarks" exist in Romeo and Juliet's Verona (*Telegraph* 2012). Tour guides in the Old City of Jerusalem take nuns on a Via Dolorosa that isn't Christ's path on the way to the crucifixion, but is rather a "more interesting" (and maybe more appealing?) path to follow (Lowenthal 1998a). Colonial Williamsburg for decades had no references whatsoever to slavery, and its outhouses used to be freshly painted in bright colors – historically inaccurate, for sure, but far easier on the eyes (Barthel 1990; Handler and Gable 1997).

Amidst these unreliable narratives, shifting standards of what ought to be preserved prevail. Most of the older European societies whose edifices current generations are now spending enormous resources to preserve cared little for ancient structures, and some of them wouldn't have given much thought to the idea that the past and present were meaningfully different. In the 1500s, St. Peter's Basilica was razed and then rebuilt, a development that was (as best we can tell) uncontroversial, even for a building of such historic importance (Lowenthal 1998b). And with so many readers having walked through the current version, do we have grounds to complain?

The question of which golden era to commemorate is one that arises across cultures. Americans' nostalgic sense of New England's small towns is more an artifact of the nineteenth century than the seventeenth. After the Civil War, a pure, agrarian, and communitarian New England helped show that the prevailing side in the conflict was always destined to emerge victorious. And later in the nineteenth century, as immigration threatened colonial revivalists' understanding of the American identity, the "fictions of New England resisted fact in order to stabilize the socially uncertain present" (Wortham-Galvin 2010). The fact that the landscape of nineteenth-century New England did not match the vision that revivalists wanted to encounter meant that New England's landscape needed to be remade. And similar questions about which "golden era" should be preserved play out in historic preservation debates in Europe. As Lowenthal explains:

> Consider Rouen Cathedral, whose sixteenth-century timber spire gave way in 1822 to a cast-iron replacement unable to bear its own weight. A new spire is now needed. Should it honour the original or the historical continuity embodied in the fraud of a nonweightbearing load? (1999)

There is no correct answer to the question. The controversy is political rather than historical. And in most preservation disputes similar issues arise.

Lowenthal does not embrace the postmodernist claim that fake history and genuine history are indistinguishable; neither should we. The Gettysburg Memorial commemorates a spot where thousands of Americans really did die, and those deaths mattered then and now. History we learn in democratic societies typically contains heavier doses of fact than fiction. The typical problem is not that historical narratives are concocted; rather it's that when the preservation domain is scarce land, facts are preserved selectively and the value choices underlying that selection are often obscured.

Yet it is becoming increasingly apparent that, as arguably our greatest living architect has put it, "preservation is overtaking us" (Koolhaas 2004).[7] We are preserving so much, and so much of what we preserve is banal, that we cannot afford to maintain and inventory everything. For cities like Venice or Bruges or Deadwood, the opportunity cost of preservation is plausibly worth bearing. These locations are centers of tourism whose glory days are a distant memory, and tourist traffic aside, they are on the periphery of economic life. But with 27 percent of the buildings in Manhattan already landmarked and with the borough on pace to landmark the majority of its buildings by 2066 (Ellen and McCabe, Chapter 4, this volume), there is a danger that preservationist instincts fed by loss aversion impulses crowd out the dynamism that created the wealth that funded the buildings with which society now seems unwilling to part (Strahilevitz 2005). To ameliorate these problems, a society might bind itself to protect no more than a fixed percentage of structures in the city, whereby in the absence of new construction, the landmarking of a new property would require the removal of another property from the landmarks registry (Glaeser 2011).

With respect to the built environment, political factors as well as historical and architectural importance influence what gets preserved and what doesn't (Noonan and Krupka 2010). As a result, there is inevitably selectivity in local government decisions about which structures should be subject to compulsory preservation.

When buildings are protected because of who lived there rather than anything having to do with the structure itself, then political choices and social values inevitably drive decision making. Add in the mix of economic factors concerning what structures are preserved or torn down by their owners, and the foreignness of the past is thrown into even sharper relief. On this view, historic preservation (like decisions about the construction of monuments, questions of who to honor on stamps and currency and airports and freeways, and controversies over the contents of state-mandated history textbooks) becomes a battlefield for purely symbolic politics that are zero-sum because of the scarcity of commemorative opportunities.

In light of these problems, perhaps it would be much better to preserve buildings at random, to serve authenticity and fairness interests, and to leave space for future creativity. That would be a strategy for implementing Rem Koolhaas's thought experiment in Beijing, where he contemplated preserving "everything in a very democratic, dispassionate way – highways, . . . monuments, bad things, good things, ugly things, mediocre things – and therefore really maintain[ing] an authentic condition" (2004). If public choices about what is worth preserving are usually flawed, then removing the element of choice may be one way to proceed. The city might decide to require the preservation of a fixed number of blocks that were constructed by a particular generation, but leave the designation of those blocks to chance.

This point can be amplified once we realize that the same sorts of intentional narrative omissions on display in The Villages – the hedges planted around the African American cemetery, the near absence of nonwhite names from the community's fictitious list of founders and settlers, the erasure of the area's Native American past – are equally present in communities celebrating their more genuine histories. Stephen Clowney's fascinating study of Lexington, Kentucky, shows the city and powerful private actors doing much the same kind of editing, with the result being a built environment that glorifies the actions of historical white figures and conceals the role of African Americans who loomed large in local history (2013). As Clowney points out, privately funded monuments to the Confederacy adorn the city's central gathering place, repelling contemporary African Americans. Thoroughbred Park, a new municipal park proposed in 1989 to commemorate Lexington's horse-racing history, occupied space between an affluent white part of the city and a less affluent black neighborhood. As Clowney tells it, both neighborhoods would be visible from the park and have easy access to the park unless something was done.

> Local business interests argued, sometimes forcefully, that the view was not conducive to Lexington's redevelopment efforts and, as a result, the large rolling hillside of Thoroughbred Park was built. The mound was "literally built for the park to effectively hide the African American residential district from view." For anyone approaching downtown from the interstate highway, Lexington's black

neighborhood – and black bodies – remain firmly out of sight, tucked neatly behind the grassy partition. An editorial in the local paper succinctly captured the dynamic; "Though aesthetically pleasing, the park is historically false. . . . The park not only ignores the black neighborhood, but also screens it from view. It is a whitewash. It is telling that almost every African American ... instantly recognizes this racial effect."

Though Clowney's case study focuses on Lexington, he marshals evidence that similar strategies are employed "throughout the South" to provide current residents and visitors with "deliberately misleading interpretations of history [that] conspire to ingrain ideas about racial hierarchy, cement conclusions about racial difference, and send messages that African Americans are not full members of the polity" (2013).

The selectivity of historic preservation and commemoration operates in more trivial ways as well. Consider the conveniently selective focus of preservationists. Communities of old smelled awful (Howes and Lalonde 1991). Mud and grit and horse manure and unpleasant body odors were omnipresent. Yet, to the best of my knowledge, there is no constituency for olfactory authenticity in preserved cities. Preservationists want to wander among old buildings and see what previous genera- tions saw. But they do not want to smell what previous generations smelled, nor to feel what previous generations felt. Historic structures should be air conditioned, after all. Nor do contemporary preservationists wish to experience the elevators of old, which were death traps (Bernard 2014). The version of historic preservation that public tastes demand is a highly sanitized fantasy about the past. "Most of the remote past is wholly gone or unrecognizably transformed" (Lowenthal 1999).

None of this analysis indicates that the preservation decisions that emerge from this process are inevitably going to be bad ones. While there is much to criticize in Lexington's approach, Clowney notes that Birmingham, Alabama, began to preserve its history in a more inclusive way after African Americans began to comprise the majority of voters there (2013). Robert Weyeneth describes efforts throughout the South to include sites associated with racial segregation on the National Register of Historic Places so that future generations will understand better through the built environment what life under Jim Crow was like for blacks and whites (Weyeneth 2005). Political processes are not always biased or broken. But the dominant ten- dencies among preservationists are evident. And those tendencies help make the case for a radical approach built on randomization.

In assessing the social welfare effects of historic preservation, property values are a sensible place to begin, though by no means a completely satisfying analytical approach. Most of the benefits of historic preservation will be felt locally. Historic preservation typically will be a local amenity. That is, if people benefit from having historic structures and neighborhoods preserved, then they will pay more to live proximate to those structures (Malani 2008). To be sure, tourists and workers who commute from elsewhere may benefit from historic preservation too, but to the extent that they do, we should expect to see a corresponding increase in the property values of hotel buildings or office towers. If real estate markets are functioning well and buyers and sellers are rational, then the long-term costs and benefits of historic preservation should be capitalized into property values. Markets leave out some considerations, such as existence value, and these externalities render real estate values an excellent though imperfect proxy for the social welfare effects of preservation. Property values also become a poor proxy when the market rewards real estate developers for catering to the preferences of white homeowners who prefer racially homogenous neighborhoods.

With those important caveats stated, what does the empirical literature tell us about the effects of historic preservation mandates on local property values? Digging into the reputable social science, there does not appear to be an absolute consensus in the economic literature as to the effects of historic preservation regulations. Case studies focused on medium-sized cities like Lincoln, Nebraska, Baton Rouge, Louisiana, and Johnson City, Tennessee, tend to find small, positive effects on property values (Chen 2013; Thompson, Rosenbaum, and Schmitz 2011; Zahirovic-Herbert and Chatterjee 2012). That said, the most sophisticated work tends to be dubious of the purported economic benefits and concerned about the resulting demographic turnover, especially in densely populated areas. Coulson and Leichenko's study of Fort Worth, Texas, found that historic preservation did not affect the residential composition of landmarked neighborhoods (Coulson and Leichenko 2004), but the same authors' work on Abilene, Texas, found that historic preservation regulations did raise property values within the landmarked district (Coulson and Leichenko 2001). By contrast, McCabe and Ellen found significant neighborhood composition effects in New York City, where the creation of a historic district was associated with subsequent increases in the socioeconomic status of the district's residents, compared to residents of otherwise comparable neighborhoods. Evidence that historic preservation decisions affect the racial composition of New York neighborhoods was weaker and not statistically significant (McCabe and Ellen 2016).

Studies of major metropolitan areas are generally more pessimistic about the economic desirability of historic preservation laws. Heintzelman and Altieri's study of historic preservation regulations in the Boston metropolitan area found associations between landmarking and *reduced* property values, though the magnitude of the effect is small with all controls, around 1 percent (Heintzelman and Altieri 2013). An impressive study that employs repeat sales hedonic fixed effects analysis, the Heintzelman and Altieri paper does a better job of dealing with endogeneity than many of the other localized studies. Similarly, another study of historic preservation in Chicago employed a small but unusual dataset that included measures of structure quality (Noonan and Krupka 2011). The authors find that landmark designation has no positive effect on property values after city property tax benefits phased out completely. Research that relies on natural experiments, such as the

Nazis' leveling parts of Rotterdam, which left historic preservation regulations in place only in the parts that hadn't been destroyed, also tends to be pessimistic about the economic effects of historic preservation regulations (Koster, Van Ommeren, and Reitveld 2012).

The gold-standard paper on the effects of historic preservation uses the largest market, has the largest dataset involving the most land transactions over the longest period of time, and employs the most careful controls (Been et al. 2016). The authors expected that the creation of a historic district would generate cross-cutting effects because such regulations can enhance beauty and open space in a neighborhood while limiting redevelopment rights. Consistent with this plausible hypothesis, Been and coauthors find that the effects of historic preservation regulations are negative to negligible in parts of New York where there is significant economic pressure to pursue higher densities (i.e., Manhattan). Outside of Manhattan, the effects on property values are positive – "they rise by about 1.4 percent per year relative to nearby properties."

A survey of the literature on the economics of historic preservation suggests the following (tentative) conclusions, then. The effects of historic preservation on neighborhood composition appear mixed, although there is some credible evidence to suggest that these regulations are associated with gentrification of neighborhoods. In areas of significant land scarcity, such as urban centers, there is little credible evidence that historic preservation regulations systematically enhance property values. Most of the rigorous evidence in fact suggests that such regulations cause property values to decline. Historic preservation restrictions on land do seem to enhance property values in lower-density areas where there is little economic pressure to redevelop property and where such regulations can promote an aesthetically appealing form of homogeneity in the streetscape that might be difficult to achieve through purely voluntary coordination among property owners.

To be sure, property values do not capture all of the potential benefits and costs of historic preservation. Such preservation, when successful, can provide current generations with guidance about how past challenges were addressed, provide present generations with an escape from their current confines, or establish continuity with the past. On the other hand, preserving the past may stifle present generations' creativity by failing to free up scarce space for future landmarks. The past can become an orthodoxy from which one deviates only at her peril.

5.3 THE LAW

In American law, it is rather clear that cities and states have a legitimate interest in promoting the preservation of historic structures, even at the expense of property values. Paradoxically, the Supreme Court case in which the right to force the continuation of existing uses is most clearly established is *Berman v. Parker*, where the proposal at issue was a slum-clearance plan designed to wipe out existing uses so that a neighborhood in Washington, DC, could start afresh. As of 1950, the area slated for redevelopment in Washington was characterized in the following terms by the Court:

> In 1950 the Planning Commission prepared and published a comprehensive plan for the District. Surveys revealed that in Area B, 64.3% of the dwellings were beyond repair, 18.4% needed major repairs, only 17.3% were satisfactory; 57.8% of the dwellings had outside toilets, 60.3% had no baths, 29.3% lacked electricity, 82.2% had no wash basins or laundry tubs, 83.8% lacked central heating. In the judgment of the District's Director of Health it was necessary to redevelop Area B in the interests of public health. The population of Area B amounted to 5,012 persons, of whom 97.5% were Negroes.

To contemporary readers, the introduction of the demographic information is unnerving. It is as though the most emphatic proof of the existing built environment's low value is the type of people who live there. In any event, in the view of the Planning Commission, Area B was characterized by an obsolete layout and a bundle of structures that was injurious to public health. In the Supreme Court's view, Congress and the District had the authority to condemn both blighted and non-blighted properties within Area B.

The fact that Berman's Department Store was, as the government conceded, not remotely blighted was irrelevant. As Justice Douglas wrote on behalf of a unanimous Court:

> Miserable and disreputable housing conditions may do more than spread disease and crime and immorality. They may also suffocate the spirit by reducing the people who live there to the status of cattle. They may indeed make living an almost insufferable burden. They may also be an ugly sore, a blight on the community which robs it of charm, which makes it a place from which men turn. The misery of housing may despoil a community as an open sewer may ruin a river.
>
> We do not sit to determine whether a particular housing project is or is not desirable. The concept of the public welfare is broad and inclusive. The values it represents are spiritual as well as physical, aesthetic as well as monetary. It is within the power of the legislature to determine that the community should be beautiful as well as healthy, spacious as well as clean, well-balanced as well as carefully patrolled. ... If those who govern the District of Columbia decide that the Nation's Capital should be beautiful as well as sanitary, there is nothing in the Fifth Amendment that stands in the way.

In this key passage, the Court articulates a broad justification for the police power. City beautification is a legitimate state interest, one that justifies overcoming the objections of an owner of a fine building who seeks to resist its condemnation by virtue of proximity to less sturdy neighboring structures. And with respect to Berman's arguments against being the victim of a collective punishment, the Court concluded that tearing down only problematic structures would do too little to prevent the neighborhood from becoming a slum again in the future, thanks to the dearth of parks, the absence of sunlight, and other deficiencies. Only a new neighborhood layout could break the "cycle of decay." In short, Berman's section of Washington, DC, to Douglas, called out for government to play the role of the Luftwaffe in Rotterdam, enabling the neighborhood to start from scratch.

Twenty-four years later, the question of the state's interest in promoting aesthetics in a community was taken for granted, though the emphasis was now on resisting modernization. The Penn Central Transportation Company, which owned Grand Central Station in New York, sued the City of New York over the application of the city's landmark preservation law to Grand Central (*Penn Central* 1978). Under that law, New York had blocked Penn Central from constructing atop Grand Central a skyscraper that would have enhanced the economic value of the parcel. Although Penn Central conceded that the landmarks preservation law fell within the city's police power, and therefore was legitimate, it argued that the Constitution compelled the city to compensate Penn Central for the diminutions in its property value resulting from the landmarks law. The legitimacy of the law's purpose was not in dispute, but the second and third paragraphs of the Court's opinion delve into the justification for historic preservation in detail.

> Over the past 50 years, all 50 States and over 500 municipalities have enacted laws to encourage or require the preservation of buildings and areas with historic or aesthetic importance. . . .
>
> New York City . . . adopted its Landmarks Preservation Law in 1965. . . . The city acted from the conviction that "the standing of [New York City] as a world-wide tourist center and world capital of business, culture and government" would be threatened if legislation were not enacted to protect historic landmarks and neighborhoods from precipitate decisions to destroy or fundamentally alter their character. The city believed that comprehensive measures to safeguard desirable features of the existing urban fabric would benefit its citizens in a variety of ways, e.g., fostering "civic pride in the beauty and noble accomplishments of the past"; protecting and enhancing "the city's attractions to tourists and visitors"; "support[ing] and stimul[ating] business and industry"; "strengthen[ing] the economy of the city"; and promoting "the use of historic districts, landmarks, interior landmarks and scenic landmarks for the education, pleasure and welfare of the people of the city."

Notice that within the span of a quarter century, the emphasis of city planners had changed from replacing the obsolete to preserving the irreplaceable. To be sure, most visitors to Grand Central regard the structure as one possessing very significant architectural merit. Contemporary Washingtonian policy makers in the 1950s did not feel any commensurate fondness for the neighborhood that was slated for destruction in *Berman v. Parker*, a discrepancy likely tied to both the quality of the structures and the perceived qualities of the people who used those structures.

The plaintiff in *Penn Central* did make one broad argument against the enterprise of historic preservation. It argued that the imposition of historic preservation requirements on it but not on other landowners was arbitrary, but the Court quickly brushed aside this argument:

> Equally without merit is the related argument that the decision to designate a structure as a landmark "is inevitably arbitrary or at least subjective, because it is basically a matter of taste," Reply Brief for Appellants 22, thus unavoidably singling out individual landowners for disparate and unfair treatment. The argument has a particularly hollow ring in this case. For appellants . . . do not even now suggest that the Commission's decisions concerning the Terminal were in any sense arbitrary or unprincipled. . . . [Q]uite simply, there is no basis whatsoever for a conclusion that courts will have any greater difficulty identifying arbitrary or discriminatory action in the context of landmark regulation than in the context of classic zoning or indeed in any other context.

Upon reflection, the Court's response to Penn Central's argument is something of a non sequitur. The company was positing that landmark designations are inherently arbitrary. The Court said by way of reply that Penn Central did not argue that the decision to designate the station as a landmark was itself arbitrary. The response seems self-contradictory. The broader argument of inevitable arbitrariness logically entails the specific argument applied to Penn Central's land. In the decades that followed, lower courts followed *Penn Central*'s lead in brushing aside questions about the discriminatory enforcement of historic preservation laws (e.g., *Mount St. Scholastica* 2007; *Van Horn* 2001). A more thoughtful (and candid) response would have suggested that landmark designation decisions are merely somewhat arbitrary – factors like neighborhood clout and voter preferences play a significant role, but so does perceived architectural merit. Or maybe the real problem is that landmark designations aren't sufficiently arbitrary.

Putting *Berman* and *Penn Central* side by side displays some of the tension that arises in historic preservation cases, though it does not show that the doctrines are contradictory. A competent government can beautify its cityscape by compelling the preservation of pleasing structures *and* by compelling the removal and replacement of displeasing structures. In that sense, *Berman* and *Penn Central* fit together coherently. But the tension arises once we begin to see the subjectivity of contemporary societal judgments about what is worth preserving and what is worth destroying. This was the argument of Penn Central's that the Court was too quick to dismiss.

To preservationists, soaring and expensive structures that are used and beloved by elites ought to be preserved, even if they become economically obsolete in their present form. But modest structures in overwhelmingly minority neighborhoods ought to be bulldozed in the name of progress. Combining the power to compel preservation with the power to compel destruction makes the government a mighty editor of the past. Systematically, when society sweeps away the latter kind of building and forces the preservation of the former, it curates the built environment in a manner that deceives future generations about what life was like in an earlier era. Compare the 27 percent of Manhattan that is landmarked to the 0.3 percent of Staten Island that is landmarked. (Ellen and McCabe, Chapter 4, this volume). What if future generations – perish the thought – decide that the lives of contemporary Staten Islanders were as worthy of commemoration as the lives of Manhattanites? From this perspective, the history that gets presented to the living becomes a history nearly as fake as what's on display in The Villages (Lowenthal 1999). When society tries to preserve and protect aesthetic greatness, it simultaneously designates winners and losers, and those political dynamics will distort the clarity of aesthetic decision making. (Recall Justice Douglas's connection between the quality of a neighborhood's buildings and the perceived quality of its residents.)

Equally troubling is the possibility that these curated choices about what history to preserve subtly signal current generations with information about who is welcome and who is not. In recent years, legal scholars have begun studying the important question of how regulations of the built environment, decisions about infrastructure placement in particular, can contribute to residential segregation (Schindler 2015). Historic preservation can and evidently does send exclusionary vibes too. But we lack an adequate understanding of the mechanisms by which it operates and the degree to which factors grounded in psychology, as opposed to pocketbook economics, explain household location choices.

As a doctrinal matter, it would appear that the evidence canvassed in Part 2 of this chapter is sufficiently mixed to authorize the continued compulsory regulation of historic structures. The best evidence suggests that historic preservation regulations do more economic harm than good in densely packed parts of the country, but they appear to be beneficial in some places, and the possibility that they may be beneficial in a given neighborhood is adequate under the law's very deferential existing standard. Moreover, a city like New York might conclude that notwithstanding the net economic harms associated with some preservation, these costs are worth bearing for the sake of continuity values that are difficult to price. There may even be good Burkean reasons for preserving things that have stood the test of time – their durability might bear witness to their value in ways that present generations do not fully recognize. At the same time, there is essentially no empirical assessment of the kind of alternative to historic preservation that The Villages represents. Historic preservation may look worse (or, depending on one's values, better) when it is compared to fake history than when it is compared to a city unmoored from both fictitious and less-fictitious pasts. And if we can imagine an inclusive version of fake history – a narrative that embraces pluralism and difference – the integration-promoting possibilities of fake history become apparent.

That said, the relationship between historic preservation regulations, fake history, and residential homogeneity sketched earlier suggests that a less deferential assessment of these strategies may be appropriate. Both historic preservation and the kind of uniformly scripted narrative on display in The Villages aim for an aesthetic homogeneity that may engender demographic homogeneity by design. When the buildings all look alike, the people living in those buildings tend to look alike too. Some of the premises taken for granted by the courts since *Penn Central* may fail to withstand a more searching form of judicial scrutiny.

5.4 CONCLUSION

The Villages' developers have gone to great lengths to develop a phony historical narrative for their fast-growing community, one that is embraced not only in retro-architecture, but with a detailed and fictitious account of the built environment's past. In so doing, they have swept away any mention of the actual history of the land and replaced it with a stylized narrative designed to appeal to today's elderly homebuyers. There is something disconcerting about the inauthenticity of The Villages.

Yet, upon reflection, it is possible that the faux history of The Villages is not all that different from the version of history presented to the public as a result of historic preservation regulations in major American cities. There too, aspects of the built environment's history are systematically ignored. Structures inhabited by the poor and by minorities tend to be replaced as soon as market forces dictate changes. Structures inhabited by elites tend to be preserved regardless of what the market demands. The result is a lasting signal about whose history is valued, whose lives mattered, and what historical events constitute successes and failures. The version of our past that Americans encounter via historic preservation regulations is at once sanitized, political, and designed to appeal to contemporary preferences. To the extent that society wants to preserve artifacts from past built environments, preserving structures at random has real advantages over our present approach.

Scholars of land use have paid too little attention to the relationship between the design of the built environment and the characteristics of the people who show up to populate it. The extraordinary and depressing racial homogeneity of The Villages, despite its very recent origins and presence in a very racially diverse part of the United States, suggests that the combination of exclusionary vibes and exclusionary amenities in age-restricted communities can be potent even in an era of Fair Housing Act enforcement. Seeing what has happened in The Villages might reveal a fast-forward version of what has happened more slowly and with less extreme results elsewhere, where an existing population dampens the salience of the signals sent by the built environment. Though we cannot isolate the effects of any particular homogeneity-promoting strategy in The Villages, the cumulative effect of multiple strategies is striking and disturbing. It would not be crazy for legal institutions to consider whether some of the techniques that might promote racial homogeneity in The Villages ought to be prohibited or at least curtailed. Indeed, it is tempting to contemplate the inclusionary possibilities of a varied approach to fake history. Imagine Lin-Manuel Miranda as a real estate developer.

Finally, the extent to which residents of The Villages have embraced the community's false history is a topic worthy of further qualitative research. The version of history presented to the world through preservation laws is never authentic. A fairer metric is to ask whether the history on display resonates within the community. If American homeowners turn out to like entirely phony history nearly as well as selectively curated history, then a hard question arises as to whether it is appropriate to impose significant financial burdens on a subset of property owners in the name of telling the story of a community in a particular, misleading way. Fake history may be inferior to real but selective history, but it is also a great deal cheaper, and the narrative can be constructed entirely by market forces. In revisiting the question of whether a legitimate societal interest remains in compulsory historic preservation, it is helpful to ask ourselves: "compared to what?" To answer that question, an examination of The Villages social experiment may prove illuminating.

AUTHOR'S NOTE

The author thanks Lee Anne Fennell, Aziz Huq, Daniel Kelly, Ben Keys, Alison LaCroix, Richard McAdams, Martha Nussbaum, Eduardo M. Peñalver, Michael Pollack, Eric Posner, John Rappaport, Julie Roin, John Tasioulas, and Laura Weinrib for comments on earlier drafts, and workshop participants at the University of Chicago Law School and the Harvard Graduate School of Design, especially Sarah Schindler, Susan Nigra Snyder, and George Thomas, for helpful conversations, Taylor Coles for skilled research assistance, and the Russell J. Parsons and Carl S. Lloyd Faculty Funds for research support.

REFERENCES

Barthel, Diane. 1990. "Nostalgia for America's Village Past: Staged Symbolic Communities." *International Journal of Politics, Culture & Society* 4: 79–93.

Bartling, Hugh. 2008. "A Master-Planned Community as Heterotopia: The Villages, Florida." In *Heterotopia and the City: Public Space in a Postcivil Society* 165 Michiel DeHaene and Lieven De Cauter, eds. New York: Routledge.

2007. "Private Governance, Public Subsidies: The Cultural Politics of Exurban Sprawl in Florida, USA." Unpublished Working Paper.

Been, Vicki, Ingrid Gould Ellen, Michael Gedal, Edward Glaeser, and Brian McCabe. 2016. "Preserving History or Restricting Development? The Heterogeneous Effects of Historic Districts on Local Housing Markets in New York City." *Journal of Urban Economics* 92: 16–30.

Bernard, Andreas. 2014. *Lifted: A Cultural History of the Elevator.* New York: New York University Press.

Blechman, Andrew D. 2008. *Leisureville: Adventures in America's Retirement Utopias.* New York: Atlantic Monthly Press.

Boddie, Elise C. 2010. "Racial Territoriality." *UCLA Law Review* 58: 401–63.

Brian, Amanda M. 2014. "The Faux History of The Villages, Florida." *Southern Cultures* 20(4): 58–71.

Chen, Ke. 2013. "The Making of a Historic District and the Economic Impact upon Housing Value: An Empirical Analysis of the Tree Streets Neighborhood in Johnson City, Tennessee." *Modern Economy* 4: 832–38.

Clowney, Stephen. 2013. "Landscape Fairness: Removing Discrimination from the Built Environment." *Utah Law Review* 2013: 1–62.

Coulson, N. Edward and Robin M. Leichenko. 2004. "Historic Preservation and Neighborhood Change." *Urban Studies* 41: 1587–1600.

　2001. "The Internal and External Impact of Historic Designation of Property Values." *Journal of Real Estate Finance & Economics* 23: 113–24.

Daly, Sean. 2010. "Mark Twain's Hannibal Retains Spirit of *Tom Sawyer, Adventures of Huckleberry Finn*." *Tampa Bay Times*. April 16.

Fandos, Nicholas. 2015. "In Renovation of Golf Club, Donald Trump also Dressed Up History." *New York Times*. November 24.

Fishleder, Sarah, Lawrence Schonfeld, Jaime Corvin, Susan Tyler, and Carla VandeWeerd. 2016. "Drinking Behavior among Older Adults in a Planned Community: Results from the Villages Survey." *International Journal of Geriatric Psychiatry* 31: 536–43.

Glaeser, Edward. 2011. *Triumph of the City: How Our Greatest Invention Makes Us Richer, Smarter, Greener, Healthier, and Happier*. New York: Penguin Press.

Gonzalez, Eloisa Ruano. 2013. "The Villages' Brownwood Paddock Square Taking Shape." *Orlando Sentinel*. February 17.

Handler, Richard and Eric Gable. 1997. *The New History in an Old Museum: Creating the Past at Colonial Williamsburg*. Durham, NC: Duke University Press.

Heintzelman, Martin D. and Jason A. Altieri. 2013. "Historic Preservation: Preserving Value?" *Journal of Real Estate Finance and Economics* 46: 543–63.

Howes, David and Marc Lalonde. 1991. "The History of Sensibilities: Of the Standard of Taste in Mid-Eighteenth Century England and the Circulation of Smells in Post-Revolutionary France." *Dialectical Anthropology* 16: 125–35.

Hurka, Thomas and John Tasioulas. 2007. "Games and the Good." *Proceedings of the Aristotelian Society* 106: 237–64.

Huxtable, Ada Louise. 1997. *The Unreal America – Architecture and Illusion*. New York: New Press.

Jacobs, Jane. 1961. *The Death and Life of Great American Cities*. New York: Random House.

Johnson, Ian. 2016. "China's Memory Manipulators." *The Guardian*. June 8.

Koolhaas, Rem. 2004. "Preservation Is Overtaking Us." *Future Anterior* 1 (Fall): 1–3.

Koster, Hans R. A., Jos van Ommeren, and Piet Reitveld. 2012. "Bombs, Boundaries and Buildings: A Regression-Discontinuity Approach to Measure Costs of Housing Supply Restrictions." 42 *Regional Science & Urban Economics* 42: 631–41.

Levi, Daniel T. 2005. "Does History Matter? Perceptions and Attitudes toward Fake Historic Architecture and Historic Preservation." 22 *Journal of Architectural & Planning Restoration* 148.

Lowenthal, David. 1999. *The Past Is a Foreign Country*. Cambridge: Cambridge University Press.

1998a. "Fabricating Heritage." *History & Memory* 10(1): 5–24.

1998b. *The Heritage Crusade and the Spoils of History*. Cambridge and New York: Cambridge University Press.

Malani, Anup. 2008. "Valuing Laws as Local Public Amenities." *Harvard Law Review* 121: 1273–1331.

McCabe, Brian J. and Ingrid Gould Ellen. 2016. "Does Preservation Accelerate Neighborhood Change? Examining the Impact of Historic Preservation in New York City." *Journal of the American Planning Association* 82: 134–46.

Ness, Bill. 2013. "The 10 Largest Active Adult Communities in America." September 2, available at https://www.55places.com/blog/the-10-largest-active-adult-communities-in-america (visited March 14, 2016).

Noonan, Douglas S. and Douglas J. Krupka. 2011. "Making – or Picking – Winners: Evidence of Internal and External Price Effects in Historic Preservation Policies." *Real Estate Economics* 39: 379–407.

2010. "Determinants of Historic and Cultural Landmark Designation." *Journal of Cultural Economics* 34: 1–26.

Olorunnipa, Toluse. 2014. "Fastest Growing Metro Area in US Has No Crime or Kids." *Bloomberg Business*, June 27, available at www.bloomberg.com/news/articles/2014–06-27/fastest-growing-metro-area-in-u-s-has-no-crime-or-kids (visited March 14, 2016).

Putnam, Robert D. 2007. "*E Pluribus Unum*: Diversity and Community in the Twenty-First Century." *Scandinavian Political Studies* 30: 137–74.

Rybczynski, Witold. 2010. *Makeshift Metropolis: Ideas about Cities*. New York: Scribner.

Schindler, Sarah. 2015. "Architectural Exclusion: Discrimination and Segregation through Physical Design of the Built Environment." *Yale Law Journal* 124: 1934–2024.

Strahilevitz, Lior Jacob. 2011. *Information and Exclusion*. New Haven, CT: Yale University Press.

2005. "The Right to Destroy." *Yale Law Journal* 114: 781–854.

Strine, Tara W., Daniel P. Chapman, Lina S. Balluz, David G. Moriarty, and Ali H. Mokdad. 2008. "The Association between Life Satisfaction and Health-Related Quality of Life, Chronic Illness, and Health Behaviors among U.S. Community-dwelling Adults." *Journal of Community Health* 33(1): 40–50.

The Telegraph. 2012. "Verona Clamps Down on Tourists Visiting Romeo and Juliet's Balcony." November 9.

The Villages Daily Sun. 2016. "Test Your Knowledge of Villages History." January 3, at D1.

Thompson, Eric, David Rosenbaum, and Benjamin Schmitz. 2011. "Property Values on the Plains: The Impact of Historic Preservation." *The Annals of Regional Science* 47: 477–91.

Uhlenberg, Peter. 2000. "Integration of Old and Young." *The Gerontologist* 40: 276–79.

U.S. Census Bureau, Quick Facts, Orlando City, Florida, available at www.census.gov /quickfacts/table/PST045215/1253000 (visited March 14, 2016).

U.S. Census Bureau, Quick Facts, The Villages CPD, Florida, available at www.census.gov/quickfacts/table/PST045215/1271625 (visited March 14, 2016).

Utsey, Shawn O., Yasser A. Payne, Ebonique S. Jackson, and Antoine M. Jones. 2002. "Race-Related Stress, Quality of Life Indicators, and Life Satisfaction among Elderly African Americans." *Cultural Diversity & Ethnic Minority Psychology* 8: 224–33.

Wells, Jeremy C. 2010. "Our History Is Not False: Perspectives from the Revitalisation Culture." *International Journal of Heritage Studies* 16: 464–85.

Weyeneth, Robert R. 2005. "The Architecture of Racial Segregation: The Challenges of Preserving the Problematical Past." *The Public Historian* 27: 11–44.

Wortham-Galvin, B. D. 2010. "The Fabrication of Place in America: The Fictions and Traditions of the New England Village." *Traditional Dwellings & Settlements Review* 21: 21–34.

Zahirovic-Herbert, Velma and Swarn Chatterjee. 2012. "Historic Preservation and Residential Property Values: Evidence from Quantile Regression." *Urban Studies* 49: 369–82.

Cases

Berman v. Parker, 358 US 26 (1954).

J.C. & Associates v. District of Columbia Board of Appeals and Review, 778 A.2d 296 (D.C. 2001).

Mount St. Scholastica, Inc. v. City of Atchison, 482 F. Supp.2d. 1281 (D. Kan. 2007).

Penn Central Transp. Co. v. New York City, 438 U.S. 104 (1978).

Van Horn v. Castine, 167 F. Supp.2d. 103 (D. Maine 2001).

Notes

1. According to the Census Bureau's website, Laguna City, California, was 84 percent Caucasian non-Hispanic in the 2010 census, and approximately 90 percent of Laguna City's population is based in the Laguna Woods Village retirement community. Sun City Center, Florida was 93 percent Caucasian non-Hispanic in the 2010 census. Sun City, Arizona was 94 percent Caucasian non-Hispanic in the 2010 census.

2. Lake Sumter Landing has 31 unique fake history plaques. Identical plaques for McCabe & McCabe Haberdashery appear outside two different nearby buildings on either side of Old Mill Run. The 56 plaques mentioned in the text exclude plaques commemorating actual history, such as the Sharon Morse Plaque at the Performing Arts Center in Spanish Springs, and two adjacent plaques commemorating the cattle industry and Florida crackers (cowboys) by the Meggison Road

entrance to Brownwood. There is also an additional fake history plaque located next to an unoccupied/façade building that is outside the three downtowns, in the residential portion of The Villages.

3. Blechman reports that on the short boat tour that operates out of Lake Sumter Landing, the captain's tour script includes a reference to "Billy Bowlegs," a Seminole chief and "a friend to whites who lived on this shore" (2008). Blechman notes that Billy Bowlegs was Holata Micco, who led a band of warriors during the Second and Third Seminole Wars.

4. A plaque in Spanish Springs references Maria Portiz Fontana "Silencio" Sanchez, who allegedly lived from 1770 to 1873. As the plaque explains, the "first female resident of Spanish Springs, Maria Sanchez arrived at what was then only a wide spot in the trail in 1788. Accompanied by her husband and their four sons, Maria helped establish the roots of the young community. . . . [S]he helped to develop the recipe for the potent local brew known as 'Mosquito Juice' and opened the budding settlement's first tavern, the Blind Mosquito. Maria earned the nickname 'Silencio' by remaining quiet for 60 years after the death of her husband in the Great Fire of 1812."

5. It is unclear whether the Sanchezes are meant to be Spaniards or immigrants from Latin America, though their status as a founding family of Spanish Springs suggests the former. Sixty-nine fictitious individuals are named on the plaques displayed in The Villages. Besides the Sanchez family, there is also one family whose surname is "Feliu," which is a Catalan surname. The Anglo-European surnames mentioned are Peterson, McCall, Seball, Lasalle, Davis, Van Patten, Metzger, Allan, Brown, Marsden, Christopher, McCabe, Hudson, Louise, Parr, Schmid, Harper, Rose, Blaise, Whitney, Marley, Sennett, Mark, Atlas, Killingsworth, Hewitt, Dzuro, Coggins, Bailey, Wise, Parker, Waggoner, Payne, Mathews, Wilcox, McDonough, Juracko, Spirodan, Shiveline, West, Coggins, Borrowman, Graham, Wahl, Roy, Upton, Krietemeyer, and Benjamin. None of the plaques indicates that any individuals referenced therein are recognizably African American, Asian American, Jewish, or Muslim. Where the national origin of individuals is mentioned on the plaques, the fictitious residents are from Germany (Seball family), New Zealand (Hudson family relatives reside there), England (Graham family), and Holland (Upton family). Several other families are described as having moved to the area from various other cities in the United States.

6. To the extent that minorities feel excluded from communities like The Villages, this may adversely affect their well-being. (Utsey et al. 2002). There are further interesting questions about whether age segregation is itself beneficial, taking into account the benefits and burdens associated with greater proximity to one's grandchildren (Uhlenberg 2000).

7. A similar sentiment was expressed by a previous generation's greatest architect, Frank Lloyd Wright, who regarded London as "senile." In Wright's view, the best parts of London should be preserved "in a great green park," but the rest of London should be opened up for new buildings (Lowenthal 1999).

6

Losing My Religion: Church Condo Conversions and Neighborhood Change

Georgette Chapman Phillips

Limestone. Granite. Stained glass. Ornamental gold. Richly polished wood. All are found in the beautiful historic churches in America's cities. But the church is more than liturgical space. The church welcomes immigrants (often with services in their native tongues), engages in outreach by feeding the poor, and serves as a political mobilizing workspace. In short, it becomes one with the community. However, as church membership and attendance slide downward (coupled with demographic shifts of parishioners moving out of the neighborhood), these once graceful structures are increasingly underutilized, undermaintained, and potentially abandoned.

First African Baptist Church in Philadelphia serves as a powerful example of this trend. Founded in 1809 (the building was erected in 1906), it was once the home of the country's oldest African American congregation. Years of deferred maintenance (estimated at $5 million) and a shrinking congregation (from 1,000 to 100) led to its closing. The building was sold for $1 million to a developer on Christmas Eve 2015. The neighborhood, South Philadelphia, has been called a "white hot real estate market." The area has become a part of the city's millennial renaissance, with luxury apartments and high-end condos with garages and decks that offer views of the city skyline (Simmons 2016). An ad for another church around the corner from First African that has been acquired by developers reads: "Development opportunity in hot neighborhood bustling with new construction and vibrant community." A proposed new use for the former First African Baptist Church is residential condominiums.

This spate of redevelopment rides the coattails of a new population surge in the central neighborhoods of America's cities. People are moving back into the central city and bringing a demand for housing with them. A phenomena sweeping through cities is the conversion of churches to residential use (either condominiums or rentals). For the city, this constitutes a victory on several fronts. Abandoned (and previously tax-exempt) property is put to use. New residents spark new business development. Tax revenues are enhanced. For the neighborhood, though, the sale of a church represents not just a demise of worship space, it is also the loss of a communal anchor. Death of the church severs the thread that ran through the neighborhood – the thread of community.

This chapter examines the trend of church conversions into residential use from several perspectives. It will begin with a review of the historical foundations of the role of churches in neighborhood life in the United States. Although the religious significance served as a magnet, the nonreligious activities act as glue. A key fact, though, is that the churches are, generally, right in the middle of residential areas. From a zoning perspective, this has engendered legal challenges as the churches increasingly engaged in nonreligious activity. The auxiliary uses that make a church more than a religious structure also challenge the zoning exemptions that permit churches to exist in residential neighborhoods.

In order to capture the magnitude of this potential conversion market, the demographics of church attendance and church real estate will be reviewed. The northeastern and north-central United States figure prominently in this discussion because this area has not only decreasing church attendance, but concomitantly has a high concentration of older gothic church structures that are architecturally stunning but expensive to maintain. I concentrate on mainline Protestant (Episcopal, Lutheran, Methodist, and Presbyterian) and Catholic churches because these are the denominations where one is most likely to find concentrations of large church buildings that are attractive for redevelopment.

All of this is happening against the backdrop of a central city renewal. Between 2010 and 2013, city growth outpaced suburban growth (Frey 2014). People, especially the millennials, are flocking to the city for the ease of walkability and social interaction (Leinberger and Doherty 2011). Church conversions are most often architecturally stunning and therefore quite appealing to a younger/more affluent buyer. In many instances, church conversions are taking place in transitional neighborhoods, which leads to consideration of gentrification and changes in community identity.

These streams of inquiry will be brought together to examine what happens when a church is converted into another use. Although there are instances of reusing a shuttered church as a school or community center, when a neighborhood church is converted to luxury apartments and/or condominiums, the clash of gentrification rings loudly. Because many of the churches have significance far beyond the bricks and mortar, community voices are raised in opposition. Unlike the "fake history" recounted by Lior Strahilevitz (Chapter 5, this volume), the history of the church in these neighborhoods is quite real. The interplay of historical significance (if not outright historical preservation), community spirit, and local governments' desire for growth combine in a unique fashion.

ROLE OF THE CHURCH IN NEIGHBORHOOD LIFE

Religious services constitute only a fraction of a church's impact in the neighborhood. A church often serves as a social service and community anchor. Churches

can be institutional agents that impact the communal trajectory of the neighborhood (McRoberts 2003, 123). One scholar noted that the breadth of community
impact spans the gamut from health care to political power to physical nourishment
(Day 2014, 61).[1]

As waves of foreign immigrants swept into U.S. cities, the church created (or, in
many cases, recreated) a common language, heritage, and social structure for the
migrants. African American migrants moving from the South into Northern cities
experienced the same assimilation pattern into neighborhood churches (McRoberts
2003, 105). Religious beliefs and the physical structures that house that belief serve as
"ballast for immigrants as they struggle to adapt to their new homeland" (Hirschman
2004, 1211). In a city that is a sea of "other," the immigrant church serves as not only a
spiritual refuge, but also a social one. One scholar has noted that in many immigrant
churches, although there may be a common ethnicity, language, and place of origin,
the communal functions the church provided are shared by those who do not
necessarily share the same religious values (Ley 2008, 2062). Whether it be
English language instruction, job services, food support, or just plain socialization,
the immigrant church plays a pivotal role. Continuing into today, the church serves
as a place of refuge and assimilation for immigrants. Even after the first immigrants
move away, the church welcomes the next wave (Ley 2008, 2070).

Research has also highlighted the importance of the neighborhood church in the
area of public health. Because there is collective identity and an established support
system, church congregations are ideal forums for public health initiatives through
behavioral outcomes (Eng et al. 1985, 82). Through models such as Parish nurses,
the church can promote wellness by "holistically addressing the physical, emotional
and spiritual needs of congregational community members" (Miskelly 1995, 1). One
pointed example is the work that churches have done in promoting HIV/AIDS
testing by providing not just the opportunity to test, but also community support for
making the decision (Day 2014, 80).

As far back as W. E. B. Du Bois, scholars have highlighted the social and
political power of the church within the community (Du Bois 1903). Because of
the social capital and linkages forged in the congregation, churches are often a
pivotal player in political activism. As intermediaries between the state and the
individual (Greenberg 2000, 380), the social networks in the congregation serve
as fertile grounds for political discourse. Interestingly, attendance at church is
not the catalyst for political activism. Political activism is linked to the church
actually encouraging its congregants to become politically active (Brown and
Brown 2003, 634).

The church's role in the neighborhood often extends beyond its congregation. In
a study by the Partners for Sacred Places organization, a stunning 81 percent of the
beneficiaries of church-based social services were not members of the congregation
(Sacred Places 2008, 11). Quantifying the "halo effect" of church activity in economic terms has begun. Preliminary results indicate that the 12 congregations in the

Partners for Sacred Places study contributed $52 million to the common good each year (Day 2014, 68).

In recent times, the social interaction of the church and the neighborhood has grown in both size and institutionalization. After a period of increased social service spending by government between 1994 and 2002, spending on social services dropped almost 16 percent between 2002 and 2007 (Gais 2009, 13). The Great Recession exacerbated this downward trend. The social services provided in the churches are not *in addition* to government-provided social services – often they are substitutes for decreasing government-provided services. Churches have taken up the slack left by the government's exit. Several studies show that between 87–92 percent of churches support at least one social program (Wuthnow 2006, 28–32). As of 2011, 59 percent of Catholic parishes reported performing social services for their communities (Gray 2011, 2). In fact, the increased involvement of churches was an explicit government policy of the federal government when George W. Bush established the Office of Faith-Based and Community Initiatives in 2002 (Wuthnow 2006, 14).[2] Whether congregations are categorized as "caring communities" (with a set of shared values, beliefs, understandings, traditions, and norms) or "service organizations" (with arms-length, or contractual understandings) (64 et seq.), they serve as the social safety net for many people. While the religious services of a church may signify its existential existence, its ancillary activities tie it to the social fabric of the neighborhood.

ZONING LAW AND RELIGIOUS USE

One reason that the church is such a powerful community-building institution is that it often sits squarely in the residential neighborhood. While religious exemptions to residential use through special use permits are common, the question becomes much more difficult as churches branch out to use their structures for more than religious services. Ancillary uses such as daycares, meeting spaces, and soup kitchens may fulfill the missionary commitment of the church, but often fly in the face of existing zoning regulation. The legal question to be answered is whether these ancillary activities are deemed part of religious practice (thus permitted under zoning regulation) or outside religious use (thus not permitted under zoning regulation). Stated another way: can the government restrict ancillary activities without infringing on religious practice? The jurisprudential route to this answer has been circuitous as the courts and lawmakers look for a way to balance the freedom of religion with the government's need for consistency and neighborhood stability.

In 2000, Congress passed the Religious Land Use and Institutionalized Persons Act (The Religious Land Use and Institutionalized Persons Act, 42 U.S.C. § 2000cc ("RLUIPA")), with the stated goal of protecting religious freedoms in a way that is compatible with municipal objectives. The legislation was enacted to meet the need for special safeguards of religious worship in the United States. Germane to the present discussion, RLUIPA focuses on the treatment of "land use of religious institutions as 'religious exercise'" (Adams 2002, 2364; 42 U.S.C. §§ 2000cc, 2000cc-5), and extends the use of the property as eligible for the same rights and protections as other forms of religious practice (Adams 2002, 2364).[3]

RLUIPA provides that no government may enact a land use regulation that "imposes a substantial burden on the religious exercise of a person, including a religious assembly or institution, unless the government demonstrates that imposition of the burden on that person, assembly, or institution is in furtherance of a compelling governmental interest; and is the least restrictive means of furthering that compelling governmental interest." Further, RLUIPA defines religious exercise as: "any exercise of religion, whether or not compelled by, or central to, a system of religious belief. The use, building, or conversion of real property for the purpose of religious exercise shall be considered to be religious exercise of the person or entity that uses or intends to use the property for that purpose" (42 U.S.C. § 2000cc-5).[4]

RLUIPA "calls for responsible religious freedom and responsible government: the statute protects churches that are attentive to neighbors and community, and affirms municipalities that address adverse impacts of religious land use with controls that are direct, carefully tailored, and evenhandedly applied" (Carmella 2009, 488–90). This well-choreographed dance between local municipalities and the religious institutions within their boundaries contributes to the social capital of society, allowing these institutions to provide for their communities while at the same time enacting zoning provisions that promote the safety and welfare of the community (Carmella 2009, 488).

In the years before RLUIPA, the law was murkier; courts were reluctant to interfere with local zoning laws. Courts, as well as cities and their inhabitants, had become used to the tight controls and monitored growth of zoning codes, wary of the instability that might ensue with less stringent land use controls (Carmella 2009, 494; Sunstein 1989, 473).[5] Courts saw zoning ordinances as a stabilizing force in communities and were reluctant to shake things up, preferring instead to see the benefits and stability of anticipated land use patterns that the zoning ordinances provide (Carmella 2009, 496–97). The courts' opinions, particularly in reviewing religious land use and auxiliary uses, varied greatly depending on a number of factors, including the location of the church and the specificity of local ordinances (Galvan 2006, 219).

Recognizing the importance of auxiliary uses to a church, the court sometimes ruled in favor of claimants even if the practice was not fundamental to the religion. In *St. Johns Evangelical Lutheran Church v. City of Hoboken*, for instance, the city of Hoboken tried to close a homeless shelter that provided meals and a place to sleep for dozens of individuals (479 A.2d 935, 939 (1983); Stout 2011, 465). The church argued that offering sanctuary was a tradition firmly entrenched in its history and that closing the shelter would put many people at risk. While it was clear that imminent harm would result if the church were forced to cease its operations as a homeless shelter, the court acknowledged that the city's concerns for following health and safety protocols should also be addressed. The New Jersey Superior Court found that it would be a "travesty of justice and compassion" for the city to prevent the church from operating a homeless shelter. The court reasoned that providing for the poor was a principal use of the church, protected from the reach of the city's zoning power (*St. Johns v. City of Hoboken*, 479 A.2d 935, 939 (1983)). In an effort to comply with health and safety standards, the church agreed that it would reduce the number of occupants to 20 and was then permitted to carry on its operations (939).

RLUIPA clarified the protection of what constitutes the free exercise of religion. Religious practice is many things to many people. It can range from actual prayer in an organized fashion within the walls of a church to daycare or social services that the church provides, or even educational or recreational activities. This breadth of possible over-inclusive activity has been cited by one court as possibly including "parking lots and playgrounds, convents, rectories, and monasteries ... day care centers, drug rehabilitation centers, and softball fields" (*Warner v. Phuoc Long Buddhist Temple of CT, Inc.*, 2010 WL 4352716, citing Rathkopf and Rathkopf 1978, 20–53). Too broad a reading would allow RLUIPA to cover all auxiliary uses, permit these uses to function outside of regular land use regulation, and perhaps grant religious landowners an immunity of sorts from local ordinances (Galvan 2006, 209). One commentator has questioned whether RLUIPA allows churches too much lenience to the detriment of the community (Hamilton 2012, 959).

RLUIPA broadly defines religious exercise as any exercise of religion, whether or not it be central to religious belief; the building in which these things take place is an extension of that exercise (RLUIPA. 42 U.S.C. § 2000cc), thereby removing the necessity of analyzing whether a particular use is integral to an individual's or organization's religious exercise (*Midrash Sephardi, Inc. v. Town of Surfside*, 366 F.3d 1214 (11th Cir. 2004)). The rationale behind accessory uses is to allow religious organizations to carry out the principal use, to "operate fully with the necessary and appropriate accessory uses allowed" (Saxer 2008, 596). This expansive view would pull in any use of the property if the church can tie that use to furtherance of its religious mission. The social services and community endeavors of a church are safeguarded simply because of this linkage to religion.

There are limitations, however. The fact that an accessory use is employed by a religious entity does not automatically guarantee it protection as a religious exercise (Saxer 2008, 619). In *Westchester Day School v. Village of Mamaroneck* (386 F.3d 183, 189 (2d Cir. 2004)), for instance, the district court granted summary judgment in favor of a religious school whose application to make improvements to its building had been denied. The district court did not address the issue of whether the expansion of the school was for religious purposes. Rather, the court reasoned that the project was religious in nature because the school was a religious school attended by students who wished to further their religious education and was therefore protected from local land use ordinances under RLUIPA (189). On appeal, the 2nd Circuit argued that under this logic, if two schools applied for the expansion of their gymnasium with the only difference being that one was a religious school, the zoning board would not be allowed to reject the application of the religious institution (189). The circuit court vacated the decision and remanded the case back to the district court to review, among other issues, whether the scope of RLUIPA manages to protect the free exercise of religion without conferring special benefits to religion.[6]

This requirement of furtherance of religious practice in order to withstand scrutiny under RLUIPA will be vital in answering the question of how to replace social services provided by a church that is now a residential structure. It will not simply be an exercise of moving the services to a different location in the same neighborhood because the loss of religious exemption means that the use will most likely violate zoning regulation. As will be discussed, *infra*, the loss of community benefit without direct method of replacement differentiates the conversion of a church from other instances of development.

CHURCH CLOSINGS

Many of the churches established during the great migration to U.S. cities are standing as empty edifices with high maintenance bills and few parishioners to pay those bills. It is important to note that the conversions to condos are not causing the closing of churches. Cities such as Pittsburgh, Detroit, Philadelphia, Chicago, and Boston all suffered large population losses in the last half of the twentieth century. These urban churches have fallen victim not just to the changing demographics of urban America, but were also dealt a knockout blow of dwindling church attendance.[7]

As one scholar who studies Catholic demographic trends points out, there are beautiful religious structures in New York and Philadelphia and Cleveland – all the urban areas that have seen decreases in population (Wang 2015). She goes on to note that as population decreases, the people in the pews are elderly and are not being replaced by younger generations. In response to these and other pressures, churches are closing at a good clip. However, church closings are not evenly distributed. For example, during an earlier round of church closings by the Catholic Archdiocese in Philadelphia, there were charges that the church was abandoning the inner city (Rzeznik 2009, 73–90). Indeed the Archdiocese of Detroit learned the importance of narrative in the late 1980s when it received harsh criticism by citing "white flight" as the underlying reasons for the closings (Bridger and Maines 1998). The massive physical size of most of the churches constrains incremental downsizing. Once the decision to close is made, the entire structure becomes abandoned.

Nationally, Roman Catholic churches date, on average, from 1920, with the majority having been built between the 1940s and 1950s (Gray 2011). The number of parishes peaked around 1990 with 19,620 churches. Some of these churches closed, some merged. Many consolidated services so that many parishes share services with other parishes. According to the *CARA*, the center specializing in social science research about the Catholic Church, about a third begin a multi-parish arrangement during the period 1995–2004 and another third from 2005 or later so that 67 percent of parishes began sharing services from around the year 1995 through the present (Gray 2011).

The 2000s saw a drop in the number of Catholic churches to 1965 levels. Catholic parishes numbered about 19,000 in 2000. By 2010, the number was fewer than 17,800 (Gray 2011). The decline can be seen in specific cities. In Detroit, for instance, the Archdiocese of Detroit saw the largest number of closings in 1989, with 26 churches closed that year, many of them ethnically oriented congregations that once served the local Polish and German communities (Archdiocese of Detroit 2016). Among the reasons for the decline in Detroit parishioners was the construction of a major highway that required the demolition of 500 homes, leaving parishes without parishioners, and contributing to the decline in church attendance (Bukowczyk 1984). In one Detroit neighborhood, the area never recovered from civil unrest in 1967 and churches merged until finally the remaining church building was sold to a developer (Detroiturbex.com 2016).

The Archdiocese of New York instituted dramatic cuts in 2015 with 40 parish closings and 59 mergers (Archdiocese of New York 2015). The number of parishes in the Archdiocese of Chicago shrank considerably in 1990, with 32 closings (Archdiocese of Chicago, Archives and Records Center). In 2004, the Archdiocese of Boston announced sweeping closures and mergers. The pain was not evenly spread. Sixteen of the 66 closed or merged parishes were in the city of Boston. In the entire diocese, the number of urban churches was reduced by 27 percent (Boston.com 2016).

The loss was felt not only in the Catholic Church, but in other denominations, as well. The Presbyterian Ministry saw its highest number of closings in 2012 (Presbyterian Church Summaries of Statistics – Comparative Statistics; www.pcusa.org). The church dropped from 10,466 churches nationally in 2011 to 9,829 in 2014. The bishop explained that the closings "were necessary . . . because of shortages of cash, worshippers and priests," and were "mostly in inner-city neighborhoods and inner-ring suburbs" (O'Malley 2010). The Lutheran Church saw a steady rate of closings nationally between 2000 and 2014, with an average of 36 churches closing each year.[8] In 2002, the Episcopalian Church had 7,305 parishes nationally. By 2013, that number had shrunk to 6,622 (Episcopal Church 2013).[9]

DEMOGRAPHIC CHANGES IN AMERICA'S CENTRAL CITIES

Church closings were predicated not just by a decrease in church membership, but also by population loss. Many of these churches stood in neighborhoods that suffered through massive population hemorrhages. However, although church attendance has yet to see a significant resurgence, it is a new day of population gains in many U.S. cities. After decades of persistent population loss, it appears that American urban centers have turned the corner. The first decade of the millennium followed the demographic pattern of the preceding 50 years of suburbs growing faster than cities. However, from 2010 to 2013, the growth pattern reversed. In fact, in these three years, cities gained more people than they did in the entire preceding decade (Frey 2014). In contradistinction to stories in the popular press, Baby Boomers are not driving this urban population growth (Bahrampour 2013; Keates 2013). This urban renaissance is driven by millennials (Couture 2015). Cities such as Buffalo, Cleveland, New Orleans, and Pittsburgh (all population losers over the previous 50 years) saw a significant increase in their young, college-educated population (Miller 2014). Central Philadelphia (extending to South Philadelphia and Fishtown) has grown so much over the past 15 years that it now ranks second only to Midtown Manhattan when it comes to people living in the heart of a city (Philly 2015). Changing lifestyle preferences (walkability/public transportation,[10] the "hip" factor), coupled with the deindustrialization of the cities, are drivers of the millennial attraction to living in central cities (Brinig 2014, 160; Glaeser 2006).[11] One real estate industry spokesman went so far as to assert that "The Millennial generation is the key to a sustained real estate recovery" (RealtyTrac 2014).

The central city "recovery" comes at a time when magnificent churches are undergoing deconsecration, renovation, and conversion. No exact data draw a direct line, but the increased supply of condominiums is feeding the demand of new urban dwellers. Church conversions present an interesting offering often in areas that are more affordable as they undergo demographic transition.

CHURCH CONVERSIONS TO CONDOS – SOME EXAMPLES

From an architectural perspective, an abandoned church is a breathtaking opportunity for adaptive reuse. In fact, churches have been converted to artist studios, community centers, and even brew pubs! However, these uses invite others into the neighborhood without permanence. The focus on reuse as residential use (apartment or condominium) requires us to address the issue on a deeper level as the use introduces not just a change within the walls of the structure, but also a change in the composition of the neighborhood. Paradoxically, it is easier to convert a church to a condominium or apartment because, as noted earlier, they generally are located in a residential neighborhood and therefore the new use usually does not require a rezoning effort.

St. Anthony's of Padua Roman Catholic Church was built in 1889 to serve the Gray's Ferry neighborhood in Philadelphia. The church served as a neighborhood anchor for 113 years. Its path was in line with the now well-worn story. Where the once thriving parish had 2,000 families and five priests, it dwindled to 175 families and one priest. The church closed in 1999, and another denomination (Greater St. Matthew Baptist Church) bought the property in 1999. However, mounting maintenance costs and lack of parking sealed its fate and that congregation moved out in 2014. Neighbors met with the developer to try to convince him to use the space as a community center, but were told that only use as housing could find financing. In the end, the neighbors were consoled by the fact that the structure could not be demolished due to its historical certification so that, although the use would be housing, the building's façade would remain. It was sold to a developer that converted it to apartments. Gray's Ferry (and the whole area known as Graduate Hospital or Center City West) is quickly gentrifying. In one study, the Graduate Hospital area had the largest gains in home price–income ratio in all of Philadelphia between 2000 and 2014 (Pew Trust 2016). According to the real estate website Trulia.com, the median sales price of a home in the Graduate Hospital community was $338,000 in September 2010, peaked at $435,000 in 2014, and stood at about $405,000 in September 2015. The median rent for the area has risen from $1,800 in April 2015 to about $2,075 in 2016. Christened "Sanctuary Lofts," the apartments are leasing for $1,200–$1,650/month.

Holy Trinity German Catholic Church in Boston's South End, like other churches, was much more than a physical structure. Holy Trinity was the only German Catholic Church in Boston in the 1800s, and new immigrants joined the church to hear Mass in their native language (Holy Trinity 2016). The present structure was dedicated in 1877 (Holy Cross 2016). In recent years, it also served as base of operations for a day program for homeless adults and a center for at-risk youth, a regular concert series, and social justice ministries. The Boston Archdiocese closed the building in 2008 and deconsecrated it in 2012, citing declining attendance and increased maintenance costs (Keith 2014). Holy Trinity parishioners formed a preservation group in October 2013 and lobbied for the church to remain open. They proposed to assume all the maintenance costs of Holy Trinity Church in return for the Archdiocese authorizing one Mass there per year. That proposal was rejected (*Boston Catholic Insider* 2014). When the Archdiocese of Boston sold Holy Trinity to New Boston Ventures for $7 million in 2014, the archbishop stipulated that the use of a relegated church may be "profane but not sordid."[12] Vacant for nearly five years, it will come to life again – not as a church, but as high-priced condominiums. The South End real estate market is bursting with development amid the current hot real estate market (D. Adams 2015a). Now christened "The Lucas," the former church has been transformed into a luxury condominium building with 33 units that come with a price tag of mid-$600,000 to $4,000,000 (Pohle 2016).

WEAVING NEW NEIGHBORS IN PLACE OF RELIGION

When the new occupants of the former church move in, they bring new sensibilities to the neighborhood. Familiar refrains of gentrification ring true, but in these instances, the newcomers represent more than an addition – they represent a loss. Whether it is a community center, a food pantry, or a safe space for at-risk youth, the community loses valuable social capital in the conversion of the church in a way that other development does not engender. Just as Brinig and Garnett (2014) contend about Catholic schools, the social capital churches generate make them effective community institutions and their loss brings tangible detriment to the neighborhood. In certain respects, conversion of a church sidesteps many of the displacement arguments put forth by scholars and policy makers who oppose gentrification (Lees, Slater, and Wyly 2008, 196). No one is forced to move; no existing housing is torn down or gutted.[13] This may serve to make the repair of social capital easier. Building of social capital is another way of promoting trust building between the new and the existing neighbors. Just as Matthew Desmond notes (Chapter 7, this volume), trust in your neighbors is crucial. Trust and norms of civic cooperation are essential to well-functioning neighborhoods (Knack 1997, 1283). I suggest, in the same vein as Hankins and Walter, that we should strive for gentrification harnessed for the good of the neighborhood (Hankins and Walter 2012, 1519).

To realize the full picture, the reuse of a church must be approached with a more inclusive notion of value. Like any real estate transaction, valuation of church property for development relies on cap rates and discounted cash flows. But there is more to fold into the calculation. For instance, many of the negotiations over converting a church can center on the building itself, especially if the building is of historical significance. Whether this designation is precisely linked to higher value (a topic discussed in several chapters of this volume), smart developers recognize the amenity value of the physical structure of the church (whether or not it is historically certified) and monetize that value into the purchase price (D. Adams 2015b).[14] I submit another component of the value is the social capital generated by the ancillary activities of the church. This capital can be described as both collective efficacy[15] and actual social services. The loss of this social capital should not be borne by the community. To recoup that loss, a fee attributable to replacement value must be established and borne by either the developer or the church.

The easy solution would be to require replacement of the lost social services within the renovated structure as a condition for any development. This is an imperfect solution for two reasons: first of all, it does not capture the lost community cohesion. Second, due to the zoning issues detailed, supra, this is not a feasible alternative for legal reasons. In this instance, zoning works to the detriment of the existing neighborhood, as the value of the social services vanish upon redevelopment. Although there is no way for the new development to replace the religious services of the former church, the social services and other amenities can be shifted to other service providers in the neighborhood. I can suggest two ways to ameliorate the effect of loss of social services when a church is closed. Both require an imposition of a fee, but differ in who pays the fee: the church (seller) or the developer (buyer). The fee is shifted either backward to the seller in the form of a reduced purchase price or forward to the developer, who will most likely pass it on to the homebuyer in the form of increased price (Rosenberg 2006, 213).

One alternative shifts the payment of the fee to the seller (i.e., a reduction in the net sale price). In this scenario, a portion of the sale price is put into a set-aside or escrow by the seller. The amount of the set-aside would be a rough approximation of the cost to replace the social services provided by the church. This amount would be donated to the church's social service provider for use by other churches in the neighborhood or close proximity. This method has the advantage of placing the burden of internalizing the externalities on the party whose action causes them to occur. When the diocese (or other canonical body) decides to close a church, an inventory and cost of social and community services that take place in the building should be calculated. Upon sale, an amount sufficient to continue the activity at another location will be held back from the purchase price in the same manner as other escrow accounts (such as environmental escrow accounts).

The other alternative is to require the developer to contribute a fee to social service agencies to offset the impact of the loss of social services in the church. Akin to the Percent for Art fee in Philadelphia[16] or the fee imposed on hotel conversions in San Francisco[17] this method would be less tied to the community, but more easily assessed than a fee to the diocese. Whether this fee is shifted to the ultimate buyer in the form of a high price or paid by the developer in lower profit is open for debate (Ihlanfeldt and Shaughnessy 2004). There is even evidence of "overshifting" where the homebuyer's cost includes a multiple of the fee (Rosenberg 2006, 12). The important point is that the costs of the externalities of development are accounted for in the transaction and are not borne by the third-party members of the community.

Impact fees (or exactions) have had a long and somewhat contentious relationship with development. A fee for redeveloping a former church is a monetary imposition that would potentially be subject to heightened "exactions" scrutiny after the court's ruling in *Koontz v. St. Johns River Water Management District* (570 U.S. ___, 133 S. Ct. 2586 (2013); see also Fennell and Peñalver 2013, 335). Cynically, exactions can be described as extortion – the city holds a building permit hostage for ransom. However, they provide an efficient means to internalize externalities of development. Although some thought *Nollan v. Calif. Coastal Comm'n.* (483 U.S. 825 (1987)) *and Dolan v. City of Tigard* (512 U.S. 374 (1994) – the two decisions that set out the "nexus" and "proportionality" requirements for exactions – would slow (or even stop) municipalities from utilizing impact fees, the report of their death was greatly exaggerated.[18] The full impact of the recent decision in *Koontz* remains to be seen. Land use law commentators are split as to whether *Koontz* was the "worst takings decision ever" (Echeverria 2014, 1), or a "straightforward application" of *Nollan* and *Dolan* (Martin 2014, 39). Nevertheless, with an amenable state statute, a reasonable degree of nexus and rough proportionality, impact fees remain popularly used today to fund street widening, green space provisions, and more.[19]

Returning to the question of how to replace the loss of community services when a church is converted, the notion of an impact fee can be applied. However, in this case, instead of the municipality receiving the fee, it would be directed to an approved social service agency or other approved not-for-profit whose work can replace the loss in social services or community amenity. In light of the flourishing network of community-based organizations and faith-based social service agencies performing more and more of the social work done in America's urban centers, a fee for the impact of lost social services can be easily tied to a continuation of those services by another provider.[20]

In either of the proposed schemes, current neighborhood residents will benefit as they see that part of the purchase price is expressly dedicated to preservation of the social fabric that is now being rewoven. New residents will recognize that moving into a former church is more than a residential decision, thus hopefully sowing the seeds of neighborhood interaction from the very beginning. Community does not have to be lost when a church is converted. Through deliberate action to retain the humanitarian and social impact initiatives, it can find new life to the benefit of all.

AUTHOR'S NOTE

I would like to thank the Kreisman Initiative and the conference organizers for putting together a wonderful series of presentations. It allowed the participants (and the readers of this volume) to view housing through a kaleidoscope of perspectives, all coming back to the common theme of how law and public policy directly impact how and where we live. Thanks for outstanding research assistance goes to Jennifer Barzeski and Sam Waldorf.

REFERENCES

Adams, Caroline R. 2002. "The Constitutional Validity of the Religious Land Use and Institutionalized Persons Act of 2000: Will RLUIPA's Strict Scrutiny Survive the Supreme Court's Strict Scrutiny?" *Fordham Law Review* 70: 2361–2408.

Adams, Dan. 2015a. "Bold Plan to Convert South End Church into Condos Approved." *Boston Globe.* June 12. Accessed July 28, 2016. www.bostonglobe.com/business /2015/06/12/dramatic-design-convert-church-into-condos-gets-city-hall-approval /pcduyudEiVVORLSd9lXOxK/story.html?p1=Article_Related_Box_Article.

   2015b. "Turning Churches into Housing a Unique Challenge." *Boston Globe.* April 21. Accessed July 28, 2016. www.bostonglobe.com/business/2015/04/20 /turning-churches-into-housing-unique-challenge-for-developers/UFPYDtqote HdtjBhzhuWxL/story.html.

Archdiocese of Detroit. 2016. Accessed October 25, 2016. www.aod.org/parishes /sacramental-records/closed-parishes.

Archdiocese of New York. 2015. Accessed October 25, 2016. http://archnyarchives.org/wp-content/uploads/2013/04/Parish-Status-and-Record-Location-9.9.15.pdf.

Bahrampour, Tara. 2013. "The Kids Gone, Aging Baby Boomers Opt for City Life." *Washington Post.* August 9. Accessed July 28, 2016. www.washingtonpost.com/local/2013/08/05/1a21c1b2-fba7-11e2-a369-d1954abcb7e3_story.html.

Boston.com. 2016. "Closings at a Glance." Accessed October 25, 2016. http://archive.boston.com/news/specials/parishes/.

Boston Catholic Insider. 2014. "Boston's Holy Trinity Church up for Sale." Accessed July 28, 2016. https://bostoncatholicinsider.wordpress.com/2014/08/27/bostons-holy-trinity-church-up-for-sale/.

Bridger, Jeffrey C. and David R. Maines. 1998. "Narrative Structures and the Catholic Church Closings in Detroit." *Qualitative Sociology,* 21(3): 319–40.

Brinig, Margaret and Nicole Stelle Garnett. 2014. *Lost Classroom, Lost Community: Catholic Schools' Importance in Urban America.* Chicago: University of Chicago Press.

Brown, R. Khari and Ronald E. Brown. 2003. "Faith and Works: Church Based Social Capital Resources and African American Political Activism." *Social Forces* 82(2): 617–41.

Bukowczyk, John J. 1984. "The Decline and Fall of a Detroit Neighborhood: Poletown vs. G.M. and the City of Detroit." *Washington and Lee Law Review* 41: 49–76.

Carmella, Angela C. 2009. "RLUIPA: Linking Religion, Land Use, Ownership and the Common Good." *Albany Government Law Review* 2: 485–536.

Couture, Victor and Jessie Handbury. 2015. "Urban Revival in America 2000 to 2010." Unpublished manuscript. Last accessed April 7, 2017 http://faculty.haas.berkeley.edu/couture/download/Couture_Handbury_Revival.pdf.

Day, Katie. 2014. *Faith on the Avenue.* New York: Oxford University Press.

Detroiturbex.com. 2016. "St. Agnes / Martyrs of Uganda Parish Church." Accessed October 7, 2016. http://detroiturbex.com/content/churches/stagnes/.

Du Bois, W. E. B. 1903. *The Souls of Black Folk.* Chicago: A.C. McClurg & Co.

Echeverria, John D. 2014. "Koontz: The Very Worst Takings Decision Ever?" *New York University Environmental Law Journal* 22: 1–56.

Eng, Eugenia and John Hatch. 1985. "Institutionalizing Social Support through the Church and into the Community." *Education Behavior* 12(1): 81–92.

Episcopal Church. 2013. "Domestic Fast Facts 2013." Accessed July 28, 2016. www.episcopalchurch.org/files/domestic_fast_facts_2013.pdf.

"Table of Statistics of the Episcopal Church." Accessed July 28, 2016. www.episcopalchurch.org/files/2002TableofStatisticsoftheEpiscopalChurch.pdf.

Fennell, Lee Anne and Eduardo Peñalver. 2013. "Exactions Creep." *Supreme Court Review* 2013: 287–358.

Florida, Richard. 2002. *The Rise of the Creative Class.* New York: Basic Books.

Frey, William H. 2014. "Will This Be the Decade of Big City Growth?" Brookings Institute. www.brookings.edu/research/opinions/2014/05/23-decade-of-big-city-growth-frey.

Gais, Thomas and Lucy Dadayan. 2009. "The Decline of States in Financing the US Safety Net: Retrenchment in State and Local Social Welfare Spending 1977–2007." Paper presented at "Reducing Poverty: Assessing Recent State Policy Innovations and Strategies," Emory University, Atlanta, Georgia, November 19–20.

Galvan, Sara. 2006. "Beyond Worship: The Religious Land Use and Institutionalized Persons Act of 2000 and Religious Institutions' Auxiliary Uses." *Yale Law and Policy Review* 24: 207–39.

Gamm, Gerald. 1999. *Urban Exodus: Why the Jews Left Boston and the Catholics Stayed*. Cambridge, MA: Harvard University Press.

Glaeser, Edward L. and Joshua D. Gottlieb. 2006. "Urban Resurgence and the Consumer City." *Urban Studies* 43(8): 1275–99.

Gray, Mark M. and Mary L. Gautier. 2011. "The Changing Face of U.S. Catholic Parishes." Accessed July 28, 2016. http://cara.georgetown.edu/CARAServices /Parishes%20Phase%20One.pdf.

Greenberg, Anna. 2000. "The Church and the Revitalization of Politics and Community." *Political Science Quarterly* 115: 377–94.

Hamilton, Marci A. 2012. "RLUIPA Is a Bridge too Far: Inconvenience Is Not Discrimination." *Fordham Urban Law Journal* 39: 959–87.

Hankins, Katherine and Andy Walter. 2012. "'Gentrification with Justice': An Urban Ministry Collective and the Practice of Place-Making in Atlanta's Inner-City Neighbourhoods." *Urban Studies* 49(7): 1507–26.

Hirschman, Charles. 2004. "The Role of Religion in the Origins and Adaptation of Immigrant Groups in the United States." *International Migration Review* 38(3): 1206–33.

Holy Cross. 2016. "RG 10.08 Holy Trinity Church, Boston, Mass., Finding Aid." Accessed October 22, 2016. http://crossworks.holycross.edu/findaid_nen_rg/15/.

Holy Trinity. 2016. "History of Holy Trinity (German) Church." Accessed October 22, 2016. http://holytrinitygerman.org/HTHistory.html.

Ihlanfeldt, Keith and Timothy Shaughnessy. 2004. "An Empirical Investigation of the Effects of Impact Fees on Housing and Land Markets." *Regional Science and Urban Economics* 34: 639–61.

Keates, Nancy. 2013. "Hip, Urban, Middle Aged." *Wall Street Journal*. August 13. Accessed July 28, 2016. www.wsj.com/articles/SB10001424127887324136204 57864408045204496o.

Keith, John. 2014. "Archdiocese of Boston Lists South End Church for Sale." *Property Blog, Boston Magazine*, June 18. www.bostonmagazine.com/prop erty/blog/2014/06/18/archdiocese-boston-lists-south-end-church-sale/.

Knack, Stephen and Philip Keefer. 1997. "Does Social Capital Have an Economic Payoff? A Cross-Country Investigation." *The Quarterly Journal of Economics* 112(4): 1251–88.

Lees, Loretta, Tom Slater, and Elvin Wyly. *Gentrification*. New York: Routledge, 2008.

Leinberger, Christopher B. and Patrick C. Doherty. 2010. "The Next Real Estate Boom." Brookings Institute. November 1. Accessed October 2016. www.brook ings.edu/research/articles/2010/11/real-estate-leinberger.

Ley, David. 2008. "The Immigrant Church as an Urban Service Hub." *Urban Studies*, 45: 2057–74.

Martin, Christina. 2014. "Nollan and Dolan and Koontz – Oh My!" *Willamette Law Review* 51: 39–72.

McRoberts, Omar M. 2003. *Streets of Glory: Church and Community in a Black Urban Neighborhood.* Chicago: University of Chicago Press 2003.

Miskelly, Sandra. 1995. "A Parish Nursing Model: Applying the Community Health Nursing Process in a Church Community." *Journal of Community Health Nursing* 12(1): 1–14.

Morenoff, Jeffrey, Robert Sampson, and Steven Raudenbush. 2001. "Neighborhood Inequality, Collective Efficacy and the Spatial Dynamics of Urban Violence." *Criminology* 39: 517–60.

O'Malley, Michael. 2010. "On Other Side of Church Closings, New Reasons to Hope." *News and Announcements.* September 8. www.pcusa.org/news/2010/9 /8/other-side-church-closings-new-reasons-hope/.

Ostergren, Robert C. 1981. "The Immigrant Church as a Symbol of Community and Place in the Upper Midwest." *Great Plains Quarterly* 1(4): 224–38.

Pew Charitable Trusts. 2016. "Philadelphia's Changing Neighborhoods." May. www.pewtrusts.org/~/media/assets/2016/05/philadelphias_changing_neighbor hoods.pdf.

Philly. 2015. "(Greater) Center City's Population Second Only to Midtown Manhattan's." Accessed July 28, 2016. www.philly.com/philly/news /20150421__Greater__Center_City_s_population_now_second_only_to_Midt own_Manhattan_s.html

Pohle, Allison. 2016. "They Celebrated Life and Love in Holy Trinity Church." *Boston.* March 9. Accessed July 28, 2016. www.boston.com/news/local/massa chusetts/2016/03/09/they-celebrated-life-and-love-holy-trinity-church-now-condo -building/F9wfkPVbVjONW8GFMDA55M/story.html.

Rathkopf, Arden H. and Daren A. Rathkopf. 1978. *Rathkopf's The Law of Zoning and Planning.* New York: Clark Boardman Co.

RealtyTrac. 2014. "Millennials Moving to Markets with Jobs, Baby Boomers Downsizing to Lower-Cost Markets." Accessed July 28, 2016. www.realtytrac .com/content/foreclosure-market-report/millennials-moving-to-markets-with-jobs -baby-boomers-downsizing-to-lower-cost-markets-8143.

Rosenberg, Ronald H. 2006. "The Changing Culture of American Land Use Regulation: Paying for Growth with Impact Fees." *Southern Methodist University Law Review* 59: 177–263.

Ross Saxer, Shelley. 2008. "Faith in Action: Religious Accessory Uses and Land Use Regulation." *Utah Law Review* 2008: 593–634.

Rzeznik, Thomas. 2009. "The Church in the Changing City: Parochial Restructuring in the Archdiocese of Philadelphia in Historical Perspective." *U.S. Catholic Historian* 27(4): 73–90.

Sacred Places. 2008. "Partners for Sacred Places Is Coming to Chicago." *Sacred Places.* Spring: 10–11.

Simmons, Sheila and Damon Williams. 2016. "Luxury Housing Takes over Black Landmarks in Philly." *Philly Tribune* March 12. Accessed July 7, 2016. www.phillytrib.com/news/luxury-housing-takes-over-black-landmarks -in-philly/article_04cea27e-d93b-53ea-a1b0-40a968b7c2b5.html.

Stout, Kelli. 2011. "Tent Cities and RLUIPA: How a New Religious-Land-Use Issue Aggravates RLUIPA." *Seton Hall Law Review* 41: 465.

Sunstein, Cass R. 1989. "Interpreting Statutes in the Regulatory State." *Harvard Law Review* 103: 405, 473.

Sutherland, Mary and Charles D. Hale. 1995. "Community Health Promotion: The Church as Partner." *Journal of Primary Prevention* 16(2): 201–16.

Wang, Hansi Lo. 2015. "'It's all about Church Closings': Catholic Parishes Shrink in Northeast, Midwest." *All Things Considered.* September 14. www.npr.org/2015 /09/14/436938871/-it-s-all-about-church-closings-catholic-parishes-shrink-in -northeast.

Wuthnow, Robert. 2006. *Saving America? Faith-Based Services and the Future of Civil Society.* Princeton, NJ: Princeton University Press.

Notes

1. Unfortunately, there have also been allegations that the church's power and influence was used to the detriment of the community. For example, during the subprime crisis, it came to light that high-cost home loans were targeted to African Americans by using the black churches. See *Mayor & City of Baltimore v. Wells Fargo*, Third Amended Complaint at 21–22 (www.clearinghouse.net/detail .php?id=11725).

2. Although arguably the intertwining of federal welfare policy and religion began earlier. For example, the 1996 welfare reform legislation included a provision known as Charitable Choice. This provision made it possible for churches and other religiously oriented service organizations to receive government funds more easily.

3. The other issue RLUIPA addressed was to protect the right of institutionalized people to the free exercise of religion.

4. RLUIPA sought to provide an alternative to past legislation, building on the overly broad reach of the earlier, invalidated Religious Freedom Restoration Act that infringed on the states' autonomy (the "RFRA") (42 U.S.C. § 2000bb (1993)), and the lack of consensus regarding the never-enacted Religious Liberty Protection Act of 1998 (the "RLPA") (H.R. 4019, § 2(a)-2(b) (1998)).

5. Sunstein states, "In the aftermath of the New Deal reformation, courts have been reluctant to use the Constitution's explicit protection of property and contracts in a way that would seriously interfere with social and economic regulation" (1989, 473).

6. See also *World Outreach Conference Center v. City of Chicago*, 787 F.3d 839 (Ill. 2015), where the court questioned whether a religious organization is entitled to "more favorable treatment than a secular institution" when the organization challenged a requirement that it obtain a special use permit for an exercise facility.

7. In his book *Urban Exodus*, Gerald Gamm (1999) presents an interesting contrast between Jews and Catholics as each group pulled up stakes and left the city for the suburbs. He asserts that the relative longevity of Catholics in the city is tied to the geographic linkages with the neighborhood parish. In contrast, Jewish residents were free to recreate religious centers freed from geographic ties.
8. A high of 43 Lutheran churches closed in 2006, and a low of 19 closed in 2013. Archives of the Evangelical Lutheran Church in America, email correspondence dated September 21, 2015, with an archivist from the Episcopal Church, who drew the numbers from his microfilm database.
9. Table of Statistics of the Episcopal Church. www.episcopalchurch.org/files /2002TableofStatisticsoftheEpiscopalChurch.pdf. Domestic Fast Facts 2013. www.episcopalchurch.org/files/domestic_fast_facts_2013.pdf.
10. Interestingly, younger people are forgoing obtaining a driver's license. Not only has there been a slight uptick for 14–34-year-olds without a driver's license (from 21 percent to 26 percent), there has been marked increase in people aged 20–34 (the workers of the immediate future) without a driver's license, from 10.4 percent to 15.7 percent. www.uspirg.org/sites/pirg/files/reports/Transportation %20%26%20the%20New%20Generation%20vUS_0.pdf.
11. This "cool" factor received widespread attention following Richard Florida's (2002) book *The Rise of the Creative Class*. See Brinig and Garnett 2014, 160; see also Glaeser and Gottlieb 2006 ("[T]he desire of consumers to live in these cities has increased enormously as a result of changes in style of government, improvements in law enforcement technology and rising incomes that have raised demand for high-end urban amenities.").
12. According to the Code of Canon Law Ch.1 Can. 1222 sec 1 www.vatican.va /archive/ENG1104/_P4H.HTM, profane means that which takes place outside the temple.
13. Admittedly, though, it does contribute to the escalation of neighborhood rents.
14. One developer commented: "These are architecturally significant buildings. . . . It adds a lot of character and flavor to the city to keep them around, and I'm all for that – as long as the numbers work." www.bostonglobe.com/business/2015 /04/20/turning-churches-into-housing-unique-challenge-for-developers/UFPYD tqoteHdtjBhzhuWxL/story.html.
15. I use this term in the vein of Robert Sampson in questioning the role of institutions in contributing to neighborhood stability. See, e.g., Morenoff, Sampson, and Raudenbush (2001).
16. The Philadelphia Redevelopment Authority requires developers to contribute 1 percent of construction costs on PRA-assembled developments to a fund dedicated to the commissioning of original, site-specific works of art. www.philadel phiaredevelopmentauthority.org/percent-for-art. This same type of program has come under fire in Oakland, CA, with a lawsuit filed claiming the requirement violates the Constitution's Takings Clause. See www.bizjournals.com/sanfran cisco/blog/real-estate/2015/07/oakland-development-public-art-fee.html.
17. Upheld by the California Supreme Court in *San Remo Hotel v. City and County of San Francisco*, 27 Cal 4th 643,41 P 3rd 87 (2002).

18. For an excellent review of this topic, see Rosenberg (2006).
19. The Growth Management Act of Washington State, for instance, allows permits' impact fees to be used for: "(a) public streets and roads; (b) publicly owned parks, open space, and recreation facilities; (c) school facilities; and (d) fire protection facilities." R.C.W. Title 82, chapter 82.02.090. The Open Space Impact Fee Program of Chicago helps generate green spaces in the city. See more at www .cityofchicago.org/city/en/depts/dcd/supp_info/open_ space_impactfee.html.
20. See Wuthnow (2006, 138) for discussion of the efficacy of using faith-based organizations to provide social services.

7

How Housing Dynamics Shape Neighborhood Perceptions

Matthew Desmond

If neighborhood perceptions can drive selection into and out of certain areas, influence the concentration of social problems, exacerbate negative health outcomes, and steer urban policy, then identifying factors that influence those perceptions is crucial to understanding city life and developing effective urban policy. What shapes how we see city streets? Research has shown that perceptions of disorder are influenced less by outright signs of decay and neglect – e.g., litter, broken windows, graffiti, public nuisances, crime – than by the kinds of people who inhabit a neighborhood. As it was at the turn of the century, when Du Bois ([1899] 1996) was writing about Philadelphia, and as it was at midcentury, when Jacobs (1961) was writing about New York, race infuses our evaluations of urban neighborhoods. Sampson demonstrates that nonblack residents are more likely to leave the city if they live in neighborhoods where blacks have a growing presence (2012, 300). Quillian and Pager show that city dwellers' perceptions of crime are positively associated with the percentage of young black men in their neighborhood, controlling for crime levels and other neighborhood factors (2001).

Race casts a long shadow over neighborhood perceptions. What else does? Here, urbanists are surprisingly quiet; and their silence leaves us particularly unprepared to understand the views of residents in racially segregated neighborhoods, where the vast majority of Americans live. Most surprisingly, researchers have neglected to appreciate how housing dynamics shape neighborhood perceptions. When Du Bois ([1899] 1996, ch. 15) set out to write about "the environment" of black Philadelphians, he began by analyzing "houses and rent." Only after reviewing the cost, quality, and spatial organization of housing in the ghetto did he broaden to "sections and wards." Du Bois recognized that the house and the neighborhood were intimately linked. But this insight was largely lost on the Chicago School, whose scholars came to view neighborhoods as "moral regions" or sites of residential attainment, a preoccupation that neglected the fact that neighborhoods were also *markets* and largely owned, in the case of the inner city, by landlords who do not live within their borders. As the neighborhood became a core object of social-scientific analysis, the house faded from view. Despite the efflorescence of research on neighborhood effects (Sampson et al. 2002; Sharkey and Faber 2014), we still know relatively little about the role housing dynamics play in shaping the characteristics and perceptions of city blocks.

To understand the link between housing and neighborhood dynamics, this chapter investigates how three housing dynamics – (1) residents' reasons for moving; (2) their strategies for finding housing; and (3) the quality of their dwelling – influence neighborhood perceptions. Drawing on a novel survey of renters in Milwaukee, it finds that city dwellers who relocated to their neighborhood after an eviction, who found their apartment through a nonprofit or government agency, and who experienced long-lasting housing problems harbored lower evaluations of their neighborhoods. These findings indicate that any theory of the neighborhood will be incomplete without accounting for the influence of housing dynamics.

FORCED INTO A NEIGHBORHOOD

Social scientists have long remarked that low-income families experience high rates of residential instability without explaining why this is so. Recent research, however, has revealed the high prevalence of eviction in the lives of renters, demonstrating that poor families move so much simply because they are forced to (Desmond, Gershenson, and Kiviat 2015). Over the past decade, low-income families have watched their incomes stagnate while their housing costs have soared. Meanwhile, only one in four families who qualify for housing assistance receives it. These transformations have led to a rapid increase in severely rent-burdened households – according to the American Housing Survey, roughly half of poor renting families spend at least half of their income on housing (Eggers and Moumen 2010) – and eviction has become a common occurrence in the lives of low-income families. In Milwaukee, the setting of this study, one in eight renter households experiences an involuntary move every two years (Desmond and Shollenberger 2015). Nationwide, renters in more than 2.8 million homes believe they will be evicted soon (Desmond 2015).

While middle-class families may exert a good deal of control and intentionality over their mobility decisions, poor families often are forced from their homes.[1] In the harried aftermath of eviction, finding subsequent housing consumes renters' time and attention. Because many landlords reject recently evicted applicants, displaced families often apply to dozens of apartments before being accepted to one, their housing search stretching on for months (Desmond 2016a). When they finally do find subsequent housing, it is often substandard and located in disadvantaged neighborhoods (Desmond et al. 2015; Desmond and Shollenberger 2015). But when the alternative is homelessness, the priority of finding shelter takes precedence, even if it means moving into a run-down apartment on a dangerous block. As one mother I met during fieldwork put it to her children after their eviction: "We take whatever we can get" (Desmond 2016a).

It is one thing to enter a neighborhood voluntarily; it is quite another to relocate in the exhausting and stressful aftermath of an eviction. Yet no study has investigated the relationship between the circumstances by which families select into a neighborhood and their perceptions of that neighborhood. If many families settle for a place after their eviction, taking "whatever they can get," we might expect them to have lower evaluations of their neighborhood than those who moved under less trying circumstances. This leads to the following hypothesis:

>   Hyp.   1. *Renters whose previous move was forced will express less favorable views of their neighborhood than renters who entered the neighborhood through more voluntary means.*

FINDING A NEIGHBORHOOD

Besides overlooking *why* families move, conventional accounts of neighborhood selection also tend to ignore *how* families move (though see Farley 1996; Krysan 2008): the multiple ways they locate subsequent housing. "More often," write Ludwig and collaborators, "we do not know exactly what is driving the [neighborhood] selection process, and we should worry that selection could occur in part on the basis of factors that are not well understood or easily measured" (2008, 176). But we can study directly "what is driving the selection process," treating neighborhood selection as an important topic of inquiry in its own right (Sharkey 2013). "In examining the sources and social consequences of residential sorting," Sampson has argued, "we need to conceptualize neighborhood selection not merely as an individual-level confounder or as a 'nuisance' that arises independent of social context. Instead, neighborhood selection is part of a process of stratification that situates individual decisions within an ordered, yet constantly changing, residential landscape" (2008, 217).

The relocation strategies of urban renters may be meaningfully diverse. Some may undertake a search independently, scanning the newspaper, local media sources, or the Internet for housing options. Others may use state, municipal, or nonprofit social-service agencies. Still others may rely on network ties, relocating to neighborhoods because a family member or friend told them about a unit coming available or referred them to a landlord (Rossi [1955] 1980, 207–10). Could the ways renters find housing influence their neighborhood perceptions?

There is a qualitative difference between finding an apartment through your own efforts or those of your social network and moving into a place found or assigned by a third-party agency, such as the Public Housing Authority. It is the difference between placing yourself and being placed in a neighborhood. In the former instance, renters may have spent more time, money (e.g., application fees), and social capital during their housing search, which may kindle a psychological desire to reap returns on their efforts. Should the neighborhood be unsafe or otherwise distressed, renters who found housing alone or through their social connections have no one to blame other than themselves or their close ties, while renters who found housing through a nonprofit or government agency can blame a third party. These considerations lead to the following hypothesis:

Hyp. 2. *Renters who located housing themselves or by relying on social networks will express more favorable views of their neighborhood than renters who found housing through a government or nonprofit agency.*

SEEING YOUR NEIGHBORHOOD THROUGH CRACKED WINDOWS

Besides paying attention to the circumstances of city dwellers' previous moves, and the ways they located subsequent housing, I also consider the condition of a family's house. Housing quality in the United States has increased significantly over the past decades (Schwartz 2010). However, some low-income families still live in degrading and dangerous housing conditions. According to the American Housing Survey, 1.2 million renter-occupied units had severe physical problems in 2011 (Desmond 2016a).

For many city dwellers, most of their time spent in a neighborhood is spent in their homes. Poor housing conditions could influence residents' neighborhood perceptions in at least two ways. First, such conditions could dim their perceptions of the world in general. Studies have linked housing problems to poor mental health outcomes, including depressive symptoms, anxiety, and neurological disorders (Evans, Wells, and Moch 2003; Shaw 2004); and quasi-experimental evidence suggests that housing improvements can improve mental health outcomes (Curl et al. 2015). Negative mental health outcomes could be a mechanism through which poor housing conditions deflate residents' perceptions of their neighborhood.

Second, city dwellers with poor housing conditions may spend less time in their homes and thus may be more regularly exposed to neighborhood disorder and crime simply by virtue of heightened neighborhood usage. One way to cope with sinking bathtubs, stopped-up plumbing, and no heat is by spending as little time in your home as possible. As one resident of a low-income trailer park in Milwaukee told me: "My trailer is a hotel. ... I sleep there, and that's about it. I wake up in the morning and leave and go to bed at night, and that's it." Housing problems are concentrated in disadvantaged neighborhoods (Desmond 2016a). Residents of those neighborhoods who flee poor housing conditions may find themselves confronting a different set of problems in the form of public disorder or violence. These paired considerations lead to the following hypothesis:

Hyp. 3. *Renters living with poor housing conditions will express less favorable views of their neighborhood than renters who live in higher-quality housing.*

DATA

To test these three hypotheses, this study draws on the *Milwaukee Area Renters Study* (MARS), an original survey comprised of more than 250 unique questions asked of

1,086 tenants in Milwaukee's private housing sector (Desmond 2016b).[2] From 2009 to 2011, households were selected into MARS through multi-stage stratified sampling. Blocks were randomly selected from strata so as to create a sample generalizable to Milwaukee's rental population. This sampling strategy drew from 168 of 591 unique block groups, representing 28 percent of Milwaukee block groups. When a block was selected into the sample, interviewers visited every renter-occupied household in it, saturating the targeted areas. To bolster response rate and data quality, surveys were administered in person in English and Spanish by professional interviewers at tenants' place of residence. For each household, interviewers surveyed an adult leaseholder or, should a leaseholder be unavailable, an adult knowledgeable about household financial matters. According to the most conservative calculation (AAPOR Rate 1), MARS has an 83.4 percent response rate.

After data collection, custom design weights were calculated to reflect the inverse of selection probability, facilitated by a Lahiri (1951) procedure, based on the demographic characteristics of Milwaukee's rental population and adjusted to MARS's sample size. The Lahiri procedure allows the sampler to select probability samples (with a probability proportional to size) and to compute the selection probabilities for the resulting sample. Selection probabilities are then used to calculate the design weights for the overall sample. I use custom weights when presenting descriptive statistics.

The characteristics of Milwaukee's residents (Pager 2007) and rental market (U.S. Department of Housing and Urban Development 2009) are comparable to those of many U.S. cities. Most low-income city dwellers neither own their homes nor live in public housing (Desmond 2015; Schwartz 2010). MARS's focus on the private rental market, then, reflects the experiences of the vast majority of low-income families.[3] That said, it is important to bear in mind that the MARS sample excludes homeowners, and the extent to which these findings apply to other cities remains to be seen.

MAIN OUTCOME VARIABLES

This study relies on two measures of neighborhood perception: the degree to which renters *trust* their neighbors and the amount of concentrated *suffering* renters believe to be within their neighborhood.

Perceived Trust. Cultivating social capital and collective efficacy on the local level depends in large part on the degree to which neighbors find one another trustworthy. Studies have shown that social trust not only serves as the foundation for civic engagement and reciprocal exchanges that help families make ends meet (Putnam 2001; Sampson 2012); it also is linked to individual health outcomes and other indicators of well-being (Kawachi et al. 1997). Accordingly, I measured renters' neighborhood perceptions through the question: "How much do you trust people in your neighborhood?" Responses were recorded on a five-point scale ranging from "not at all" to "a great deal." For ease of interpretation, neighborhood trust is reported as a binary variable. Renters were considered to trust their neighbors if they reported trusting people in their neighborhood "quite a bit" or "a great deal."

Perceived Suffering. I also observed the degree to which renters believe social problems were found in their neighborhood (Sampson 2012). Each respondent was asked: "While you have been living in this neighborhood, have any of your neighbors ever: (1) been evicted; (2) been in prison; (3) been in an abusive relationship; (4) been addicted to drugs; (5) had their children taken away by social services; or (6) had a close family member or friend murdered?" This measure allowed me to observe what kind of neighborhood renters believed themselves to be living in: one relatively free of hardship, violence, and vice or one brimming over with disadvantage. I treat this measure as a count variable (score 0–6).

EXPLANATORY VARIABLES

Forced Moves. To assess if renters' neighborhood perceptions were influenced by the nature of their previous move – the housing-related circumstances that brought them to their current neighborhood – I examined if that move was induced by eviction, foreclosure, or building condemnation (Desmond and Shollenberger 2015). These are moves that were involuntary or forced, initiated by landlords or city officials (e.g., code inspectors), and involved situations where tenants had no choice other than to relocate. Forced moves are distinct not only from voluntary moves, intentional and uncoercive relocations often carried out to gain residential advantage, but also from responsive moves, motivated by housing or neighborhood conditions such as rent hikes, a deterioration in housing quality, or escalating neighborhood violence. Because retrospective data are most reliable when limited to a recent recall period (Beckett et al. 2001), I only recorded involuntary moves that occurred within two years prior to the survey. Doing so had the added benefit of conservatively biasing the estimated effect of eviction toward zero, since renters who had lived in their neighborhood for more than two years and whose previous move was involuntary were not classified as recently evicted.

Housing Search Strategies. I observed how tenants found their current residence through the question: "How did you find this place? Was it through: (a) a friend; (b) a family member; (c) a [nonprofit] agency; (d) a newspaper, Redbook, Bluebook;[4] (e) a 'for rent' sign; (f) the Internet; (g) the Housing Authority; (h) some other way?" I organized responses into three categories: *network-based searches* that relied on kin, friends, or other social ties; *agency-based searches* that relied on the Housing Authority or nonprofit organizations; and *individual searches* in which tenants located housing themselves by relying on print media or the Internet, or by calling on "for rent" signs. Nearly all renters in our sample (97 percent) found housing exclusively through one of these types of searches.[5] Although renters may have searched for housing in multiple ways, this measure records the technique that led them to the dwelling they inhabited at the time of the survey.

Housing Problems. To measure housing quality, renters were asked if they had experienced any of the following problems in their current residence in the year prior to being interviewed: at least three days with (a) a broken stove or other appliance; (b) a broken window; (c) a broken exterior door or lock; (d) mice, rats, or other pests; or (e) exposed wires or other electrical problems; or at least 24 hours with (f) no heat; (g) no running water; or (h) stopped up plumbing. Responses were summed.

CONTROLS

All models control for a number of demographic attributes related to neighborhood perception, including respondents' race and ethnicity, gender, and age (Hartnagel 1979; Quillian and Pager 2001). I also observed respondents' highest level of education, a stable measure of socioeconomic status (Sampson 2012; Soss and Jacobs 2009). I accounted for family status by observing if each respondent lived with minor children and was the only adult in the household. Living alone or with children could influence one's views of their community (Kimbro and Schachter 2011; Klinenberg 2012).

Renters who experienced recent setbacks might also harbor more negative views of their community. Accordingly, I observed if renters lost their job or experienced relationship dissolution within the previous two years. Although cost-burdened renters need not experience a major setback to invite eviction, accounting for recent job losses and breakups allowed me to observe the relationship between involuntary moves and neighborhood perceptions, conditioning on other recent shocks that could also color renters' views.

Next, I controlled for several factors related to respondents' time and experiences in their neighborhood. Long-standing residents might view their community in a different light than new arrivals (Highton 2000). Accordingly, I observed how long each respondent had lived in her or his neighborhood. In a similar vein, I controlled for the distance (in miles) between renters' current and previous addresses. Moving long distances, such as relocating from across the city or another city entirely, could influence one's views of their current community in stronger ways than moving short distances. Additionally, because renters' neighborhood experiences and perceptions are steered by their relationships with people in their community (Glynn 1986; Stack 1974), I observed how many of a respondent's "closest family members/friends" lived in her or his neighborhood.

The address of each MARS respondent was geo-coded using ArcGIS and an associated road network database. I then assigned each residence to a census block group, my neighborhood metric. In Milwaukee, the population of the average block group was 1,135 in 2010. Each block group was then linked to aggregate data from the

2010 U.S. Census and crime records from the Milwaukee Police Department. I controlled for neighborhood poverty rate: the percentage of people in a census block group below the poverty line. This is a straightforward measure of concentrated disadvantage (Sampson 2012; Wilson 1987). As discussed later, results are robust to other community-level measures, including a neighborhood disadvantage composite variable.

To account for missing data prior to estimation, I conducted multiple imputation (m = 10). Values for missing data were estimated using regression equations that relied on all in-sample variables as predictors (Allison 2002). Where appropriate, logit, ordinal logit, and negative binomial models were used, depending on the type of imputed variable. By and large, MARS has very little missing data. The average variable in our sample was missing only 1.2 percent of observations. Findings hold across imputed and non-imputed datasets. Summary statistics for all variables are presented in Table 7.1.

TABLE 7.1: *Weighted Summary Statistics*

	Mean	SD	Min	Max	Count
Perceived Trust	2.88	1.18	1	5	1,055
Perceived Suffering	0.91	1.32	0	6	1,021
Previous Move was Forced	0.10		0	1	1,063
Found Housing through Network	0.51		0	1	1,063
Found Housing through Agency	0.05		0	1	1,063
Found Housing through Self	0.44		0	1	1,063
Number of Lasting Housing Problems	0.80	1.14	0	9	1,063
Black Renter	0.34		0	1	1,060
Hispanic Renter	0.14		0	1	1,060
White Renter	0.46		0	1	1,060
Other Race Renter	0.06		0	1	1,060
Female Renter	0.62		0	1	1,062
College Graduate	0.40		0	1	1,074
Age	38.78	14.68	15	91	1,053
Months in Neighborhood	48.44	75.88	0	635	1,037
Miles from Previous Residence	47.33	309.35	0.006	5,408	1,032
Minor Children in Household	0.43		0	1	1,060
Only Adult in Household	0.47		0	1	1,063
Neighborhood Strong Ties	1.91	2.43	0	26	1,044
Recent Job Loss	0.19		0	1	1,049
Recent Relationship Dissolution	0.23		0	1	1,061
Neighborhood Poverty Rate	0.12	0.15	0	0.89	1,062
Observed Disorder	0.04		0	1	1,036
Violent Crime Rate	0.12	0.12	0	0.87	1,056
Neighborhood Disadvantage	−0.51	0.79	−1.451	2.99	1,056

Note: Milwaukee Area Renters Study, N = 1,086.

METHODS

I use regressions to examine the relationship between housing dynamics and neighborhood perceptions. When estimating neighborhood trust (o, 1), I rely on logistic regression. To investigate the association between housing dynamics and perceptions of concentrated suffering (a count variable), I employ negative binomial models. Along with the controls listed earlier, models include block-group fixed effects to account for time-invariant neighborhood factors potentially correlated with renters' perceptions of their community (Allison 2009). The identification strategy of the multivariate analyses, then, conditions both on time-variant ecological indicators of disadvantage (through neighborhood-level coefficients) and time-invariant indicators (through neighborhood fixed effects), facilitating comparisons between similar renters in similar neighborhoods who differ with respect to the reasons they entered the neighborhood, how they located their housing, and the quality of dwelling they inhabit.

To address treatment selection, I also employ propensity score matching. Applying experimentalist logic to observational data, this technique compares renters matched along several observable characteristics but who differ by whether they were exposed to a treatment: in this case, one of the three housing dynamics of interest (Rosenbaum and Rubin 1983). To predict renters' propensity for (1) selecting into the neighborhood after a forced move (e.g., eviction) and (2) finding housing through an agency, I included the following characteristics in the matching algorithm: race, age, gender, education, recent job loss, and recent relationship dissolution, as well as indicators for whether the tenant is the only adult in the household or lives with minor children. In addition to these characteristics, when predicting renters' propensity for (3) experiencing any lasting housing problem (here, a binary outcome), I also included how many months they had lived in the neighborhood, the miles between their current and previous residence, neighborhood-based strong ties, and the neighborhood poverty rate.

DESCRIPTIVE PATTERNS: FORCED MOBILITY, SEARCH STRATEGIES, AND HOUSING PROBLEMS

Looking strictly at moves that occurred within the previous two years, I found that the prior move for 1 in 10 renters in Milwaukee was a forced relocation. A nontrivial percentage of renting families, then, selected into their current home and community through an involuntary dislocation from their previous neighborhood. This was the case for 17 percent of Hispanic renters, 10 percent of black renters, and 9 percent of white renters – a disparity driven in large part by the high rate of landlord foreclosures in predominantly Latino neighborhoods during the study period (Desmond and Shollenberger 2015). Fifteen percent of renters living in neighborhoods with high concentrations of poverty (where at least 40 percent of residents

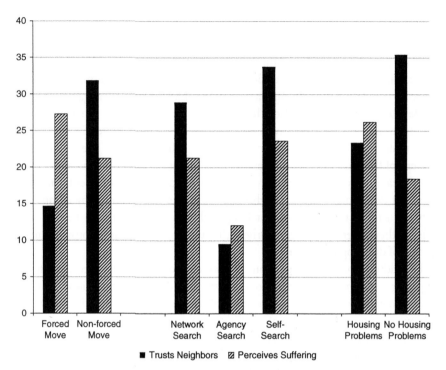

FIGURE 7.1 Perceived Neighborhood Trust and Suffering by Reasons for Moving, Housing Search Strategies, and Housing Problems (weighted percentages). Renters were considered to have housing problems if they reported at least one lasting issue. Renters were considered to trust their neighbors if they reported trusting people in their neighborhood "quite a bit" or "a great deal." Renters were considered to perceive suffering if they reported that their neighbors had experienced two or more adverse events. Milwaukee Area Renters Study, N = 1,086.

lived below the poverty line) came to their neighborhoods after an eviction, compared to 9 percent of renters residing in low-poverty areas (where less than 20 percent of residents lived in poverty).

As displayed in Figure 7.1, considerable differences appear in perceived neighborhood trust and suffering between renters who selected into their community after a forced move and those who did not. Compared to renters who had relocated to their neighborhood after a recent eviction, other renters were twice as likely to report trusting people in their neighborhood "quite a bit" or "a great deal." This difference is statistically significant (p = 0.007). Recently evicted movers were also far more likely to perceive suffering in their neighborhood (27 percent), compared to non-forced movers or long-term stayers (21 percent).

With respect to locating new housing, most Milwaukee renters (51 percent) found their current housing through a network connection: a friend, family member, church attendee, coworker, or other social tie. An additional 44 percent found their housing by themselves, through searching the newspaper or Internet, or spotting a "for rent" sign. Only 5 percent of renters found their housing through a government or nonprofit agency.

While roughly 58 percent of black renters found housing through social networks, the same was true for 50 percent of Hispanic renters and only 41 percent of white renters. The majority of white renters (54 percent) and 49 percent of Hispanic renters located housing through an independent search. Roughly 34 percent of black renters relied on a self-guided search. A small share of renters – roughly 5 percent of white renters, 8 percent of black renters, and less than 1 percent of Hispanic renters – relied on agencies. The vast majority of tenants who located housing through network ties relied on kin and friends. In sharp contrast to research suggesting that black *job* seekers receive less help from social ties than other groups (Smith 2007), I found that black *house* seekers receive more.

White, black, and Hispanic renters who searched for housing independently did so differently. Roughly 48 percent of whites who found housing on their own relied on the Internet, and 33 percent found housing after spotting a "for rent" sign. A total of only three Hispanic households who undertook a self-guided search used the Internet. The majority of them (55 percent) found housing through "for rent" signs. Only 15 percent of black households who executed an independent search relied on the Internet. A third found housing through "for rent" signs and an additional third through the newspaper or other print media. Except for white renters, looking for rental housing was largely an un-digital affair.

Figure 7.1 indicates that the ways renters found housing might influence how they perceive their neighborhoods. The difference is especially acute when it comes to trusting one's neighbors. Roughly a third of renters who located housing independently reported high levels of neighborhood trust; the same was true for 29 percent of renters who located housing through social networks. However, only 9.5 percent of renters who found housing through an agency reported high levels of neighborhood trust, a statistically significant difference when compared to non-agency search methods (p = 0.04). Surprisingly, the reverse pattern was observed with respect to perceived suffering, with renters who found housing independently and through networks being roughly twice as likely to report suffering in their communities, compared to renters who relied on agencies to locate housing.

Regarding housing quality, 44 percent of Milwaukee renters reported experiencing at least one significant and lasting housing problem. Twenty-one percent of renters reported one problem; 16 percent reported two; and 7 percent reported three or more. Black and Hispanic renters were more likely to live in poor-quality housing, with 52 percent and 42 percent, respectively, experiencing any housing problem, compared to 37 percent of white renters. Housing problems affected renters across the city, particularly those in poor communities. Forty-two percent of renters in neighborhoods with poverty rates below 20 percent reported housing problems, compared to 58 percent of renters in all other neighborhoods.

While more than a third of renters who experienced no housing problems reported high levels of trust in their neighbors, the same was true for less than a quarter of those who experienced at least one housing problem, a statistically significant difference (p = 0.03). Likewise, while 18 percent of renters who lived in decent conditions perceived suffering in their community, 26 percent of those who reported at least one lasting housing problem did.

MULTIVARIATE MODELS

To further examine these patterns in a multivariate framework, I employed logistic and negative binomial regression analyses. Table 7.2 displays the results. Separate models were estimated for each of the three explanatory variables: eviction, housing search methods, and housing problems. Models 1 and 3 include the full suit of control variables; Models 2 and 4 also employ neighborhood fixed effects.

Table 7.2 shows that renters whose previous move was forced reported significantly higher levels of perceived neighborhood suffering, all else equal. A previous eviction is estimated to increase the likelihood that renters will perceive suffering in

TABLE 7.2: *Logistic and Negative Binomial Regression Models Estimating Neighborhood Perceptions*

	Neighborhood Trust		Perceived Suffering	
	(1)	(2)	(3)	(4)
Previous Move Was Forced	−0.360	−0.171	0.241*	0.192
	(0.234)	(0.259)	(0.106)	(0.123)
Found Housing through Agency	−1.406*	−1.236*	−0.245	−0.196
	(0.549)	(0.567)	(0.205)	(0.210)
Found Housing through Networks	−0.075	0.095	−0.043	−0.068
	(0.156)	(0.173)	(0.083)	(0.090)
Lasting Housing Problems	−0.250***	−0.271***	0.174***	0.185***
	(0.066)	(0.074)	(0.023)	(0.027)

Note: Milwaukee Area Renters Study, N = 1,086. Logistic regression models are used when estimating perceived trust; negative binomial regression models are used when estimating perceived suffering. Separate regressions were used to estimate the association between eviction, housing search methods, and housing problems on neighborhood perceptions. Models 2 and 4 include neighborhood fixed effects. All models control for months in neighborhood; miles from previous residence; the race, age, gender, and education of respondents; if respondents live with other adults or children; if respondents recently experienced job loss or relationship dissolution; how many of each respondent's strong ties live in the neighborhood; and the neighborhood (block group) poverty rate.
* p < 0.05; ** p < 0.01; *** p < 0.001 (two-tailed)

their neighborhood by 27 percent. However, the association between eviction and perceived suffering becomes insignificant when neighborhood fixed effects are introduced. No model documented a statistically significant relationship between eviction and neighborhood trust.

I did, however, document such a relationship when the explanatory variable was housing search strategies. Specifically, renters who located housing through agencies expressed lower levels of neighborhood trust. All else equal, finding housing through an agency is predicted to reduce renters' levels of neighborhood trust by 71 percent, a finding robust to neighborhood fixed effects. No relationship between housing search strategies and perceived neighborhood suffering was documented.

My findings also indicate that housing problems are associated with lower levels of perceived neighborhood trust and higher levels of perceived neighborhood suffering. After controlling for several relevant factors and including neighborhood fixed effects, each lasting housing problem a renter experiences is expected to decrease her or his odds of trusting neighbors by 24 percent and increase her or his level of perceived suffering by 20 percent. Renters who lived with more housing problems thought less of their neighborhoods.

All else equal, older renters and those with at least some college education reported higher levels of neighborhood trust, while Hispanic renters expressed lower levels of perceived suffering (results available upon request). Renters who had lived in the neighborhood longer and who counted more of their neighbors among their closest family members and friends reported higher levels of perceived suffering. This suggests that those who spend more time in a neighborhood and who are intimately connected with their neighbors may have a heightened sensibility of the adversity surrounding them. That housing dynamics remained a significant and substantially large predictor of more negative neighborhood perceptions after a number of relevant controls were introduced indicates that the circumstances that led families to select into a neighborhood, how they selected in, and the conditions of their home are critically important to understanding how they see their local community.

ROBUSTNESS CHECKS

Across models, the neighborhood poverty rate was negatively associated with perceived trust and positively associated with perceived suffering, indicating that renters living in more economically disadvantaged neighborhoods harbor dimmer views of their community. To test whether the results were robust to alternative ecological specifications, I replicated the fixed effects models displayed in Table 7.2, replacing block-group poverty rate with three alternative neighborhood-level measures. The first was *Observed Disorder*, a binary variable that takes the value of 1 if survey interviewers documented abandoned buildings and litter on a respondent's street. Renters' perception of their community might be dragged down if they lived on streets displaying visible signs of distress.

I also substituted neighborhood poverty with *Violent Crime* rates, the latter being among the most important indicators of neighborhood disadvantage (Sampson 2012; Wilson 1987) and may affect cognitive functioning (Margolin and Gordis 2000; Sharkey and Sampson 2015) Drawing on data supplied by the Milwaukee Police Department, I estimated each neighborhood's violent crime rate as the sum of all counts of homicide, kidnapping, assault, arson, robbery, and weapon-related incidents per 100 people in the year a renter was surveyed.

Last, I created the composite variable, *Neighborhood Disadvantage*, via factor analysis, loading seven block-group characteristics onto a single scale: median household income, violent crime rate, and the percentages of families below the poverty line, of the population under 18, of residents with less than a high school education, of residents receiving public assistance, and of vacant housing units. This measure provides a more comprehensive estimate of neighborhood quality.

Separate models were estimated for each neighborhood-level control. The results are displayed in Table 7.3. In addition to using neighborhood fixed effects, these

TABLE 7.3: *Fixed Effects Models with Alternative Neighborhood Controls*

	Observed Disorder	Violent Crime	Neighborhood Disadvantage
Neighborhood Trust			
Previous Move Was Forced	−0.177	−0.145	−0.126
	(0.267)	(0.260)	(0.260)
Found Housing through Agency	−1.104[+]	−1.251[*]	−1.252[*]
	(0.574)	(0.568)	(0.570)
Lasting Housing Problems	−0.251[**]	−0.270[***]	−0.270[***]
	(0.074)	(0.074)	(0.074)
Perceived Suffering			
Previous Move Was Forced	0.200	0.182	0.180
	(0.124)	(0.124)	(0.123)
Found Housing through Agency	−0.207	−0.201	−0.191
	(0.216)	(0.211)	(0.210)
Lasting Housing Problems	0.190[***]	0.182[***]	0.183[***]
	(0.027)	(0.027)	(0.027)

Note: Milwaukee Area Renters Study, N = 1,086. Logistic regression models are used when estimating perceived trust; negative binomial regression models are used when estimating perceived suffering. These models include all individual- and household-level control variables used in Table 7.2. *Observed Disorder* = 1 if survey interviewers noticed abandoned buildings and litter on a given block. *Violent Crime* is the sum of all counts of homicide, kidnapping, assault, arson, robbery, and weapon-related incidents (categories based on Incident-Based Reporting codes) per 100 people per year. *Neighborhood Disadvantage* is a composite variable created via factor analysis, with seven block-group characteristics loading onto a single scale: median household income, violent crime rate, and the percentages of families below the poverty line, of the population under 18, of residents with less than a high school education, of residents receiving public assistance, and of vacant housing units.
[+] $p < 0.1$; [*] $p < 0.05$; [**] $p < 0.01$; [***] $p < 0.001$ (two-tailed)

TABLE 7.4: *Propensity Score Matching Estimates, Average Treatment Effects*

	Neighborhood Trust	Perceived Suffering
Previous Move Was Forced	0.041	0.348*
	(0.061)	(0.173)
Found Housing through Agency	−0.224***	−0.277
	(0.036)	(0.198)
Lasting Housing Problems	−0.098**	0.619***
	(0.031)	(0.113)

Note: Milwaukee Area Renters Study, N = 1,086. Here, *Lasting Housing Problems* is a binary variable, with 1 indicating having experienced any problems.
* $p < 0.05$; ** $p < 0.01$; *** $p < 0.001$ (two-tailed)

models include all individual- and household-level control variables employed in Table 7.2. The results are robust to alternative neighborhood specifications. Across all models, renters who worked with an agency to find housing reported lower levels of neighborhood trust, and those living in substandard conditions expressed more negative views of their local community.

As a final robustness check, I employed propensity score matching to estimate differences in neighborhood trust and perceived suffering by eviction, agency-based housing searches, and experiencing at least one housing problem. The results are displayed in Table 7.4. The findings indicate that agency-based searches and housing problems are negatively related to neighborhood trust, while previous involuntary moves and housing problems are positively associated with perceived suffering.

DISCUSSION

Most of the chapters in this volume focus on housing markets and their regulation, with the primary actors being real estate investors, policy makers and enforcers, and homeowners. This study, by contrast, increased the magnification to focus on the relationship between housing and neighborhood dynamics in an American city, understood through the experiences of urban renters, many of whom live below the poverty line. An analysis of a unique dataset of Milwaukee renters found that those who had relocated to their neighborhood after an eviction or other kind of involuntary displacement, located their apartments through a government or nonprofit agency, or experienced multiple housing problems saw their neighborhood in a lesser light. With the exception of the finding pertaining to the estimated effect of eviction on neighborhood perceptions, the results of this study are robust to multiple measures of neighborhood quality as well as to neighborhood fixed effects.

What mechanisms help explain these patterns? Consider, first, the relationship between eviction and negative neighborhood perceptions. This study found some evidence that renters whose previous move was involuntary reported higher levels of perceived suffering, although this finding was not robust to neighborhood fixed effects specifications. Eviction can be a demoralizing process involving families being forced from a community in which they were invested to a neighborhood they consider undesirable (Desmond 2016a). If processed through the court system, an eviction comes with a record, which can result in families moving into worse neighborhoods and substandard housing (Desmond and Shollenberger 2015). Even if evicted families relocate to equivalent housing and similar neighborhoods, they may still *feel* that their surroundings are of lower quality because they were accepted under acute duress; after all, the effect of eviction on local trust remained after controlling for neighborhood poverty rate and housing quality. Alternatively, eviction can affect one's mental health, heightening depressive symptoms and stress levels (Desmond and Kimbro 2015), which could cast a pall over renters' outlooks in general, including their views on the local community.

A more puzzling finding, however, concerns the observation that renters who located their housing through a government or nonprofit agency had a dimmer view of their neighborhoods. These renters did live in more disadvantaged neighborhoods: the poverty rate for the average agency-assisted renter was 28 percent, compared to 11 percent for all other renters. However, the link between locating housing through a third party and lower levels of community trust remained after conditioning on several ecological characterizes and including neighborhood fixed effects. When attempting to understand this pattern, it is important to recognize, first, that the vast majority of these renters (91 percent) did not receive housing assistance. So this finding should not be interpreted as reflecting the perceptions of voucher holders. On the contrary, two-thirds of renters who located housing through a government or community organization relied on a nonprofit agency; and roughly 40 percent sought help from the Housing Authority. By and large, then, most renters who located housing through a government or nonprofit agency did not receive additional help, like rent assistance, and relied on nonprofit organizations.

To further investigate possible dynamics beneath this pattern, I examined the reasons these renters offered as to why they moved into their neighborhoods. Some renters who relied on agencies to find housing expressed a lack of options when it came to neighborhood choice. "This is what the Housing Authority had open," one renter said. "Couldn't find anywhere else to go," said another. As these comments attest, finding housing through an agency can be a stressful and rushed experience, owing to time limits affixed to assistance and limited staff capacity. This may influence how renters see the neighborhood into which they eventually select.

This finding suggests a pair of implications for policy makers. First, expanding a city's stock of temporary housing would allow housing organizations to operate with more slack. When the alternative is homelessness, an organization assisting a family in need is more likely to identify housing options quickly and to encourage clients to accept whatever is available. However, if that family were able to stay in temporary housing for some duration of time, organizations could provide families more housing options. This could boost low-income families' neighborhood quality and their level of community trust. Agencies assisting families in crisis operate under considerable pressure not only because those families have an acute need to be housed quickly, but also because many landlords turn away assisted renters. Landlords in most states are not obligated to accept families with housing vouchers, for example, and many make inferences about the quality of tenants based on their relationships with government or nonprofit agencies (DeLuca, Garboden, and Rosenblatt 2013). A second policy implication from this study, then, has to do with expanding and enforcing source-of-income discrimination laws, which would increase the housing and neighborhood options of low-income, assisted families.

Besides renters' motivations for moving and strategies for locating housing, the quality of their dwellings also appears to color their neighborhood perceptions. Renters who experienced more housing problems were far less likely to trust their neighbors and more likely to perceive suffering around them. As suggested earlier, a potential explanation for this finding pertains to neighborhood usage. Renters living in worse housing conditions might spend less time in their homes and more on the street than those in higher-quality housing. If this were the case, we might expect housing problems to be positively associated with indicators of neighborhood involvement or exposure. Following this line of thought, I replicated the fixed effects negative binomial regression model displayed in Table 7.2 on a new outcome: *Local Assistance*, a measure of how meaningfully engaged renters were with their neighbors. Respondents were asked: "While you have been living in this neighborhood, have you ever helped a neighbor (1) pay bills or buy groceries; (2) get a job; (3) fix their house or their car; (4) by supporting them emotionally, as they went through a hard time; or (5) by watching their kids?" Answers were summed to create a measure of local assistance (min = 0, max = 5). The models found that renters who experienced more housing problems reported higher levels of local assistance (b = 0.086; p < 0.001). This finding is robust to the three alternative measures of neighborhood quality discussed earlier.

Material hardship could be the underlying cause of both heightened exposure to housing problems and neighborhood engagement, relied on to make ends meet. All else equal, renters who live in disadvantaged neighborhoods report higher levels of local assistance (Desmond and An 2015). However, I observed a significant association between housing problems and neighborhood engagement *net of* indicators of material hardship, such as having experienced a recent job loss or breakup, as well as controls for the length of time and the number of strong ties in a community and neighborhood fixed effects. Renters who have experienced more housing problems report higher levels of neighborhood involvement, compared to similar renters in similar neighborhoods. This suggests that housing problems spur community exposure, as renters leave their homes to escape degrading conditions or to address such conditions by seeking help from neighbors.

This study's identification strategy pertains to similar renters in similar neighborhoods having different housing-related experiences that influence how they perceive their local community. Those perceptions are steered not only by objective neighborhood disadvantage, like crime, but also by multiple housing dynamics: *why* city dwellers moved, *how* they found subsequent housing, and the *conditions* of their dwelling. A neighborhood's outlook, whether it will improve or decline, depends in significant part on how its residents see it. If people see their community as a special, cherished thing, they will work to protect and improve it (Fischel, Chapter 1, this volume). However, if they fear their neighborhood or become ashamed of it, they will look for ways to leave or burrow behind locked doors, ignoring the streets around them (Rosenblatt and DeLuca 2012). When neighbors work together, they can improve their community and drive down crime by establishing effective local practices or lobbying elected representatives. "Our failures with city neighborhoods are, ultimately, failures in localized self-government," wrote Jane Jacobs. "And our successes are successes at localized self-government" (1961, 114).

A prerequisite for successful self-management is the cultivation of a palpable optimism about the capacity of the local community (McAdam 1982; Piven and Cloward 1977), a belief in and familiarity with one's neighbors. But negative neighborhood perceptions can compromise a community's civic efficacy and thwart community-based organizing (Desmond and Travis 2016; Sampson 2012), directly contributing to neighborhood decline through depopulation (when families move out) and disinvestment (when families withdraw from their own community). It follows, then, that those hoping to identify ways to cultivate collective efficacy and raise people's expectations of their community should strive to apprehend why people see their neighborhood in this or that light.

The findings of this study indicate that if we wish to understand neighborhood perceptions, we have to pay attention to housing dynamics. A long-standing interest in housing discrimination and gentrification notwithstanding (Massey and Denton 1993; South and Crowder 1997), research on neighborhood effects largely overlooks housing dynamics. Because city dwellers' immediate environment – the house – is fundamentally linked to their broader ecological surroundings, future investigations into the role housing markets play in shaping neighborhood perceptions and local dynamics could advance urban studies in significant ways. This chapter has contributed to uniting the sociology of housing and of neighborhoods, but much work remains undone. Indeed, many chapters in this volume reflect the tendency of research on housing markets to ignore neighborhood characteristics, which in turn are critical to understanding market dynamics. For example, despite the fact that racial residential segregation directly contributed to the foreclosure crisis (Rugh and Massey 2010), scholarship on the crisis trains most of its attention on regulatory failures and financial instruments.

If housing and neighborhood dynamics are bound together in a tight knot, then policy interventions focused on one will likely have an effect on the other. The findings of this chapter indicate that initiatives designed to prevent eviction, for example, not only could promote family stability and well-being, but may also promote community investment since renters that select into neighborhoods under more voluntary circumstances see their communities in a more positive light. Similarly, if housing problems color renters' perceptions of their neighborhoods, then initiatives designed to improve housing quality could benefit not just individuals but communities as well.

Negative neighborhood perceptions can thwart community cohesion, impede the formation of social capital, spur residential turnover, and invite social problems. Addressing these issues by confronting such perceptions requires understanding the factors that deeply influence how we see our communities. When it comes to promoting neighborhood trust and pride, a good place to start is the home.

AUTHOR'S NOTE

I thank Kathleen Cagney, Lee Anne Fennell, Benjamin Keys, and participants at the Kreisman Initiative on Housing Law and Policy, University of Chicago Law School, for critical feedback on earlier drafts. This research was supported by the John D. and Catherine T. MacArthur Foundation, through its "How Housing Matters" initiative.

REFERENCES

Allison, Paul. 2009. *Fixed Effects Regression Models*. New York: Sage Publications. 2002. *Missing Data*. New York: Sage Publications.
Beckett, Megan, Julie DaVanzo, Narayan Sastry, Constantijn Panis, and Christine Peterson. 2001. "The Quality of Retrospective Data: An Examination of Long-Term Recall in a Developing Country." *Journal of Human Resources* 36: 593–625.
Coulton, Claudia, M. Zane Jennings, and Tsui Chan. 2013. "How Big Is My Neighborhood? Individual and Contextual Effects on Perceptions of Neighborhood Scale." *American Journal of Community Psychology* 51: 140–50.
Curl, Angela, Ade Kearns, Phil Mason, Matthew Egan, Carol Tannahill, and Anne Ellaway, 2015. "Physical and Mental Health Outcomes Following Housing Improvements: Evidence from the GoWell Study." *Journal of Epidemiology and Community Health* 69: 12–19.
DeLuca, Stefanie, Philip Garboden, and Peter Rosenblatt. 2013. "Segregating Shelter: How Housing Policies Shape the Residential Locations of Low-Income Minority Families." *The Annals of the American Academy of Political and Social Science* 647: 268–99.

Desmond, Matthew. 2016a. *Evicted: Poverty and Profit in the American City.* New York: Crown.

———. 2016b. *Milwaukee Area Renters Study.* Cambridge, MA: Harvard University Dataverse.

———. 2015. "Unaffordable America: Poverty, Housing, and Eviction." *Fast Focus: Institute for Research on Poverty* 22: 1–6.

Desmond, Matthew and Weihua An. 2015. "Neighborhood and Network Disadvantage among City Dwellers." *Sociological Science* 2: 329–50.

Desmond, Matthew, Carl Gershenson, and Barbara Kiviat. 2015. "Forced Relocation and Residential Instability among Urban Renters." *Social Service Review* 89: 227–62.

Desmond, Matthew and Rachel Tolbert Kimbro. 2015. "Eviction's Fallout: Housing, Hardship, and Health." *Social Forces* 94: 295–324.

Desmond, Matthew and Tracey Shollenberger. 2015. "Forced Displacement from Rental Housing: Prevalence and Neighborhood Consequences." *Demography* 52: 1751–72.

Desmond, Matthew and Adam Travis. 2016. "Political Consequences of Survival Strategies among the Urban Poor." Harvard University: Working Paper.

Du Bois, W. E. B. (1899) 1996. *The Philadelphia Negro: A Social Study.* Philadelphia: University of Pennsylvania Press.

Eggers, Frederick and Fouad Moumen. 2010. *Investigating Very High Rent Burdens among Renters in the American Housing Survey.* Washington, DC: U.S. Department of Housing and Urban Development.

Evans, Gary, Nancy Wells, and Annie Moch. 2003. "Housing and Mental Health: A Review of the Evidence and a Methodological and Conceptual Critique." *Journal of Social Issues* 59: 475–500.

Farley, Reynolds. 1996. "Racial Differences in the Search for Housing: Do Whites and Blacks Use the Same Techniques to Find Housing?" *Housing Policy Debate* 7: 367–86.

Glynn, Thomas. 1986. "Neighborhood and Sense of Community." *Journal of Community Psychology* 14: 341–52.

Hartnagel, Timothy. 1979. "The Perception and Fear of Crime: Implications for Neighborhood Cohesion, Social Activity, and Community Affect." *Social Forces* 58: 176–93.

Highton, Benjamin. 2000. "Residential Mobility, Community Mobility, and Electoral Participation." *Political Behavior* 22: 109–20.

Hill, Terrence and Ronald Angel. 2005. "Neighborhood Disorder, Psychological Distress, and Heavy Drinking." *Social Science and Medicine* 61: 965–75.

Hirano, Keisuke and Guido Imbens. 2001. "Estimation of Causal Effects Using Propensity Score Weighting: An Application to Data on Right Heart Catheterization." *Health Services and Outcomes Research Methodology* 2: 259–78.

Jacobs, Jane. 1961. *The Death and Life of Great American Cities.* New York: Random House.

Kawachi, I., B. Kennedy, K. Lochner, and D. Prothrow-Stith. 1997. "Social Capital, Income Inequality, and Mortality." *American Journal of Public Health* 87: 1491–98.

Kimbro, Rachel Tolbert and Ariela Schachter. 2011. "Neighborhood Poverty and Maternal Fears of Children's Outdoor Play." *Family Relations* 60: 461–75.

Klinenberg, Eric. 2012. *Going Solo: The Extraordinary Rise and Surprising Appeal of Living Alone.* New York: Penguin.

Krysan, Maria. 2008. "Does Race Matter in the Search for Housing? An Exploratory Study of Search Strategies, Experiences, and Locations." *Social Science Research* 37: 581–603.

Lahiri, D. B. 1951. "A Method of Sample Selection Providing Unbiased Ratio Estimates." *Bulletin of the International Statistical Institute* 33: 133–40.

Ludwig, Jens, Jeffrey Liebman, Jeffrey Kling, Greg J. Duncan, Lawrence F. Katz, Ronald C. Kessler, and Lisa Sanbonmatsu. 2008. "What Can We Learn about Neighborhood Effects from the Moving to Opportunity Experiment?" *American Journal of Sociology* 114: 144–88.

Margolin, Gayla and Elana Gordis. 2000. "The Effects of Family and Community Violence on Children." *Annual Review of Psychology* 51: 445–79.

Massey, Douglas and Nancy Denton. 1993. *American Apartheid: Segregation and the Making of the Underclass.* Cambridge, MA: Harvard University Press.

McAdam, Doug. 1982. *Political Process and the Development of Black Insurgency, 1930–1970.* Chicago: University of Chicago Press.

Pager, Devah. 2007. *Marked: Race, Crime, and Finding Work in an Era of Mass Incarceration.* Chicago: University of Chicago Press.

Park, Robert. 1925. "The City: Suggestions for the Investigation of Human Behavior in the Urban Environment." In *The City,* Robert Park, Ernest Burgess, and Roderick McKenzie, eds., 1–46. Chicago: University of Chicago Press.

Piven, Frances Fox and Richard Cloward. 1977. *Poor People's Movements: Why They Succeed, How They Fail.* New York: Pantheon Books.

Putnam, Robert. 2001. *Bowling Alone: The Collapse and Revival of American Community.* New York: Simon and Schuster.

Quillian, Lincoln and Devah Pager. 2001. "Black Neighbors, Higher Crime? The Role of Racial Stereotypes in Evaluations of Neighborhood Crime." *American Journal of Sociology* 107: 717–67.

Rosenbaum, Paul and Donald Rubin. 1983. "The Central Role of the Propensity Score in Observational Studies for Causal Effects." *Biometrika* 70: 41–55.

Rosenblatt, Peter and Stefanie DeLuca. 2012. "'We Don't Live Outside, We Live in Here': Neighborhood and Residential Mobility Decisions among Low-Income Families." *City and Community* 11: 254–84.

Ross, Catherine and John Mirowsky. 2009. "Neighborhood Disorder, Subjective Alienation, and Distress." *Journal of Health and Social Behavior* 50: 49–64.

Rossi, Peter. (1955) 1980. *Why Families Move.* 2nd Edition. Beverly Hills: Sage Publications.

Rugh, Jacob and Douglas Massey. 2010. "Racial Segregation and the American Foreclosure Crisis." *American Sociological Review* 75: 629–51.

Sampson, Robert. 2012. *Great American City: Chicago and the Enduring Neighborhood Effect*. Chicago: University of Chicago Press.

2008. "Moving to Inequality: Neighborhood Effects and Experiments Meet Social Structure." *American Journal of Sociology* 114: 189–231.

Sampson, Robert, Jeffrey Morenoff, and Thomas Gannon-Rowley. 2002. "Assessing 'Neighborhood Effects': Social Processes and New Directions in Research." *Annual Review of Sociology* 28: 443–78.

Schwartz, Alex. 2010. *Housing Policy in the United States*, 2nd Edition. New York: Routledge.

Sharkey, Patrick. 2013. *Stuck in Place: Urban Neighborhoods and the End of Progress toward Racial Equality*. Chicago: University of Chicago Press.

Sharkey, Patrick and Jacob Faber. 2014. "Where, When, Why, and for Whom Do Residential Contexts Matter? Moving Away from the Dichotomous Understanding of Neighborhood Effects." *Annual Review of Sociology* 40: 559–79.

Sharkey, Patrick and Robert Sampson. 2015 "Violence, Cognition, and Neighborhood Inequality in America." In *Social Neuroscience: Brain, Mind, and Society*, Russell Schutt, Matcheri Keshavan, and Larry Seidman, eds. Cambridge, MA: Harvard University Press.

Shaw, Mary. 2004. "Housing and Public Health." *Annual Review of Public Health* 25: 397–418.

Smith, Sandra. 2007. *Lone Pursuit: Distrust and Defensive Individualism among the Black Poor*. New York City: Russell Sage Foundation.

Soss, Joe and Lawrence Jacobs. 2009. "The Place of Inequality: Non-participation in the American Polity." *Political Science Quarterly* 124: 95–125.

South, Scott and Kyle Crowder. 1997. "Escaping Distressed Neighborhoods: Individual, Community, and Metropolitan Influences." *American Journal of Sociology* 102: 1040–84.

Stack, Carol. 1974. *All Our Kin: Strategies for Survival in a Black Community*. New York: Basic Books.

U.S. Department of Housing and Urban Development. 2009. *50th Percentile Rent Estimates for 2010*. Washington, DC: U.S. Department of Housing and Urban Development.

Wilson, William Julius. 1987. *The Truly Disadvantaged: The Inner City, the Underclass, and Public Policy*. Chicago: University of Chicago Press.

Zorbaugh, Harvey. 1926. "The Natural Areas of the City." In *The Urban Community*, Ernest Burgess, ed., 217–29. Chicago: University of Chicago Press.

Notes

1. Until recently, national data collection efforts have placed heavy emphasis on volitional moves, overlooking involuntary displacements. The American Housing Survey only began asking respondents if they have moved because of an eviction in 2005. Before that, the only types of forced moves the survey

recorded were those attributed to disaster (fire), government order (eminent domain), changes or repairs to the unit, or the owner moving into the unit.

2. The MARS dataset, instrument, and documentation are available at the Harvard Dataverse (dataverse.harvard.edu).

3. The MARS sample excluded renters living in public housing but not those in the private market in possession of a housing voucher.

4. "Redbooks" and "Bluebooks" were free glossy advertisements distributed in inner-city bodegas.

5. For ease of interpretation, I recoded the housing search strategies of the small number of renters who relied on multiple methods, making them exclusive. If renters looked for housing by relying on network ties and other means, I counted them among those who conducted a network-based search. And if renters looked for housing themselves and by soliciting help from an agency, I counted them among those who conducted agency-based searches.

PART III

Housing as Wealth Building: Consumers and Housing Finance

8

Behavioral Leasing: Renter Equity as an Intermediate Housing Form

Stephanie M. Stern

We are accustomed to thinking of residential property as an asset or an arrangement of legal rights. Yet, property forms are also behavioral, with the property interests and incentives of housing forms enabling or supporting behaviors and commitments. By choosing a residential property form, such as owning or renting, we commit ourselves to a range of opportunities, behaviors, and built-in, ongoing incentives for those behaviors. Homeownership is attractive in significant part for its behavioral and consumption benefits – contrary to the expectations of most homeowners, inflation-adjusted asset appreciation is startlingly modest (Shiller 2015, 27–30). The benefits of homeownership include greater control and governance rights, opportunities for "forced" or automatic savings through mortgages, incentives to maintain and improve property, and stronger rights to stay put.

Viewing property as behavioral, while overbroad, suggests a different starting place for understanding and innovating property forms: focusing on the behaviors we wish to enable and how to produce them. One application is to the rather cramped residential leasehold form, with its shallow possessory rights, weak incentives for property improvement, and limited opportunities for asset building. Can we provide an interested subset of renters a measure of the rights, behaviors, or benefits of homeownership? One way to accomplish this, albeit sometimes coarsely, is to adjust homeownership. A number of proposals in the scholarly literature have sought to create variants of the homeownership form, with the intent of producing some of the behaviors and benefits of homeownership while increasing affordability or adjusting risk (Fennell 2008, 1070–77; Arruñada and Lehavi 2011, 26–33). There has been less progress in creating alternative housing forms that don't require equity investment, putting them in reach of lower-income renters.

A behavioral perspective suggests one possibility for innovating rental: the use of incentives and commitment strategies to support alternative property forms and certain ownership-like behaviors and effects. Yet, applying these psychological tools to rental seems an uneasy fit with residential property law, which has tended to rely on equity interests and legal rules to produce ownership effects (e.g., Fischel 2001). Is incentivizing such behaviors inevitably too costly, complex, and vulnerable to unintended motivational effects to be successful?

This chapter examines renter equity, an emerging and understudied intermediate form of housing between homeownership and traditional rental (Cornerstone Renter Equity 2016; Renting Partnerships 2016). This fledging property form, in operation at four affordable housing sites in Cincinnati, Ohio, puts into practice the kind of psychology-informed policy design and finer-grained division of property rights that have been of so much recent theoretical interest (e.g., Fennell 2008, 179–85; Thaler and Sunstein 2008, 3–44). The renter equity form monetizes and allocates to tenants a share of the financial value created by their upkeep and participation in the property – and frames that allocation as an incentive in order to support a range of homeownership-like behaviors and benefits. Specifically, the lease provides renters the right to earn savings credits for a constellation of property-enhancing behaviors (Drever et al. 2013, 16–20; Renting Partnerships 2016). In turn, the reduced property management and vacancy costs fund the renter savings accounts.

Renter equity has sparked increasing interest and attention from investors, think tanks, and government (HUD 2011; Williams 2012, 1–2). Andrea Levere, president of the Corporation for Economic Enterprise, has proposed using HUD funding, including Sustainable Communities Initiative funding, the Community Development Block Grant, and HOME investment partnership funds, to expand the renter equity model on a national scale (Williams 2012, 2). The Cornerstone Corporation, which manages three renter equity sites, recently trademarked the name "renter equity," presumably with an eye toward licensing or franchising it to other providers of low-income affordable housing services. Renting Partnerships, a newer and similar housing form, envisions expanding to a network of affiliates (Margery Spinney, pers. comm.).

In academic circles, renter equity has been a much quieter innovation, with no scholarship to my knowledge addressing this housing form. In this chapter, I examine renter equity as an emerging innovation and a model of the potential, and the pitfalls, of leveraging incentives and commitments to support alternative housing forms. The chapter proceeds in five parts. Part 1 highlights some of the key behavioral options and benefits that renters lack and suggests that one consequence of landlord-tenant reform has been to reduce the incentives and commitment strategies available to tenants. Part 2 describes renter equity and a newer, similar form called *renting partnerships*. I use the term *renter equity* throughout this chapter to refer to the core property configuration shared by both renter equity and renting partnerships. Part 3 identifies the conceptual underpinnings of renter equity as well as legal and policy gaps in its implementation. In Part 4, I address behavioral and social concerns about renter equity incentives. Part 5 concludes by briefly discussing renter equity's potential as an alternative property form and the lessons of renter equity for incentive-based "behavioral leasing."

8.1 CONFINES OF THE RENTAL FORM

Splitting possession from residual ownership (i.e., renting) confers a number of valuable benefits on renters, including greater residential mobility, allocating property management and repair obligations to landlords, and avoiding the financial risks of equity ownership. In other ways, however, this division is binary and often crude from the standpoints of tenant preferences, landlords' interests, and social and community needs (Fennell 2008, 188–90). Renters, particularly long-term renters, miss out on a number of behavioral options and corresponding benefits allocated to their homeowning counterparts. This section highlights some of the behavioral confines of the rental form.

First, the division of property rights in rental reduces incentives for tenants to maintain and improve the rental property and local neighborhood. Beyond the benefits to consumption, the rental form does not monetize or compensate tenants for their investments in upkeep, safety, or improvements that increase residential value or enhance their local communities (cf. Lerman and McKernan 2007, 1–2). Indeed, there are explicit disincentives for such tenant efforts: the risk of increased rent and gentrification (2). In some cases, landlords may compensate tenants implicitly for upkeep and improvements through lower rent. However, the standard lease offers no formal mechanism of compensation on which renters can rely. Concededly, renters have lower consumption motivations for such behaviors because they can exit more cheaply to satisfy consumption elsewhere and have limited control over rental duration (Rohe and Stewart 1996, 45). However, renters still engage in some property-benefiting behaviors and presumably would engage in more if they could capture the value of their actions.

Not only do renters lack incentives to invest in property, they typically lack legal rights to do so. Standard residential leases make tenants liable for damages and subject to eviction for altering their units (e.g., appliances, flooring, even wall color) or making repairs without landlord consent. Renters also lack rights to participate in governance and decision making affecting common areas and residential management (cf. Davis 2009, 29–31). For some, offloading upkeep and improvement to landlords is an attraction of renting (Freddie Mac 2016, 6, 16). Others, however, desire more intensive participation – perhaps particularly renters who anticipate less attentive landlords or who lack future prospects for ownership. Paucity of control can frustrate tenant preferences, and, some research suggests, produce negative psychological states (Manturuk 2012, 409–22) and impair control over "image presentation" (Downs 1981, 466). It is not surprising, or objectionable, that landlords have strong interests in protecting their property from value dissipation. Yet, some reallocations of consumption-oriented rights to tenants may be possible (e.g., limited tenant decision making subject to standards and a budget or tenant voting within owner-approved choice sets).

Landlord tenant reforms, while salutary in some regards, have narrowed opportunities for tenants to invest and participate in property by creating a harder-edged boundary between possessory rights in rental and ownership interests. In the 1970s, post-industrialization changes in housing needs and failures of rental market competition prompted the "reform era" of landlord-tenant law (Kelley 1995, 1563–74). These reforms shifted the treatment of leaseholds from a conveyance of property to a hybrid of contract and property (Glendon 1982, 503–05; Merrill and Smith 2001, 820–31). The shift toward contract law enabled courts to impose common law contract doctrines such as unconscionability and the implied warranty of habitability (obligation of the landlord to ensure fit and habitable rental premises), with some of these protections later codified (Korngold 1998, 707–07; cf. Super 2011, 389–400). These reforms also made many tenant protections non-waivable (Geurts 2004, 356–60).

One consequence of landlord-tenant reform has been to limit tenants' ability to rent premises more cheaply, improve or maintain them, and realize the value of below-market rent for their lease term. Landlord-tenant laws regulating and limiting escrows (e.g., security deposits) also constrain the ability of tenants to contract with landlords for tenant alterations by escrowing additional money as security against damage. In the face of a complex framework of tenant protections, landlords are leery of contracting for tenants to provide maintenance or repair, make alterations, or assume greater governance or management roles. Even if landlords are willing to engage in such contracting, certain protections, such as the landlord warranty of habitability, cannot be waived in many states (Rabin 2011, 80). In some cases, tenant "sweat equity" arrangements may occur informally. For example, sociologist Matthew Desmond's ethnography of urban renters describes instances where landlords allowed tenants to make up back rent and avoid eviction by working on the property (Desmond 2016, 129). Landlords who countenance such arrangements risk running afoul of landlord-tenant and labor laws.

A second constraint of the rental form is that renters lack ongoing, long-term rights to stay put. The legal duration of a typical residential lease is one year or month-to-month; after the lease term expires, the landlord can opt not to renew or to increase rent. Unlike homeowners who lock in ongoing possessory rights and a purchase price (and often a mortgage interest rate), tenants face rent increases and the accompanying risk of dislocation (Sinai and Souleles 2005, 785–86). The lack of control over housing costs and mobility is a significant drawback to renting that can frustrate tenant preferences, increase psychological stress, and undermine financial security (Desmond 2016). Limited control over residential duration also weakens incentives for tenants to invest in local communities.

Third, tenants have less ability than homeowners to use housing as a commitment device to bind their future selves to certain actions or decisions. Commitment strategies address bounds on willpower and self-control by removing a future temptation or option entirely or raising the costs of exercising that option. The illiquidity of the owned home (i.e., the expense and difficulty of asset transfer) acts as a commitment strategy for longer residential duration and the social, personal, and financial effects that entails. Homeownership also enables buyers to commit at the time of purchase to a hedging strategy against housing cost inflation. Compared to renters, owners pay higher upfront costs to purchase, but face lower risk of housing cost escalation over time (Sinai and Souleles 2005, 785–86).

One of the most important "commitment benefits" of homeownership is lodged not in the property form, but in its financing: forced saving. Much of the financial value of homeownership derives not from appreciation, but from long-term home-owners who pay down the principal each month on traditional, self-amortizing mortgages (the most common mortgage choice) (Shiller 2015, 27-30; U.S. Census Bureau 2013, table 1016). The mortgage is a powerful commitment device that makes the consequences of not paying one's mortgage costly, disruptive, and humiliating. Homeowners accumulate far greater lifetime savings than similarly-situated renters, as a result of the forced saving component of traditional mortgages, homeowner-ship's relative illiquidity, and its tax subsidy.

Self-amortizing mortgages, which fuse the monthly principal and interest payment into one amount due, create automatic asset-building – an important point in light of the behavioral law and economics research showing marked improvements in saving when contributions are made automatic and set as the default (Benartzi and Thaler 2004, S166-85; Thaler and Sunstein 2008 103–17; cf. Moulton et al. 2015, 55–74). Of course, lenders can deter or unravel home-based savings with products such as interest-only and negatively amortizing loans, cash-out refinancing, and home equity lines of credit. Saving through home-ownership is suboptimal due to these escape hatches and the undiversified nature of the home investment. However, this form of savings has nonetheless proven financially meaningful, as well as culturally resonant and highly attrac-tive to Americans – in large part due to its advantages as a psychological commitment strategy. The dearth of comparable supports for renter asset-build-ing recently prompted Josh Barros to propose that renters self-fund a savings portion, automatically paid on top of their rent, which would be directed monthly to federal MyRA accounts (Barro 2014).[1]

For their part, landlords contend with renters who are, as Julie Roin and Lee Fennell term it, "understaked" to their residential property and the community (Fennell and Roin 2010, 16–18). The lack of an equity interest and, in some cases, a strong social stake increases delinquent rent, property damage, and turnover. To date, many of the legal tools available to landlords to address these harms are unpopular with tenants (e.g., fees for late rent), expensive and adversarial (e.g., legal process for eviction), or limited to ex-post compensation rather than prevention (e.g., deducting repair costs from the security deposit). In addition, some state statutes limit the penalties that landlords can impose for delinquent rent and other violations (e.g., Cal. Civ. Code § 1671 (d)).

The shortcomings of the rental form have not only frustrated the preferences of a large subset of renters, but have motivated premature and unstable moves to home-ownership (Reid 2013, 152–54). Some tenants prefer to rent, particularly at earlier and later life stages; however, most report a preference to own (MacArthur Foundation 2014; Pew Research Center 2011). While abundant survey research establishes the strong inclination toward ownership (MacArthur Foundation 2014, 30; Pew Research Center 2011), it is harder to tease from this data relative preferences for different aspects of homeownership.[2] The preference to own is likely due in part to government subsidy of ownership, a benefit I do not focus on in this chapter (e.g., Poterba and Sinai 2008, 84–89). The desire to stay in place for a longer period of time appears to be an important trigger for homebuying (Sinai and Souleles 2005, 785). There is also evidence that renters' thin control over rental property and inability to build assets through housing drive preferences for homeownership (Rohe and Lindblad 2013, 7–18).

8.2 PRODUCING OWNERSHIP EFFECTS THROUGH INCENTIVE-BASED LEASES

Can any of the benefits and behaviors of homeownership be produced for renters, particularly low-income renters without prospects for ownership? A variety of pro-posals have sought to create more particularized divisions of residential property rights that redistribute the archetypic benefits of renting and homeowning. Lee Anne Fennell has conceptualized this process as "unbundling" property forms to enable valuable divisions of risk and consumption values and proposed a "home-ownership 2.0" form to accomplish this (Fennell 2008, 1070–77). Other approaches, such as limited equity cooperatives, focus on increasing homeownership affordabil-ity by limiting equity stake to small shares and restricting rights to appreciation on resale (Davis 2009, 29–30; Diamond 2009, 88–109). There have also been a number of proposals to redistribute property risks through alternative financing of home-ownership. Most prominently, Andrew Caplin has proposed a residential shared appreciation mortgage where a lender contributes a percentage of the total equity needed by the homebuyer in exchange for rights to a percentage of appreciation upon resale (Caplin et al. 2008, 5–11; see also Arruñada and Lehavi 2011, 26–33).

There has been decidedly less excitement about alternative property forms based in rental. Municipal rent control has collapsed in discredit, with economic evidence of its ultimate harm to tenants (Green and Malpezzi 2003, 126). Subsidized housing alternatives such as rental mutual housing, which gives tenants permanent lease rights at subsidized rates, have mixed records (Krinsky and Hovde 1996, 148–49). Lease-purchase contracts (rent-to-own) show some promise, but have suffered from predatory practices. These contracts often target renters with poor credit, particularly African Americans, who purchase expensive, nonrefundable options only to find later that they cannot qualify for mortgage financing (Way 2009, 132, 147).

In this chapter, I explore renter equity, an emerging housing paradigm that uses lease-based incentives and commitments to support an alternative rental form.

8.2.A *Renter Equity*

Renter equity began with the vision of creating an intermediate property form for low-income renters interested in greater commitment, participation, and opportunities for life improvement through housing. In 2000, the nonprofit Cornerstone corporation opened the first of three renter equity apartment complexes in the Over-the-Rhine neighborhood of Cincinnati. Cornerstone's mission is to "help residents of affordable housing reap the potential financial and social rewards of homeownership" (Drever et al. 2013, 9). Renter equity allows renters to earn monthly renter equity credits (i.e., savings credits) in exchange for three behaviors: paying their rent on time, participating in a resident community association and attending its monthly meetings, and completing their assigned property upkeep task in common areas (for ease of monitoring, the typical work assignments require tenants to maintain specified physical spaces in the building or its grounds). The upkeep task takes each tenant approximately one to two hours per week.

The Renter Equity Agreement, which is part of the lease, gives renters rights to earn up to $10,000 in savings credits over 10 years. The monthly savings credit amount increases over time (reminiscent of the principal in a self-amortizing mortgage) (19). Once the resident earns the credit, it automatically deposits into a savings account (Cornerstone Renter Equity 2016). Tenants do not have the ability to access the savings for five years. This provides a measure of homeownership's behavioral benefits of "forced savings" since the credits must accumulate untouched for at least five years and up to 10 years. If tenants depart prior to the saving credits vesting in year five, they lose their savings credits. Renter equity leases do not specify what happens to the savings credits in the event a tenant is evicted before vesting. It seems the evicted tenant would lose his or her savings credits – a rule that creates incentives for strategic landlord behavior.

High occupancy, reduced turnover, and lower maintenance costs fund the renter credits (i.e., no additional subsidy is required for asset building). Management costs range from 4–12 percent according to industry reports (Muela 2017). Estimates peg the cost of apartment turnover at a minimum of $1,000 per unit, with turnover rates of more than 25 percent for subsidized tenants (Barker 2003, 3; Lee 2013, 67). A recent evaluation of Cornerstone reported a 95 percent occupancy rate (Drever et al. 2013, 38). A comparison of one Cornerstone site (St. Anthony's) with three comparable federally subsidized low-income housing properties in the same neighborhood found that Cornerstone had similar operating expenses even after funding the savings credits and at least 75 percent less "bad debt" from delinquent rent payment (43).

Another key element of renter equity is the Resident Association Agreement, which establishes the resident association and describes tenants' obligations and rights of shared governance. The resident association is reminiscent of the legal cooperative or "co-op" form of common interest ownership. In renter equity housing, the resident association works in concert with management and the board to manage certain aspects of the property. The association's duties include reporting maintenance issues, recommending improvements, coordinating measures to increase safety, and conflict resolution (Drever et al. 2013, 17–18). Resident participation and limited self-governance mark renter equity as a property form rather than an incentive contract. However, this balance between property and contract may be shifting with Cornerstone's recent changes to management and trademarking of renter equity as an operations model.

Compared to homeownership and traditional renting, renter equity offers a middle ground for residential stability. The renter equity form supports and incentivizes medium-term residential stability through a five-year vesting rule and a 10-year maximum schedule for earning (increasingly larger) savings credits. Renter equity leases do not require tenants to move at the 10-year mark. However, they cannot earn further credits and are unlikely to continue property upkeep and participation – a problematic situation. Unlike homeownership, renter equity does not provide tenants with legal rights to stay put or lock in housing costs long-term. In practice, affordable housing protections and nonprofit involvement provide renter equity tenants greater de facto control over exit and rent costs than traditional renters, but still less than owners. A form similar to renter equity, renting partnerships, has proposed restructuring within land trusts to offer tenants full stability of tenure (Spinney, pers. comm.).

By design, enter equity grafts onto small to mid-size Low-Income Housing Tax Credit (LIHTC) housing and nonprofit affordable housing developments. More than 2 million housing units have been created by the Low-Income Housing Tax Credit Program since 1995, most of which have remained low-income housing past the required 15-year time span (HUD 2012, 49). Government subsidies tend to reward bricks-and-mortar units constructed, as opposed to housing innovation or services. For this reason, private developers of affordable housing have limited incentives to adopt innovations like renter equity; they make sufficient profits without it. This may be beginning to change. Some states now set aside percentages of their LIHTC funds for "innovation rounds" to consider development projects with innovative features (Kimura 2014).

The empirical evidence supporting renter equity is limited, with only one study to date. In 2013, the Ohio Housing Finance Agency and the Corporation for Enterprise Development completed an evaluation of Cornerstone based on surveys and interviews of residents and a review of the renter equity records. The study found that of residents who stayed more than five years, approximately two-thirds earned a median equity amount of $2,600 (26). More than 50 percent of tenants earn credits each month. Most residents used their savings to pay debts or medical expenses. Notably, renter equity has produced median savings comparable to state Individual Development Accounts that provide matched savings to low-income Americans (Miller 2007, 26). On measures of housing satisfaction, a high majority of renter equity residents (85–95 percent depending on the specific measure) reported they were satisfied with the unit, the building, and the management (Drever et al. 2013, 93–98).

These findings, while promising, should be interpreted conservatively. This was a single study, sought by Cornerstone. The study design does not rule out selection effects (i.e., the characteristics of tenants attracted to renter equity and able to complete its rigorous application process may have produced these outcomes). In future research, it would be interesting to explore how different aspects of tenant self-selection drive outcomes. For example, would renters who opt for renter equity's locked-up savings credit have different outcomes than a group that selected a version of renter equity with cash rebates or unrestricted savings? What if tenants were randomized?

Beyond outcomes for renter equity tenants, important and unanswered questions remain about the displacement effects of renter equity on other forms of housing. If renter equity proves successful at providing a share of the benefits of homeownership, might the form attract would-be homebuyers? Renter equity may appeal to scrappy and debt-burdened millennials or working-class retirees who might otherwise purchase homes. It is possible that renter equity could reduce unstable or unsustainable home purchase and help renters to save for down payments. At the same time, renter equity produces less wealth accumulation than homeownership, does not convey the same level of tax benefits, and provides limited liquidity (renter equity tenants have access to a small emergency loan fund). On balance, the magnitude of these displacement effects is likely small. Renter equity's displacement of homeownership should be modest or minimal under renter equity's current structure. On the demand side, the upkeep tasks in renter equity are unattractive to many middle- and upper-income individuals, as are the lack of tax benefits and stay-put rights. Supply-side, renter equity would not interest private landlords who have low turnover costs and can exploit opportunities for increasing rent with new tenants (Barker 2003, 10).

Renter equity also raises issues of tenant sorting and selection and price discrimination. Households use a variety of means to sort themselves into communities that share similar tastes, goals, and, sometimes, less legitimate factors (cf. Strahilevitz 2011, 16–19). Low-income renters have a similar set of concerns about resident composition, but reduced capacity to differentiate among their fellow tenants in affordable housing. Moreover, low-income tenants typically have greater exposure to negative spillovers given the density of rental housing and its disproportionate siting in urban or low-income areas. Renter equity facilitates tenant sorting into more fine-grained and like-minded groups. The renters who apply to renter equity programs report that they are highly concerned about safety, desire a stronger commitment to their residence and sense of community, and want to build savings (Spinney, pers. comm.). The application process also exerts pressure on selection: tenants must complete three in-person orientation sessions to secure an apartment.

Because tenants self-select into renter equity, the form reveals information about applicants' preferences for savings, financial aspirations, anticipated residential stability, tastes for cooperation, and inclination toward upkeep. If there is a draw to renter equity for private landlords, it is in its ability to attract high-quality tenants that are less likely to cause property damage and disturbances. More concerning, renter equity could also be a way for landlords to indirectly draw a certain demographic of tenant. For example, the Cornerstone study found that residents in renter equity were more likely to be female, older, and better educated than the median renter at a similar income level (Drever et al. 2013, 50).

Renter equity facilitates price discrimination by offering higher-quality tenants better housing at a lower rate – it uses a specific system of renter equity savings credits to deliver differentiated pricing. To some extent, price discrimination occurs informally in traditional rental housing as higher-quality tenants negotiate better housing deals or lower rent increases over time. However, the less precise and efficient price discrimination mechanisms in traditional renting often mean that high-quality tenants pay a share of the costs of lower-quality tenants in the form of higher rents. By the same token, one consequence of renter equity's superior ex ante sorting and ex post pricing differentiation (via savings credits) may be to leave lower-quality, and more vulnerable, renters worse off in terms of rental access and affordability. This poses a normative and distributional question of whether it is socially desirable for higher-quality tenants to subsidize lower-quality ones.

8.2.B Renting Partnerships

In 2014, the creator of the renter equity model, Margery Spinney, departed from Cornerstone to launch a housing form called renting partnerships and launch its first apartment site. Renting partnerships uses the same incentive and leasing structure as renter equity: renter equity savings credits for on-time rent, participation, and upkeep jobs, credit vesting after five years, a tenants' association, and resident access to an emergency loan fund (Renting Partnerships 2016). Unlike Cornerstone renter equity, renting partnerships makes extensive rights of participation and sense of community the fundamental elements of the property form. In the founder's view, the incentives function more as a measure of residential participation and personal development rather than as a motivation for it (Spinney, pers. comm.). Accordingly, there is a stronger emphasis on ensuring that renters have input into policies affecting their rentals, including the use of trained facilitators to oversee the tenant association meetings and ensure meaningful participation (McKenzie 1994, 16–19; Resident Association Membership Agreement 2016, 1).

The legal structure of renting partnerships reflects these priorities. Renting partnerships leases the property from the owner and subleases to the tenants. The Renter Equity Agreement (savings credits) and the Resident Association Agreement run between renting partnerships and the tenants (Renting Partnerships Legal Structure 2016). Renting partnerships chose this legal structure so that it could extend strong and well-enforced tenant rights of participation and make the renting partnership directly accountable to tenants. However, interposing the renting partnership as a lessee of the owner increases costs compared to renter equity, which operates as a manager under contract with the owner.

8.2.C *Federal Lease-Based Incentives: The Family Self-Sufficiency Program*

The closest analog to the renter equity model, and another example of the recent interest in behavioral leasing, comes from the federal HUD Family Self-Sufficiency Program (FSS) enacted in 1990. FSS aims to motivate tenants to increase their earnings through lease-based incentives in the form of savings credits. Typically, low-income residents receiving HUD assistance must pay higher levels of rent as their income increases. In the FSS program, HUD deposits the increment of rent attributable to higher income in a savings account for the tenant. Tenants can withdraw the savings once they fulfill their Contract of Participation. This typically occurs in five years and requires that the family head be employed full-time and no other family members receive welfare. FSS is available to residents of HUD public housing as well as to Housing Choice Voucher recipients dispersed in private rentals. Housing Choice Voucher recipients pay 30 percent of their monthly adjusted gross income to rent apartments in the private market, with a voucher from their local housing authority covering the balance (24 C.F.R. §982.1(a)(3) (2016)).

A 2011 study that tracked 191 FSS participants found that at year four of five in the FSS program, 24 percent had met program requirements and graduated with an average escrow account of $5,300, 37 percent left the program before graduating, and 39 percent were still enrolled and accumulating savings (HUD FSS Evaluation 2011, 32–33).[3] It is possible that FSS has stronger effects on asset building than on employment. Interim results from a study of New York City participants report effective asset building, but only show positive employment effects for the subgroup of residents who were not employed at all when they entered FSS (Nuñez et al. 2015, 26, 140–41).

8.3 LEASE-BASED INCENTIVES AS SURROGATES FOR EQUITY

Far from an elegant model, renter equity is a veritable patchwork of property rules, institutions, and incentives. Into this jumble, it mixes psychological elements of commitment strategies and framing, the theme of life improvement via housing, a savings credit schedule reminiscent of mortgage principal accumulation, and the ability to use housing for liquidity (the resident emergency loan fund). The core innovation of the renter equity approach is to allocate to tenants the right to some of the value of their property-benefiting behaviors – and then to explicitly frame and market that right as an illiquid incentive payment in order to support a range of behaviors. This form offers a model of how psychology, in the form of behavioral incentives and commitment devices, can produce certain ownership effects – a model that raises intriguing possibilities as well as legal and policy concerns.

8.3.A Creating Rights to the Value of Property-Benefiting Behaviors

The renter equity agreement creates a limited right for tenants to a share of the value of their property-benefiting behaviors. This is an innovation that simultaneously lessens two key shortcomings of rental: disincentives for tenants to maintain and improve property and lack of asset-building opportunities. It also capitalizes on certain efficiencies of possession for maintenance and management. By virtue of being on site daily, tenants often possess a great deal of information relevant to upkeep, maintenance, and aspects of management. In typical rentals, tenants cannot capture the investment or management value of their property-benefiting actions, only the consumption value. As a result, tenants typically engage in less upkeep, improvement, and beautification of rental property than comparable owners (Rohe and Stewart 1996, 48), though not necessarily less local volunteering or civic engagement (DiPasquale and Glaeser 1999, 382–84; Stern 2011, 102–04).

The renter equity savings credit is not a prototypical property right. It is not an equity share with rights to property appreciation, and there is only a rough correspondence between the behaviors sought by renter equity and the savings credits. Appreciation is difficult to measure in advance of sale, particularly for rent-restricted affordable housing, which does not appreciate in a typical fashion (HUD 2012, 24). Instead, renter equity uses a predetermined schedule of credits based, presumably conservatively, on a tenant's anticipated share of the savings from reduced maintenance and turnover (e.g., $60 in month 1, $62 in month 2, etc.). Calculating credits based on a share of annual operating savings might be more efficient or motivating, but would decrease certainty, breed resentment if payouts fall short of expectations, and potentially mute the incentive's salience by using a share rather than a concrete dollar amount.

Because the money for the savings credits comes from management savings and reduced turnover, renter equity solves a common problem of incentives: the need for a costly stream of subsidy (cf. Galle 2012, 814–16).[4] At the same time, renter equity adds a unique, asset-building component to rental. Despite increasing national attention and funding for asset building for low-income Americans, effective savings programs for this cash-constrained group are rare (Schreiner and Sherraden 2007). Renters have dramatically lower levels of savings and multiple barriers to asset building (Joint

Center for Housing Studies 2013, 13). The lack of renter assets is particularly concern-ing because renter households are increasing at a rate not seen in the past half century and the percentage of middle-aged renter households is rising (1–3).

Renter equity has proven effective at building a modest level of assets for tenants by creating rights to the value of their property-benefiting behaviors (i.e., the savings credits). However, it has failed to articulate its goals for savings (e.g., pay debts, develop emergency fund, or long-term savings), which leaves the form vulnerable to the criticism of "savings for savings' sake." It is also not clear that housing, particularly rental housing, is the optimal vehicle for savings. Renter equity savings is undiversified and has less legal protection than retirement accounts, securities, or home equity. As I will discuss in Section 8.3.C, illiquid savings accounts can also be problematic.

In attempting more fine-grained allocations, renter equity exposes shared or overlapping interests between tenants and owners and the difficulty of teasing apart respective rights and obligations. Owners are justifiably concerned that renters will create costly misallocations or negative externalities that the owner will bear the cost of correcting (cf. Fennell 2009, 16). Also landlords may worry about violating landlord-tenant laws and habitability provisions (though liability seems unlikely since landlords retain responsibility for major maintenance and repairs). In practice, the renter equity lease has only partially resolved these issues by vesting responsi-bility for major alterations, major maintenance, and residual upkeep (i.e., what the tenants do not accomplish) in the landlord, while tenants participate in the annual operating budget, upkeep and minor maintenance, house rules, and decorating. If private landlords are to adopt renter equity in any number, they will require additional assurances against damage and greater ex ante clarification of their rights to intervene if tenant action dissipates value.

Renter equity's reallocation of property rights and responsibilities also raises concerns about unregulated labor and labor efficiency. Do we want unregulated tenant labor to displace regulated labor in renter equity apartments? Renter equity is likely not subject to labor and wage standards because the tenants have management duties and serve on managerial committees (cf. *Simpson v. Ernst & Young*, 1996, 434–44). There is also an efficiency issue of whether residents are the best providers of maintenance and upkeep. Would it be more efficient for tenants or landlords to hire out upkeep tasks? Renter equity does not allow such substitution, in part because of the emphasis on building community. In practice, the constraints of affordable housing may mitigate these concerns. At affordable housing sites, it is not a simple choice between regulated and unregulated labor. Absent resident participation via renter equity, some of the upkeep would not occur at all.

8.3.B *Framing Incentives to Produce Ownership Behaviors and Benefits*

The renter equity model frames the value of residential contributions as an incentive for tenant participation and adherence to the property form. Indeed, the savings incentive might inspire less action, or more conflict, if renters thought of the credits as property rights that should have been recognized previously. The savings credits accrue monthly, which provides what psychologists refer to as periodic reinforcement, rather than a less motivating schedule such as annual accounting. Even the term *renter equity* is compelling, suggesting both financial accumulation and personal stake. This is not to claim that incentives, however artfully defined and marketed, will persuade highly resistant renters. Instead, the incentives support ownership-like behaviors in concert with preexisting tenant motivations (selection), legal rules and expectations for the required renter equity behaviors, and the development of norms of resident participation (cf. Drever et al. 2013, 34).

Psychologically, incentives have a number of advantages for altering behavior. First, incentives increase the salience of certain behaviors. They communicate what is important to the entity providing the incentive, draw attention to those behaviors, and serve as ongoing reminders over time (Karlan et al., 2016, 2, 16). Second, incentives provide positive reinforcement of the desired behavior that increases its frequency (and may eventually create habits). Incentives can also help maintain the renter equity system against free riding and other collective action problems. Third, there is some evidence that incentives maintain good relations between parties by cultivating positive associations with the people connected to the incentive (Tyler and Blader 2000, 41). It is possible that penalties, taken from residents' existing assets, may be more effective than incentives at producing desired behaviors due to loss aversion (Kahneman, Knetsch, and Thaler 1990, 1325–48; Kahneman and Tversky 1979, 263–74). However, for behaviors that are not part of traditional lease obligations, such as upkeep, penalties seem misplaced (cf. Galle 2012, 834) and likely illegal under some tenant protection laws. Moreover, penalties are costly to enforce and often impossible to collect against judgment-proof tenants.

Residential leases have strengths as instruments of behavior change. They enable access to tenants and typically operate based on monthly rent, which can demarcate or deliver incentives. There is often preexisting rental management in place that can lower the incremental cost of administering incentives. Of course, incentives need not, and often should not, be tied to property. However, we might structure incentives within the property form in certain instances, such as when the target behaviors are residential or associated with property, the incentive is more efficiently monitored or administered on site, or the incentive payment is the housing itself.

In renter equity, the savings incentive supports behaviors that track homeownership, albeit in smaller magnitude and altered form. These behaviors include upkeep obligations, participation rights and limited self-governance, longer durations of residence, asset building, and a more "ownership-like" relationship to one's residence. The incentives directly reward three behaviors (upkeep, the monthly resident meeting, and paying rent on time). The resident association and the vesting rules for renter equity then sweep into the incentives' ambit a host of other behaviors, including participation in social events, creating and enforcing the house rules, and residential longevity.

Notably, renter equity frames the incentive not as a bald payment, but rather as an "equity-like" savings credit that represents opportunities for life improvement (evocative of homeownership). By emphasizing these positive connotations, the form likely produces stronger behavioral effects than it would otherwise. An immediate cash payment or shopping gift card is also motivating, but would undermine renter equity's attraction to lower-income tenants as an alternative to traditional renting and an asset-building vehicle.

The flip side of the psychological power of incentives is their vulnerability to abuse. If incentive-based behavioral leasing proliferates, the legal system may need to address misleading or deceptive incentives as landlords attempt to capture the value created from tenant contributions. For example, less scrupulous landlords may mislead tenants about incentives or offer incentives in complex forms that are difficult to understand. These practices have occurred with other consumer incentives, such as loyalty points programs (Dougherty 2013).

8.3.C Renter Equity as a Commitment Device

Renter equity employs what psychologists refer to as commitment strategies to shield tenants' savings from later willpower failings and time-inconsistent preferences (Ayres 2010, 45–47; Kurth-Nelson and Redish 2012, 1–2). A large body of research in psychology, law, and economics converges on the finding that commitment strategies are an important tool to mitigate bounds on willpower and address present bias and hyperbolic discounting (Ayres 2010, 20–55). For example, making a visible public commitment to exercise, agreeing to pay a penalty for not exercising, and selling your car so you must walk to work all reduce the likelihood of yielding to sedentary temptations.

As David Laibson recognized two decades ago, illiquid investments, including housing, offer a mechanism for commitment (1997, 444). He refers to such illiquid instruments as "golden eggs" that increase savings (and that can be undermined by financial products that enable instant borrowing against the illiquid asset) (445, 465). Housing illiquidity offers one strategy for insulating people's "future selves" from the temptation to spend, as well as to relocate. For example, research by Thomas Davidoff suggests that homeowners use housing illiquidity to save for long-term care rather than purchasing long-term care insurance (2008, 15–22).

Renter equity offers a potent commitment device for ensuring tenants save: it makes the savings illiquid for five years. This is similar, though not identical, to the illiquidity of home equity (at least prior to the advent of cash-out refinancing and reverse mortgages). Of course, illiquidity can also have undesirable effects, particularly for low-income renters. When new situations or economic shocks arise, it may make sense for tenants to access savings. In the face of a liquidity crisis, tenants may accept punishing interest on payday loans or defer needed health care, for example, because they cannot access their renter equity funds. Renter equity only partially addresses this problem through a resident loan fund for residents who need short-term loans for emergencies and move-in expenses.

Renter equity may not appeal to the renters who need commitment devices for savings the most. A significant subset of the population misestimates how time and flagging willpower will affect their future decisions (i.e., they don't believe they will have self-control problems). Non-mandatory or opt-in commitment devices are often not effective for this subset, who choose not to adopt them. Ted O'Donoghue and Matthew Rabin suggest an interesting solution. They describe a hypothetical policy where people opt into a combined potato chip tax and carrot subsidy. People who recognize that they have imperfect control will opt in to this commitment device. However, so will "naifs" who don't realize their limited self-control and view the policy as a gratis subsidy (they believe they will only consume carrots) (O'Donoghue and Rabin 2003, 186–90). Renter equity or other renter savings programs might experiment with this approach. For example, they could offer a savings account that tenants may withdraw from at any time and then an opt-in policy. The opt-in would impose a tax on early withdrawal and a bonus (subsidy) for allowing the money to accumulate for a certain period of time or periodic subsidies for each year the money remains untouched. Individuals who want to build savings and realize they have self-control problems will opt into the program, but so will those who are unaware of their self-control problems. Of course, if the costs of illiquidity are too high relative to its benefits, tenants either won't opt in or may opt in to their detriment because they also misestimate their liquidity needs or are overoptimistic about the perceived subsidy.

In addition to savings, the five-year vesting period also provides a commitment strategy for residential stability. The commitment structure allows renters, like owners, to embed ex ante preferences for residential stability into their housing by choosing a form (renter equity) that increases the costs of exit. Lodging the value of tenants' property-benefiting behaviors in late-vesting savings accounts provides incentives to stay put and, by design, distorts exit decisions. This undermines some of the virtues of rental: mobility and low costs of exit that enable tenants to respond to changed preferences and new opportunities. On the other hand, duration tends to increase both social ties and social contribution, which are important to the renter equity model. As a practical matter, a substantial percentage of renter equity residents are disabled or chronically ill; for these groups, geographic mobility tends to be lower anyway (Spinney pers. comm.).

There may be ways to lessen stability distortions in renter equity. Renter equity might integrate elements of the Family Self-Sufficiency Program by allowing residents to withdraw their savings early without penalty, and possibly an additional financial bonus, for achieving income that disqualifies them from subsidized housing. If renter equity were to proliferate, presumably via government or nonprofit support, a transfer system could evolve to allow tenants to move between different (possibly subsidized versus unsubsidized) rental equity sites. Renter equity could also shorten the time period for vesting. This would decrease asset accumulation for tenants as well as the amount of renter equity the landlord could provide, as turnover would increase. Another option would be to keep a five-year vesting rule but allow immediate, partial vesting if tenants leave their rental or if the building is sold. Either a shorter vesting period or an escape hatch approach would enable greater mobility and discipline against landlords' temptations to lessen services or otherwise exploit tenants' desire to stay in place for the five-year vesting window. These options also lessen renter equity's downsides for marketability: landlords want flexibility to sell their buildings without narrowing their market to those willing to manage the building with renter equity (tenant buy-out provisions may also address market-ability, albeit at a cost to landlords).

8.4 PSYCHOLOGICAL PITFALLS OF RENTER EQUITY AND MITIGATING EFFECTS

Renter equity leverages psychology to structure and support its alternative housing form. Like any policy tool, psychology can fail. This section considers the potential for psychology to unravel or have unintended consequences in practice. Specifically, I examine the risk that incentives will crowd out intrinsic motivation and voluntary behavior and the potential harms from renter equity's behavioral control of tenants.

8.4.A *Crowding Out Motivation and Behavior*

In some circumstances, incentives may reduce or "crowd out" the target behavior (Frey and Jegen 2001, 591–96). When this happens, people put forth less effort and produce less behavior than they would have in the absence of any incentive. Crowding out happens most commonly in the long run after an incentive is removed, but it can also occur when the incentive is still in place (Gneezy, Meier, and Rey-Biel 2011, 193). The research literature offers several explanations for crowding out: a loss of intrinsic motivation in the face of external rewards (Deci 1971, 105–10), the inference from payment that the task is unpleasant (Bénabou and Tirole 2003, 479–89), and compromise of one's image when prosocial behavior follows from payment (Ariely et al. 2009, 544–55). Incentives appear particularly vulnerable to crowding out when the incentive is visible to others and the behavior is "noble" or prosocial (Kamenica 2012, 13:18). This suggests a reason for not offering explicit incentives for residential activities such as volunteering in the community.

Why didn't the renter equity incentives produce the calamitous effects predicted by the research on crowding out? Based on the limited evidence available, the data from the Cornerstone study and my interviews with renting partnerships, the savings credit incentive supported on-time rent, created more attractive and better-maintained housing, and increased residential participation, satisfaction, and sense of community. These results may be due to attributes of the residents themselves, who self-select into the program following an extensive orientation process. Perhaps more to the point given the inevitable issue of selection bias, what factors might we expect would make incentives less at-risk for poor behavioral outcomes in renter equity or other forms of behavioral leasing?

First, the long-term nature of incentives in the renter equity form is a major protective factor against declining effort and reduced behavior output. Behavior can dwindle while incentives are in effect. But this is much less common and appears to occur when the incentive is not large enough, communicates a message of low social regard, or is so oversized as to induce anxiety and "choking" (Gneezy and Rustichini 2000, 791–98; Heyman and Ariely 2004, 787–90). The self-funding nature of the renter equity incentive enables an ongoing stream of incentive payments (renter equity keeps money in the operating reserves so that if cost savings are not realized for a discrete period, the incentive will still be paid). We might expect problems when the 10-year period for renter equity ends and residents stop collecting credits, which is just beginning to occur at Cornerstone. In that case, it seems unlikely tenants will continue to engage in upkeep or participate as frequently in tenant meetings. Renting partnerships does not place an expiration date on earning savings credits for this reason (Renting Partnerships 2016).

Second, the structure of renter equity may buffer against motivational harms. Homeownership offers a paradigm of embedding incentives and cloaking them with positive social meaning. Similarly, renter equity affords tenants more control and decision-making power and has connotations with ownership – a desirable social status. These positive meanings may reframe the incentive in a more personally and socially admirable light. The form of the incentive may reduce crowding out as well. There is evidence that crowding out occurs most commonly for monetary payments. In renter equity, the incentives take the form of a monthly savings "credit" that goes into an account for five years rather than an immediate cash payment. Of course, not all aspects of the savings credit are desirable or empowering. Renter equity tenants receive their savings credits on the judgment of a third-party administrator who monitors the defined spaces that each tenant maintains. This may suggest low trust, signal negative perceptions of residents, or alter the nature of relations from social to monetized or hierarchical. This point suggests a symbolic importance to renter equity's participatory structures. Some amount of resident governance (though perhaps less than the full amount envisioned by renter equity and especially renting partnerships) seems necessary to prevent renter equity from taking on the paternalistic flavor of an allowance for chores or becoming a labor contract.

Last, practically speaking, concerns about crowding out are often overblown for the simple reason that many behaviors subject to financial incentives would not have occurred but for the incentive. For example, low-income renters have a negative savings rate and are very unlikely to save voluntarily. Even among middle-income households, the savings rate is startlingly low (Guidolin and La Jeunesse 2007, 491–94, 512). With respect to upkeep and residential participation, the motivational picture is more complex. For example, a tenant may voluntarily pick up litter when he passes it or plan a resident gathering, but he would not voluntarily engage in the one to two hours of weekly upkeep of common areas that renter equity requires. Paying rent on time is perhaps the behavior most vulnerable to crowding out. However, this behavior is subject to a stick (the lease obligation to pay rent and remedies such as eviction) as well as a carrot (the savings credit).

Beyond specific behaviors, could savings credits crowd out one's civic or altruistic orientation toward residential living or stymie the more "owner-like" personal dispositions that renter equity seeks to cultivate? The psychology and economics research on incentives is less illuminating here because it has focused on measurable behaviors, with less attention to dispositions or attitudes. Even if we assume that a crystallized, prosocial orientation toward residential living exists, it is not clear whether incentives linked to renter equity support or undermine it given renter equity's positive connotations with savings, life improvement, and a social "equity stake" in housing.

8.4.B Controlling Personal and Social Behaviors

Linking scarce housing to financial incentives for upkeep tasks and participation in resident meetings could be seen as classist or coercive – or a possible gateway to leases that attempt to incentivize more personal behaviors and choices. Renter equity exercises a substantial amount of social control over tenant behaviors and interactions. Residents must join and participate in the tenant association to earn renter equity credits as well as consent to extensive house rules that include obligations to escort guests out the door, report safety concerns, forego long-term houseguests, and engage in peer mediation of conflicts (House Rules 2016, 1–2). Incentivizing or requiring certain behaviors as part of one's lease is an uneasy fit with notions of autonomy and liberty, as well as theories of property's particular role in securing liberty (cf. Ely 2008, 43). Homeownership incentives, in contrast, are intrinsic, less direct and visibly controlling, and the product of a choice to buy. It may feel and mean something different to perceive that your behavior is influenced by ownership of your property versus a rental incentive payment.

Another criticism might be that the renter equity model imposes a class-based notion that low-income residents need only adopt a better work ethic or habits of participation to improve their lot in life and become more productive citizens. To some, the upkeep tasks may seem insulting. As a practical matter, however, low-income tenants often receive barebones property upkeep services and may prefer to have an option to coordinate with other tenants to provide a higher level of service.

The pivotal issue for tenant liberty and dignity interests may be whether residents have a meaningful choice to opt into renter equity, with its mandated social structures and "sweat equity" component. The lack of affordable housing for low-income renters is severe, with only 32 housing units available for every 100 very low-income renters (Furman Center 2012, 3). Should renter equity expand, it is not clear whether residents competing over a severe undersupply of affordable units can choose whether or not to enter into a behavioral lease – indeed, this may be a new twist on the concerns of "unequal bargaining power" that animated landmark landlord-tenant cases (e.g., *Javins v. First Natl. Realty Corp* (D.C. Cir. 1970)). Yet, discarding forms such as renter equity and renting partnerships based on concerns about choice would foreclose housing options from tenants, a result that seems both undesirable and ironic.

Beyond renter equity, there is a broader question of whether we are starting down a "path of behaviorism" in leasing that may lead to other, more objectionable attempts to control the personal behaviors and choices of tenants. This is a deeper question, beyond the scope of this chapter. For now, I note that while fair housing acts provide some safeguards against overreaching, there may be a danger to acclimating ourselves to behavioral leases that regulate or incentivize personal behaviors.

8.5 CONCLUSION

Renter equity fills a gap between traditional rental and homeownership – but, in certain respects, rests uneasily within it. The form offers a number of innovations. It enables asset building for renters through their rental interests. Renter equity also offers relief from the stranglehold of traditional renting by allowing tenants greater control and governance. Focus group research by Cornerstone has found substantial interest among low-income renters for renter equity (asset building), greater participation in their residence, and safer housing (Spinney, pers. comm.). With respect to neighborhoods, while the renter equity sites have not deconcentrated poverty, they may deconcentrate dysfunction by drawing more responsible, motivated, and educated low-income residents to distressed neighborhoods (Dawkins 2011, 35–37; Drever et al. 2013, 35–36).

To expand, renter equity will need to resolve a number of legal and policy issues. These questions include how the form will address stay-put rights, incentives for residential stability, disbursals of savings credits upon eviction, and landlord abuse or fraud with respect to the tenants' savings credits. Until recently, Cornerstone renter equity was content to limit the program to three carefully tended sites (Spinney, pers. comm.). As a result, there has been limited development of or experimentation with the renter equity form. For example, it is not clear if all of the many moving parts of renter equity are necessary to sustain the form. Less elaborate structures of participation and community building would make the renter equity form more "scalable" to other sites, but could undermine the program's success.

Perhaps renter equity's most important contribution is as a model of innovation of an intermediate housing form for renters, supported by lease incentives. Traditionally, the residential lease divided the respective property rights and obligations of the landlord and tenant along the standard dimensions of possession and residual ownership. This division was cast at the time of lease signing and frozen into place for the term of the lease. Neither the historical property-bound view of leases nor the post-1970s contractual paradigm contemplated explicit, ongoing incentives in residential leases. Renter equity, and other behavioral leases, represent a novel iteration of the rental form – one that increases the continuum of housing options and raises new issues for property law.

REFERENCES

Ariely, D., Bracha, A., and S. Meier 2009. "Doing Good or Doing Well? Image Motivation and Monetary Incentives from Behaving Pro-socially." *American Economic Review* 99: 544–55.

Arruñada, Benito and Amnon Lehavi. 2011. "Prime Property Institutions for Subprime Era: Towards Innovative Models of Homeownership." *Berkeley Business Law Journal* 8(1): 1–34.

Ayres, Ian. 2010. *Carrots and Sticks: Unlock the Power of Incentives to Get Things Done.* New York: Bantam Books.

Barker, David. 2003. "Length of Residence Discounts, Turnover, and Demand Elasticity. Should Long-Term Tenants Pay Less than New Tenants?" *Journal of Housing Economics* 12(1): 1–11.

Barro, Josh. 2014. "How to Turn Renters into Savers." *TheUpshot* (blog). *New York Times.* May 14. www.nytimes.com/2014/05/15/upshot/how-to-turn-renters-into -savers.html?_r=1.

Bénabou, R. and J. Tirole. 2003. "Intrinsic and Extrinsic Motivation." *Review of Economic Studies* 70: 489–520.

Benartzi, Shlomo and Richard H. Thaler. 2004. "Save More Tomorrow: Using Behavioral Economics to Increase Employee Savings." *Journal of Political Economy* 112: 1, S164–S187.

Caplin, Andrew, Noel B. Cunningham, Mitchell Engler, and Frederick Pollock. 2008. "Facilitating Shared Appreciation Mortgages to Prevent Housing Crashes and Affordability Crises" (discussion paper, The Hamilton Project, The Brookings Institution). www.brookings.edu/~/media/Research/Files/Papers /2008/9/mortgages-caplin/0923_mortgages_caplin.PDF.

Cornerstone Renter Equity. Accessed January 17, 2016. http://cornerstone -equity.org/.

Davidoff, Thomas. 2008. "Illiquid Housing as Self-Insurance: The Case of Long Term Care." Available at SSRN: http://papers.ssrn.com/sol3/papers.cfm ?abstract_id=1009738.

Davis, John E. 2009. "Shared Equity Housing: Designed to Last." *Communities & Banking* 20(4): 29–31.

Dawkins, Casey J. 2011. "Exploring the Spatial Distribution of Low Income Housing Tax Credit Properties." *United States Department of Housing and Urban Development Office of Policy Development and Research* 1–39.

Deci, E. L. 1971. "Effects of Externally Motivated Rewards on Intrinsic Motivation." *Journal of Personality and Social Psychology* 18: 105–15.

Desmond, Matthew. 2016. *Evicted: Poverty and Profit in the American City.* New York: Crown Publishers.

Diamond, Michael R. 2009. "The Meaning and Nature of Property: Homeownership and Shared Equity in the Context of Poverty." *St. Louis University Public Law Review* 29(1): 85–112.

DiPasquale, Denise and Edward L. Glaeser. 1999. "Incentives and Social Capital: Are Homeowners Better Citizens?" *Journal of Urban Economics* 45(2): 354–84.

Downs, Anthony. 1981. *Neighborhoods and Urban Development.* Washington, DC: Brookings Institution.

Dougherty, Carter. 2013. "Credit-Card Rewards Programs Examined by U.S. Consumer Bureau." *BloombergBusiness.* November 14. www.bloomberg.com /news/articles/2013–11-15/credit-card-rewards-programs-examined-by-u-s-consu mer-bureau.

Drever, Anita, Cara Brumfield, Meredith Decker, Lebaron Sims, Benjamin Passty, and Stuart Wilson. 2013. *Cornerstone's Renter Equity Property Management System: Final Evaluation Report.* Washington, DC: Corporation for Enterprise Development. http://cornerstone-equity.org/wp-content/uploads/2013/12 /CornerstoneEvaluation-FinalReport.pdf.

Ely, James W. 2008. *The Guardian of Every Other Right: A Constitutional History of Property Rights.* New York: Oxford University Press.

Fennell, Lee Anne. 2008. "Homeownership 2.0." *Northwestern University Law Review* 102(3): 1047–1118.

Fennell, Lee Anne and Julie A. Roin. 2010. "Controlling Residential Stakes." *University of Chicago Law Review* 77(1): 143–76.

Fischel, William A. 2001. *The Homevoter Hypothesis: How Home Values Influence Local Government Taxation, School Finance, and Land-Use Policies.* Cambridge, MA: Harvard University Press.

Freddie Mac. 2016. *Profile of Today's Renter: Multi-family Renter Research.* www.freddiemac.com/multifamily/pdf/Consumer_Omnibus_Results_Jan_Feb _2016.pdf

Frey, Bruno S. and Reto Jegen. 2001. "Motivation Crowding Theory." *Journal of Economic Surveys* 15: 591–96.

Furman Center. 2012. *What Can We Learn about the Low-Income Housing Tax Credit Program by Looking at the Tenants?* New York: Furman Center.

Galle, Brian. 2012. "The Tragedy of the Carrots: Economics and Politics in the Choice of Price Instruments." *Stanford Law Review* 64: 797–850.

Glendon, Mary Ann. 1982. "The Transformation of American Landlord-Tenant Law." *Boston College Law Review* 23: 503–76.

Gneezy, U., S. Meier, and P. Rey-Biel. 2011. "When and Why Incentives (Don't) Work to Modify Behavior." *Journal of Economic Perspectives* 24(4): 191–210.

Gneezy, Uri and Aldo Rustichini. 2000. "Pay Enough or Don't Pay at All." *Quarterly Journal of Economics* 115: 791–810.

Green, Richard K. and Stephen Malpezzi. 2003. *A Primer on U.S. Housing Markets and Housing Policy*. Washington, DC: Urban Institute Press.

Geurts, Tom G. 2004. "The Historical Development of the Lease in Residential Real Estate." *Real Estate Law Journal* 32: 356–65.

Guidolin, Massimo and Elizabeth A. La Jeunesse. 2007. "The Decline in the U.S. Personal Saving Rate: Is It Real and Is It a Puzzle?" *Federal Reserve Bank of St. Louis Review* 89(6): 491–514.

Heyman, J. and Ariely, D. 2004. "Effort for Payment: A Tale of Two Markets." *Psychological Science* 15: 787–93.

Karlan, Dean, Margaret McConnell, Sendhil Mullainathan, and Jonathan Zinman. 2016. "Getting to the Top of Mind: How Reminders Increase Savings." *Management Science Articles in Advance* 19 January 2016.

John D. and Catherine T. MacArthur Foundation. 2014. *How Housing Matters: The Housing Crisis Continues to Loom Large in the Experiences and Attitudes of the American Public.* www.macfound.org/media/files/How_Housing_Matters_2014_FINAL_REPORT.pdf.

Joint Center for Housing Studies of Harvard University. 2013. *America's Rental Housing: Evolving Markets and Needs.* www.jchs.harvard.edu/sites/jchs.harvard.edu/files/jchs_americas_rental_housing_2013_1_0.pdf.

Kahneman, Daniel, Jack L. Knetsch, and Richard H. Thaler. 1990. "Experimental Tests of the Endowment Effect and the Coase Theorem." *Journal of Political Economy* 98(6): 1325–48.

Kahneman, Daniel and Amos Tversky. 1979. "Prospect Theory: An Analysis of Decision under Risk." *Econometrica* 47(2): 263–92.

Kamenica, Emir. 2012. "Behavioral Economics and Psychology of Incentives." *Annual Review of Economics* 4: 13.1–13.26.

Kelley, Robert H. 1995. "Any Reports of the Death of the Property Law Paradigm for Leases Have Been Greatly Exaggerated." *Wayne Law Review* 41(4): 1563–1607.

Kimura, Donna. 2014. "LIHTC Allocators Discuss Development Costs, QAP Changes." *Affordable Housing Finance*. November 24. www.housingfinance.com/finance/lihtc-allocators-discuss-development-costs-qap-changes_0.

Kleinbard, Edward. 2010. "Tax Expenditure Framework Legislation." *National Tax Journal* 63: 353–82.

Korngold, Gerald. 1998. "Whatever Happened to Landlord Tenant Law?" *Nebraska Law Review* 77: 703–18.

Krinsky, John and Sarah Hovde. 1996. *Balancing Acts: The Experience of Mutual Housing Associations and Community Land Trusts in Urban Neighborhoods*. New York: Community Service Society of New York.

Kurth-Nelson, Zeb and A. David Redish. 2012. "Don't Let Me Do That – Models of Precommitment." *Frontiers in Neuroscience* 138(6): 1–9.

Laibson, David. 1997. "Golden Eggs and Hyperbolic Discounting." *Quarterly Journal of Economics* 112(2): 465–69.

Lee, Christopher. 2013. *NAAHQ Executive Summary: 2013 Survey of Operation Expenses in Rental Apartment Communities.* www.naahq.org/sites/default/files /naa-documents/income-expenses-survey/2013-Income-Expenses-Summary.pdf.

Lerman, Robert I. and Signe-Mary McKernan. 2007. "Promoting Neighborhood Improvement While Protecting Low-Income Families." *Urban Institute* 8: 1–3.

Manturuk, Kim. 2012. "Urban Homeownership and Mental Health: Mediating Effect of Perceived Sense of Control." *City & Community* 11(4): 409–30.

McKenzie, Evan. 1994. *Privatopia: Homeowner Associations and the Rise of Residential Private Government.* New Haven, CT: Yale University Press.

Merrill, Thomas W. and Henry E. Smith. 2001. "The Property/Contract Interface." *Columbia Law Review* 101: 773–852.

    2000. "Optimal Standardization in the Law of Property: The Numerus Clausus Principle." *Yale Law Journal* 110: 1–70.

Miller, Rae-Ann. 2007. "Individual Development Accounts and Banks: A Solid 'Match.'" *FDIC Quarterly* 1(1): 22–31. www.fdic.gov/bank/analytical/quarterly /2007_vol1/quarterly_jun07_web.pdf.

Moulton, Stephanie, Anya Samek, and Cäzilia Loibl. 2015. "Save at Home: Building Emergency Savings One Mortgage Payment at a Time." In *A Fragile Balance: Emergency Savings and Liquid Resources for Low-Income Consumers,* J. Michael Collins, ed., 55–74. New York: Palgrave Macmillan.

MRDC. www.mdrc.org/sites/default/files/Building_Self-Sufficiency_for_Housing _Voucher_Recipients_FR.pdf.

Muela, Jordan. Property Management Fees Part I. 2017. www.managemyproperty.com /articles/property-management-fees-part-i-10

National Association of REALTORS. (NAR) 2015. "2015 Profile of Home Buyers and Sellers." *Highlights from the 2015 Profile of Home Buyers and Sellers.* November 5. www.realtor.org/reports/highlights-from-the-2015-profile-of -home-buyers-and-sellers.

Nuñez, Stephen, Verma Nandita, and Edith Yang. 2015. *Building Self-Sufficiency for Housing Voucher Recipients: Interim Findings from the Work Rewards Demonstration in New York City.* MDRC Report. www.mdrc.org/sites/default /files/Building_Self-Sufficiency_for_Housing_Voucher_Recipients_FR.pdf.

O'Donoghue, Ted and Matthew Rabin. 2003. "Optimal Paternalism, Illustrated by a Model of Sin." *American Economic Review.* 93(2): 186–91.

Pew Research Center. 2011. "Home Sweet Home. Still." *Social & Demographic Trends.* April 12. www.pewsocialtrends.org/2011/04/12/home-sweet-home-still/.

Poterba, James and Todd Sinai. 2008. "Tax Expenditures for Owner-Occupied Housing: Deductions for Property Taxes and Mortgage Interest and the Exclusion of Imputed Rental Income." *American Economic Review* 98(2): 84–89.

Rabin, Edward H. 2011. *Fundamentals of Modern Property Law.* New York: Foundation Press.

Reid, Carolina. 2013. "To Buy or Not to Buy? Understanding Tenure Preferences and the Decisionmaking Processes of Lower-Income Households in Homeownership Built to Last." Paper presented at the Homeownership Built to Last: Lessons from the Housing Crisis on Sustaining Homeownership for

Low-Income and Minority Families symposium, Harvard Business School, Boston, MA, www.jchs.harvard.edu/sites/jchs.harvard.edu/files/hbtl-14.pdf.

Renting Partnerships: Equity for Renters. Accessed February 20, 2016. www.renting partnerships.org/.

Rohe, William M. and Mark Lindblad. 2013. "Reexamining the Social Benefits of Homeownership after the Housing Crisis." Paper presented at the Homeownership Built to Last: Lessons from the Housing Crisis on Sustaining Homeownership for Low-Income and Minority Families symposium, Harvard Business School, Boston, MA. www.jchs.harvard.edu/sites/jchs .harvard.edu/files/hbtl-04.pdf.

Rohe, William M. and Leslie S. Stewart. 1996. "Homeownership and Neighborhood Stability." *Housing Policy Debate* 7(1): 37–81.

Schreiner, Mark and Michael Sherraden. 2007. *Can the Poor Save? Saving and Asset Building in Individual Development Accounts*. New Brunswick, NJ: Transaction Publishers.

Section 8 Tenant-Based Assistance: Housing Choice Voucher Program, 24 C.F.R. §982.1(a)(3) (2016).

Shiller, Robert J. 2015. *Irrational Exuberance*. 3rd Edition. Princeton, NJ: Princeton University Press.

Sinai, Todd and Nicholas S. Souleles 2005. "Owner Occupied Housing as a Hedge against Rent Risk." *Quarterly Journal of Economics* 120(2): 785–86.

Smith, Henry E. 2004. Property and Property Rules. *New York University Law Review* 79: 1719–98.

Stern, Stephanie M. 2011. Reassessing the Citizen Virtues of Homeownership, *Columbia Law Review* 100: 101–50.

Strahilevitz, Lior Jacob. 2011. *Information and Exclusion*. New Haven, CT: Yale University Press.

Super, David A. 2011. "The Rise and Fall of the Implied Warranty of Habitability." *California Law Review* 99: 389–63.

Thaler, Richard H. and Cass R. Sunstein. 2008. *Nudge: Improving Decisions about Health, Wealth, and Happiness*. New Haven, CT: Yale University Press.

Tyler, Tom R. and Steven L. Blader. 2000. *Cooperation in Groups*. Philadelphia, PA: Psychology Press.

U.S. Census Bureau. 2013. *American Housing Survey: National Summary Tables – AHS 2013*. www.census.gov/programs-surveys/ahs/data.html.

U.S. Department of Housing and Urban Development (HUD). 2011. "Informing the Next Generation of Rental Housing Policy." *Evidence Matters* (blog). Spring. www.huduser.gov/portal/periodicals/em/spring11/highlight1.html.

U.S. Department of Housing and Urban Development Office of Policy Development and Research. 2011. *Evaluating the Family Self-Sufficiency Program: Prospective Study*. www.huduser.gov/Publications/pdf/FamilySelfSufficiency.pdf.

U.S. Department of Housing and Urban Development Office of Policy Development and Research. 2012. *What Happens to Low Income Tax Credit Properties at Year 15 and Beyond?* www.huduser.gov/portal/publications /what_happens_lihtc_v2.pdf.

U.S. Government Accountability Office. 2013. *Rental Housing Assistance. HUD Data of Self-Sufficiency Programs Should Be Improved.* GAO-13–581. www.gao.gov/assets/660/655797.pdf.

Way, Heather K. 2009. "Informal Homeownership in the United States and the Law." *St. Louis University Public Law Review* 29(1): 113–92.

Williams, Lauren. 2012. "Affordable Housing as an Asset-Building Platform." *The Inclusive Economy* (blog). *Corporation for Enterprise Development.* October 3. http://cfed.org/blog/inclusiveeconomy/affordable_housing_as_an_asset-building _platform/index.html.

Notes

1. This proposal seems unlikely to catch fire, in part because it requires renters to voluntarily opt in to additional savings and because renters, who are poorer on average and receive less government subsidy than owners, are more cash-constrained. Procedurally, funneling savings through rent seems to be an increasing possibility due to the proliferation of online intermediaries for collecting rent payments.

2. Surveys that ask about homebuying motivations, such as the data collection completed annually by the National Association of Realtors, tend to use broad, under-differentiated response categories. For example, the primary reason respondents selected for purchasing a home was the "desire to own a home of my own" (NAR Profile of Home Buyers and Sellers 2015, 7).

3. Similarly, interim findings from the ongoing MRDC study of the New York FSS and FSS plus incentives (additional cash incentives for seeking education and working) found that four years into the program, 50 percent of participants accumulated savings with almost a third reporting more than $5,000 (Nuñez et al. 2015, 26).

4. However, this does not mean there is no subsidy involved in the renter equity sites. Both the development of the building and their operating reserves are initially subsidized by tax credits and charitable contributions, as is frequently the case for affordable housing.

9

Housing, Mortgages, and Retirement

Christopher J. Mayer

Many policy makers and business experts have expressed concern about the deteriorating savings and retirement readiness of older Americans. The Federal Reserve 2015 *Survey of Household Economics and Decisionmaking* states that "Thirty-one percent of non-retired respondents report that they have no retirement savings, including 27 percent of non-retired respondents age 60 or older." Measurements from the Boston College National Retirement Risk Index show "52 percent of households are 'at risk' of not having enough to maintain their living standards in retirement."[1] Fidelity Investments notes that "More than half of Americans [are] at risk of not covering essential expenses in Retirement."[2]

Several factors may be contributing to the growing financial challenges facing older Americans, including reduced pensions, increasing debt, and low savings. In previous generations, retirees relied on defined benefit plans offered by larger employers and Social Security to cover retirement expenses. Yet today "only half of American workers have access to an employer-based retirement plan."[3] As well, Social Security is facing its own financial challenges, and many experts are proposing an increase in the retirement age.[4]

At the same time that the coverage of pension plans is shrinking, debt among the elderly and near elderly is growing. According to researchers at the Federal Reserve Bank of New York,[5] "Debt held by borrowers between the ages of 50 and 80 ... increased by roughly 60 percent (between 2003 and 2015)." See Figure 9.1.

The predominant factor driving increased debt was mortgages taken out in the 2000s; credit card debt actually fell over the same period for older households.[6] This result is not surprising. After all, Greenspan and Kennedy (2005) pointed out that homeowners extracted $564 billion of home equity *per year* from 2001 to 2005.

Unfortunately, as debt is rising, most Americans of retirement age still have low balances of financial assets. According to the U.S. Census Bureau, median net worth excluding home equity in 2011 for the elderly aged 65 to 69 was only $43,921 (Figure 9.2).

Thus it is not surprising that Poterba and colleagues (2011) show that "Even if households used all of their financial assets ... to purchase a life annuity, only

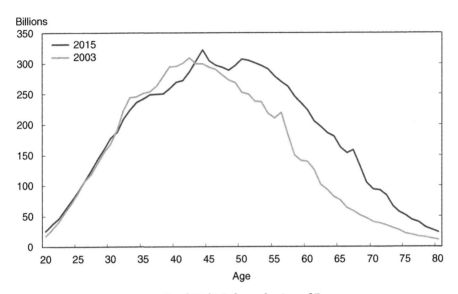

FIGURE 9.1 Total Debt Balance by Age of Borrower
Source: Federal Reserve Bank of New York Consumer Credit Panel/Equifax, Liberty
Street Economics Blog post, "The Graying of American Debt," February 24, 2016

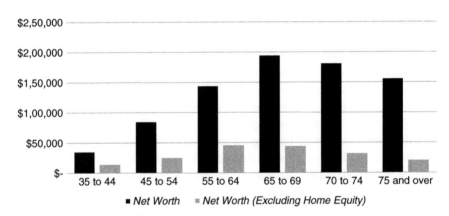

FIGURE 9.2 Median Net Worth in 2011
Source: Author's calculations using U.S. Census data

47 percent of households between the ages of 65 and 69 in 2008 could increase their life-contingent income by more than $5,000 per year." Savings are not large enough at this point to address the growing needs of the elderly.

For older households struggling to finance retirement, owning a home may explain how many retirees are able to successfully get by.[7] As shown in Figure 9.3,

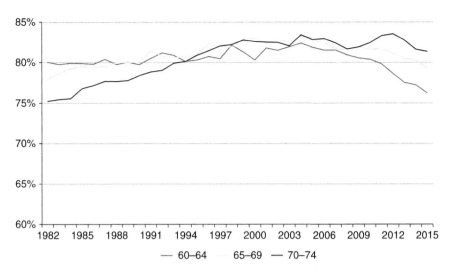

FIGURE 9.3 Homeownership Rate for Elderly Households, 60–74 Years Old
Source: Author's calculations using U.S. Census data

the share of elderly households owning their home increased by about five percentage points from 1982 to 2012 to a peak of nearly 84 percent of those aged 70 to 74. Since that time, the rate has fallen a bit (to 81 percent), but the vast majority of the elderly own their primary residence today. Owning a home can substantially reduce expenses and risk associated with retirement (Sinai and Souleles 2005).

Homeowners appear more prepared for retirement than renters in almost every way. Census data show that median net worth including home equity is considerably larger than without (Figure 9.2) – almost $195,000 for households aged 65 to 69 in 2011. Poterba and colleagues (2011) show that housing and real estate wealth exceeds the total of financial assets and personal retirement accounts for households of the same age. Even more striking, the authors show that real estate represents almost 80 percent of the present value of Social Security income.

In what follows, I examine the growth in mortgage debt and home equity for the elderly using the Survey of Consumer Finances (SCF) and consider how retirees are able to manage debt and utilize home equity in retirement with data from the Health and Retirement Survey (HRS). Previous academic research often examines home equity as a share of net worth without considering the amount of mortgage debt.[8] Indebtedness is important to consider in its own right given the way many households now pay for their costs in retirement, predominantly financing expenditures from cash flow rather than spending down their stock of assets. As Poterba and colleagues (2011) point out, the typical household appears to treat home equity and non-annuitized wealth like precautionary savings, which they spend only very late in life.

The data show a striking increase in mortgage debt at or near retirement age since 1992. For example, about 40 percent of households age 66–71 have a mortgage in 2013, up from 25 percent two decades earlier. At the same time, the average amount of mortgage debt (in 2013$) has almost tripled from less than $20,000 to more than $55,000. By contrast, real home equity in 2013 is at about the same level as it was almost 15 years earlier for most older homeowners. These data make clear that the growth of housing debt in the boom prior to the Great Recession remains on the balance sheets of many older households today.

Next I consider the evolution of mortgage debt versus financial assets over time. Debt is not necessarily a problem if homeowners have more assets to pay back the debt. Unfortunately, not only has debt increased as a share of home values, it has also increased relative to financial assets. About 40 percent of homeowners with a mortgage aged 65–69 had more mortgage debt than the sum total of all of their financial assets in 2012, up from about 28 percent in 1992.

Having established the growth in housing debt, I examine data from previous cohorts of older homeowners to examine how these households have historically managed mortgage debt and spent down home equity and financial assets over time. This analysis builds on a pair of papers by Poterba and colleagues (2012, 2015) that examine the net worth of the elderly in the year just prior to death as well as examining the evolution of assets from retirement age to just before death.[9]

The evidence shows that few homeowners spend down home equity until very late in life. For a sample of borrowers first observed at age 53–63 in 1994 and who die within 18 years, the share without home equity increased slightly from 31 percent to 34 percent. For elderly first observed over age 70 in 1992 and who die within 15 years, the share without home equity doubled from 22 percent to 44 percent.[10] Even for the oldest households in the sample, however, the majority own a home in the year prior to death.

Next I examine the link between home equity and financial assets. Poterba and colleagues (2015) show that for households entering retirement with assets, most of those assets remain unspent unless the household has a disruption in family composition or a member with an important medical event. I expand on their analysis by separating assets into home equity and financial assets. The results show that most older households only spend down home equity in the years just prior to death when they enter assisted living. By contrast, households spend down 30 percent to 40 percent of financial assets. Homeowners with larger amounts of financial assets are slightly less likely to reduce home equity, potentially because they have the resources to age in place in their home rather than selling the home and moving to assisted living.

Putting these results together, my findings suggest that the prognosis for financial stability in retirement is getting worse because more households are entering retirement age with greater amounts of debt. This trend is likely to continue as younger cohorts are nearing retirement age with more debt than previous cohorts, whether measured in real dollars or as a share of home value (loan-to-value ratios are also rising). While many elderly have large amounts of home equity (which often exceeds other financial assets, including retirement accounts), most do not use that home equity to fund retirement.

This chapter has two empirical sections. The first examines the Survey of Consumer Finances to determine changes in household balance sheets and borrowing when heading into retirement. The second examines data from the Health and Retirement Survey to study how households spend down home equity and financial assets. This chapter concludes with ideas about a future policy and research agenda.

HOUSING DEBT IN RETIREMENT

To begin, I examine data from the Survey of Consumer Finances to track homeownership and borrowing by families at or near retirement age. The analysis is conducted by age as well as by following cohorts of borrowers in six-year age intervals from 1992 to 2013. The six-year age intervals were designed to allow the reader to compare housing behavior of some cohorts.

Data Description

The Survey of Consumer Finances (SCF) is sponsored by the Federal Reserve Board in cooperation with the Department of Treasury. It is a cross-sectional survey of families in the United States that has taken place every three years since 1983. I start with the 1992 survey, which was the first date that the SCF was built to provide a nationally representative sample, using waves in 1992, 1995, 1998, 2001, 2004, 2007, 2010, and the latest published wave in 2013. The survey collects information on assets, liabilities, pensions, income, and demographics. About 6,500 families participate in each wave of the survey, which means that it can be difficult to separate into smaller groups of elderly without some sampling error. The yearly survey data were downloaded directly from the Federal Reserve website. Dollar-denominated variables are reported in 2013($) to allow comparisons across years. The primary variables used are X14 (age), X805 (balance still owed on first mortgage), X808 (mortgage payment), X701 (homeownership), X809 (payment frequency), X5729 (income), and X507 (value of primary residence). Sample weights (X42oo) were applied throughout the data.

The term "family" is defined in the SCF by examining a household unit and dividing into a primary economic unit (PEU) – the family – and everyone else in the household (Board of Governors of the Federal Reserve System 2014). The PEU is intended to be the economically dominant single person or couple (whether married or living together as partners) and all other persons in the household who are financially interdependent with that economically dominant person or couple. In this regard, the definition of families in the SCF is more comparable to the definition of households in other government surveys.

The data are analyzed in four six-year age groups beginning in 1992 and based on the age of the head of the family: 54–59, 60–65, 66–71, and 72–77-year-olds. The cohorts were then aged every six years, the same intervals that align with years that cohorts are observed in the SCF. While the SCF takes place every three years, the data are aggregated into six-year age intervals to ensure a large enough sample for appropriate inferences. In the last year of study, the oldest cohort went from being 42–47 in 1992 to 72–77 years in 2013.

Analysis

To start, I examine changes in housing debt, homeownership, and home equity by age. Table 9.1 reports the share of families without a mortgage in the various age groups. Families with a mortgage in retirement may be at greater risk of losing their homes without working or obtaining additional income above and beyond Social Security.

The data show a consistent downward trend in the share of homeowners with a paid-off home entering retirement age. For families whose head was over age 65 (in this case, age 66–71), the share without a mortgage fell from a high of 75 percent in 1992 to 69 percent in 2004, just prior to the financial crisis. By 2007, the percentage without a mortgage had fallen to 61 percent and remained around 59 percent in 2010 and 2013. Families with a head aged 72–77 years old exhibit a similar large decline in the share of borrowers without mortgages. Older borrowers appear to have strongly contributed to the growth in borrowing during the mid-2000s. By contrast, the share of borrowers aged 54 to 59 without a mortgage has remained relatively stable at between 35 percent and 42 percent. Thus the increase in debt appears to be a result of borrowers not paying off their mortgage as they approach and enter retirement age.

TABLE 9.1: *Percent of Households with No Mortgage by Age*

	1992	1995	1998	2001	2004	2007	2010	2013
54–59	41%	42%	42%	42%	41%	35%	37%	39%
60–65	56%	53%	55%	57%	54%	47%	46%	48%
66–71	75%	72%	70%	68%	69%	61%	59%	59%
72–77	90%	82%	83%	83%	80%	76%	67%	70%

Source: Author's calculations using Survey of Consumer Finances data

TABLE 9.2: *Homeownership Rate by Age*

	1992	1995	1998	2001	2004	2007	2010	2013
54–59	76%	83%	77%	77%	80%	79%	70%	69%
60–65	76%	79%	78%	79%	77%	81%	76%	74%
66–71	74%	76%	76%	75%	78%	78%	78%	79%
72–77	75%	78%	75%	76%	78%	74%	75%	77%

Source: Author's calculations using Survey of Consumer Finances data

TABLE 9.3: *Percent with Housing Payments by Age*

	1992	1995	1998	2001	2004	2007	2010	2013
54–59	69%	65%	67%	67%	67%	72%	74%	73%
60–65	57%	58%	57%	55%	58%	62%	65%	64%
66–71	44%	45%	47%	49%	47%	52%	54%	53%
72–77	33%	36%	38%	37%	38%	44%	50%	45%

Source: Author's calculations using Survey of Consumer Finances data

One possible explanation for the decline in the share of families with fully paid-off mortgages is that the homeownership rate was rising for older families during this same time period. As a result, some families who might have been renters in previous years became homeowners. Although these "new" homeowners may not have fully paid off their mortgage, they might have accumulated enough home equity to make retirement more financially stable than if they had not owned a home at all. Table 9.2, in fact, documents that the homeownership rate was rising over this time period for families whose head is age 66 and above.[11]

One way to address this issue is to examine the share of families with some housing payment.[12] In this case, a homeowner with a mortgage might be treated similarly to a renter, at least from the perspective that both groups may require additional income relative to a homeowner with a fully paid-off mortgage. In fact, data from the Joint Center for Housing Studies of Harvard (2014) documents that about 30 percent of elderly households with a mortgage pay more than one-half of their income in housing expenses, a similar share as elderly renters. Thus mortgage payments could present an appreciable burden on elderly retirees just as rental payments might.

The data in Table 9.3 show that after 2007, a sharply higher share of families whose head is over the age of 65 fall into the category of owners with mortgage payment or renters. While in 2004, 47 percent of those aged 66 to 71 had some housing payment, by 2010 that number had risen to 54 percent. For the oldest families (with a head aged 72 to 77), the share rose from 38 percent to

TABLE 9.4: *Real Mortgage Amount (2013$) by Age among Homeowners with a Mortgage*

	1992	1995	1998	2001	2004	2007	2010	2013
54–59	$ 32,610	$ 39,559	$ 44,860	$ 52,574	$ 62,471	$ 68,561	$ 67,174	$ 69,954
60–65	$ 23,118	$ 28,023	$ 43,512	$ 47,562	$ 63,578	$ 69,082	$ 69,099	$ 71,418
66–71	$ 18,304	$ 23,342	$ 31,997	$ 40,180	$ 43,219	$ 66,052	$ 54,790	$ 54,828
72–77	$ 16,419	$ 23,359	$ 34,113	$ 34,662	$ 47,338	$ 36,677	$ 46,892	$ 40,360

Source: Author's calculations using Survey of Consumer Finances data

50 percent. While the data in 2013 show a small decline in the share of elderly with a mortgage, the overall pattern documents that housing payments have become much more common among retirement-age families after the financial crisis.

Next, I examine the amount of mortgage debt held by families in this age group who own a home. Table 9.4 shows the average mortgage debt by age for homeowners with a mortgage and documents an appreciable rise over time in the amount of mortgage debt held by older borrowers.

Overall real mortgage debt among 66–71-year-olds increased from about $18,000 in 1992 (in 2013 dollars) to about $55,000 in 2010 and 2013. This is a sharp growth in borrowing for an age group that is at or near retirement. At first glance, it is surprising that the amount of borrowing grew throughout the 1990s and early 2000s, in seeming contradiction of the Greenspan and Kennedy (2005) result showing a much sharper increase in mortgage borrowing in the early 2000s than the 1990s. However, the data on the share of homeowners with a mortgage can reconcile this seeming contradiction. Table 9.3 shows that the share of families without a mortgage fell from 2001 to 2007. This suggests that the mortgage excesses of the 2000s resulted in increases in mortgage debt on both the intensive and extensive margins; not only did borrowers take on more housing debt, but a larger share of older borrowers had a mortgage than in previous years.

Of course, families may have seen an increase in home values that offset the larger overall borrowing amounts. Table 9.5 reports loan-to-value (LTV) ratios for the same age groups, once again conditioned on having an outstanding mortgage.[13] While mortgage debt grew steadily prior to 2007, the overall LTVs for these age groups only increased slightly between 1998 and 2007. This suggests that the typical family increased its borrowing roughly in proportion with the overall rise in home prices. However, after the housing crash, LTVs exhibited a large increase. By 2013, the typical older borrower over age 65 had an LTV of almost 50 percent, up more than 10 percentage points from 1998. The data suggest that mortgage debt for older families increased when home values rose, but that borrowers did not decrease their mortgage debt when prices fell.

While the SCF data from 2016 are not yet available, it is possible that the trend of increasing LTVs might reverse itself. Between 2013 and 2016, home values have risen

TABLE 9.5: *Mean Loan-to-Value (LTV) Ratio among Homeowners with a Mortgage*

	1992	1995	1998	2001	2004	2007	2010	2013
54–59	32%	40%	43%	43%	43%	42%	56%	59%
60–65	29%	36%	37%	43%	39%	40%	52%	58%
66–71	22%	33%	34%	36%	38%	41%	50%	48%
72–77	17%	32%	37%	37%	43%	40%	41%	49%

Source: Author's calculations using Survey of Consumer Finances data

TABLE 9.6: *Home Equity (Real 2013$) among All Homeowners*

	1992	1995	1998	2001	2004	2007	2010	2013
54–59	$ 101,904	$ 98,258	$ 104,718	$ 123,660	$ 145,815	$ 162,934	$ 120,013	$ 119,124
60–65	$ 80,939	$ 77,683	$ 117,603	$ 109,922	$ 163,279	$ 170,605	$ 133,546	$ 122,818
66–71	$ 83,006	$ 70,088	$ 94,357	$ 110,136	$ 114,036	$ 162,783	$ 109,641	$ 114,094
72–77	$ 97,417	$ 73,644	$ 92,530	$ 93,666	$ 110,457	$ 92,719	$ 114,158	$ 82,193

Source: Author's calculations using Survey of Consumer Finances data

about 20 percent according to the Case and Shiller National Home Value Index.[14] Thus LTVs today would be close to their historical average of 40 percent as long as mortgage balances have not gone up for elderly borrowers, which would be consistent with data showing the overall size of mortgage borrowing has been flat over this time period.[15]

Finally, I examine overall home equity. Table 9.6 reports home equity in real 2013 dollars for all families who own a home. Not surprisingly, given the data on LTVs, home equity has been relatively stable around $100,000 since the early 2000s for families aged 66–71, with the exception of a large increase in 2007 followed by a decline in 2010.[16] This is consistent with studies finding that owners have large amounts of home equity, even those older homeowners with a mortgage.

The data from this section show that a growing number of families are entering retirement age with mortgage debt that will not be paid off for many years to come. The increasing amounts of mortgage debt will likely challenge retirement stability for some homeowners.

SPENDING HOME EQUITY AND FINANCIAL ASSETS IN RETIREMENT

Next, I turn to the questions of how mortgage debt has evolved relative to assets for older homeowners, as well as how these homeowners spend down their assets in retirement. Here, this chapter uses information in the Health and Retirement

Survey (HRS), following closely the analysis in Poterba and colleagues (2015). These authors take advantage of the panel feature of the HRS to identify assets in the last wave prior to death and compare them to assets that the same household had when it first entered the HRS up to 20 years earlier. The point of the analysis is to understand how households spend down assets, including both housing and other financial assets in typical retirement years. An important advantage of the HRS for this analysis is the opportunity to observe a large sample of respondents in the very late stages of life.

Data Description

The University of Michigan Health and Retirement Study is a nationally representative survey of Americans over the age of 50. The survey has interviewed a sample of approximately 20,000 individuals every two years since its inception in 1992. Eleven waves of the study are included in this dataset.

Two of the six age cohorts of the HRS are included in our dataset. They are the base HRS cohort and the AHEAD cohort. The HRS cohort includes individuals born from 1931 to 1941 and are ages 51 to 61 in 1992. The AHEAD cohort began as part of a different study (The Study of Assets and Health Dynamics among the Oldest Old) in 1993 and includes individuals born before 1924. The AHEAD cohort was interviewed once more in 1995 before being added to the general HRS interview for the 1998 study. For the purposes of this study, the 1993 AHEAD cohort responses are added to the 1994 HRS study responses (wave 2) and the 1995 AHEAD cohort responses are added to the 1996 HRS study responses (wave 3). I drop the first wave of the HRS (1992 sample) due to data problems, so the sample begins with wave 2. The data file used is the RAND HRS Data (Version O) file. The RAND HRS Data file is a cleaned version with derived variables of all the core interviews of all waves of the HRS. All data are listed under the respondent level, but wealth variables are collected on the household level and can be identified through a household ID (HHID).

As I am predominantly interested in assets at end of life, responses for this study are limited only to respondents who died during the survey time period (after 1993 and prior to 2012). The data choices that follow closely track those in Poterba and colleagues (2015). Respondents with spouses who are not eligible for the HRS due to their age, and any respondents who left for reasons other than death are also dropped. When looking at the change in assets up to the year prior to death, the analysis is limited to respondents who joined the study at the beginning (i.e., 1994 for HRS and 1993 for AHEAD). This includes the majority of respondents from these years (wave 2). Variables indicating which survey year the respondent enters the survey (FYO – First Year Observed) and when the respondent last fully completes the survey (LYO – Last Year Observed) are created. The LYO variable can range from only a few months to two years before the time the respondent dies. On average, given that the HRS is conducted every two years, the LYO is about a year before death. The HRS provides separate codes for respondents who exit the sample due to death versus attrition; I consider only those who died in determining LYO.

Wealth assets are computed in multiple categories and converted into 2012 dollars using the Consumer Price Index. Housing wealth comes from housing equity (home value net of mortgage debt). Other wealth is made up of non-housing real estate equity, vehicles, business, and second home equity minus other debt. Annuity wealth includes both the respondent's and their spouse's pension and Social Security wealth. Financial wealth is made up of IRA accounts, stocks, checking accounts, CDs, bonds, and other financial assets.

Health variables for specific conditions are dummies that indicate whether a condition appears from the FYO to the LYO. The general health variable is a percentile index created as described in Poterba and colleagues (2013) with a range from one to 100, with one being the lowest. For all health conditions and dummies, the value is made positive if either the respondent or their spouse reports the issue. This way, the respondent-level health data more closely resemble the household-level wealth data.

Education variables are constructed by years of education. Family pathway variables are constructed using the marriage status variable. The family pathways indicate whether the respondent stays single, stays married, or goes from married to single. There were too few responses for single to married to be included in the study.

Analysis

To start, I examine additional metrics describing the ability of borrowers to retire their mortgage. Figure 9.4 uses all waves of the HRS starting in 1998 along with sample weights to compare the amount of mortgage debt relative to financial assets. The goal is to determine whether households have enough financial assets to pay off their mortgages if they chose to do so. In 1998, only 25 percent of those with a mortgage had a larger mortgage balance than financial assets. In other words, about three-quarters of mortgage borrowers could retire their mortgage if they chose to do so.[17] However, the share unable to retire their mortgage has been steadily increasing, up to 40 percent in 2012.

Another way to consider the burden associated with carrying a mortgage is to examine the extent to which borrowers who start with a mortgage end up paying it off before passing away. To do this, Table 9.7 reports data on mortgage amounts for all households in first and last year observed for the AHEAD and HRS samples. The data suggest that the bulk of borrowers who start retirement age with a mortgage do not fully pay it off by the time of their death. Among the younger HRS borrowers who enter the sample at ages 53 to 63 in 1994, the share with a mortgage increases from 62.5 percent to 71.8 percent. In other words, of the 37.5 percent with a

TABLE 9.7: *Mortgage Debt*

	HRS		AHEAD	
	First Year Observed	Last Year Prior to Death	First Year Observed	Last Year Prior to Death
< = 0	62.5%	71.8%	89.0%	93.4%
$1–$50k	19.7%	11.3%	2.4%	1.2%
$50,001–$100k	8.7%	9.0%	5.1%	2.7%
$100,001–$250k	7.8%	6.8%	2.2%	1.5%
$250,001–$500k	1.2%	1.1%	1.2%	1.1%
> 500k	0.1%	0.0%	0.1%	0.2%
Total	100.0%	100.0%	100.0%	100.0%

HRS Sample: Respondents age 51–61 in 1992 who died prior to 2012
AHEAD Sample: Respondents age 70+ in 1993 who died prior to 2012
Source: Author's calculations using the Health and Retirement Survey data

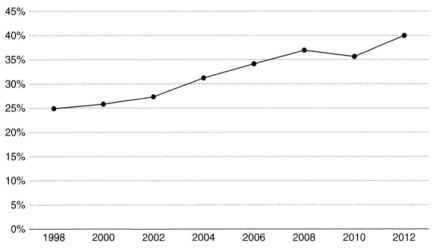

FIGURE 9.4 Percent of Homeowners with a Mortgage Aged 60–69 with More Mortgage
Debt than Financial Assets
Source: Author's calculations using Health and Retirement Survey data

mortgage, only about one-quarter of households (9.3 percent) pay off their mortgage
up to the year prior to death. Not surprisingly, the bulk of those that pay off the
mortgage appear to be borrowers with mortgage debt under $50,000 in 1994. In the
AHEAD group of borrowers entering the sample at age 70 and above, a much higher
share of borrowers start the sample without debt (89 percent) and more than 40
percent of the remainder pay off their mortgage prior to death. In both cohorts,

however, most borrowers who enter retirement age with a mortgage will have at least some mortgage payments up to the year prior to passing away.

Next, I examine the amount of home equity and compare it to financial assets. The goal is to examine whether the type of asset is related to the likelihood that a household liquidates the asset over time to help fund retirement. Tables 9.8 and 9.9 compare the distribution of home equity and financial assets for those in the HRS sample (age 53–63 in 1994) and the AHEAD sample (over age 70 in 1993).

First consider the older AHEAD respondents. Panel 1 in Table 9.8 shows that households over age 70 in 1993 held significant amounts of home equity; on average 48 percent had more than $100,000 ($2012) and another 23 percent had more than $50,000.[18] In fact, housing wealth represents the bulk of wealth for households. Almost 23 percent of respondents had more than $50,000 in home equity and less than $50,000 in financial assets, whereas only 8.3 percent had the opposite – more than $50,000 in financial assets and less than $50,000 in home equity. Alternatively, about 44 percent of respondents had home equity that was at least one category higher than financial assets, whereas 39 percent had at least one more category of financial assets. At the top end of the wealth distribution, there is an appreciable proportion of households (17 percent) that have more than $250,000 in financial assets, but less in home equity. Thus for the elderly with high net worth, housing is less important as a share of total assets, whereas at the lower end of the wealth distribution, home equity is much more important.

Of particular interest with the HRS (and AHEAD sample) is the ability to look at respondents just prior to death at much older ages than would be possible with other data. Panel 2 in Table 9.8 shows the same comparison of home equity and financial assets in the last wave observed prior to death.

One striking feature is the sharp increase in households who appear to have liquidated their home and own no home equity. More than 43 percent of respondents report having no home equity versus 22 percent in the first year surveyed (1993) from Panel 1. As well, another 15 percent of respondents report having less than $50,000 in home equity and more than $50,000 in financial assets. Overall, almost one-half now report having at least one more bucket of financial assets relative to home equity (26.5 percent have at least one category more of home equity).

It is also striking just how many respondents hit the last stage of their life having completely exhausted their financial assets (a point first made by Poterba et al. 2012). Almost 36 percent have less than $10,000 in financial assets and another 21 percent have less than $50,000 in financial assets. Two-thirds of those with less than $10,000 of financial assets (23.5 percent) also have no home equity. These households are ill-prepared to fund unreimbursed medical expenses and other costs. Many of these elderly will end up on Medicaid in addition to Medicare, with the government funding all of the costs associated with the last stages of their lives.[19]

TABLE 9.8: *Home Equity vs. Financial Assets, AHEAD Sample (respondents aged 70+ in 1993 who died prior to 2012).*

Panel 1.
Responses in 1993

		Total Financial Assets						
		<= 0	$1–$10k	$10,001–$50k	$50,001–$100k	$100,001–$250k	$250,001–$500k	>500k	Total Financial
	<= 0	6.2%	5.0%	6.1%	1.5%	1.9%	0.9%	0.6%	22.2%
	$1–$10k	0.5%	0.4%	0.9%	0.0%	0.1%	0.0%	0.0%	1.9%
Total	$10,001–$50k	2.4%	2.2%	4.5%	1.2%	1.3%	0.6%	0.2%	12.4%
Home	$50,001–$100k	2.2%	2.1%	7.5%	3.2%	4.2%	2.6%	1.2%	23.0%
Equity	$100,001–$250k	1.9%	1.9%	5.6%	4.8%	8.1%	5.0%	4.2%	31.5%
	$250,001–$500k	0.2%	0.2%	0.8%	0.9%	2.0%	1.2%	1.9%	7.2%
	> 500k	0.0%	0.0%	0.5%	0.0%	0.1%	0.2%	1.1%	1.9%
	Total Home	13.4%	11.8%	25.9%	11.6%	17.7%	10.5%	9.2%	100.0%

Note: All data reported in $2012; N = 5,581
22.9 percent of respondents have less than 50k in financial wealth and more than 50k in home equity
8.3 percent of respondents have less than 50k in home equity and more than 50k in financial assets

Panel 2.
Responses in Last Year in Sample Prior to Death

	Total Financial Assets							
	<= 0	$1–$10k	$10,001–$50k	$50,001–$100k	$100,001–$25ok	$250,001–$500k	>500k	Total Financial
<= 0	12.7%	10.8%	8.4%	3.2%	4.1%	2.2%	2.3%	43.7%
$1–$10k	0.4%	0.4%	0.5%	0.1%	0.1%	0.0%	0.0%	1.5%
$10,001–$50k	1.9%	2.1%	3.2%	1.1%	0.9%	0.4%	0.4%	10.0%
Total $50,001–$100k	1.7%	2.6%	4.5%	2.3%	2.8%	1.4%	1.3%	16.6%
Home $100,001–$25ok	1.0%	1.6%	4.0%	2.9%	5.0%	3.2%	3.3%	21.0%
Equity $250,001–$500k	0.2%	0.4%	0.6%	0.8%	1.1%	0.8%	1.7%	5.6%
>500k	0.0%	0.1%	0.1%	0.1%	0.2%	0.2%	1.2%	1.9%
Total Home	17.9%	18.0%	21.3%	10.5%	14.2%	8.2%	10.2%	100.0%

Note: All data reported in $2012; N = 5,581
16.80 percent of respondents have less than 50k in financial wealth and more than 50k in home equity
14.80 percent of respondents have less than 50k in home equity and more than 50k in financial assets
Source: Author's calculations using Health and Retirement Survey data

Table 9.9 repeats this same analysis using younger households in the HRS sample (age 53–63 in 1994). The HRS respondents appear to head into retirement age in similar circumstances as AHEAD households (Panel 1). The younger HRS respondents with low net worth still hold portfolios disproportionately concentrated in home equity, whereas the respondents with higher net worth have a more balanced portfolio. Almost 20 percent have more than $50,000 ($2012) in home equity and less than $50,000 in financial assets, whereas only 9 percent have the reverse situation. However, unlike their older AHEAD counterparts, few HRS respondents have liquidated their housing equity in the year prior to death. In their last year observed, about two-thirds still own their home. About 18 percent have more than $50,000 ($2012) in home equity and less than $50,000 in financial assets, versus less than 8 percent in the reverse situation. And nearly 32 percent have at least one category more in home equity than financial assets as in Table 9.9. The comparison with the AHEAD cohort seems to suggest that households do not spend down home equity until they reach much older ages. The oldest respondents in the HRS sample would have died by age 81, whereas the AHEAD cohort has been observed into much older ages.[20]

To better understand how households spend housing and financial wealth as they age, I examine the determinants of assets in the last year observed as a function of assets when households are first surveyed plus demographic and health controls. The regressions in Table 9.10 follow the same format and include the same control variables as in Poterba and colleagues (2015), tables 3.1 and 3.2.[21] However, I make two adjustments. First, the regressions address skewness in observed wealth data by removing the top and bottom 3 percent of the dependent variable. Trimming the data results in more consistent estimates in the following regressions, although the overall findings are little changed. Second, I decompose assets in the form of home equity and financial wealth. The goal is to determine whether the type of asset has an impact on the likelihood that a household liquidates that asset to pay for expenses in retirement. Given that home equity is much less liquid than financial assets, it would not be surprising that households spend down these assets at different rates.[22]

The results in the basic regression in Panel 1 of Table 9.10 are surprising at first blush – household assets in the last year observed are very similar to or slightly larger than assets in the first year observed. In other words, households do not appear to spend down assets, even by the year prior to death. These results remain whether looking at the younger HRS sample or the older AHEAD cohort, with coefficients on beginning of sample assets between 1.02 and 1.08. In Panel 1, and in the remaining two panels, the R-squared increases modestly with the inclusion of time between first and last year observed, as well as demographic, health, and household type variables. Many of these control variables are statistically significantly different from zero with the expected sign. However, the inclusion of these control variables does not change the interpretation of the regressions, although it slightly reduces the size and significance of the coefficient on beginning of sample asset balances.

TABLE 9.9: *Home Equity vs. Financial Assets, HRS Sample (respondents aged 53–63 in 1994 who died prior to 2012).*

Panel 1.
Responses in 1994

		Total Financial Assets						
		<= 0	$1–$10k	$10,001–$50k	$50,001–$100k	$100,001–$250k	$250,001–$500k	>500k	Total Financial
	<= 0	15.2%	6.5%	4.9%	1.0%	1.7%	1.0%	0.4%	30.7%
	$1–$10k	1.3%	0.7%	0.7%	0.2%	0.2%	0.0%	0.0%	3.1%
Total	$10,001–$50k	4.7%	3.9%	4.8%	1.9%	1.9%	0.6%	0.4%	18.2%
Home	$50,001–$100k	3.7%	3.5%	5.7%	2.8%	3.1%	1.3%	0.7%	20.8%
Equity	$100,001–$250k	1.3%	1.5%	3.4%	2.6%	6.0%	3.6%	3.5%	21.9%
	$250,001–$500k	0.1%	0.1%	0.3%	0.6%	1.2%	0.9%	1.2%	4.4%
	> 500k	0.0%	0.0%	0.0%	0.0%	0.0%	0.0%	0.7%	0.7%
	Total Home	26.3%	16.2%	19.8%	9.1%	14.1%	7.4%	6.9%	100.0%

Note: All data reported in $2012

N = 2,154

19.6 percent of respondents have less than 50k in financial wealth and more than 50k in home equity

9.3 percent of respondents have less than 50k in home equity and more than 50k in financial assets

Panel 2.
Responses in Last Year in Sample Prior to Death

		Total Financial Assets						
	<= 0	$1–$10k	$10,001–$50k	$50,001–$100k	$100,001–$250k	$250,001–$500k	> 500k	Total Financial
<= 0	15.5%	8.3%	6.0%	1.1%	1.6%	0.6%	0.5%	33.6%
$1–$10k	0.6%	0.6%	0.8%	0.0%	0.1%	0.0%	0.0%	2.1%
$10,001–$50k	4.1%	3.0%	4.7%	1.5%	1.4%	0.8%	0.2%	15.7%
$50,001–$100k	2.6%	2.1%	5.2%	2.7%	3.0%	1.1%	0.7%	17.4%
$100,001–$250k	1.5%	1.6%	3.9%	3.2%	4.6%	2.8%	3.8%	21.4%
$250,001–$500k	0.3%	0.1%	0.8%	1.0%	1.4%	1.3%	2.2%	7.1%
> 500k	0.0%	0.0%	0.1%	0.1%	0.4%	0.0%	1.8%	2.4%
Total Home	24.6%	15.7%	21.5%	9.6%	12.5%	6.6%	9.2%	100.0%

(Row group label: Total Home Equity)

Note: All data reported in $2012; N= 2,154
18.20 percent of respondents have less than 50k in financial wealth and more than 50k in home equity
7.80 percent of respondents have less than 50k in home equity and more than 50k in financial assets
Source: Author's calculations using Health and Retirement Survey data

TABLE 9.10: *Determinants of Assets in Last Year Observed, HRS Sample (respondents aged 53–63 in 1994 who died prior to 2012); AHEAD Sample (respondents aged 70+ in 1993 who died prior to 2012)*

Panel 1.
Regression of Net Worth in Last Year Observed

	Dependent Variable: Net Worth – Last Year Observed			
	(1)	(2)	(3)	(4)
	HRS	HRS	AHEAD	AHEAD
Net Worth – First Year Observed	1.078***	1.022***	1.058***	1.005***
Health Controls	N	Y	N	Y
Demographics	N	Y	N	Y
Household Type Controls	N	Y	N	Y
Time between First/Last Observed	N	Y	N	Y
Constant	37946.0***	−35902.7	22452.0***	−5994.8
Number of Observations	1414	1414	2526	2526
R-Squared	0.676	0.690	0.674	0.683

* $p < 0.05$, ** $p < 0.01$, *** $p < 0.001$

Panel 2.
Regression of Home Equity in Last Year Observed, Separate Controls for Home Equity and Financial Assets

	Dependent Variable: Home Equity – Last Year Observed			
	(1)	(2)	(3)	(4)
	HRS	HRS	AHEAD	AHEAD
Home Equity – First Year Observed	0.69***	0.614***	0.81***	0.78***
	(29.30)	(25.16)	(53.58)	(50.49)
Financial Assets – First Year Observed	0.083***	0.077***	0.021***	0.016***
	(18.08)	(17.22)	(5.15)	(3.84)
Health Controls	N	Y	N	Y
Demographics	N	Y	N	Y
Household Type Controls	N	Y	N	Y
Time between First/Last Observed	N	Y	N	Y
Constant	27853***	−25029.9**	3022	−1635
Number of Observations	1414	1414	2526	2526
R-Squared	0.578	0.617	0.575	0.592

* $p < 0.05$, ** $p < 0.01$, *** $p < 0.001$

Panel 3.
Regression of Financial Assets in Last Year Observed, Separate Controls for Home Equity and Financial Assets

	Dependent Variable: Financial Assets – Last Year Observed			
	(1)	(2)	(3)	(4)
	HRS	HRS	AHEAD	AHEAD
Home Equity – First Year Observed	0.39***	0.31***	0.57***	0.53***
	(8.04)	(6.09)	(21.00)	(19.38)
Financial Assets – First Year Observed	0.77***	0.74***	0.64***	0.62***
	(37.97)	(35.04)	(47.71)	(43.81)
Health Controls	N	Y	N	Y
Demographics	N	Y	N	Y
Household Type Controls	N	Y	N	Y
Time between First/Last Observed	N	Y	N	Y
Constant	11632**	−47736.5**	−2830	−51074.9***
Number of Observations	1414	1414	2526	2526
R-Squared	0.614	0.63	0.608	0.618

* $p < 0.05$, ** $p < 0.01$, *** $p < 0.001$
Source: Author's calculations using Health and Retirement Survey data

The next two panels present separate regressions using a dependent variable for first year observed home equity (Panel 2) and financial assets (Panel 3). These results suggest it is important to examine the type of asset when considering changes in asset balances over time.

The home equity regressions show that respondents decrease home equity from the beginning of sample values, as we found in Tables 9.8 and 9.9, with coefficient estimates around 0.65 (HRS) and 0.8 (AHEAD). However, the extent to which the elderly reduce home equity does not appear to depend nearly as much on first-year observed financial assets, with coefficients of only 0.08 (HRS) to 0.02 (AHEAD). All of these coefficients are strongly statistically different than zero.

To better understand these findings, I examine where households live if they have no home equity in the year prior to life. More than two-thirds of borrowers with no home equity are living in a nursing home or assisted living in the last year observed. Thus, rather than selling the home to utilize the assets to support the costs of retirement, most people appear to sell their home as a result of a health care event. The fact that the coefficient on home equity prior to death is well below 1.0 seems to be predominantly a function of when or if a household moves into assisted living. In fact, most households remain homeowners throughout their lives and do not access their housing wealth prior to death. The fact that home equity is partly related to financial assets might be explained by wealthier households having resources to live longer at home.

By contrast, the last year observed financial assets in Panel 4 is highly correlated with the first year observed home equity, with coefficients of about 0.35 (HRS) to approximately 0.55 (AHEAD). This result appears consistent with those in Panel 2. After all, if most homeowners sell their home due to a medical event and move into assisted living, the remaining home equity would be converted into financial assets when the home is sold. This interpretation is consistent with the coefficient on home equity being larger for the AHEAD sample, as the oldest households are more likely to sell a home and move into assisted living.

The pattern of spending down beginning of period financial assets, by contrast, shows an opposite pattern with coefficients around 0.75 (HRS) and 0.6 (AHEAD). Again, it is not surprising that older households spend down financial assets more quickly than younger households. Younger households who die may do so unexpectedly early and thus be left with more assets, whereas older households may be more willing to spend down assets. Nonetheless, households have more than one-half of their first year observed assets in the year prior to death.

Decomposing asset types shows that the mix of assets is an important determinant of the extent to which a household spends assets later in life. While the initial regression that combines assets together suggests that there is little spend down of wealth by the elderly, separating the behavior of housing assets and financial assets gives a much more nuanced view. Households have a much greater propensity to spend financial assets, but not housing wealth.

CONCLUSION

The relationship between housing wealth, mortgages, and retirement readiness is taking on increasing importance as many more households enter retirement age without defined benefit retirement accounts and are thus reliant on assets to support their lifestyle. Home equity is the largest asset for the vast majority of retirement-age households. According to the U.S. Census, in 2011, median net worth including home equity for 65–69-year-olds was $194,000, whereas median net worth without home equity was only $44,000.

This chapter presents some new evidence to better understand the challenges facing near retirees. First, this chapter separately examines changes over time in the movement of mortgage debt, homeownership, and home equity. Often in previous research, the existence of growing mortgage debt is hidden in computations of home equity, which has remained roughly steady over the past 15 years, even as real home prices have risen. Second, I reexamine how households spend down assets up to the year prior to death, separately analyzing home equity and financial assets rather than combining them into a single measure of net worth.

For households with a head aged 66 to 71 and thus of traditional retirement age, the results suggest twin challenges – a large increase in mortgage debt at the same time that more households are paying a mortgage. Real mortgage debt ($2012) rose from $18,000 in 1992 to almost $55,000 in 2013 in this age group. At the same time, the share of households with a mortgage has risen from 25 percent to 41 percent. The combined effect is that more households face a larger debt burden. However, real home equity has remained roughly flat since 2001 at about $110,000, although it is up about $30,000 since 1992. Loan-to-value ratios are up from 22 percent to 48 percent. By any measure, older homeowners today are facing more financial challenges than in previous decades.

Historically, retiring without mortgage debt has been key to financial stability. Homeowners older than age 65 who are paying off a mortgage appear nearly as financially constrained as renters. The Joint Center for Housing Studies of Harvard (2014) reports that 30 percent of owners with a mortgage pay more than one-half of their income in housing costs, leaving few resources available to cover other basic expenses and health care. Similarly, about 30 percent of all older renters pay 50 percent of more of their income in housing expenses.[23]

A second question is whether homeowners can leverage existing home equity or financial assets to help cover their mortgage or other retirement expenses. Here I examine past behavior of elderly homeowners.

The data show, historically speaking, that most households entering retirement age with a mortgage do not fully retire the mortgage debt in retirement. In fact, only about 25 percent to 35 percent of older homeowners with a mortgage in 1992 had paid off their mortgage by the year prior to death. As well, the bulk of homeowners entering retirement age do not appear to spend down home equity, except when they move out of their home to enter assisted living. The elderly appear more willing to spend financial assets while living independently, although households have more than one-half of financial assets remaining in the year prior to death. Unfortunately, about 40 percent of all homeowners with a mortgage have more mortgage debt than financial assets.

In response to these challenges, many households report that they will work longer. The Federal Reserve 2015 *Survey of Household Economics and Decisionmaking* reports that more than one-half of respondents expect to either retire after age 65 or to never retire.[24] The plan to work longer is a recent phenomenon and appears to be driven more by financial necessity than a longer life expectancy. The Employee Benefit Research Institute (Helman et al. 2015) has been surveying individuals for 25 years about their retirement preparedness and expectations. The share of respondents stating that they expected to work after age 65 has grown from 11 percent in 1991 to 23 percent in 2000, to 46 percent by 2015.[25] See Figure 9.5.

Similarly, the EBRI data point out that borrowers who have debt or lack a retirement plan are much less confident in their ability to have enough money to fund retirement.

The problem with working longer, however, is that it may not be feasible for many of the elderly, either due to health problems or the inability to keep or obtain a job, especially for the middle-income or low-income households that this study shows have the largest increase in housing debt. In the EBRI survey, the share of people

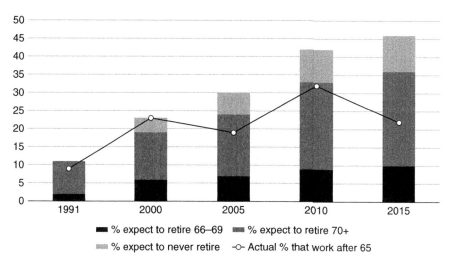

FIGURE 9.5 Late Retirement Expectations vs. Actual Retirement Age
Source: Author's calculations using Employee Benefit Retirement Institute data

actually working after age 65 (22 percent) is about one-half as large as the share who say they intend to work after age 65 (46 percent).[26] This is a striking change from 15 years ago, when worker expectations about working longer seemed to match the reality in the data. A recent Pew study[27] showed that 19 percent of people aged 65 and above are working full- or part-time, up from 13 percent in 2000. This share of the elderly who are working has grown steadily, but the largest increases are in high-income professions like management, sales, and legal, whereas three of the four largest declines are in low-paid professions like food preparation, construction, and production.

Despite these apparent challenges, the elderly poverty rate remains near record lows, so many elderly are getting by with what they have. Of course, the traditional measurement of poverty does not consider asset or debt balances, and the measurement of health care expenses is difficult. Future research should examine the implications of growing debt in retirement and how households manage home equity. How are households paying this debt? Will poverty rates continue to grow? And how do these trends impact taxpayers? Are indebted households more likely to tap Medicaid to pay for at home or nursing home care?

Policy makers and business leaders have proposed a number of solutions to address these challenges. Some propose reform in the type of advice given to workers, the cost of delivering retirement products, and/or the creation of greater incentives for workers to save. Others suggest the development of new or more cost-effective financial products to tap home equity without selling the home[28] or to annuitize existing savings. Nonetheless, the results in this chapter suggest something will need to change in order for many older Americans to have a more comfortable and satisfying retirement.

AUTHOR'S NOTE

The opinions, analysis, and conclusions of this chapter are those of the author. Monica Clodius provided excellent research assistance. This chapter benefited from the help of Jim Poterba and Steve Venti, who shared programs and insights from their previous analysis of the Health and Retirement Survey; Stephanie Moulton, who added helpful suggestions; and Luigi Zingales, who provided great thoughts as the discussant. The research was supported by the Paul Milstein Center for Real Estate at Columbia Business School. Christopher Mayer is CEO of Longbridge Financial, a start-up reverse mortgage lender. Any errors are those of the author.

REFERENCES

Banerjee, Sudipto. 2015. "A Look at the End of Life Financial Situation in America." *EBRI Notes* 36(April): 2–10.
Benartzi, Shlomo, Alessandro Previtero, and Richard H. Thaler. 2011. "Annuitization Puzzles." *Journal of Economic Perspectives* 25(4): 143–64.
Benítez-Silva, Hugo, Selçuk Eren, Frank Heiland, and Sergi Jiménez-Martín. 2010. "Using the Health and Retirement Study to Analyze Housing Decisions, Housing Values, and Housing Prices." *Cityscape* 12(2): 149–58.
Board of Governors of the Federal Reserve System. 2016. "Report on the Economic Well-Being of US Households in 2015." May.
 2014. "Changes in U.S. Family Finances from 2010 to 2013: Evidence from the Survey of Consumer Finances." *Federal Reserve Bulletin* 100(4): 1–41.
Brown, Meta, Donghoon Lee, Joelle Scally, Katherine Strair, and Wilbert van der Klaauw. 2016. "The Graying of American Debt" posted on the blog *Liberty Street Economics*, February 24.
Chetty, Raj, Michael Stepner, Sarah Abraham, Shelby Lin, Benjamin Scuderi, Nicholas Turner, Augustin Bergeron, and David Cutler. 2016. "The Association between Income and Life Expectancy in the United States, 2001–2014." *Journal of the American Medical Association* 315(16): 1750–66.
Coile, Courtney, Kevin S. Milligan, and David A. Wise. 2016. "Health Capacity to Work at Older Ages: Evidence from the U.S." NBER Working Paper No. 21940, January.
Consumer Financial Protection Bureau (CFPB). 2014. "Snapshot of Older Consumers and Mortgage Debt." Report issued by the Office for Older Americans, May.
 2012. "Reverse Mortgages." Report to Congress, June 28.
DeNardi, Mariacristina, Eric French, and John Bailey Jones. 2016. "Savings after Retirement: A Survey." *Annual Review of Economics* 8: 177–204.

Helman, Ruth, Craig Copeland, and Jack VanDerhei. 2015. "The 2015 Retirement Confidence Survey: Having a Retirement Savings Plan a Key Factor in Americans' Retirement Confidence." EBRI Issue Brief No. 413, April.

Greenspan, Alan and James Kennedy. 2005. "Estimates of Home Mortgage Originations, Repayments, and Debt on One-to-Four-Family Residences." Finance and Economics Discussion Series no. 2005–41.

Joint Center for Housing Studies of Harvard University. 2014. *Housing America's Older Adults Meeting the Needs of an Aging Population.*

Korenman, Sanders and Dahlia Remler. 2013. "Rethinking Elderly Poverty: Time for a Health-Inclusive Poverty Measure?" NBER Working Paper No. 18900.

Lucas, Deborah. 2015. "Hacking Reverse Mortgages." MIT Mimeo, October 26.

Moulton, Stephanie, Donald Haurin, Maximilian Schmeiser, and Samuel Dodini. 2016. "How Home Equity Extraction and Reverse Mortgages Affect the Financial Well-Being of Senior Households." Ohio State Working Paper.

Poterba, James, Steven Venti, and David Wise. 2015. "What Determines End-of-Life Assets? A Retrospective View." NBER Working Paper No. 21682, October.

2013. "Health, Education, and the Post-retirement Evolution of Household Assets." *Journal of Human Capital* 7(4): 297–339. Winter.

2012. "Were They Prepared for Retirement? Financial Status at Advanced Ages in the HRS and AHEAD Cohorts." In *Investigations in the Economics of Aging*, David A. Wise, ed., 21–69. Chicago: University of Chicago Press.

2011. "The Composition and Drawdown of Wealth in Retirement." *Journal of Economic Perspectives* 25(4): 95–118.

Short, Kathleen. 2015. "The Supplemental Poverty Measure: 2014." *Current Population Reports*, September.

Sinai, Todd and Nicholas S. Souleles. 2005. "Owner Occupied Housing as a Hedge against Rent Risk." *Quarterly Journal of Economics* 120(2): 763–89.

Trawinsky, Lori A. 2012. "Nightmare on Main Street: Older Americans and the Mortgage Market Crisis." AARP Public Policy Institute Research Report #2012–08.

Wimer, Christopher and Lucas Manfield. 2015. "Elderly Poverty in the United States in the 21st Century: Exploring the Role of Assets in the Supplemental Poverty Measure." Boston College Center for Retirement Research Working Paper 2015–29.

Notes

1. See http://crr.bc.edu/special-projects/national-retirement-risk-index/. The report further notes that "Explicitly including health care in the Index further drives up the share of households 'at risk.'"

2. Fidelity Investments Biennial Retirement Savings Assessment. January 7, 2016. www .fidelity.com/about-fidelity/individual-investing/americas-savings-rate-improves.

3. See the Brookings Institution Retirement, Savings and Pension project at www
   .brookings.edu/research/topics/retirement.
4. In 1940, the average woman (man) aged 21 had only a 61 percent (54 percent)
   chance of living to age 65. By 1990, those odds had risen to 83.4 percent (72.3
   percent). The average woman (man) hitting age 65 today will live more than 21
   (19) years, an increase of 2 (4) years since 1990. (See www.ssa.gov/history/life
   expect.html and www.ssa.gov/OACT/population/longevity.html.) As well,
   recent evidence shows that higher-income earners (who collect higher benefits)
   are living longer (Chetty et al. 2016).
5. See the blog post on Liberty Street Economics titled "The Graying
   of American Debt" by Meta Brown, Donghoon Lee, Joelle Scally,
   Katherine Strair, and Wilbert van der Klaauw (February 24, 2016). http://
   libertystreeteconomics.newyorkfed.org/2016/02/the-graying-of-american-debt
   .html#.Vot8ppMrI6g.
6. Auto loans and student loans also grew for older borrowers, although the overall
   amounts were low.
7. Large majorities of both workers and retirees in annual surveys conducted by the
   Employee Benefit Research Institute appear to be very or somewhat confident
   that they will have enough resources in retirement to cover basic expenses,
   health care costs, and long-term care costs. The high rate of confidence in a
   financially stable retirement has not changed a lot in the past 25 years, even as
   the data show fewer households being prepared for retirement. This seeming
   contradiction seems worthy of future research.
8. That said, policy analysts at the New York Fed (Brown et al. 2016), the
   Consumer Financial Protection Bureau (CFPB 2014), and the AARP
   (Trawinsky 2012) have been warning about a potential coming crisis with
   growing mortgage debt for the elderly.
9. See also Banerjee (2015). DeNardi, French, and Jones (2016) point to uncertainty about medical costs and bequest motives as potentially explaining the
   slow spend down of financial assets.
10. The HRS began as two surveys in its early years. The main HRS sample
    surveyed borrowers ages 51–61 beginning in 1992 and every two years afterward.
    The AHEAD group sampled borrowers aged 70 and above starting in 1993 and
    the same survey years beginning in 1998. The HRS did not track households in
    the intermediate age group until future waves when the data were expanded.
11. While not directly comparable due to different age ranges, the data on home-
    ownership in Table 9.2 are similar to those reported in the U.S. Census data on
    homeownership (reported in Figure 9.3), which has a much larger sample. Due
    to the small sample in the SCF, it is not possible to make inferences about exact
    differences between age groups and years. However, the overall pattern of
    changes over time and across age groups is consistent between these two
    different data sources.
12. These computations assume that all households headed by someone over age 65
    who do not own are renters with a rental payment. This might slightly overstate
    the share of elderly with a housing payment if some of the poorest elderly have

housing that is entirely paid for by one or more government or charitable programs. If an elderly person lived with family, that person would not be considered an independent household.

13. Data from the SCF utilize self-report home values, which have been shown to be slightly over-reported by the elderly (Benítez-Silva et al. 2010). Thus the LTV might be understated.

14. The Case and Shiller National Home Price Index rose from 144.35 in January 2013 to 175.26 in January 2016, an increase of 20.6 percent.

15. According to the Federal Reserve, aggregate mortgage balances have grown only slightly from $13.3 trillion to $13.5 trillion between 2012 and 2015 (Flow of Funds Table L4 as of Q4, 2015).

16. The data for 72–77-year-olds show a slight decline in 2007 relative to 2004 and then a slight increase in 2010. This is likely an anomaly due to measurement error and a small sample size for borrowers in that age group.

17. This ignores any possible tax consequents associated with selling assets in a tax-deferred retirement account like an IRA or a 401(k).

18. Using data from the SCF data in the previous section, older households today likely have even more housing wealth.

19. While it is possible that ending life with few assets was a strategic decision to "spend down" assets in order to qualify for Medicaid (or give away the assets to family members), "look back" provisions in Medicaid have substantially cut down on such strategic behavior. While the "look back" provisions were not in force during the entire sample period, the bulk of households with little to no wealth at end of life also had little wealth entering retirement age, so strategic behavior is likely limited.

20. Whereas 81 years old might seem like an old age, the life expectancy for a single man or woman at age 65 would be 82 and 84 years old, respectively, so many of the HRS sample would have outlived the last wave observed in the survey.

21. The coefficients, sample size, and standard errors differ slightly from Poterba and colleagues (2015) based on differences in sample definition. Results in Panel 1, columns 1 and 3 are materially similar to those in table 3.1 in Poterba and colleagues (2015).

22. Households could use a reverse mortgage to spend down home equity, but reverse mortgages were quite rare during this time period, representing only 2 to 3 percent market share of all eligible elderly homeowners (Consumer Financial Protection Bureau, 2012).

23. More than one-half of older renters pay at least 30 percent of their income in housing expenses.

24. Among respondents who provided an expected retirement age or indicated that they do not expect to ever retire.

25. It is important to note that the retirement age for Social Security is rising over this period, although by a small amount each year, from 65 to 67. The change in the Social Security retirement age is quite gradual, increasing by a year per decade of birth year, whereas these survey results seem to move in a cyclical manner.

26. More than half report retiring earlier than expected due to health problems or disability, while other common reasons for early retirement include changes in the workplace and having to care for a spouse or another family member.
27. See "More older Americans are working, and working more, than they used to," by Drew Desilver, June 20, 2016, Pew Research Center Blog (www .pewresearch.org/fact-tank/2016/06/20/more-older-americans-are-working-and -working-more-than-they-used-to/).
28. See Moulton and colleagues (2016) for a more complete discussion of the various options for tapping home equity among the elderly and Lucas (2015) for a proposal to reform reverse mortgages.

10

The Rise and (Potential) Fall of Disparate Impact Lending Litigation

Ian Ayres, Gary Klein, and Jeffrey West

10.1 INTRODUCTION

For generations, the civil rights community understandably focused its fair housing efforts largely on minority access to affordable housing. Fair Housing Act litigation resources were generally concentrated on whether minority renters and homebuyers were being denied housing opportunities in the first instance. More recently, the focus of some litigation has changed, at least in the context of homeownership, to disparities in the price at which housing is available. In the context of mortgage credit, a series of important private class actions and government investigations under both the Fair Housing Act and the Equal Credit Opportunity Act have focused on discrimination in practices that appear to have driven black and Latino families into higher-cost loans on more onerous terms than similarly situated borrowers. The cases and investigations described in this chapter are grounded largely in the disparate impact of pricing practices that appear to have resulted in hundreds or sometimes thousands of dollars in additional annual credit costs for minority homeowners.

Disparate impact has often been viewed as the poor stepchild of civil rights litigation. Even though the Supreme Court first ruled in 1971 that a discrimination claim based on disparate impact was cognizable,[1] and Congress reaffirmed its status in 1991,[2] the Justice Department's Civil Rights Division didn't bring its first disparate impact case until almost 2010.[3] At the same time, however, there has been a growing recognition by academics as well as by courts that disparate treatment claims were becoming less well suited to combat a variety of civil rights problems (Kreiger and Fiske 2006). Discretionary decision making tainted by unconscious racism can fly below the radar screen of traditional civil rights scrutiny (Lawrence 1987). Disparate impact has offered an alternative approach to combating the detrimental effects of implicit racial bias (Hart 2005; Primus 2010).

This chapter argues that disparate impact proof of discrimination is especially well suited for application to loan transactions, because it can be thoroughly investigated based on the lender's own data records. The commodification of lending has created a system of mass retail selling. While many borrowers see themselves as unique and their financial history as opaque, lenders almost always use algorithmic underwriting standards applied to a core set of underwriting variables. Assessing whether a lender's policies allowing the final price to then be set based on other non-objective factors produced an unjustified disparate impact is straightforward because lenders' own underwriting datasets are, by design, intended to capture information about the variables that the lending industry itself believes are germane to originating and setting the terms of loans. The key statistical evaluation is to ascertain, after controlling for the variables that the lenders themselves have gathered and evaluated, whether minority borrowers were more likely than non-minority borrowers to be charged higher credit costs.

To be sure, there is discretion in choosing the factors evaluated in algorithmic underwriting, but the most important form of discretion is ceded to the sales force who set the ultimate terms of the mortgage and who receive commissions to maximize profit. An important and widespread policy of lenders was to give brokers the discretion to price gouge consumers – if they could induce the borrower to agree to a supra-competitive interest rate or supra-competitive fees. Lenders who were not aware of the race of borrowers at the time of lending could nonetheless be liable for setting up systems that allowed salespeople (who do know the race of their customers) to exercise discretion in way that disproportionately exposed minorities to predatory terms and high-cost loans.

This chapter tracks the rise of disparate impact lending litigation and how subsequent decisions of the Supreme Court and circuit courts have limited the viability of such claims. Part 2 details the history of mortgage lending lawsuits and the kinds of information plaintiffs were able to bring to bear in such cases. Part 3 then discusses the growing judicial resistance to these kinds of claims, particularly in *Wal-Mart Stores, Inc. v. Dukes*, 564 U.S. 338 (2011). Part 4, in speculating on possible futures for disparate impact liability, describes the Consumer Financial Protection Bureau's (CFPB) recent auto-lending initiatives.

10.2 HISTORY OF "REVERSE REDLINING" MORTGAGE LENDING DISPARATE IMPACT LITIGATION

Over the past two decades, a large number of academic studies have explored the relationship between borrower race and the availability or the cost of obtaining residential mortgage loans in the United States. Two literature reviews can be found in White (2009) and Courchane (2007). As explained in greater detail in these reviews, early academic studies focused on the relationship between mortgage denials and the racial composition of neighborhoods (Munnell et al. 1996). Early studies also included audits of lenders. For example, a 1999 study by the Urban Institute found that minorities were offered mortgages at higher rates than whites in similar circumstances (Turner and Skidmore 1999). The Urban Institute findings were based in part on paired audit testing conducted by the National Fair Housing Alliance that was carried out by people of different racial and ethnic backgrounds in a sample of seven cities. Each group of testers – including one white and one or more minorities – told lenders it had similar credit histories, incomes and financial histories, and the same type of mortgage needs. The testing found that minorities were less likely to receive information about loan products, and received less time from loan officers. Most important for our purposes, this audit study found that minorities "were quoted higher interest rates in most of the cities where tests were conducted" (Turner and Skidmore 1999, 2).[4]

These earlier studies were suggestive of significant racial effects, but suffered from an absence of controls for credit risk and other underwriting considerations when examining substantial samples of actual loan originations as opposed to more limited audit tests. Over time, as government reporting requirements improved and litigation and various investigations offered more complete datasets, researchers were able to include a number of additional controls in their studies and developed more complete empirical models of the residential mortgage origination process. Some focused on the impact of race on credit spreads and found statistically significant racial disparities (Avery et al. 2005; Bocian, Ernst, and Li 2006; Fishbein and Woodall 2005, 2006). Later studies expanded this analysis by controlling for loan channels, and found reduced, but still statistically significant racial effect on the APR of mortgage loans (Courchane 2007, LaCour-Little 2009; White 2009). Yet other studies found statistically and economically significant racial disparities in the amount of compensation mortgage brokers earned on residential mortgage originals and in FHA closing costs charged to borrowers (Jackson and Burlingame 2007; Woodward 2008).

The notion that minority borrowers may pay more for home loans than similarly situated white borrowers is not altogether surprising. A wide body of literature has shown that individuals can be influenced (even subconsciously) by race. The theory that the racial disparities in borrowing costs are the by-product (at least in part) of racially influenced credit-pricing decisions in no way implies that loan officers and brokers must harbor animus toward minorities or that they are engaging in intentional discrimination. For example, a number of studies have found that economic decision makers are influenced by racially conscious or unconscious stereotypes (Kirschenman and Neckerman 1991). For example, the Implicit Association Tests[5] suggest that many people of professed goodwill find it impossible to avoid treating African American pictures differently from white pictures when asked to perform a simple sorting exercise. These tests are part of a growing literature documenting unconscious bias against African Americans and other minorities (Chen and Bargh 1997; Dovidio et al. 1986; Niemann et al. 1988; Vanman et al. 1997).

To the extent that economic decision makers often harbor unconscious, but biased racial stereotypes, it becomes more plausible that the subjective pricing process that mortgage lenders established for setting loan terms (in which a loan officer or broker can often plausibly deny that its treatment of an individual consumer was based on some attribute other than race) might mask what are in fact racially influenced decisions. In *Watson v. Fort Worth Bank & Trust, supra*, the Supreme Court's recognition of the existence of subconscious stereotypes was cited as one of the reasons for approving the use of a disparate impact analysis to evaluate the subjective decision-making processes at issue in that case (ibid. at 990). ("Furthermore, even if one assumed that any such discrimination can be adequately policed through disparate treatment analysis, the problem of subconscious stereotypes and prejudices would remain.") Similar reasoning impacted the Supreme Court's decision in *Texas Department of Housing & Community Affairs v. The Inclusive Communities Project, Inc.*, 135 S. Ct. 2507 (2015), where the court held that "[r]ecognition of disparate-impact liability under the FHA plays an important role in uncovering discriminatory intent: it permits plaintiffs to counteract unconscious prejudices and disguised animus that escape easy classification as disparate treatment."

10.2.A Measuring the Effects of Discretionary Decisions on Mortgage Prices

A number of class-action cases have been brought against various lenders regarding the alleged disparate impact resulting from discretionary pricing policies.[6] Plaintiffs in these cases asserted that the defendant lenders engaged in discretionary pricing policies under which the lenders' loan officers, brokers, and correspondent lenders could impose subjective, discretionary charges and interest rate markups in the loans that they originated. These subjective charges are added to the objective, risk-based rates already established by the defendants. Plaintiffs alleged that the defendants' policies for access to their loan products subjected minority customers to a significantly higher likelihood of exposure to discretionary points, fees, and interest rate markups.

These allegations were brought pursuant to the Fair Housing Act (FHA) and the Equal Credit Opportunity Act (ECOA). Although it has been a question of substantial dispute, both civil rights laws clearly permit use of proof of disparate impact to establish discrimination. For the FHA, the Supreme Court recently confirmed this long-standing conclusion of every court of appeals that had considered the question in *Texas Department of Housing & Community Affairs v. The Inclusive Communities Project, Inc., supra*.[7] Both the courts and the CFPB, the agency charged with interpreting the ECOA under the Dodd-Frank Act, have found that that statute also allows for a disparate impact cause of action.[8]

In this section, we focus on *In re Wells Fargo Mortgage Lending Discrimination Litigation* as an exemplar of the kinds of evidence that plaintiffs were able to adduce in these cases.[9] Wells Fargo, like many lenders, made loans both as a retail lender through its branches and mortgages offices and as a wholesale lender through ostensibly independent mortgage brokers. In either channel, Wells Fargo set its core loan prices by using an algorithm applied across a wide range of the borrower's credit characteristics, but allowed its employees and its brokers to earn a commission, within certain limits, by marking up and adding costs to the algorithmically derived price. These markups were at the discretion of Wells Fargo's employees and brokers, were not tethered to credit risk, and yielded a commission, based on a formula for the employee or broker that set them. Wells Fargo published price sheets that showed its core prices (subject to underwriting), the scope of the permitted markup, and the commission structure by which the sales commission for the loan would be tied to the markup. By maximizing discretionary markups, the sales force increased the loan price and maximized commissions.

The case against Wells Fargo asserted that Wells Fargo's sales force used markups most aggressively to increase loan costs for African American and Hispanic borrowers such that Wells Fargo's markup policy resulted in a measurable disparate impact across Wells Fargo's mortgage lending business.[10] To the extent that the markups were imposed by nonemployee brokers, Plaintiffs relied on the longstanding agency principles applicable to the discrimination laws.[11]

The evidence at issue was designed to show the amount by which the loan costs for African American and Hispanic borrowers exceeded those of similarly situated white borrowers. The statistical evaluation presented the actual costs of borrowers with virtually identical credit characteristics as determined in Wells Fargo's underwriting process. In particular, the following tables are taken from the report of Professor Howell Jackson, who served as the plaintiffs' economic expert and provided the crucial statistical tests of disparate impact. Table 10.1 summarizes both the average difference in loan costs (as measured by the Annual Percentage Rate (APR)) for Wells Fargo borrowers of different races as well as the racial differences after controlling for a host of underwriting risk factors. Professor Jackson estimated that the present value of the defendant's overcharges had cost minority borrowers, in aggregate, approximately half a billion dollars.

Of course, simple difference in the average APR charged to minorities and whites might be justified by difference in creditworthiness. Even though statistically significant average APR differences might be prima facie evidence of actionable disparate impacts and therefore shift the burden of justification to the defendant, plaintiffs routinely go further to establish that the disparities persist after controlling in regressions for standard underwriting variables. Because regression analysis remains opaque to many triers of fact, plaintiffs often show that average racial APR disparities persist within individual credit score ranges. Thus, Professor Jackson's report showed (reproduced here as Table 10.2) that within most FICO score bins, the average APR charged to whites was lower – often by dozens of basis points – than the average APR charged to minority borrowers. The persistence of racial APR

TABLE 10.1: *Summary of Disparate Impact and Monetary Relief*

	African Americans	Hispanics	Total
Mean APR for Given Minority	6.940%	6.511%	
Mean APR for Whites	6.266%	6.266%	
Difference	0.674%	0.245%	
Difference after Controlling for Relevant Risk Factors with Regressions	0.101%	0.064%	
Present Value of Relief over Five Years ($Millions)	$297.7	$329.2	$627.0
Number of Loans	294,983	452,471	747,454
Avg. Present Value of Relief per Loan over Five Years ($)	$1,009	$728	$839

Source: Class Certification Report of Howell E. Jackson, In re Wells Fargo Residential Mortgage Lending Discrimination Litigation, M: 08-md-01930 MMC (N.D. Cal. Aug. 6, 2010), at 6, 53

differences even among borrowers with similarly high credit scores particularly underscores that Professor Jackson's finding is not driven by the possibility that minority borrowers tend to have poorer credit scores than white borrowers.

The core evidence of unjustified disparate impacts comes, however, from regressions. Thus, for example, in the following table, Jackson reported four nested specifications testing for racial disparities:

The simplest regression (Model 1) reported in Table 10.3 only includes controls for the borrower race – and in this and the other models the reported coefficients represent the estimated APR differences measured in basis points between the indicated minority race and non-Hispanic white borrowers. Thus, Model 1 indicates that African American borrowers' APRs averaged 67 basis points more than white borrowers. Model 1 in essence provides evidence for a disparate racial impact without considering whether it is business justified. Models 2 and 3 respectively add fixed effects controls for the month in which the interest rate lock occurred and for the FICO score bins reported in Table 10.2. These models show that African American and Hispanic borrowers continued to pay statistically higher APRs than non-Hispanic white borrowers – but that the differentials are roughly halved when one controls for borrowers' FICO score. Finally, Model 4 adds to Model 3 controls for the comprehensive set of underwriting variables listed in the notes to Table 10.3, including loan amount, debt-to-income ratio, loan-to-value ratio, loan type, loan purpose, loan term, occupancy type, property type, borrower history of bankruptcies, foreclosures, collections, and late payments, documentation type, loan amortization type, loan product category (e.g., 30-year fixed, 5-year ARM), prepayment penalty length, and the borrower's state and metropolitan area (MSA). Professor Jackson's specification includes a multitude of controls that could provide plausible business justifications for charging borrowers different APRs. After controlling for all these

TABLE 10.2: *Mean Annual Percentage Rate (APR) by Race and Credit Score, 2001–2007*

	African American		Hispanic		White		Difference Mean between Af. Amer. APR & Mean White APR	Difference between Mean Hisp. APR & Mean White APR
	Loans	Mean APR	Loans	Mean APR	Loans	Mean APR	APR	Mean White APR
Missing score	24,994	6.370	33,811	6.336	190,503	5.986	0.384	0.350
300–539	10,506	8.847	5,163	8.609	25,806	8.875	-0.028	-0.266
540–559	8,615	8.395	5,171	8.149	26,662	8.279	0.116	-0.131
560–579	13,573	8.286	8,752	7.906	45,688	7.954	0.332	-0.048
580–599	18,144	7.984	13,375	7.648	70,260	7.618	0.367	0.031
600–619	22,675	7.609	20,145	7.251	107,043	7.181	0.428	0.070
620–639	29,809	7.333	32,065	7.014	165,535	6.882	0.452	0.133
640–659	30,519	7.086	37,265	6.807	218,907	6.630	0.456	0.177
660–679	31,058	6.776	46,209	6.567	294,162	6.395	0.381	0.172
680–699	29,454	6.562	52,537	6.416	365,036	6.246	0.315	0.170
700–719	26,177	6.424	52,855	6.335	412,046	6.169	0.255	0.166
720–739	22,676	6.355	49,844	6.268	450,023	6.126	0.229	0.143
740–759	21,136	6.263	50,019	6.194	525,970	6.071	0.192	0.123
760–779	18,679	6.171	46,681	6.111	617,954	6.019	0.152	0.092
780–799	14,106	6.124	33,932	6.053	563,555	6.014	0.110	0.039
≥ 800	4,990	6.125	10,610	6.045	211,130	6.055	0.070	-0.010
All Credit Scores	327,111	6.940	498,434	6.511	4,290,280	6.266	0.674	0.245

Source: Class Certification Report of Howell E. Jackson, In re Wells Fargo Residential Mortgage Lending Discrimination Litigation, M: 08-md-01930 MMC (N.D. Cal. Aug. 6, 2010), at 35

TABLE 10.3: *Effect of Race on APR (Basis Points) Using Regressions Estimated on All Loans*

Race	Model (1)	Model (2)	Model (3)	Model (4)
African American	67.39***	62.53***	26.24***	10.10***
	(0.29)	(0.26)	(0.22)	(0.16)
Hispanic	24.53***	24.69***	13.41***	6.39***
	(0.19)	(0.16)	(0.14)	(0.11)
Observations	5,654,985	5,654,985	5,654,985	5,654,985
R-Squared	2.6%	30.7%	46.4%	70.5%
Adjusted R-Squared	2.6%	30.7%	46.4%	70.5%

Note: Standard errors in parentheses.
*** Statistically significant at 1%, ** Statistically significant at 5%, * Statistically significant at 10%.
Coefficients and standard errors for other explanatory variables are shown in Appendix 5 of Professor Jackson's expert report.
Explanatory variables for each model consist of:
Model (1): Race dummy variables only.
Model (2): Race dummy variables and interest rate lock month dummy variables.
Model (3): Same as Model (2), but add FICO score bin dummy variables.
Model (4): Same as Model (3), but add loan amount bin dummy variables, total debt-to-income ratio bin dummy variables, housing debt-to-income ratio dummy variables, loan-to-value (LTV) bin dummy variables, combined loan-to-value (CLTV) bin dummy variables, loan type (conventional, FHA, VA, or RHS) dummy variables, self-employed borrower/co-borrower dummy variable, loan purpose dummy variables, loan term dummy variables (e.g., 15-year, 20-year, 30-year), dummy variables for occupancy type interacted with property type, property subclass dummy variables, dummy variables for credit report items (such as the presence of bankruptcies, foreclosures, collections, and late payments), documentation type dummy variables, loan amortization type dummy variables, loan product category dummy variables (e.g., 30-year fixed, 5-year ARM), escrow waiver dummy variables, length of rate lock dummy variables, rate float-down option dummy variables, lender-paid mortgage insurance dummy variable, combination loan dummy variable, prepayment penalty length dummy variables, state dummy variables, and metropolitan area (MSA) dummy variables.
Source: Class Certification Report of Howell E. Jackson, In re Wells Fargo Residential Mortgage Lending Discrimination Litigation, M: 08-md-01930 MMC (N.D. Cal. Aug. 6, 2010), at 37

underwriting influences, the regression tests find that African Americans and Hispanics still pay higher APRs than non-Hispanic whites who are similarly situated with regard to plausible business justifications – respectively 10.1 and 6.4 basis points higher. Moreover, the regression indicates that these disparities were highly statistically significant ($p < 0.01$). Model 4 thus represents the second stage of testing (and in this case showing) that the disparate racial impact persists after controlling for plausible business justifications.

Professor Jackson used these two racial APR differentials estimated in Model 4 to estimate the monetary relief due to the plaintiff class. Portions of his calculations for monetary relief are reprinted here as Table 10.4.

Professor Jackson calculated how much less the monthly payment for minority borrowers would have been if these borrowers had been charged the expected APR for similarly situated white borrowers. He then calculated the present value of this

TABLE 10.4: *Present Value of Monetary Relief to Wells Fargo Minority Borrowers Using the APRs Predicted by Model (4)*

	African Americans	Hispanics	Total
Present Value of Relief over Entire Loan Term ($Millions)	$923.0	$996.7	$1,919.7
Present Value of Relief over 10 Years ($Millions)	$539.8	$592.9	$1,132.7
Present Value of Relief over Five Years ($Millions)	$297.7	$329.2	$627.0
Number of Loans*	294,983	452,471	747,454
Avg. Present Value of Relief per Loan over 5 Years ($)	$1,009	$728	$839

Note: *Monetary relief calculations are restricted to those loans in Wells Fargo's loan database with APR data.

Source: Class Certification Report of Howell E. Jackson, In re Wells Fargo Residential Mortgage Lending Discrimination Litigation, M: 08-md-01930 MMC (N.D. Cal. Aug. 6, 2010), at 53

monthly differential (discounting at the Treasury rate) under different assumptions of about how long the minority borrowers were subjected to the higher monthly payments. Thus, Table 10.4 shows that if the average minority borrower pays for just five years of inflated fees (before paying off or refinancing their loans), the present value of the expected additional payments is more than $600 million.[12]

10.2.B Predatory Terms

While we have focused on litigation challenging disparate racial impact with regard to the cost of borrowing, a number of lawsuits have alleged that minority borrowers were disproportionately subjected to potentially predatory mortgage terms that artificially increased the risk of default. For example, loan characteristics described as potentially predatory in these lawsuits include higher interest rates reportable under the rate spread thresholds established by the Home Mortgage Disclosure Act (HMDA) regulations,[13] subprime status, high LTVs, high debt-to-income ratios, interest-only payment periods, balloon payments, prepayment penalties, negative amortization, "stated" or no documentation requirement during loan underwriting, and teaser rates (in which the loan's initial interest rate was substantially lower than the interest rate that could be imposed later during the life of the loan).[14] Moreover, some banks used distinct marketing tactics and product development strategies in communities of color that some have argued lead to more expensive loans in those communities. An example is a case that resulted in a $3.5 million jury verdict: *Jones et al. v. Wells Fargo Bank NA, et al.*, Case No.

BC337821 (Ca. Super. Court, LA Cty., 2011). Certainly it would make sense to study whether loan terms are, on average, more favorable at suburban institutions where loan officers are more common, for example, than in urban branches of large national banks where mortgages are more often made through loan brokers. Similarly, examination of advertisements and other marketing materials available in different communities and possibly a renewed focus on paired testing may be useful.

Municipalities, including the cities of Atlanta, Baltimore, Cleveland, Memphis, Los Angeles, Miami, Miami Gardens, and Oakland, have pursued lawsuits against some or all of the four largest lenders (Bank of America, Wells Fargo, JPMorgan Chase, and Citibank), alleging that these lenders disproportionately originated loans with predatory terms to minority borrowers, which increased their likelihood of default, resulted in more foreclosures, and caused the municipalities to suffer damages through losses in property taxes (through decreased property values) and increased municipal services.[15] The defendant lenders argued that the FHA does not cover municipalities seeking monetary recovery for these types of claims. The Supreme Court recently ruled that the municipalities have standing under the FHA and that the cases may go forward, albeit with some admonitions to the underlying courts to consider the question of whether the violations proximately caused the injuries complained of. *Bank of America Corp., v. City of Miami*, Slip Op., 581 U.S. ___ (May 1, 2017) (Stern 2017).

10.2.C DOJ Settlements

The Justice Department's Civil Rights Division during the Obama administration in a series of enforcement actions aggressively pursued disparate impact theories against major mortgage lenders.

10.2.C.1 Countrywide (2011)

In December 2011, the U.S. Department of Justice settled an investigation against Countrywide alleging FHA and ECOA violations between 2004 and 2008. The U.S. Department of Justice alleged that "more than 200,000 Hispanic and African-American borrowers paid Countrywide higher loan fees and costs for their home mortgages than non-Hispanic White borrowers, not based on their creditworthiness or other objective criteria related to borrower risk, but because of their race or national origin" (Complaint, *U.S. v. Countrywide*, 2).[16] The U.S. Department of Justice also alleged that, between 2004 and 2007, "more than 10,000 Hispanic and African-American wholesale borrowers received subprime loans, with adverse terms and conditions such as high interest rates, excessive fees, prepayment penalties, and unavoidable future payment hikes, rather than prime loans from Countrywide, not based on their creditworthiness or other objective criteria related to borrower risk, but because of their race or national origin" (3).

The Justice Department's core evidence was quite similar to the kinds of evidence used in the previous class-action suits (exemplified by Professor Jackson's analysis discussed earlier). The Department found that Hispanic and African American borrowers paid between 13 and 28 basis points more in interest than similarly situated non-Hispanic white borrowers in Countrywide's retail Consumer Markets Division channel from 2004 to 2008, and these disparities were statistically significant (39–40). The Department also found that Hispanic and African American borrowers paid between 12 and 67 basis points more in broker fees than similarly situated non-Hispanic white borrowers in Countrywide's wholesale channel from 2004 to 2008 (65–68). With respect to allegations of steering, the Department concluded:

> Statistical analyses of loan data kept by Countrywide on wholesale 30-year term prime and subprime loans originated by Countrywide between January 2004 and August 2007 demonstrate that on a nationwide basis Hispanics who qualified for a Countrywide home mortgage loan and who obtained wholesale loans from Countrywide had odds between approximately 2.6 and 3.5 times higher than similarly-situated non-Hispanic White borrowers of receiving a subprime loan instead of a prime loan, after accounting for objective credit qualifications. Those odds ratios demonstrate a pattern of statistically significant differences between Hispanic and non-Hispanic White borrowers with respect to their placement by Countrywide in one of these two loan product categories even after controlling for objective credit qualifications such as credit score, loan amount, debt-to-income ratio, loan-to-value ratio, and others. (34)

Moreover, the Department's causal explanation for these disparities emulated the discretionary-pricing theories of the plaintiff class litigation.

> The disparate placement of both Hispanic and African-American wholesale borrowers whom Countrywide determined had the credit characteristics to qualify for a home mortgage loan into subprime loan products, when compared to similarly-situated non-Hispanic White borrowers . . . resulted from the implementation and interaction of Countrywide's policies and practices that: (a) permitted mortgage brokers and Countrywide's own employees to place an applicant in a subprime loan product even if the applicant could qualify for a prime loan product; (b) did not require mortgage brokers or its employees to justify or document the reasons for placing an applicant in a subprime loan product even if the applicant could qualify for a prime loan product; (c) did not require mortgage brokers to notify subprime loan applicants that they could qualify for a prime loan product; (d) created a financial incentive for brokers to place loan applicants in subprime loan products; (e) allowed brokers and Countrywide loan officers and underwriters to request and to grant underwriting exceptions in a subjective, unguided manner; and (f) failed to monitor these discretionary practices to ensure that borrowers were being placed in loan products on a nondiscriminatory basis. (37–38)

The Department settled the case for $335 million.[17]

10.2.C.2 *Wells Fargo (2012)*

In July 2012, using some of the same evidence described earlier, the Justice
Department resolved allegations that Wells Fargo Bank engaged in a pattern or
practice of discrimination against qualified African American and Hispanic borrowers in its mortgage lending from 2004 through 2009 (Complaint, *U.S. v. Wells
Fargo*, 15–16).[18] The Department's investigation showed that the odds that an African
American borrower of a Wells Fargo wholesale channel loan would receive
a subprime loan rather than a prime loan were approximately 2.9 times as high as
the odds for a similarly situated non-Hispanic white borrower from 2004 to 2008.
Over the same time period, the same odds for an African American borrower of
a Wells Fargo retail channel loan were 2.0 times the odds for a similarly situated non-
Hispanic white borrower. The odds that a Hispanic borrower of a Wells Fargo
wholesale channel loan would receive a subprime loan rather than a prime loan
were approximately 1.8 times as high as the odds for a similarly situated non-
Hispanic white borrower from 2004 to 2008. Over the same time period, the same
odds for a Hispanic borrower of a Wells Fargo retail channel loan were 1.3 times the
odds for a similarly situated non-Hispanic white borrower. All of these disparities
were statistically significant (15–16). The Department also found that Wells Fargo
charged minority borrowers in its wholesale channel up to 78 basis points more in
broker fees than similar white borrowers (26).

The settlement provided $125 million in compensation to wholesale borrowers
who were steered into subprime mortgages or who paid higher fees and rates than
white borrowers because of their race or national origin (Consent Order,
U.S. v. Wells Fargo, 13).[19] In addition, Wells Fargo agreed to internally review its
retail mortgage lending policies and to compensate African American and Hispanic
retail borrowers who were placed into subprime loans when similarly qualified white
retail borrowers received prime loans (21–22). Wells Fargo also agreed to provide
$50 million in down payment assistance for new loans to borrowers in communities
around the country that were especially hard hit by the housing crisis (18–19).

10.2.C.3 *Sage Bank (2015)*

In 2015, the Justice Department reached a smaller settlement on similar theories
with Massachusetts-based Sage Bank. The United States alleged that Sage had set
a target price for each mortgage loan and allowed loan officers to mark up loans
above that target (Complaint, *U.S. v. Sage Bank*).[20] It further alleged that the
discretion was exercised in a manner that resulted in higher prices for African
American and Hispanic borrowers. Sage agreed to practice changes and to create
a fund of just over $1 million in compensation for affected borrowers (Consent
Order, *U.S. v. Sage Bank*, 4–10).[21]

10.3 REJECTION OF STATISTICAL ANALYSIS AS A BASIS FOR CERTIFICATION OF A DISPARATE IMPACT CLASS

In *Dukes v. Wal-Mart Stores, Inc.*, plaintiffs brought an ambitious broad-based challenge to Wal-Mart's treatment of its female employees. Although the plaintiffs successfully sought class certification in the district court in a decision that was ultimately affirmed both by a panel of the Ninth Circuit and by the Ninth Circuit sitting *en banc* (603 F. 3d 571 (9th Cir. 2010)), the Supreme Court reversed in a far reaching decision on what it means to have a "common question" under the class-action rule and on the use of statistical analysis to establish commonality in a disparate impact case (*Wal-Mart Stores, Inc. v. Dukes*, 564 U.S. 338 (2011)).

From its inception, the *Wal-Mart* class action involved claims of both disparate treatment and disparate impact regarding the hiring and promotion of more than a million female employees. The plaintiffs alleged that the company delegated employment decisions to local managers who intentionally discriminated against women. The Supreme Court held that if employment discrimination is alleged to occur because local managers are exercising discretion in a discriminatory manner, no common issue exists for purposes of class certification. The Court explained that the company essentially had a policy against having uniform employment practices (355). Accordingly, managers "were left to their own devices" to determine criteria for making hiring and promotion decisions for millions of employees (355). The Court concluded (in a 5–4 decision) that granting employees discretion was the antithesis of having a policy:

> The only corporate policy that the plaintiffs' evidence convincingly establishes is Wal-Mart's "policy" of allowing discretion by local supervisors over employment matters. On its face, of course, that is just the opposite of a uniform employment practice that would provide the commonality needed for a class action; it is a policy against having uniform employment practices. (355)

The Court thus found that where there was no challenge to a uniform policy or practice, a court would need to look at millions of individual decisions by the local managers (352). The Court explained there needs to be "some glue holding the alleged reasons for all those decisions together" to meet the commonality requirement (352). Class certification was therefore not possible.[22]

In reaching this conclusion, the Court rejected the plaintiffs' view that adequate statistical analysis could function as "glue" by establishing that Wal-Mart's grant of discretion had a statistically significant overall discriminatory impact on female employees. Notably, this rejection appears to be inconsistent with the driving impetus behind a "disparate impact" claim itself and is therefore an implicit rejection of *Watson* and perhaps even *Griggs*.

The "impact" of any policy is represented by its aggregate effects. Where those effects tend to fall negatively on a protected class, a conclusion of discrimination is appropriate even if not every class member is affected. In *Griggs*, for example, some

African American applicants apparently did have high school diplomas; nevertheless, the Supreme Court correctly recognized that the overall effect of the diploma requirement fell more heavily on African American applicants. Similarly, some applicants, with or without diplomas, would properly be denied employment irrespective of their educational background.[23] A disparate impact claim arises from the negative impact of being subjected to the policy in the first instance, particularly if the impact is demonstrated by a measurable factor such as loan cost. A policy that results in an average increase in the amount charged to members of a protected class affects borrowers both above and below the mean loan payment. That is, a disparate impact claimant paying below the mean might have a payment even further below the mean absent the impact of the policy.

It would be well-nigh impossible for the individual evidence of the impact of any corporate policy in employment or lending, particularly one granting discretionary autonomy to those making subjective decisions, to point in a single direction across a large group of individuals. *Wal-Mart's* class certification rubric, taken at face value, may thus render any group private remedy for disparate impact unachievable.[24] Despite this, the Supreme Court explicitly declined to overrule *Watson v. Fort Worth Bank and Trust*, 487 U.S. 977 (1988) in which the court concluded:

> We are also persuaded that disparate impact analysis is in principle no less applicable to subjective employment criteria than to objective or standardized tests. In either case, a facially neutral practice, adopted without discriminatory intent, may have effects that are indistinguishable from intentionally discriminatory practices. ... If an employer's undisciplined system of subjective decision-making has precisely the same effects as a system pervaded by impermissible intentional discrimination, it is difficult to see why Title VII's proscription against discriminatory actions should not apply. ... We conclude, accordingly, that subjective or discretionary employment practices may be analyzed under the disparate impact approach in appropriate cases. (990–91)

As one judge noted in *Miller v. Countrywide*, 571 F.Supp.2d 251, 258 (D. Mass. 2008), a mortgage lending discrimination case against Countrywide:

> Where the allocation of subjective decision-making authority is at issue, the "practice" amounts to the absence of a policy, that allows racial bias to seep into the process. Allowing this "practice" to escape scrutiny would enable companies responsible for complying with anti-discrimination laws to "insulate" themselves by "refrain[ing] from making standardized criteria absolutely determinative." *Watson*, 487 U.S. at 990. This is especially the case in this context. Unlike in the employment context, subjective criteria, unrelated to creditworthiness, should play no part in determining a potential borrower's eligibility for credit.

By neglecting to recognize that a policy permitting discretionary decision making can let bias enter the system and that the overall effect of that bias can present a common question, the Supreme Court's analysis of class certification of a disparate impact claim in *Wal-Mart* undermines, or perhaps eviscerates, *Watson*. To reconcile *Wal-Mart* and *Watson*, if it's possible, one needs to look carefully, on a case-by-case basis, at the nature of the available proof.

If *Wal-Mart* makes sense as a rubric for disparate impact, it is perhaps only in connection with evaluating which individuals are entitled to damages. Absent analysis of each individual outcome, it is perhaps difficult to assess the monetary impact of the discriminatory effect in order to provide appropriate compensation. Traditionally, courts dealt with this by awarding injunctive relief and disgorgement or other forms of equitable penalties to be split among those exposed to the policy.[25] More recently, however, cases like *Coleman v. GMAC* made clear that any relief for the individual effects of discrimination was unavailable to be awarded in conjunction with class certification for injunctive relief (Cubita, Willis, and Selkowitz 2015).

Wal-Mart put a final nail in this coffin. Not only was certification for injunctive relief rejected, but by rejecting statistical evidence of the disparate effect of discretion as a valid basis for evaluating commonality under the class-action rule, one never gets to the question of whether injunctive relief, let alone whether monetary relief consistent with the injunction, is available. This is because finding commonality under Rule 23(a)(2) is a prerequisite to evaluating whether injunctive relief under 23(b)(2) is available at all.[26] Absent the injunction, monetary relief incidental to the injunction never comes into play.

After *Wal-Mart*, almost no class remedies based on the impact of discretionary decision making remain.[27] Remarkably, in *Rodriguez v. National City Bank*,[28] the Court concluded that a bank could not even choose to settle a disparate impact mortgage lending claim against it for a class, because commonality under the class-action rule was necessary to approve the settlement. Seven million dollars that the bank was willing to pay to African American and Hispanic mortgage borrowers to settle claims was therefore returned to the bank and the class members were left with no remedy.

For private plaintiffs, *Texas Department of Housing & Community Affairs v. The Inclusive Communities Project, Inc., supra*, provides little comfort.[29] Although *Inclusive Communities* does reaffirm the availability of disparate impact to establish discrimination under the FHA, it imposes restrictions on disparate impact claims that would doom any but the least ambitious disparate impact cases. *Inclusive Communities* emphasizes the importance of adequate safeguards at the *prima facie* stage to make sure that the prospect of disparate impact liability does not "almost inexorably lead" to the imposition of quotas and thus raise "serious constitutional questions." In particular, *Inclusive Communities* exhorts judges to apply a "robust causality requirement" under which "a statistical disparity must fail if the plaintiff cannot point to a defendant's policy or policies causing that disparity" (Hancock and Glass 2015). Moreover, even when plaintiffs can establish a *prima facie* case of disparity, the *Inclusive Communities* decision arguably expanded the scope of the defendant's business necessity defense by finding that "policies are not contrary to the disparate-impact requirement unless they are 'artificial, arbitrary, and unnecessary barriers.'" It is hard to see how this restriction can apply in the context of subjective decision-making processes that tend to result in biased choices. Again, *Watson* and its progeny may be nothing but dead letters.

Perhaps, after *Wal-Mart*, the Court is starting to move back toward the science of statistics as a tool for evaluating class cases. In *Tyson Foods, Inc. v. Bouaphakeo*, 136 S. Ct. 1036 (2016), the Court concluded that average time to don and doff equipment could be a basis fairly to award damages to class members with Fair Labor Standards Act claims for uncompensated time that they spent preparing for work.[30] The Court concluded that statistical evidence may be used to certify and provide relief in a class action if the same sampling techniques could be used to establish liability in an individual action. Perhaps this points to an approach to measuring impact. If individuals can use representative statistics to show that their loan price exceeds what they might have paid if they were white, that same evidence should be equally available to the group.

10.4 POSSIBLE FUTURES

The foregoing impediments to private class-action litigation have coincided with the emergence of the CFPB as an active enforcer of ECOA disparate impact claims. The CFPB has been aggressive in "reminding" lenders that ECOA prohibits policies that result in a disparate racial impact unless those policies "meet a legitimate business need that cannot reasonably be achieved as well by means that are less disparate in their impact" (CFPB 2012). The Bureau has been aggressive in interpreting ECOA to apply to so-called "indirect lenders" – who, for example, may have arrangements to purchase loans from car dealerships at pre-established "buy rates" (CFPB 2013). A CFPB Bulletin explains:

> Some indirect auto lenders may be operating under the incorrect assumption that they are not liable under the ECOA for pricing disparities caused by markup and compensation policies because Regulation B provides that "[a] person is not a creditor regarding any violation of the [ECOA] or [Regulation B] committed by another creditor unless the person knew or had reasonable notice of the act, policy, or practice that constituted the violation before becoming involved in the credit transaction." This provision limits a creditor's liability for another creditor's ECOA violations under certain circumstances. But it does not limit a creditor's liability for its own violations – including, for example, disparities on a prohibited basis that result from the creditor's own markup and compensation policies. (CFPB 2013)

Notwithstanding the *Wal-Mart* finding that granting discretion is "opposite of a uniform employment practice," the CFPB has notified indirect lenders that discretion-granting policies that "permit dealers to increase consumer interest rates and that compensate dealers with a share of the increased interest revenues" may be actionable (CFPB 2013).

The Bureau's aggressive stance has not been limited to just its interpretation of ECOA's scope, but also in calling for "institutions subject to CFPB jurisdiction, including indirect auto lenders" to develop "a robust fair lending compliance management program" that includes regular assessment of lending policies "for potential fair lending violations, including potential disparate impact." To avoid liability, indirect and direct lenders "should take steps to ensure that they are operating in compliance with the ECOA and Regulation [B]," including possibly "imposing controls on dealer markup" or "eliminating dealer discretion to mark up buy rates and fairly compensating dealers using another mechanism, such as a flat fee per transaction" (CFPB 2013). Thus, the CFPB has felt empowered to call on indirect lenders such as GMAC or Ford Motor Credit to exert their influence to substantially restructure dealership compensation or to engage in an ongoing manner in the same kinds of number-crunching undertaken by plaintiffs in the previous section.

The Bureau has translated these regulatory positions into a series of enforcement actions that have resulted in a series of multimillion-dollar settlements that have attracted the lending industry's attention and ire. For example, in December 2013, the CFPB and the Justice Department ordered Ally Bank to pay $80 million in damages to consumers harmed by Ally's auto loan pricing policies. The agencies found that "Ally's markup policy resulted in African-American, Hispanic, Asian and Pacific Islander borrowers paying more for auto loans than similarly situated non-Hispanic white borrowers" (Ficklin 2016).

Other actors, including cities and counties as well as national and local groups, that can assert standing under the civil rights laws may continue to pursue disparate impact claims that do not require class certification. Unfortunately, it is less clear that these actions can provide specific and targeted remedies for the economic harm to individuals that is associated with disparate pricing.

Finally, the principles described in this chapter may not apply to class-action cases designed to test the discriminatory impact of discrete practices, unrelated to discretion available to decision makers, that may lead to either disparate treatment or disparate impact claims. For example, if a bank assigns mortgage officers to its branches in white communities[31] while making loans through a network of high-cost brokers in minority communities, class certification and class remedies may remain viable. Some of these practices may emerge most clearly as explanatory in communities of color where rates of foreclosure remain persistently high.

Some may argue that litigation remedies, whether initiated by private actors or governmental entities, are among the least efficient methods for establishing discipline and fairness in the housing market. Whether one accepts this premise turns on one's views about voluntary compliance with new regulation, including the changes associated with Dodd-Frank, as well as one's beliefs about the effectiveness of competition to regulate markets, and about whether new tools can achieve more complete consumer understanding of complex transactions. Others in this volume address those issues directly or indirectly (see, e.g., Bostic and Orlando, Chapter 13, this volume). Our view is that absent effective enforcement mechanisms, including meaningful opportunities for aggregation of claims, new mechanisms will be found to discriminate by manipulating the cost of housing credit for those least able to afford high credit prices.

10.5 CONCLUSION

The motivating force behind applying disparate impact theories to mortgage lending has been the happenstance that the defendants collect and retain all of the borrower characteristics that are relevant to the defendants' underwriting decisions. Defendants are, in an important sense, estopped from criticizing plaintiffs' regressions for not controlling relevant variables when the plaintiffs have controlled for all the variables that defendants relied on in their own underwriting.

However, given the increased hostility to class actions and private disparate impact claims, it is uncertain whether private plaintiffs can feasibly pursue such claims. At the moment, it seems most likely that disparate impact discipline of lenders will come from government enforcers, especially the CFPB.

AUTHORS' NOTE

The authors were involved as lawyers or expert consultants on a number of cases raising claims of disparate racial impacts in mortgage lending. Mr. Klein worked on many of the cases discussed in this chapter as a partner at Klein Kavanagh Costello, LLP before joining the Massachusetts attorney general's office. The views expressed in this chapter are not necessarily the views of the Massachusetts attorney general's office.

REFERENCES

Avery, Robert B. et al. 2005. "New Information Reported Under HMDA and Its Application in Fair Lending Enforcement." *Federal Reserve Bulletin* (Summer): 344–94.

Bocian, Debbie Gruenstein, Keith S. Ernst, and Wei Li. 2006. "Unfair Lending: The Effect of Race & Ethnicity on the Price of Subprime Mortgages." *Center for Responsible Lending.* May 31. www.responsiblelending.org/mortgage-lend ing/research-analysis/rr011-Unfair_Lending-0506.pdf.

Case Note. 2015. "Fair Housing Act – Disparate Impact and Racial Equality – Texas Department of Housing & Community Affairs v. Inclusive Communities Project, Inc." Harvard Law Review 129(1): 321–330.

"CFPB and DOJ Order Hudson City Savings Bank to Pay $27 Million to Increase Mortgage Credit Access in Communities Illegally Redlined." 2015. *Consumer*

Finance Protection Bureau. September 24. www.consumerfinance.gov/about -us/newsroom/cfpb-and-doj-order-hudson-city-savings-bank-to-pay-27-mil lion-to-increase-mortgage-credit-access-in-communities-illegally-redlined/.

"CFPB Bulletin 2013–02: Indirect Auto Lending and Compliance with the Equal Credit Opportunity Act." 2013. *Consumer Finance Protection Bureau*. March 21. http://files.consumerfinance.gov/f/201303_cfpb_march_-Auto-Finance-Bulletin.pdf.

"CFPB to Pursue Discriminatory Lenders." 2012. *Consumer Finance Protection Bureau*. April 18. www.consumerfinance.gov/about-us/newsroom/consumer -financial-protection-bureau-to-pursue-discriminatory-lenders/.

Chen, Mark and John A. Bargh. 1997. "Nonconscious Behavioral Confirmation Processes: The Self-Fulfilling Consequences of Automatic Stereotype Activation." *Journal of Experimental Social Psychology* 33(5) (September): 541–60.

Courchane, Marsha J. 2007. "The Pricing of Home Mortgage Loans to Minority Borrowers: How Much of the APR Differential Can We Explain?" *Journal of Real Estate Research* 29(4) (November): 399–439.

Cubita, Peter N., Christopher J. Willis, and Jonathan E. Selkowitz. 2015. "Auto Finance and Disparate Impact: Substantive Lessons Learned from Class Certification Decisions." *Consumer Financial Services Law Report* 18(21) (May 1): 6–11.

Dovidio, John F. et al. 1986. "Racial Stereotypes: The Contents of Their Cognitive Representations." *Journal of Experimental Social Psychology* 22(1) (January): 22–37.

Ficklin, Patrice. 2016. "Harmed Ally Borrowers Have Been Sent $80 Million in Damages." *Consumer Finance Protection Bureau*. January 29. www.consumer finance.gov/about-us/blog/harmed-ally-borrowers-have-been-sent-80-million -in-damages/.

Fishbein, Allen J and Patrick Woodall. 2006. "Subprime Locations: Patterns of Geographic Disparity in Subprime Lending." *Consumer Federation of America*. September 5. www.consumerfed.org/pdfs/SubprimeLocationsStudy090506.pdf.

2005. "Subprime Cities: Patterns of Geographic Disparity in Subprime Lending." *Consumer Federation of America*. September 8. www.consumerfed.org/pdfs/Subprimecities090805.pdf.

Hancock, Paul and Andrew C. Glass. 2015. "The Supreme Court Recognizes but Limits Disparate Impact in Its Fair Housing Act Decision." *Supreme Court of the United States Blog*. June 26. www.scotusblog.com/2015/06/paul-hancock -fha/.

Hart, Melissa. 2005. "Subjective Decisionmaking and Unconscious Discrimination." *Alabama Law Review* 56(3): 741–91.

Heckman, James J. 1998. "Detecting Discrimination." *Journal of Economic Perspectives* 12(2): 101–16.

Jackson, Howell E. and Laurie Burlingame. 2007. "Kickbacks or Compensation: The Case of Yield Spread Premiums." *Stanford Journal of Law, Business, and Finance* 12(2): 289–361.

Kirschenman, Joleen and Kathryn M. Neckerman. 1991. "'We'd Love to Hire Them But . . .': The Meaning of Race to Employers." In *The Urban Underclass*, Christopher Jencks and Paul E. Peterson, eds., 203. Washington, DC: The Brookings Institution.

Krieger, Linda H. and Susan T. Fiske. 2006. "Behavioral Realism in Employment Discrimination Law: Implicit Bias and Disparate Treatment." *California Law Review* 94(4): 997–1062.

LaCour-Little, Michael. 2009. "The Pricing of Mortgages by Brokers: An Agency Problem?" *Journal of Real Estate Research* 31(2) (October): 235–64.

Lawrence, Charles R., III. 1987. "The Id, the Ego, and Equal Protection: Reckoning with Unconscious Racism." *Stanford Law Review* 39(2) (January): 317–88.

Munnell, Alicia H. et al. 1996. "Mortgage Lending in Boston: Interpreting HMDA Data." *American Economic Review* 86(1) (March): 25–53.

Niemann, Yolanda F. et al. 1998. "Intergroup Stereotypes of Working Class Blacks and Whites: Implications for Stereotype Threat." *Western Journal of Black Studies* 22(2): 103–08.

Perez, Thomas E. 2011. "Assistant Attorney General for the Civil Rights Division Thomas E. Perez Speaks at the National Community Reinvestment Coalition Annual Conference Luncheon." U.S. Department of Justice. April 15. www.justice.gov/opa/speech/assistant-attorney-general-civil-rights-divi sion-thomas-e-perez-speaks-national-community.

Primus, Richard. 2010. "The Future of Disparate Impact." *Michigan Law Review* 108 (8): 1341–87.

Rugh, Jacob S., Len Albright, and Douglas S. Massey. 2015. "Race, Space, and Cumulative Disadvantage: A Case Study of the Subprime Lending Collapse." *Social Problems* 62(2): 186–218.

Stern, Mark Joseph. 2017. "Will Fair Housing Stay?" *Slate*. May 1. http://www.slate .com/articles/news_and_politics/jurisprudence/2017/05/in_bank_of_ameri ca_v_miami_the_supreme_court_strengthens_the_fair_housing.html.

Turner, Margery Austin and Felicity Skidmore. 1999. *Mortgage Lending Discrimination: A Review of Existing Evidence*. Washington, DC: The Urban Institute.

Vanman, Eric J. et al. 1997. "The Modern Face of Prejudice and Structural Features That Moderate the Effect of Cooperation on Affect." *Journal of Personality & Social Psychology* 73(5) (November): 941–59.

White, Alan M. 2009. "Borrowing While Black: Applying Fair Lending Laws to Risk-Based Mortgage Pricing." *South Carolina Law Review* 60(3): 677–706.

Woodward, Susan E. 2008. "A Study of Closing Costs for FHA Mortgages." U.S. *Department of Housing & Urban Development*. May. www.huduser.gov /Publications/pdf/FHA_closing_cost.pdf.

Zatz, Noah. "Disparate Impact and the Unity of Equality Law." *Boston University Law Review* 97 (forthcoming). http://ssrn.com/abstract=2730845.

Notes

1. *Griggs v. Duke Power Co.*, 401 U.S. 424 (1971).
2. Civil Rights Act of 1991 Pub. L. No. 102–166, 105 Stat. 1071 (codified in various sections of 42 U.S.C (Supp. III 1992)).
3. Perez (2011). ("A [disparate impact] case of this nature would not have been brought in the previous administration, because disparate impact claims were not allowed, even though every circuit in the country where the issue has been presented has determin[ed] that disparate impact theory is viable.")
4. See also Turner and Skidmore (1999, 30–31) (interest rate offered African Americans statistically greater than those offered whites only in Atlanta tests). The report also found:

   > One early analytic study found discrimination against Blacks and Hispanics in interest rates and loan fees but not in loan maturities. Another also found discrimination against Blacks in the setting of interest rates. Both studies used extensive statistical controls to isolate the effect of race and ethnicity from the effects of other factors. Two more recent studies examine discrimination in overages, defined as the excess of the final contractual interest rate over the lender's official rate when it first commits to a loan. Both of these studies find cases in which the overages charged to Black and Hispanic borrowers are higher than those charged white customers by a small but statistically significant amount.

   Ibid. at 19. Paired audit studies have been questioned however for adequately controlling for unobservables (Heckman 1998).
5. *Project Implicit*, at https://implicit.harvard.edu/implicit/.
6. Such claims were found viable and withstood dismissal in at least seven reported district court opinions: *Miller v. Countrywide Bank, N.A.*, 571 F. Supp. 2d 251 (D. Mass. 2008); *Ramirez v. GreenPoint Mortg. Funding, Inc.*, 633 F. Supp. 2d 922 (N.D. Cal. 2008); *Ware v. Indymac Bank*, 534 F. Supp. 2d 835 (N.D. Ill. 2008); *Zamudio v. HSBC North America Holdings, Inc.*, No. 07-C-4315, 2008 WL 517138 (N.D. Ill. Feb. 20, 2008); *Martinez v. Freedom Mortg. Team, Inc.*, 527 F. Supp. 2d 827 (N.D. Ill. 2007); *Newman v. Apex Financial Group, Inc.*, No. 07 C 4475, 2008 WL 130924 (N.D. Ill. Jan. 11, 2008); *Jackson v. Novastar Mortg., Inc.*, 645 F. Supp. 2d 636 (W.D. Tenn. 2007).
7. See also *infra* note 27 and accompanying text. The Massachusetts Attorney General's Office appeared in the Supreme Court as an amicus party in support of this aspect of the holding. It did not take a position on other issues in that case discussed in this chapter.
8. See, e.g., *Wise v. Union Acceptance Corp.*, No. IP 02–0104-C-M/S, 2002 WL 31730920 at *3 (S.D. Ind. Nov. 19, 2002) (gathering cases). The text of the ECOA clearly implies that disparate impact is a method of proving discrimination under that statute: "In determining the amount of [punitive] damages in any action, the court shall consider, among other relevant factors, the amount of any actual damages awarded, the frequency and persistence of failures of compliance by the creditor, the resources of the creditor, *the number of persons adversely affected*, and *the extent to which the creditor's failure of compliance was intentional*." 15 U.S.C. § 1691e(b) (emphasis added). This is consistent with the applicable regulatory determination. 12 C.F.R. Pt. 202, Supp. I, § 202.6(a)2.

Official Staff Interpretations. See also *Smith v. City of Jackson*, 544 U.S. 228, 244 (2005) (agency interpretation that disparate impact analysis is applicable to discrimination statute is entitled to deference) (Scalia J. concurring).

9. In re Wells Fargo Residential Mortg. Lending Discrimination Litigation, M: 08-md-01930 MMC (N.D. Cal. 2011). We were involved as lawyer and consultants in this matter. We also conducted statistical analyses of disparate impact against minorities in similar cases against several other lenders. See In re First Franklin Financial Corp., No. C08-01515JW (HRL) (N.D. Cal. 2010); *Ramirez v. Greenpoint Mortg. Funding, Inc.*, 268 F.R.D. 627 (N.D. Cal. 2010); *Barrett v. Option One Mortg. Corp.*, 2012 WL 407465 (D. Mass., Sept. 18, 2012); In re: Countrywide Financial Corp. Mortg. Lending Practices Litigation, 708 F.3d 704 (6th Cir. 2013); *Rodriguez v. Nat'l City Bank*, 726 F.3d 372 (3d Cir. 2013); *Guerra v. GMAC LLC*, 2:08-CV-01297-LDD, 2009 WL 449153 (E.D. Pa. Feb. 20, 2009).

10. Some of the Wells Fargo cases also alleged steering, mostly by asserting that minority applicants who qualified for prime loans were instead steered into less favorable loan channels, or were otherwise pressured to accept subprime loans. Those claims were supported, in part, by testimony of ex-employees who alleged patterns of intentional discrimination. The statistical record on this issue was inconclusive and is not discussed here.

11. E.g., *Marr v. Rife*, 503 F.2d 735, 741 (6th Cir. 1974).

12. Because loan servicing has become unmoored from loan origination, lenders retained relatively little data on the performance of the loans they made during the time period relative to these cases. Recent evidence that higher loan costs lead to increased foreclosures is not surprising. Charging higher prices to those least able to afford them makes foreclosure a self-fulfilling prophecy. Indeed, as foreclosures in certain neighborhood multiply, the impact on property values can contribute to a spiraling foreclosure problem. See Rugh, Albright, and Massey (2015).

13. For loans originated from 2004 to 2010, the spread between a loan's APR and a benchmark Treasury security of comparable maturity would be reported if the spread was three percentage points for first-lien loans or five percentage points for subordinate-lien loans. For loans originated since 2010, the spread between a loan's APR and survey-based estimate of APRs offered on prime mortgages of a comparable type would be reported if the spread was 1.5 percentage points for first-lien loans or 3.5 percentage points for subordinate-lien loans. Federal Financial Institutions Examination Council, *History of HMDA*, www.ffiec.gov/hmda/history2.htm.

14. See, e.g., *Adkins v. Morgan Stanley*, No. 1:12-cv-7667-HB (S.D. N.Y. filed Oct. 15, 2012); *Saint-Jean v. Emigrant Mortg. Co.*, No. 1:11-cv-02122-SJ (E.D. N.Y. filed Apr. 29, 2011); *City of Los Angeles v. Bank of America Corp.*, Case No. 2:13-cv-09046-PA (AGRx) (C.D. Cal. filed Dec. 6, 2013). Two of us have served as consultants on these cases.

15. See, e.g., *Mayor of Baltimore v. Wells Fargo Bank, N.A.*, No. 1:08-cv-00062-JFM (D. Md. filed Oct. 21, 2010); *City of Memphis v. Wells Fargo Bank, N.A.*, No. 2:09-

cv-02857x-STA-dkv (W.D. Tenn. filed Apr. 7, 2010); *City of Los Angeles v. Wells Fargo & Co.*, No. 2:13-cv-09007-ODW (RZx) (C.D. Cal. filed Dec. 5, 2013); *City of Los Angeles v. Citigroup, Inc.*, No. 2:13-cv-09009-SVW (JCx) (C.D. Cal. filed Dec. 5, 2013); *City of Miami v. JPMorgan Chase & Co.*, No. 1:14-cv-22205-WPD (S.D. Fla. filed Nov. 30, 2015), *City of Miami Gardens v. Wells Fargo & Co.*, No. 1:14-cv-22203-FAM (S.D. Fla. filed Sept. 21, 2015); *City of Oakland v. Wells Fargo & Co.*, No. 3:15-cv-04321-EMC (N.D. Cal. filed Sept. 21, 2015). Many of these cases are in active litigation at the writing of this chapter, and two of us have served as consultants on several of these matters.

16. Complaint, *U.S. v. Countrywide Financial Corp.*, No. 2:11-cv-10540-PSG-AJW (C.D. Cal. filed Dec. 21, 2011), at 2.

17. Consent Order, *U.S. v. Countrywide Financial Corp.*, No. 2:11-cv-10540-PSG-AJW (C.D. Cal. Dec. 28, 2011), at 5.

18. Complaint, *U.S. v. Wells Fargo Bank, NA*, No. 1:12-cv-01150 (D.D. C. filed July 12, 2012). We served as consultants for the Department of Justice in its investigation of Wells Fargo.

19. Consent Order, *U.S. v. Wells Fargo Bank*, NA, No. 1:12-cv-01150 (D.D.C. July 12, 2012), at 13.

20. Complaint, *U.S. v. Sage Bank*, No. 1:15-cv-13969 (D. Mass. Nov. 30, 2015).

21. Consent Order, *U.S. v. Sage Bank*, No. 1:15-cv-13969 (D. Mass. Nov. 30, 2015), at 4–10.

22. After *Wal-Mart*, a number of courts reconsidered a prior grant of class certification in disparate impact cases with varied outcomes. Compare, e.g., *Ellis v. Costco Wholesale Corporation*, 285 F.R.D. 492 (N.D. Cal. 2012) (reaffirming class certification in an employment discrimination case after remand from the 9th Circuit – (See *Ellis v. Costco Wholesale Corp. ("Ellis II ")*, 657 F.3d 970 (9th Cir.2011)) – requiring reconsideration in light of *Wal-Mart*) with *Barrett v. Option One Mortg. Corp.*, 2012 WL 4076465 (D. Mass., Sept. 18, 2012) (decertifying a class in mortgage discrimination case after Wal-Mart).

23. See Zatz (forthcoming) (noting the statistical certainty of status causation for some in a disparate impact class even though it is impossible to know which ones).

24. Discovery costs alone would sink even the most deeply injured plaintiff (and any well-intentioned counsel) from pursuing an individual claim based on statistical analysis of the impact of a policy on a large group. In the discrimination cases described here, discovery costs in each case were hundreds of thousands of dollars, dwarfing any potential individual claim.

25. In *Allison v. Citgo Petroleum Corp.*, 151 F.3d 402, 411, 415 (5th Cir.1998), the Fifth Circuit held that "at least some form or amount of monetary relief" is available in (b)(2) class actions if it flows "directly from liability to the class as a whole on the claims forming the basis of the injunctive or declaratory relief."

26. The structure of the rule makes clear that to certify a class, all elements of Rule 23(a) must be satisfied, including commonality under Rule 23(a)(2), before evaluating whether at least one of the prongs of Rule 23(b) applies. As the Advisory Committee note to the 1966 amendment to the rule states

"Subdivision (a)" contains "necessary but not sufficient conditions for a class action. . . . Subdivision (b) describes the additional elements which in varying situations justify the use of a class action."

27. After *Wal-Mart*, plaintiffs were unable to achieve class certification in almost all of the unresolved mortgage cases discussed in this chapter. See In re Countrywide Financial Corp. Mortg. Lending Practices Litigation, 708 F.3d 704 (6th Cir. 2013); In re Wells Fargo Residential Mortg. Lending Discrimination Litigation, 2011 WL 3903117 (N.D. Cal., Sept. 06, 2011); *Barrett v. Option One Mortg. Corp.*, 2012 WL 4076465 (D. Mass., Sept. 18, 2012) (decertifying a class of mortgage discrimination claimants in light of *Wal-Mart*).

28. 726 F.3d 372 (3d Cir. 2013). Compare *Harris v. Citigroup, Inc.*, Case 1:08-cv-10417-MLW, Doc. No. 128 (D. Mass. August 10, 2012) (finding commonality for the purposes of certifying the class for settlement). The judge in *Citigroup* concluded that the common question was whether the plaintiffs were entitled to an injunction to end the discretionary pricing policy of the lender. Ibid., Doc. No. 105 (D. Mass., Mar. 6, 2012).

29. See also Case Note (2015).

30. Notably, Wal-Mart was hit recently hit with a similar class certification decision in Pennsylvania and, after class certification, the Supreme Court refused to grant certiorari. *Braun v. Wal-Mart Stores, Inc.*, 106 A. 3d 656 (Pa. 2014), *cert. denied*, 136 S. Ct. 1512 (2016).

31. There is a renewed potential for redlining claims where banks simply fail to do business (CFPB 2015).

PART IV

Housing and the Financial System: Risks and Returns

Household Debt and Defaults from 2000 to 2010: The Credit Supply View

Atif Mian and Amir Sufi

11.1 INTRODUCTION

From 2000 to 2007, the United States experienced the most dramatic boom and bust in household debt since the Great Depression. Household debt increased at a steady pace through the 1990s, and then jumped by $7 trillion from 2000 to 2007. The boom in debt ended badly: by 2009, the delinquency rate on debt had reached above 10 percent, much higher than seen since the Great Depression. Figure 11.1 shows these patterns.

Our previous research on the housing and household debt cycle of 2000 to 2010 in the United States, summarized in Mian and Sufi (2014a), made four main points:

- From 2002 to 2005, there was an expansion in the supply of mortgage credit for home purchase toward marginal households that had previously been unable to obtain a mortgage, and this expansion was unrelated to improved economic circumstances of these individuals. We have referred to this fact as the *extensive margin* of mortgage credit expansion.
- The expansion in mortgage credit availability and the increase in house prices were closely connected, but the expansion in credit was not merely a passive response to higher house price growth. Credit expansion was prevalent even in areas that experienced slow house price growth, and there is substantial evidence that house price growth during the boom was itself a result of credit expansion.
- Existing homeowners borrowed aggressively against the rise in home equity values through cash-out refinancing and home equity loans, and this behavior explains the substantial rise in the household debt to GDP ratio from 2000 to 2007. This borrowing was strong among the bottom 80 percent of the credit score distribution. Only the top of the credit score distribution was unresponsive. We have referred to home equity–based borrowing as the *intensive margin* of mortgage credit expansion in previous research.

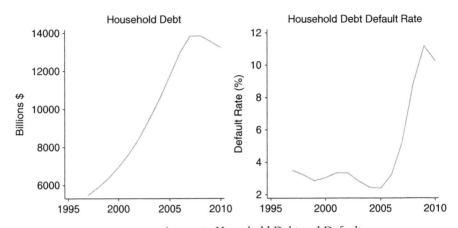

FIGURE 11.1 Aggregate Household Debt and Defaults
The left panel of this figure (Panel 1) plots nominal household debt according to the Federal Reserve Flow of Funds. The right panel (Panel 2) plots the default rate on household debt according to our sample of credit reports.
Source: Authors' calculations using Federal Reserve Flow of Funds data (Panel 1), Equifax credit bureau data (Panel 2)

- The sharp rise in delinquencies on household debt in 2007 was driven primarily by lower credit–score individuals living in areas where the house price boom and bust was most severe.

We have argued that these four points collectively support the *credit supply view* in which an increase in credit supply unrelated to fundamental improvements in income or productivity was the shock that initiated the household debt boom and bust shown in Figure 11.1.

In this study, we provide new evidence and highlight other research that supports the previously listed four points. In the process, we also discuss criticism of the credit supply view, which argues that credit played only a passive role in the housing boom and bust of 2000 to 2010. In this *passive credit view*, put forward most strongly by Foote, Gerardi, and Willen (2012) and Adelino, Schoar, and Severino (2016), mortgage credit simply followed the housing bubble and played no independent role.[1] This alternative view is difficult to reconcile with numerous studies that show that the expansion in mortgage credit had a causal effect on house prices during the boom. The dramatic growth in house prices from 2000 to 2006 depended at least in part on the expansion of credit availability.

The credit supply view is not incompatible with the idea that unreasonable house price growth expectations were important. In particular, the initial credit supply shock may have been due to lenders having unrealistic beliefs about house prices.

Further, existing homeowners likely borrowed so aggressively because they believed house prices would continue to rise. But the expansion in credit supply intermediated by the financial sector was a necessary ingredient in generating the boom and bust in household debt seen in Figure 11.1. This view has been formally modeled in a number of recent studies, including Favilukis, Ludvigson, and Van Nieuwerburgh (2017) and Justiniano, Primiceri, and Tambalotti (2015).[2]

Why are we still debating the causes of the housing boom and bust, eight years after the height of the mortgage default crisis? Determining whether credit played an active or passive role is important for a number of reasons. First, in the credit supply view, the financial sector plays an important role in explaining the mortgage boom and bust. As a result, an analysis of financial-sector activities during the boom such as incentives in securitization or fraudulent underwriting of mortgages is important to understanding what happened. Further, distributional issues come to the forefront because the financial sector transforms savings of some into borrowing by others. In contrast, under the passive-credit view, the financial sector is largely a sideshow. It simply followed the housing bubble like everyone else, and its actions had little independent effect on either the boom or the bust. Put differently, finance and capital structure play no role in this alternative view.

Second, the two views have different implications for economic modeling and our understanding of boom-and-bust episodes. A large body of research has shown a systematic relation between increases in household debt and subsequent economic downturns and financial crises (e.g., Jordà, Schularick, and Taylor 2016; Mian, Sufi, and Verner 2015). A growing body of theoretical models relies on changes over time in borrowing constraints, credit supply, or risk premia (as opposed to productivity shocks) to explain fluctuations in house prices, debt levels, and the real economy (e.g., Farhi and Werning 2016; Favilukis, Ludvigson, and Van Nieuwerburgh 2017; Justiniano, Primiceri, and Tambalotti 2015; Korinek and Simsek 2016; Martin and Philippon forthcoming; Schmitt-Grohé and Uribe 2016). We believe the experience of the Great Recession supports the assumptions and conclusions of these models. The evidence and theory line up nicely, and they suggest that we have a solid understanding of the drivers of severe economic downturns. On the other hand, in the passive-credit view, we have little understanding of the ultimate causes behind boom-and-bust episodes such as the one we witnessed in the United States from 2000 to 2010.[3]

Third, and closely related to the previous point, the policy conclusions one reaches are different depending on which narrative is true. In the passive-credit view, regulation can accomplish little. For example, Foote, Gerardi, and Willen (2012) write that "critics might contend that treating bubbles like earthquakes is reminiscent of a doctrine often associated with Alan Greenspan: policy makers should not try to stop bubbles, which are not easily identified, but should instead clean up the damage left behind when they burst. To some extent, we concur with this doctrine, because we believe that policy makers and regulators have little ability to identify or to burst bubbles in real time."

In contrast, the credit supply view argues that a consistent pattern emerges from the data: debt-fueled asset price booms, especially in real estate, typically end badly, and should therefore raise a red flag for regulators. The credit supply view suggests that more equity-based contracts may help reduce the amplitude of real estate booms, and make their busts less painful. Policies such as macro-prudential regulation targeting household debt-to-income ratios also follow naturally from the credit supply view. These policies are theoretically justified (e.g., Farhi and Werning 2016; Korinek and Simsek 2016), and they have been implemented by the Bank of England, the Bank of Israel, the Bank of Korea, and the Swedish financial supervisory authority.

We use a number of datasets in the analysis that follows. We will describe most of the datasets as we utilize them, and others are already described in our previous research. The main dataset we utilize is individual-level Equifax credit bureau data, which is the same dataset used in Mian and Sufi (2011). It is based on a 0.45 percent random sample of individuals in 1997 who were residing in ZIP codes for which Fiserv Case Shiller Weiss data are available. We sample these individuals and then obtain yearly credit bureau data through 2010. Although this sample is based on a limited number of ZIP codes, and new entrants are not included, the aggregate debt patterns for this sample closely match aggregate debt from the Federal Reserve Flow of Funds. We discuss these issues in more detail in the appendix.

11.2 MORTGAGE CREDIT EXPANSION ON THE EXTENSIVE MARGIN

The first main fact supporting the credit supply view is that lenders from 2002 to 2005 became more willing to extend home purchase mortgages to households that were traditionally denied credit. The increased willingness to extend credit to these households was not due to an improvement in the permanent income or productivity of these individuals. Let us first examine the aggregate evidence, and then we will present evidence from microeconomic data.

11.2.1 *Aggregate Evidence*

Levitin and Wachter (2012) show a dramatic expansion of mortgage credit originated and sold into the private-label, mortgage-backed security market from 2002 to 2005. The private-label, mortgage-backed security market went from 22 percent of originations in 2002 to 46 percent of originations in 2004 and then more than 50 percent in 2005. The total dollar amounts originated jumped from $200 billion to $800 billion (see 1198, fig. 2). As they put it, this was a market designed for "nonprime, nonconforming conventional loans." In terms of interest rates, Demyanyk and Van

Hemert (2011) show that there was a steady decline in the subprime mortgage to prime mortgage interest spread from 2001 through 2006 once loan and borrower characteristics are taken into account. They also suggest that their calculation understates the decline in the risk-adjusted spread because unobservable characteristics likely deteriorated more for subprime than prime borrowers.

During the mid-2000s, there was a simultaneous *increase* in the quantity of credit originated for nonprime borrowers and a *decline* in the interest rates faced by nonprime borrowers, exactly as would be expected with an expansion in credit supply.

Data from the American Community Survey show an increased willingness of lenders to originate credit for households that were traditionally denied mortgages. In Figure 11.2, we present the average characteristics of survey respondents who say that they both moved within the prior year and have a mortgage. We refer to these

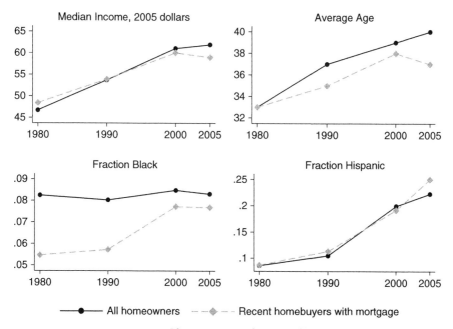

FIGURE 11.2 Characteristics of Marginal Borrowers
This figure plots the characteristics of individuals with a mortgage that bought a home within the prior year and the characteristics of all homeowners. Compared to recent homebuyers in 2000, 2005 recent homebuyers with a mortgage saw a decline in income, a decline in age, and an increase in the fraction that was Hispanic.
Source: Authors' calculations using American Community Survey and U.S. Census data

households as "recent homebuyers with a mortgage." As a comparison, we also plot
characteristics of all homeowners. The three characteristics we examine are income,
age, and race. We pick these three characteristics because ZIP code–level evidence
from 1997 reveals higher denial rates on mortgage applications for individuals living
in lower-income, younger, more Hispanic, and more black ZIP codes.

As the top left panel of Figure 11.2 shows, from 2000 to 2005, the real median
income of recent homebuyers with a mortgage actually *fell*. This is the only time
from 1980 to 2005 such a decline occurred. The individuals buying a home with
a mortgage in 2005 had lower real income than those who bought a home with
a mortgage in 2000, which is strong evidence that a credit supply shift toward more
marginal borrowers occurred during these years. As a comparison, real median
income for all homeowners grew from 2000 to 2005, but at a slower pace than
previously.

Over the same time period, the average age of recent homebuyers with a mortgage
fell, which is also the only time this happened in the 1980 to 2005 period.
The fraction of recent homebuyers with a mortgage who are of Hispanic origin
increased substantially, while the fraction who was black remained constant.
Relative to 2000, recent homebuyers with a mortgage in 2005 had lower income,
and they were younger and more likely to be Hispanic. These are all characteristics
associated with higher mortgage denial rates prior to 2000. These changes were
unique to recent homebuyers with a mortgage: the average characteristics of all
homeowners remained on a similar trend.

The expansion of credit to marginal borrowers is also seen in homeownership
rates. As the left panel of Figure 11.3 shows, the homeownership rate increased
sharply from 2002 to 2004, falling only slightly in 2005. However, we believe the
homeownership rate is not the ideal measure of an increase in homeownership due
to credit expansion. The homeownership rate is measured as the number of owner-
occupied units scaled by the number of owner-occupied and renter-occupied housing units. This measure is problematic for two reasons. First, because the number of
owner-occupied units is in both the numerator and denominator, an increase in the
number of owned units will mechanically have a reduced effect on the homeownership rate through an increase in the denominator. Second, movements in the
number of renter-occupied units can have an effect on the homeownership rate,
and such movements are not directly related to extensive margin changes in homeownership. We discuss these two issues at more length in the appendix. A better
measure of the extensive margin of expansion in homeownership is the total number
of owner-occupied homes scaled by the adult population. We plot this ratio in the
right panel of Figure 11.3, which shows a sharp rise from 2002 to 2004, and continues
to rise from 2004 to 2005. A disadvantage of this measure is the numerator is only
available from 2000 onward.

The homeownership rate data are collected by the Census. The Census also
provides homeownership rates by subgroups including race, age, and income.

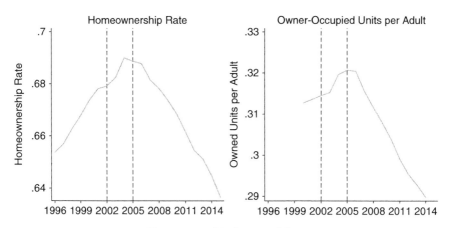

FIGURE 11.3 Homeownership Increased from 2002 to 2005
The left panel (Panel 1) plots the homeownership rate, which is defined as the number
of owner-occupied housing units divided by the total number of occupied housing units.
The right panel (Panel 2) shows the owner-occupied units per adult ratio, which is
defined as the number of owner-occupied housing units divided by the total population
of individuals 15 years old and above.
Source: Authors' calculations using U.S. Census data.

Table 11.1 shows the change in the homeownership rate from 2002 to 2005, and from 2003 to 2005 for these subgroups. We provide the changes for both time periods because the homeownership rate for subgroups tends to be noisy. Consistent with the evidence from the American Community Survey, the Census homeownership rate shows a large increase in homeownership rates for young and Hispanic households for 2002 to 2005 or for 2003 to 2005. However, the evidence on income is less conclusive. From 2002 to 2005, the homeownership rate increased by more for households above median income, but from 2003 to 2005 we see the opposite pattern.

In general, homeownership rates by income from the Census are especially noisy. The coefficient of variation for the quarterly homeownership rate from 2000 to 2006 for those below the median income is substantially larger than the coefficient of variation for the U.S. homeownership rate. We have some evidence that potentially illustrates why. In 2010, the Census changed its methodology to impute income for households that do not report income. As a result of the imputation, the homeownership rate for individuals below the median increased by 1.9 percentage points in 2015 relative to without this imputation. It increased by only 0.2 percentage points for those above median family income. In other words, there appears to be systematic bias in the households that do not report income: they tend to be poorer. It is difficult to know whether this bias leads the Census to understate or overstate the rise in homeownership from 2002 to 2005 among low-income individuals. But we believe

TABLE 11.1: *Change in Homeownership Rates during the Mortgage Credit Boom*

This table plots the change in the homeownership rate during the mortgage credit boom by age, race, and family income. All data come from the Census.

	Change in Homeownership Rate by Age				
	Age < 35	35 ≤ Age < 45	45 ≤ Age < 55	55 ≤ Age < 65	65 ≤ Age
Δ 2002 to 2005	1.025	0.725	0.050	−0.075	−0.075
Δ 2003 to 2005	1.550	0.875	0.150	−0.100	0.200

	Change in Homeownership Rate by Race		
	White	Black	Hispanic
Δ 2002 to 2005	1.075	0.800	2.525
Δ 2003 to 2005	0.475	0.125	2.825

	Change in Homeownership Rate by Family Income	
	Above Median	Below Median
Δ 2002 to 2005	1.525	0.850
Δ 2003 to 2005	0.575	1.125

Source: Authors' calculations using the American Community Survey and U.S. Census

both the noisiness of the data and the fact that there is systematic bias in who reports income levels should lead researchers to use extreme caution with these data.[4]

11.2.2 *ZIP Code– and Individual-Level Evidence*

In Mian and Sufi (2009), we utilized ZIP code–level data from Equifax and the Home Mortgage Disclosure Act (HMDA), and we showed stronger growth in home-purchase mortgage originations in ZIP codes with a higher share of subprime borrowers as of 1996. We split ZIP codes into quartiles based on the fraction of subprime borrowers in 1997. From 1991 to 2002, the total dollar amount of home-purchase mortgages grew at a similar rate for the top and bottom quartile. However, from 2002 through 2005, the home-purchase mortgage amounts skyrocketed in low credit–score ZIP codes. The expansion of mortgage credit on the extensive margin in low credit–score ZIP codes from 2002 to 2005 was unprecedented in the 1991 to 2008 period.

In Figure 11.4, we use data from DataQuick by CoreLogic on the number of housing transactions in a ZIP code. In order to isolate housing transactions that are purchased for owner occupation, we match the address of the property to the address of the buyer where tax documents are sent.[5] We also isolate the sample to transactions in which a mortgage was present.[6] So Figure 11.4 measures the growth in owner-occupied transactions in which a mortgage is present, which should purge any effect coming from investment purchases. Similar to the analysis in Mian and

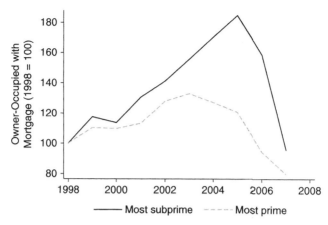

FIGURE 11.4 Number of Owner-Occupied Transactions, ZIP Code–Level Evidence
This figure shows that both the number of owner-occupied housing purchases financed
with a mortgage grew rapidly in low credit–score ZIP codes from 2002 to 2005. ZIP codes
are split into quartiles based on the share of individuals with a credit score below 660 in
1997, and we show the top quartile (most subprime) and bottom quartile (most prime) by
this measure. The number of owner-occupied transactions with a mortgage uses data
from DataQuick by CoreLogic. All series are normalized to be 100 in 1998. The sample of
ZIP codes is those that are in the Mian and Sufi (2009) sample and are located in counties
for which DataQuick has transaction data available for 1998 through 2010.
See the appendix for more details.
Source: Authors' calculations using data from DataQuick by CoreLogic

Sufi (2009), we split ZIP codes into quartiles based on the fraction of subprime
borrowers in 1997.

As Figure 11.4 shows, the number of owner-occupied housing transactions in the
most subprime 25 percent of ZIP codes was similar from 1998 to 2000 relative to the
most prime ZIP codes. There is a slight increase from 2000 to 2002, and then a large
increase from 2002 to 2005. The number of properties bought for primary residence
with a mortgage grew much more rapidly in low credit–score ZIP codes during
exactly the period when credit supply expanded along the extensive margin.

Owner-occupied transactions increased substantially more in low credit–score
ZIP codes from 2002 to 2005. In Table 11.2, we test whether investors increased their
presence in these same low credit–score ZIP codes. Using DataQuick, we classify
investor purchases in two ways. First, we classify a purchase as an investor purchase if
the street name is different on the tax mailing address compared to the property
address. Second, we use the ZIP code on the tax mailing address compared to the
property address. Table 11.2 shows that, if anything, there was a relative *decline* in the
investor share of purchases from 2002 to 2005 in low credit–score ZIP codes. Investor
purchases cannot explain the larger mortgage credit and transaction growth in low
credit–score ZIP codes from 2002 to 2005.

TABLE 11.2: *Did the Investor Share of Purchases Rise in Low Credit–Score ZIP Codes?*
This table uses DataQuick data from CoreLogic to examine whether the change in the investor share of purchases from 2002 to 2005 was larger in low credit–score ZIP codes. In columns 1 and 2, the definition of an investor is based on whether the street name of the tax mailing address is different that the street name of the property purchased. In columns 3 and 4, the definition is based on whether the ZIP code of the tax mailing address is different than the ZIP code of the property purchased. The sample includes ZIP codes from Mian and Sufi (2009) that are also in DataQuick.

	Δ Investor Share 2002 to 2005, Street		Δ Investor Share 2002 to 2005, ZIP Code	
	(1)	(2)	(3)	(4)
Fraction Subprime	−0.078*	−0.052**	−0.018	−0.012
Borrowers, 1996	(0.030)	(0.017)	(0.027)	(0.015)
Constant	0.042**	0.034**	0.025**	0.023**
	(0.010)	(0.006)	(0.009)	(0.005)
County FE?	No	Yes	No	Yes
Observations	1923	1923	1925	1925
R^2	0.003	0.778	0.000	0.779

Growth patterns in mortgage debt among low credit–score individuals are also consistent with an expansion of credit along the extensive margin. In Figure 11.5, we use the individual-level Equifax data and we split the sample into five quintiles based on the Vantage Score in 1997. Individuals are placed into one of these five quintiles based on their 1997 credit score, and they remain in the same quintile throughout the sample period. Given the large number of individuals with zero debt, we aggregate the debt of all individuals within the category before estimating the growth rates, as opposed to taking the average of the individual growth rates. As the left panel shows, the bottom 20 percent of the credit score distribution saw a 300 percent increase in debt from 2000 to 2006. The growth rates are uniformly smaller as the credit score gets larger.

Is the higher growth rate in debt among lower credit–score individuals purely a function of age? Individuals in the low credit–score bin are younger, with an average age as of 1997 of 37 versus 44 for the middle quintile and 58 for the highest quintile (see the appendix for the differences across credit score quintiles). However, there is enough variation in age for individuals within the same credit score quintile that we can extract the growth effect independent of age. To produce the right panel of Figure 11.5, we first aggregate individuals into credit score by age bins, where we use the five quintiles of credit scores and age as of 1997 for the age bin. For each year of the sample, we regress annual growth of credit for each credit score by age bin on a set of age indicator variables and indicators for the five credit score bins. The coefficients on the credit score bins then give us the differential growth rate for each credit score quintile, controlling for age.

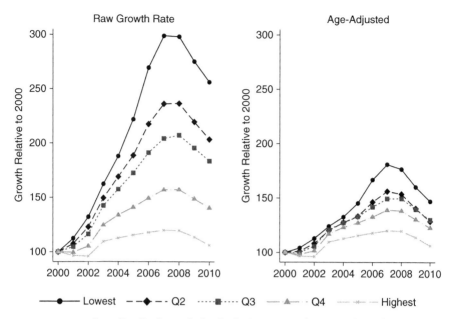

FIGURE 11.5 Low Credit–Score Individuals Experienced Largest Growth in Debt
This figure plots debt growth for individuals in credit bureau data, sorted by their credit score in 1997. Each quintile contains 20 percent of the population. In the right panel, we partial out age fixed effects to ensure that stronger growth for the lowest credit–score individuals is not merely an artifact of their younger age on average.
Source: Authors' calculations using data from Equifax

As the right panel of Figure 11.5 shows, such an age adjustment decreases the relative growth rate of the low credit–score quintile over the other quintiles. But even with these detailed controls for age, low credit–score individuals saw the largest growth in debt from 2000 to 2006. Finally, controlling for age in such a rigorous manner is an example of too many control variables. Prior to the debt boom, younger individuals were more likely to be denied credit. As a result, stronger mortgage credit growth by younger individuals could be interpreted as evidence of an expansion of mortgage credit on the extensive margin. Nonetheless, mortgage credit grew by more for low credit–score individuals, even taking out the age effect.

While Mian and Sufi (2009) and the findings presented earlier emphasize the shift in credit supply toward marginal borrowers previously denied credit, credit supply likely expanded on other margins as well. For example, even consumers with high credit scores applying for mortgages may have faced lower interest rates or less stringent verification of income during the mortgage boom.

11.2.3 *Other Research*

In addition to Mian and Sufi (2009), several other studies conclude that the early 2000s witnessed a dramatic expansion in mortgage credit toward marginal borrowers. For example, Mayer, Pence, and Sherlund (2009) use a variety of datasets on subprime mortgages and conclude that "lending to risky borrowers grew rapidly in the 2000s ... we find that underwriting deteriorated along several dimensions: more loans were originated to borrowers with very small down payments and little or no documentation of their income or assets in particular."

Demyanyk and Van Hemert (2011) conducted one of the first academic explorations of the LoanPerformance data. As they wrote, "we uncover a downward trend in loan quality ... we further show that there was a deterioration of lending standards and a decrease in the subprime-prime mortgage rate spread during the 2001–2007 period. Together, these results provide evidence that the rise and fall of the subprime mortgage market follows a classic lending boom-bust scenario, in which unsustainable growth leads to the collapse of the market." Levitin and Wachter (2012) come to a similar conclusion: the "[housing] bubble was, in fact, primarily a *supply-side* phenomenon, meaning that it was caused by excessive supply of housing finance ... the supply glut was the result of a fundamental shift in the structure of mortgage-finance market from regulated to unregulated securitization."

Justiniano, Primiceri, and Tambalotti (2016) use the FRBNY Consumer Credit Panel and CoreLogic data to show that both mortgage debt growth and house price growth were stronger from 2000 to 2006 in ZIP codes with a high fraction of subprime borrowers as of 1999. This is similar to the results shown previously, and suggests that the results are robust to using alternative data sources. The authors further show that such a finding can be rationalized in a model where the fundamental shock is an outward shift in credit supply.

The results are also confirmed by Adelino, Schoar, and Severino (2016), who show in their summary statistics that home-purchase mortgage credit growth from 2002 to 2006 was strongest in ZIP codes with the lowest per capita income as of 2002. They show this using both the total amount of the mortgages, and the total number of mortgages. They also show that these same low-income ZIP codes saw the worst income growth from 2002 to 2006.

The fact that mortgage credit expanded along the extensive margin toward more marginal borrowers was viewed as relatively uncontroversial until recently. For example, Foote, Gerardi, and Willen (2012) wrote, "to our knowledge, no one has disputed the fact that from 2002 to 2006, credit availability increased far more for subprime borrowers than for prime borrowers – this growth was widely discussed as it occurred."

11.3 MORTGAGE CREDIT AND HOUSE PRICE GROWTH

In this section, we discuss the large body of evidence showing that expansion in mortgage credit availability caused an increase in house price growth; the evidence contradicts the argument that credit passively followed the housing boom.

11.3.1 *Evidence from Mian and Sufi (2009)*

In Mian and Sufi (2009), we conducted two main tests to support the view that the expansion of mortgage credit pushed up house prices. First, we showed that house price growth was significantly stronger in low credit–score ZIP codes, despite the fact that these ZIP codes saw a *decline* in income compared to high credit–score ZIP codes within the same city. This was especially true in cities where geographical barriers induce a low elasticity of housing supply. To our knowledge, proponents of the passive credit view have never addressed this pattern. An explanation for the housing boom must explain why house prices rose the most in low credit–score neighborhoods within inelastic housing supply cities. The credit supply view provides a clear explanation: mortgage credit for home purchase was expanding rapidly in these neighborhoods, which pushed up housing demand. In inelastic housing supply cities, house prices rose in response to the demand shock.

The second technique we used in Mian and Sufi (2009) to support the view that credit supply pushed up house prices was to examine very elastic housing supply cities. In cities with very elastic housing supply, there was little house price growth from 2002 to 2006 and there was little reason to expect house price growth from an *ex ante* perspective. Yet even in these cities, mortgage credit expanded by more in low credit–score ZIP codes seeing a decline in income growth. When we shut down the house price growth expectations channel by focusing on elastic housing supply cities, we still see an expansion in mortgage credit to low credit–score individuals. This supports the view that the expansion in mortgage credit supply was not simply a function of house price growth or house price growth expectations. To our knowledge, advocates of the passive-credit view have not addressed this test from Mian and Sufi (2009). If the expansion of mortgage credit supply to marginal households was purely a function of house price growth expectations, why did such an expansion occur even in elastic housing supply cities with no house price growth?

Neither of these results implies the absence of a feedback effect from house price growth onto credit. As we acknowledged in Mian and Sufi (2009), "we want to emphasize that there may be a feedback mechanism between credit growth and house price growth ... increasing collateral value may also increase credit availability for previously constrained households, which forces a cycle by further pushing up collateral value ... in fact, our results lend support to such a feedback effect."

11.3.2 *Evidence from Other Research*

The idea that an increase in mortgage credit supply caused an increase in house prices prior to the Great Recession is supported by an extensive body of research. Di Maggio and Kermani (forthcoming) use variation in state anti-predatory laws in combination with the federal preemption of national banks in 2004 from such laws as an instrument for credit supply. They show that an exogenous increase in credit supply increased house price growth significantly. As they write, "a 10% increase in loan origination, through a local general equilibrium effect, leads to a 3.3% increase in house price growth, which resulted in a total increase of 10% in house prices during the 2004 to 2006 period." They also show that credit supply expansion predicts the decline in house prices during the bust.

Landvoigt, Piazzesi, and Schneider (2015) build an assignment model designed to understand the sources of house price growth within a city. They focus on San Diego county during the early 2000s to quantify the model. They conclude that "cheaper credit for poor households was a major driver of prices, especially at the low end of the market." Using a completely different methodology, Landvoigt, Piazzesi, and Schneider (2015) come to a similar conclusion as Mian and Sufi (2009): mortgage credit expansion caused an increase in house price growth, especially in neighborhoods with a disproportionate number of individuals previously denied mortgage credit.

Favara and Imbs (2015) exploit the deregulation of restrictions on bank branching across the United States from 1994 to 2005. They show that such deregulation caused an increase in mortgage credit supply, and that the expansion in mortgage credit supply caused a rise in house prices. They also show that the effect of deregulation on house prices is mitigated in elastic housing supply cities, consistent with the idea that a credit-induced rise in housing demand increases house prices more in inelastic housing supply areas. The magnitude is large: the authors show that between one-third and one-half of the increase in house prices from 1994 to 2005 can be explained by the expansion in mortgage credit supply. While the sample period is not exactly the 2002 to 2006 period studied by others, the findings show that house price growth is affected by increases in mortgage credit supply.

Adelino, Schoar, and Severino (2014) also show that exogenous increases in mortgage credit supply affect house prices. They exploit exogenous changes in the conforming loan limit set by the Federal Housing Finance Agency, and they find that houses that become eligible for cheaper funding because of these changes see a rise in value. While the average effect is small, they find that credit supply shifts "have a strong impact on particularly constrained households."

It is worth mentioning that these studies each use a different empirical methodology to isolate exogenous shifts in mortgage credit supply. And they all find that an expansion in mortgage credit supply causes a rise in house prices. While the exact magnitude remains a debated point, the core conclusion does not: *movements in house prices should not be viewed as independent of changes in mortgage credit supply.*[7]

11.3.3 *Investors, Speculation, and Housing Supply Elasticity*

While the expansion of credit supply to marginal households was a chief determinant of house price growth during the 2000 to 2007 period, we do not mean to suggest it was the only factor. A recent body of research argues that speculation by investors, defined broadly as individuals or companies buying for a purpose other than residing in the property, was an important determinant of house price growth (Chinco and Mayer 2016; Gao, Sockin, and Xiong 2016; Nathanson and Zwick 2016).[8]

One of the key insights from these studies is that house price growth and construction were strong in some cities in the medium part of the housing supply elasticity distribution such as Phoenix, Las Vegas, and the Central Valley in Northern California. The studies show that strong house price growth in these cities was related to purchases by investors who were speculating on house prices. This point is related to the critique given by Davidoff (2013; 2016) that housing supply elasticity is not a legitimate instrument for house price growth.

These studies convincingly show that the presence of investors was higher in elastic housing supply cities experiencing strong house price growth. In Table 11.3, we explore this finding to see how it is related to credit supply expansion. The house price growth data are from CoreLogic, and the housing supply elasticity measure is from Saiz (2010). All of the regressions are weighted by the total population in the Core-based-statistical area (CBSA).

In columns 1 and 2, we follow Gao, Sockin, and Xiong (2016) by regressing house price growth in a city on both the linear and squared housing supply elasticity measure. There is a very strong negative correlation between house price growth and housing supply elasticity, and the squared term is positive in column 2. However, the $R2$ is not 1, and so there are outliers to the relation.

In columns 3 through 5, we include measures of the presence of marginal borrowers in the city before the housing boom. In contrast to the within-city ZIP code–level variation in the presence of marginal borrowers used in Mian and Sufi (2009), we focus here on the between-city variation in the presence of marginal borrowers.

As columns 3 through 5 show, after controlling for housing supply elasticity, house price growth in a city from 2000 to 2006 is strongly positively related to the presence of marginal borrowers. The fraction of subprime borrowers is positively related to house price growth, and higher *ex ante* homeownership rates and income levels are negatively related to house price growth. The statistical power is very strong: the $R2$ including the income variable increases by 0.06.

The results in columns 3 through 5 of Table 11.3 show that the residual variation in house price growth after controlling for housing supply elasticity is closely related to

TABLE 11.3: *House Price Growth and Housing Supply Elasticity: The Outliers*

This table presents CBSA-level regressions relating measures of house price growth from 2000 to 2006 to housing supply elasticity. As has been pointed out, housing supply elasticity does not fully explain house price growth. However, controlling for housing supply elasticity, the extent to which marginal borrowers live in the CBSA prior to the housing boom has a strong effect on house price growth. All regressions are weighted by the total number of households in the CBSA as of 2000.

	House Price Growth, 2000 to 2006				
	(1)	(2)	(3)	(4)	(5)
Housing Supply Elasticity	−0.246**	−0.471**	−0.494**	−0.543**	−0.428**
	(0.022)	(0.047)	(0.046)	(0.047)	(0.052)
Housing Supply Elasticity Squared		0.041**	0.043**	0.046**	0.037**
		(0.008)	(0.008)	(0.008)	(0.008)
Fraction Subprime Borrowers, 2000			1.422**		
			(0.324)		
Ln(average income per capita, 2000)				−0.638**	
				(0.119)	
Homeownership Rate, 2000					−0.568*
					(0.282)
Constant	1.129**	1.351**	0.911**	8.064**	1.655**
	(0.045)	(0.060)	(0.116)	(1.252)	(0.162)
Observations	253	253	253	253	253
R^2	0.339	0.405	0.448	0.467	0.415

Source: Authors' calculations using data from DataQuick by CoreLogic, Fiserv Case Shiller Weiss, and Saiz (2010), and the U.S. Census

the presence of marginal borrowers in the city prior to the boom. This is not to say that the investor channel proposed in the existing research is incorrect. But it does suggest that between-city variation in credit supply may have been an important factor explaining why some elastic housing supply cities saw rapid price growth. Indeed, Davidoff (2013) suggests the exact same mechanism in his critique of housing supply elasticity as an instrument. He points to the fact that Washington Mutual, one of the most aggressive subprime mortgage lenders of the 2002 to 2005 period, had a large market share as of 2001 in many of the elastic housing supply cities that saw strong house price growth.

11.4 HOME EQUITY–BASED BORROWING ON THE INTENSIVE MARGIN

The expansion of credit supply to marginal borrowers alone could not possibly explain the tremendous rise in household leverage from 2000 to 2007. Marginal borrowers are a small part of the population, especially if one weighs by *ex ante* debt amounts in 2000. In Mian and Sufi (2011), we showed that the rise in household debt was driven primarily by existing homeowners borrowing heavily against the rise in house prices. While the marginal propensity to borrow out of a rise in home equity was strongest among low credit–score individuals, it was also positive among all but the top 20 percent of the distribution.

This fact can be seen in Mian and Sufi (2014b), where we show the marginal propensity to borrow against home equity by credit score. Using the Vantage Score from Equifax as of 1997, we show that the marginal propensity to borrow out of a one-dollar rise in home value was 0.25 for individuals having a credit score below 700, 0.22 for individuals having a credit score between 700 and 799, and 0.10 for individuals between 800 and 899. For individuals with credit scores above 900, the marginal propensity to borrow is almost exactly zero. In our sample of homeowners, only 10 percent of individuals had a credit score above 900 as of 1997. In other words, homeowners throughout almost the entire distribution borrowed against home equity; only the very top of the distribution was unresponsive. While both Mian and Sufi (2011) and Mian and Sufi (2014b) use various strategies to isolate causality as best as possible, the basic insight can be seen in correlations. In Table 11.4, we use the individual-level Equifax data and we split the sample by both credit score in 1997 and house price growth from 2000 to 2007 of the ZIP code in which the individual lived in as of 2000. Each credit score bin contains exactly 20 percent of the population, and each house price growth bin also contains approximately 20 percent of the population.

The top panel in Table 11.4 shows the distribution of the population. If house price growth and 1997 credit scores were uncorrelated, there would be 4 percent of individuals in each bin. This is not the case, as low credit–score individuals tend to live in ZIP codes experiencing stronger house price growth from 2000 to 2007 (Mian and Sufi 2009). As the second panel shows, the level of debt in 2000 is closely related to credit scores, with the lowest credit–score individuals having the smallest amount of debt. As a result, even though the growth in debt was quite dramatic for these low credit–score individuals (reflecting the expansion of credit on the extensive margin), the increase in the total level of debt should be expected to be less dramatic than the growth rates.

Figure 11.6 shows how the level of debt evolved for individuals in each quintile based on 1997 credit scores. The level of debt went up substantially for the bottom 60 percent of the credit score distribution. It went up the least for the top 20 percent of the distribution. The total level of debt went up by the highest amount for individuals in the 20th to 60th percentile of the credit score distribution.

The bottom panel of Table 11.4 shows that the rise in the level of debt was closely related to house price growth. It presents the share of the total aggregate rise in debt by both 1997 credit score and house price growth from 2000 to 2007 bins. The six cells at the top right of the panel represent the low and middle credit–score individuals living in the high house price–growth ZIP codes. These individuals

TABLE 11.4: *Share of Rise in Debt, by Credit Score and House Price Growth*

This table shows means by 1997 credit score quintile and by house price growth from 2000 to 2007. Each individual is assigned the house price growth from 2000 to 2007 of the ZIP code in which he or she resided in 2000. The bottom panel shows the share of total debt increase from 2000 to 2007 for each cell.

Credit Score Quintile	Share of Population, 1999 (%)				
	House Price Growth Category				
	lt 40%	40–75%	75–105%	105–130%	gt 130%
1	3.7	3.2	3.7	3.7	5.4
2	3.8	3.8	4.0	3.6	4.8
3	3.9	4.2	4.1	3.5	4.1
4	4.0	4.8	4.4	3.5	3.5
5	3.7	5.1	4.5	3.7	3.4

Credit Score Quintile	Debt level, 2000 (thousands $)				
	House Price Growth Category				
	lt 40%	40–75%	75–105%	105–130%	gt 130%
1	32.3	34.0	32.4	33.9	28.9
2	63.6	69.0	65.4	68.8	59.5
3	75.4	84.2	76.8	82.1	73.8
4	65.2	78.0	66.3	68.7	64.0
5	76.0	90.1	77.1	84.0	76.3

Credit Score Quintile	Share of Debt Increase, 2000 to 2007 (%)				
	House Price Growth Category				
	lt 40%	40–75%	75–105%	105–130%	gt 130%
1	2.2	3.2	3.6	4.1	5.6
2	3.3	5.7	5.9	5.7	6.9
3	3.7	6.2	5.4	5.1	5.6
4	2.8	4.5	3.8	3.3	3.4
5	1.6	3.0	1.9	1.9	1.7

Source: Authors' calculations using data from Equifax and Fiserv Case Shiller Weiss

account for 33 percent of the aggregate rise in household debt, despite making up only 25 percent of the total population.

Further, as Table 11.4 shows, every credit score bin shows a larger rise in household debt as house price growth increases with the exception of the top credit score bin. There is no relation between house price growth and the rise in debt for the top credit score bin. Individuals with the highest credit scores were unresponsive to higher house price growth, as shown in Mian and Sufi (2011) and Mian and Sufi (2014b).

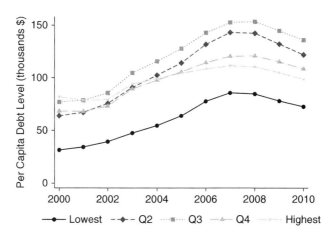

FIGURE 11.6 Increase in the Level of Debt, by Credit Score
This figure plots the average level of debt for individuals in the Equifax data, sorted by their credit score in 1997. Each quintile contains 20 percent of the population.
Source: Authors' calculations using data from Equifax

11.5 DEFAULTS

In Mian and Sufi (2009), we argued that the mortgage default crisis as of 2007 was "significantly amplified in subprime ZIP codes, or ZIP codes with a disproportionately large share of subprime borrowers as of 1996." In Mian and Sufi (2011), we showed that the default rate for low credit–score home-owners who had borrowed aggressively against home equity during the boom rose sharply in 2007 and 2008. These facts suggest that credit expansion on the extensive margin in combination with aggressive borrowing against home equity by low credit–score homeowners were main factors explaining the initial sharp rise in defaults in 2007. Mortgage defaults triggered losses among large financial firms, and these losses mark the beginning of the financial crisis episode that peaked in the fall of 2008.

A real-time analysis of the media in 2007 confirms that the mortgage default crisis was triggered by defaults on mortgages to low credit–score individuals, and subprime mortgages in particular. For example, a MarketWatch story from February 27, 2007 reports: "shockwaves have been rippling through financial markets as more signs emerge that relaxed lending standards during the housing boom of recent years are leading to escalating defaults and rising losses for lenders and owners of securities backed by such loans." New Century Financial Corporation, described in an article by Reuters on March 9, 2007 as "the largest independent U.S. subprime mortgage lender," saw its shares fall 17 percent on March 9, 2007. In a March 13, 2007 article titled "Subprime shakeout could hurt CDOs," MarketWatch discussed how losses in the subprime mortgage market would impact financial institutions through the mortgage-backed securities market.

In July and August 2007, the media emphasized losses on Bear Stearns' hedge funds with large subprime mortgage exposure. An article on the German press website Spiegel Online on August 15, 2007 led with the sentence: "The US subprime mortgage crisis has hit banks and stock markets worldwide." Regulators were also emphasizing problems in the subprime market quite early in 2007. For example, on May 17, 2007, Chairman Ben Bernanke gave a speech on rising defaults in the subprime mortgage market. This explains why the first wave of academic research focused on this market (i.e., Demyanyk and Van Hemert 2011; Keys, Mukherjee, Seru, and Vig 2010; Mayer, Pence, and Sherlund 2009).

The individual-level credit bureau data confirm the anecdotal evidence from the media. Figure 11.7 shows the default rate among individuals based on their credit score as of 1997. As it shows, the default rate from 2005 to 2007 increased by seven percentage points for individuals in the lowest 20 percent of the credit score distribution. The default rate hardly budged for those in the top 40 percent of the distribution. In 2008 and 2009, default rates rose significantly for even higher credit–score individuals. However, this likely reflects the fallout of the initial mortgage default crisis, as banks pulled back heavily on mortgage lending and house prices began to rapidly fall. At the very least, the default rate among higher credit score individuals in 2008 and 2009 cannot be viewed as independent of the subprime mortgage crisis that erupted in 2007.

One concern about the default rate evidence in Figure 11.7 is that while default rates may be high for low credit–score individuals, the total credit outstanding to low credit–score individuals was quite small. We examine the total *amount* in default in the left panel of Figure 11.8. Recall that our Equifax sample is based on a 0.45 percent random sample of ZIP codes that make up about 45 percent of the U.S. population. We scale up the defaulted amounts by this sampling frequency to obtain total defaults.[9]

In 2007, of the $900 billion of delinquent household debt, $660 billion came from the bottom 40 percent of the credit score distribution. Only $81 billion came from the top 40 percent of the credit score distribution and $160 billion from the middle quintile. Put another way, let us suppose that borrowers in the top 60 percent of the credit score distribution did not default on one single dollar of debt. Even in such a counterfactual, total delinquent household debt would have been $660 billion in 2007, which is *twice* as much as the *total* delinquent debt as of 2003. Such a large amount of delinquent debt would have constituted an unprecedented default crisis, even had individuals in the top 60 percent of the credit score distribution avoided defaults entirely. Table 11.5 shows the share of all delinquent debt in 2007 by credit score quintile and house price growth quintile. Individuals in the bottom 40 percent of the credit score distribution with the highest house price growth during the boom

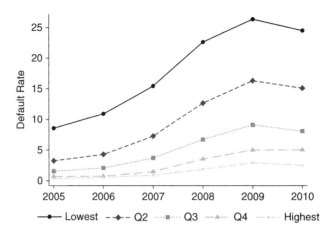

FIGURE 11.7 Default Rate, by 1997 Credit Score
This figure plots the default rate for individuals in credit bureau data based on their
1997 credit score. Each quintile contains 20 percent of the sample.
Source: Authors' calculations using data from Equifax

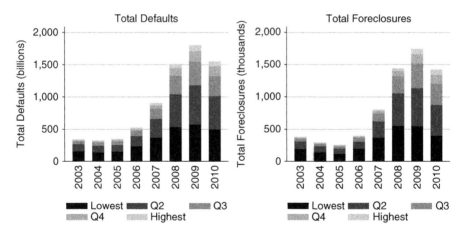

FIGURE 11.8 Total Defaults and Foreclosures, by 1997 Credit Score
This figure plots the total defaults and foreclosures for individuals in our credit bureau
data based on their 1997 credit score. Each quintile contains 20 percent of the sample.
The left panel (Panel 1) plots the total amount in delinquency for each quintile.
The right panel (Panel 2) shows total foreclosures, which is measured as a flag in credit
bureau data for a foreclosure in the past 24 months. We scale up the total defaults and
foreclosures by the sampling frequency to obtain aggregates.
Source: Authors' calculations using data from Equifax

TABLE 11.5: *Share of Delinquencies, by Credit Score and House Price Growth*

This table shows the share in delinquencies in 2007 by 1997 credit score quintile and by house price growth from 2000 to 2007. Each individual is assigned the house price growth from 2000 to 2007 of the ZIP code in which he or she resided in 2000.

| | Share of Delinquent Debt, 2007 (%) | | | | |
| | House Price Growth Category | | | | |
Credit Score Quintile	lt 40%	40–75%	75–105%	105–130%	gt 130%
1	5.6	6.8	7.6	7.9	12.8
2	4.5	5.8	6.7	6.6	9.7
3	2.3	3.5	3.3	3.8	4.6
4	1.0	1.4	0.9	1.1	1.2
5	0.4	0.9	0.5	0.3	0.8

Source: Authors' calculations using data from Equifax and Fiserv Case Shiller Weiss

make up more than 22 percent of defaults in 2007, despite being only 10.4 percent of the population.

By 2008 and 2009, the default crisis spread to higher credit–score borrowers. However, the bottom 40 percent of the initial credit score distribution continued to account for the lion's share of delinquencies: 69 percent in 2008 and 66 percent in 2009. Individuals in the top 40 percent of the initial credit score distribution never accounted for more than 15 percent of total dollars in delinquency, even at the height of the mortgage default crisis. As the right panel shows, the exact same pattern is seen for foreclosures, where we use the flag in the credit bureau data for an individual experiencing a foreclosure in the past 24 months.

Our reading of the evidence in Figure 11.8 is that the default crisis was primarily associated with defaults among low credit–score individuals, especially at the beginning of the crisis during the financial sector meltdown.

11.6 CONTRASTING WITH RECENT RESEARCH

In this section, we describe some of the reasons for disagreement in recent research on the source of the mortgage credit boom and bust. We begin with two conceptual points, and then discuss more detailed data issues that lead to different conclusions.

11.6.1 *The Extensive versus Intensive Margin of the Rise in Household Debt*

One source of disagreement in recent research is based on confusion between the extensive margin and intensive margin of household debt expansion. The analysis in Mian and Sufi (2009) was focused uniquely on the *extensive margin* of credit expansion, or the expansion of credit that allowed households that previously were unable to obtain a mortgage to buy a home. The article does not claim that expansion in mortgage credit for home purchase to marginal borrowers explains the rise in aggregate household debt.

This point is emphasized in our follow-up work: in Mian and Sufi (2014a), we wrote, "let's recall that households in the United States doubled their debt burden to $14 trillion from 2000 to 2007. As massive as it was, the extension of credit to marginal borrowers alone could not have increased aggregate household debt by such a stunning amount. In 1997, 65% of U.S. households already owned their homes. Many of these homeowners were not marginal borrowers – most of them already had received a mortgage at some point in the past." Mian and Sufi (2011) and Mian and Sufi (2014b) focused on the rise in aggregate household debt, and these studies show that home equity extraction by all but the top 20 percent of the distribution was the most important factor in explaining the rise in aggregate household debt.

Many of the findings in Adelino, Schoar, and Severino (2016) support the credit supply view of expansion on the extensive margin. Their summary statistics show that low-income ZIP codes saw stronger growth in home-purchase mortgage originated amounts from 2002 to 2006, while households in these ZIP codes saw lower income growth. They also show in the aggregate that the share of mortgages for home purchase by low-income ZIP codes increased from 2002 to 2006.

Adelino, Schoar, and Severino (2016) also show that the growth in average mortgage size conditional on origination is positively correlated with IRS income growth. As we show in Mian and Sufi (2017), this finding is an artifact of improper calculation of total mortgage size in Adelino, Schoar, and Severino (2016). More specifically, Adelino, Schoar, and Severino (2016) treat first and second liens as separate mortgages instead of combining them when calculating the total mortgage size used in a home purchase. Second liens are smaller than first liens, and second liens expanded more in low income–growth ZIP codes, which makes it appear as if average mortgage size decreased in low income–growth ZIP codes. Once first and second liens are properly combined, Mian and Sufi (2017) show that average mortgage size increased in low credit–score, low income–growth ZIP codes during the mortgage credit boom.

In general, it is crucial to emphasize that the credit supply view of the mortgage boom does not imply that the lowest-income or lowest credit–score individuals were responsible for the aggregate rise in household debt. The aggregate rise in household debt was driven by homeowners borrowing against the rise in home equity, and as already mentioned, this was prevalent in most of the distribution except at the very top. The key finding in Mian and Sufi (2009) is that credit expanded to marginal households previously unable to obtain credit, and this was unrelated to improvements in income.

11.6.2 *Falling House Prices versus Credit Expansion?*

A second conceptual point is the assertion in some studies that falling house prices "caused" the mortgage default crisis, and therefore the credit supply view is incorrect. This is a conceptually flawed assertion. A homeowner with positive equity will never default on her mortgage. Instead, she will sell the house, pay off the mortgage, and pocket the equity value of the home. As a result, negative equity is a *necessary* condition for default. In any hypothesis explaining the mortgage default crisis, a decline in house prices will be necessary to generate a rise in defaults. Put differently, the fact that falling house prices generate a default crisis is almost a tautology: it does not help discern different hypotheses for why the default crisis occurred.

The key question is: what explains the rise and fall in house prices? As already mentioned, a substantial body of evidence shows that the expansion in mortgage credit supply pushed up house prices, and this expansion was unsustainable given that it was not based on fundamental improvements in income. There are also convincing studies showing the role of speculators, investors, and mortgage fraud in explaining the rise and fall in house prices. But any hypothesis for what caused the mortgage default crisis must take a stand on the fundamental cause of the dramatic rise and fall in house prices. Simply stating that house price declines caused mortgage defaults is insufficient.

11.6.3 *Using Share of Defaults over Time*

The evidence in Figures 11.7 and 11.8 show that default rates and total defaulted amounts were highest for low credit–score individuals during the mortgage default crisis. However, recent research questions this conclusion, asserting that middle and even high credit–score borrowers played a more important role (Adelino, Schoar, and Severino 2016). What explains this disagreement?

The main source of this disagreement is how the basic facts are interpreted. Adelino, Schoar, and Severino (2016) in particular focus on the *share* of total defaults over time, and they show that the share of total defaults for richer and higher credit–score individuals went up during the mortgage default crisis relative to previous years. There is no disagreement on this basic fact; one can see this also in our Figure 11.8.

The fact that the share of defaults increased for high credit–score individuals is interesting, and perhaps informs us on important questions about the default crisis. However, in our view, this fact does not imply that high credit–score individuals drove the default crisis. Even with a higher share of total defaults in 2008, individuals in the top 40 percent of the credit score distribution had total delinquent debt of only $178 billion. Individuals in the bottom 20 percent of the credit score distribution had $530 billion of delinquent debt in 2008, three times larger.

A focus on the change in the share of defaults over time can lead to faulty conclusions on the source of overall defaults during the crisis. For example, in 2003, the top 20 percent of the credit score distribution made up only 2.3 percent of total defaults. In 2008, their share increased to 3.9 percent of defaults. This rise is a large increase in the share of defaults relative to the baseline in 2003. But in 2008, the top 20 percent had a total amount in default of $59 billion, which is only one-third the amount of defaults by the lowest 20 percent of the credit score distribution *in 2003*. Defaults in the crisis by the top 20 percent of the credit score distribution were small even relative to defaults of the lowest credit score bin in a normal year. In general, we believe the best way of assessing who drove the default crisis is to look at who made up most of the dollar amount in default during the crisis, not by a comparison of default shares in a crisis versus non-crisis year. It is unambiguous that low credit–score individuals accounted for the lion's share of defaults during the crisis.

11.6.4 *Other Data Issues*

Two other data issues help explain some of the disagreements in recent research. First, the use of fraudulently overstated income reported on mortgage applications leads to incorrect conclusions. While Adelino, Schoar, and Severino (2016) confirm that total mortgage origination growth for home purchase is negatively correlated with IRS income growth in a ZIP code from 2002 to 2005, they find a *positive* correlation between total mortgage origination growth and the growth in income reported on mortgage applications in a ZIP code.

The reason for this finding is that income reported on mortgage applications was fraudulently overstated during the mortgage credit boom, and this fraudulent over-statement was pronounced in ZIP codes with low income growth. The fact that fraudulent overstatement of income was a prominent part of the mortgage credit boom is one of the most rigorously established facts in the literature (Avery et al. 2012; Blackburn and Vermilyea 2012; Garmaise 2015; Jiang, Nelson, and Vytlacil 2014; Mian and Sufi 2017). We address this issue in more detail in a companion piece (Mian and Sufi 2017) and we show that researchers should not use mortgage application income in low credit–score ZIP codes as true income. It leads to mistaken conclusions on the nature of the credit supply expansion.

A second data issue is the measurement of credit scores. Our research always sorts individuals or ZIP codes based on their credit score prior to the mortgage credit boom, and then follows the same group over time. We sort based on *ex ante* credit scores because credit scores become endogenous to the mortgage credit boom from 2002 to 2006. In contrast, many researchers dynamically sort individuals into groups based on their credit score during the boom. For example, Adelino, Schoar, and Severino (2016) sort individuals into groups based on the credit score at origination on home purchase mortgages in 2006.

Sorting on credit scores during the mortgage credit boom mechanically biases the correlation between credit scores and default rates upward because credit scores increased more for individuals in high house price–growth areas who were borrowing heavily against home equity. As we show in Mian and Sufi (2011), low credit–score individuals living in high house price growth areas saw a sharp decline in defaults from 1997 to 2005 (see the middle panel of their figure 5). In that study, we argue lower default rates were due to the ability of homeowners in high house price–growth areas to extract equity to avoid default in case of a negative shock such as unemployment (e.g., Hurst and Stafford 2004). When house prices crashed, the pattern reverses and default rates increase by far more for the same households that saw the largest drop in default rates during the boom.

Because of lower default rates during the boom, low initial credit–score homeowners in high house price–growth areas saw the largest increase in their credit scores from 2000 to 2006. Table 11.6 shows that the largest increase in credit scores occurred among the lowest 40 percent of the credit score distribution living in high house price–growth areas (the top right four cells). We know from Table 11.5 that these individuals made up the largest share of defaults during the crisis. In other words, conditional on the 2006 credit score, the increase in credit scores from 2000 to 2006 predicts higher defaults during the crisis.

We confirm this result in a regression framework reported in Table 11.7. Using the individual-level Equifax data, we first show that a higher credit score as of 2006 predicts a lower propensity to default during the crisis. However, conditional on the credit score in 2006, an *increase* in the credit score from 1998 to 2006 is *positively* related to defaults during the crisis. As column 5 shows, the increase in credit scores from 2002 to 2006 in particular strongly predicts defaults. This shows the endogeneity of credit scores during the mortgage credit boom, and it shows that sorting on

TABLE 11.6: *Change in Credit Scores, by Credit Score and House Price Growth*

This table shows the change in the Vantage Score from 2000 to 2006 by 1997 credit score quintile and by house price growth from 2000 to 2007. Each individual is assigned the house price growth from 2000 to 2007 of the ZIP code in which he or she resided in 2000.

| | Change in Vantage Score, 2000 to 2006 | | | | |
| | House Price Growth Category | | | | |
Credit Score Quintile	lt 40%	40–75%	75–105%	105–130%	gt 130%
1	30.1	40.0	38.6	43.1	43.9
2	31.2	42.2	45.1	47.6	48.5
3	32.1	38.7	40.5	43.4	43.4
4	22.7	26.3	24.7	26.8	24.6
5	11.1	10.3	8.2	8.8	8.1

Source: Authors' calculations using data from Equifax and Fiserv Case Shiller Weiss

TABLE 11.7: *Increases in Credit Scores during Boom Predicts Default during Bust*

This table presents regressions in individual-level credit bureau data of the probability of default during the crisis on credit scores prior to 2007. While the level of the credit score in 2006 is negatively correlated with subsequent defaults, the change in credit scores from 1998 to 2006 is positively related to subsequent defaults.

	(1) Default in 2008	(2) Default in 2008	(3) Default in 2009	(4) Default in 2010	(5) Default in 2010
Credit Score, 2006	-12.527^{**} (0.061)	-13.423^{**} (0.068)	-12.731^{**} (0.069)	-12.153^{**} (0.068)	-12.424^{**} (0.070)
Δ Credit Score, 1998 to 2006		2.318^{**} (0.079)	3.655^{**} (0.084)	3.981^{**} (0.083)	
Δ Credit Score, 1998 to 2000					2.279^{**} (0.116)
Δ Credit Score, 2000 to 2002					3.653^{**} (0.126)
Δ Credit Score, 2002 to 2004					4.775^{**} (0.127)
Δ Credit Score, 2004 to 2006					5.717^{**} (0.126)
Constant	114.384^{**} (0.534)	120.476^{**} (0.576)	114.819^{**} (0.580)	109.569^{**} (0.577)	111.899^{**} (0.591)
Observations	245308	244299	244299	244299	240502
R^2	0.213	0.216	0.176	0.161	0.165

Source: Authors' calculations using data from Equifax

credit scores during the boom will mechanically push up the correlation between credit scores and default propensities.

11.7 CONCLUSION

In their classic history of financial crises, Kindleberger and Aliber (2011) provide an axiom: "asset price bubbles depend on the growth in credit." They show that even classic asset price bubble episodes such as the tulip mania in the Netherlands in the seventeenth century were associated with significant leverage. An established body of economic models shows how changes in leverage can have a causal effect on asset prices (e.g., Allen and Gale 2000; Geanakoplos 2010). We believe that the evidence from the United States during the first decade of the twenty-first century is most consistent with the view that credit expansion played a prominent role in explaining the rise in house prices.

The view in which credit expansion played no independent role in the mortgage debt boom and subsequent default crisis is inconsistent with the evidence. Further, it leads to a mistaken conclusion that we have no understanding of the nature of boom-and-bust episodes.

This not to say we understand everything about the U.S. experience from 2000 to 2010. There are a number of open questions. For example, what was the fundamental driver of the increase in credit supply? The increase in global savings, especially from East Asian and oil-producing countries, is a likely culprit. Levitin and Wachter (2012) make a compelling case that private-label securitization took on a fundamentally different character in the early 2000s. Research by Bruno and Shin (2015), Miranda-Agrippino and Rey (2015), and Rey (2015) suggests that monetary policy is also an important driver of credit supply shifts. A rise in income inequality in the United States may have helped fuel higher credit availability.

Also, what is the exact interaction between behavioral biases, fraud, and leverage? In one extreme view, the originators of mortgage credit knew that they were feeding an unsustainable bubble, and were preying on both the buyers of homes and the ultimate holders of the mortgage-backed securities. On the other extreme, perhaps the originators of mortgage credit expanded lending because of their own beliefs about house prices. Cheng, Raina, and Xiong (2014) provide evidence to support the latter view. However, the sheer scale of the fraud by mortgage originators and banks is difficult to resolve with the view that the financial sector was an innocent bystander simply caught up in a bubble (e.g., Griffin and Maturana 2016b; Piskorski, Seru, and Witkin 2015). Regardless of whether lenders had flawed expectations or not, their decision to extend credit was an important driver of the housing boom.

Finally, models in which a credit supply shock drives house prices typically do not take into account the feedback effect of house prices on consumption. While the credit supply view holds that the fundamental shock is an expansion in credit supply, the macroeconomic effects are mainly driven by homeowners borrowing against the rise in home equity. This feedback effect should be present in models, and research is needed to understand exactly why homeowners borrow so aggressively. Flawed expectations formation or other behavioral biases are likely important.

AUTHORS' NOTE

This research was supported by funding from the Initiative on Global Markets at Chicago Booth, the Fama-Miller Center at Chicago Booth, and Princeton University. We thank Seongjin Park, Jung Sakong, and Xiao Zhang for excellent research assistance. Any opinions, findings, or conclusions or recommendations expressed in this material are those of the authors and do not necessarily reflect the view of any other institution. We appreciate the comments from many colleagues at various universities. A previous version of this manuscript circulated as: "Household Debt and Defaults from 2000 to 2010: Evidence from Credit Bureau Data." The appendix is available on our websites at this link: http://faculty .chicagobooth.edu/amir.sufi/data-and-appendices/miansufi_creditsupplyviewap pendix.pdf. Mian: (609) 258–6718, atif@princeton.edu; Sufi: (773) 702–6148, amir.sufi@chicagobooth.edu.

REFERENCES

Adelino, Manuel, Antoinette Schoar, and Felipe Severino. 2016. "Loan Originations and Defaults in the Mortgage Crisis: The Role of the Middle Class." *The Review of Financial Studies* 29(7): 1635–670.

2014. "Credit Supply and House Prices: Evidence from Mortgage Market Segmentation." Available at SSRN 1787252.

Allen, Franklin and Douglas Gale. 2000. "Bubbles and Crises." *The Economic Journal* 110(460): 236–55.

Avery, Robert, Neil Bhutta, Kenneth Brevoort, Glenn B Canner, et al. 2012. "The Mortgage Market in 2011: Highlights from the Data Reported under the Home Mortgage Disclosure Act." *Federal Reserve Bulletin* 98(6): 1–46.

Bhutta, Neil. 2015. "The Ins and Outs of Mortgage Debt during the Housing Boom and Bust." *Journal of Monetary Economics* 76: 284–98.

Blackburn, McKinley L. and Todd Vermilyea. 2012. "The Prevalence and Impact of Misstated Incomes on Mortgage Loan Applications." *Journal of Housing Economics* 21(2): 151–68.

Bruno, Valentina and Hyun Song Shin. 2015. "Capital Flows and the Risk-Taking Channel of Monetary Policy." *Journal of Monetary Economics* 71: 119–32.

Cheng, Ing-Haw, Sahil Raina, and Wei Xiong. 2014. "Wall Street and the Housing Bubble." *The American Economic Review* 104(9): 2797–2829.

Chinco, Alex and Chris Mayer. 2016. "Misinformed Speculators and Mispricing in the Housing Market." *The Review of Financial Studies* 29(2): 486–522.

Davidoff, Thomas. 2016. "Supply Constraints Are not Valid Instrumental Variables for Home Prices because They Are Correlated with Many Demand Factors." *Critical Finance Review* 5(2): 177–206.

2013. "Supply Elasticity and the Housing Cycle of the 2000s." *Real Estate Economics* 41(4): 793–813.

Demyanyk, Yuliya and Otto Van Hemert. 2011. "Understanding the Subprime Mortgage Crisis." *The Review of Financial Studies* 24(6): 1848–80.

Di Maggio, Marco and Amir Kermani. Forthcoming. "Credit-Induced Boom and Bust." *Review of Financial Studies*.

Farhi, Emmanuel and Ivan Werning. 2016. "A Theory of Macroprudential Policies in the Presence of Nominal Rigidities." *Econometrica* 84(5): 1645–704.

Favara, Giovanni, and Jean Imbs. 2015. "Credit Supply and the Price of Housing." *The American Economic Review* 105(3): 958–92.

Favilukis, Jack, Sydney C Ludvigson, and Stijn Van Nieuwerburgh. 2017. "The Macroeconomic Effects of Housing Wealth, Housing Finance, and Limited Risk-Sharing in General Equilibrium." *Journal of Political Economy* 125(1): 140–223.

Foote, Christopher L., Kristopher S Gerardi, and Paul S Willen. 2012. "Why Did so Many People Make so Many Ex Post Bad Decisions? The Causes of the

Foreclosure Crisis." *Federal Reserve Bank of Boston Public Policy Discussion Paper Series* 12–2.

Gao, Zhenyu, Michael Sockin, and Wei Xiong. 2016. "Housing Supply, Speculation and Cycles." Working paper.

Garmaise, Mark J. 2015. "Borrower Misreporting and Loan Performance." *The Journal of Finance* 70(1): 449–84.

Geanakoplos, John. 2010. "The Leverage Cycle." In *NBER Macroeconomics Annual 2009*, Volume 24: 1–65. Chicago: University of Chicago Press.

Griffin, John M. and Gonzalo Maturana. 2016a. "Did Dubious Mortgage Origination Practices Distort House Prices?" *The Review of Financial Studies* 29(7): 1671–1708.

      2016b. "Who Facilitated Misreporting in Securitized Loans?" *The Review of Financial Studies* 29(2): 384–419.

Haughwout, Andrew, Donghoon Lee, Joseph S. Tracy, and Wilbert Van der Klaauw. 2011. "Real Estate Investors, the Leverage Cycle, and the Housing Market Crisis." *FRB of New York Staff Report* (514).

Hurst Erik and Frank Stafford. 2004. "Home Is Where the Equity Is: Mortgage Refinancing and Household Consumption." *Journal of Money, Credit and Banking* 36(6): 985–1014.

Jiang, Wei, Ashlyn Aiko Nelson, and Edward Vytlacil. 2014. "Liar's Loan? Effects of Origination Channel and Information Falsification on Mortgage Delinquency." *Review of Economics and Statistics* 96(1): 1–18.

Jordà, Òscar, Moritz Schularick, and Alan M. Taylor. 2016. "The Great Mortgaging: Housing Finance, Crises and Business Cycles." *Economic Policy* 31(85): 107–52.

Justiniano, Alejandro, Giorgio E Primiceri, and Andrea Tambalotti. 2016. "A Simple Model of Subprime Borrowers and Credit Growth." *The American Economic Review Papers and Proceedings* 106(5): 543–47.

      2015. "Credit Supply and the Housing Boom." Technical report. The National Bureau of Economic Research.

Keys, Benjamin J., Tanmoy Mukherjee, Amit Seru, and Vikrant Vig. 2010. "Did Securitization Lead to Lax Screening? Evidence from Subprime Loans." *The Quarterly Journal of Economics* 125(1): 307–62.

Kindleberger, Charles P. and Robert Z Aliber. 2011. *Manias, Panics and Crashes: A History of Financial Crises*. London: Palgrave Macmillan.

Korinek, Anton and Alp Simsek. 2016. "Liquidity Trap and Excessive Leverage." *The American Economic Review* 106(3): 699–739.

Landvoigt, Tim, Monika Piazzesi, and Martin Schneider. 2015. "The Housing Market(s) of San Diego." *The American Economic Review* 105(4): 1371–1407.

Levitin, Adam J. and Susan M Wachter. 2012. "Explaining the Housing Bubble." *The Georgetown Law Journal* 100(4): 1177–1258.

Martin, Philippe and Thomas Philippon. Forthcoming. "Inspecting the Mechanism: Leverage and the Great Recession in the Eurozone." *The American Economic Review*.

Mayer, Christopher, Karen Pence, and Shane M Sherlund. 2009. "The Rise in Mortgage Defaults." *The Journal of Economic Perspectives* 23(1): 27–50.

Mian, Atif and Amir Sufi. 2017. "Fraudulent Income Overstatement on Mortgage Applications during the Credit Expansion of 2002 to 2005." *Review of Financial Studies* 30: 1831–64.

2014a. *House of Debt: How They (and You) Caused the Great Recession, and How We Can Prevent It from Happening Again.* Chicago: University of Chicago Press.

2014b. "House Price Gains and U.S. Household Spending from 2002 to 2006." Technical report. National Bureau of Economic Research.

2011. "House Prices, Home-Equity Based Borrowing, and the U.S. Household Leverage Crisis." *The American Economic Review* 101(5): 2132–56.

2009. "The Consequences of Mortgage Credit Expansion: Evidence from the U.S. Mortgage Default Crisis." *The Quarterly Journal of Economics* 124(4): 1449–96.

Mian, Atif R., Amir Sufi, and Emil Verner. 2015. "Household Debt and Business Cycles Worldwide." Technical report. The National Bureau of Economic Research.

Miranda-Agrippino, Silvia and Hélène Rey. 2015. "World Asset Markets and the Global Financial Cycle." Technical report. National Bureau of Economic Research.

Nathanson, Charles G. and Eric Zwick. 2016. "Arrested Development: Theory and Evidence of Supply-Side Speculation in the Housing Market." Working paper.

Piskorski, Tomasz, Amit Seru and James Witkin. 2015. "Asset Quality Misrepresentation by Financial Intermediaries: Evidence from the RMBS Market." *The Journal of Finance* 70(6): 2635–78.

Rey, Hélène. 2015. "Dilemma Not Trilemma: The Global Financial Cycle and Monetary Policy Independence." Technical report. National Bureau of Economic Research.

Saiz, Albert. 2010. "The Geographic Determinants of Housing Supply." *The Quarterly Journal of Economics* 125(3): 1253–96.

Schmitt-Grohè, Stephanie and Martín Uribe. 2016. "Downward Nominal Wage Rigidity, Currency Pegs, and Involuntary Unemployment." *Journal of Political Economy* 124(5): 1466–514.

Notes

1. Adelino, Schoar, and Severino (2016): "these results provide a new picture of the mortgage expansion before 2007 and suggest that cross-sectional distortions in the allocation of credit were not a key driver of the run-up in mortgage markets and the subsequent default crisis. In contrast, our results point to an explanation where house prices increases and drops played a central role during the credit expansion and in the subsequent defaults." Foote, Gerardi, and Willen (2012): "the facts suggest that the expansion occurred simply because people believed that house prices would keep going up – the defining characteristic of an asset bubble. Bubbles do not need securitization, government involvement, or non-traditional lending products to get started."

2. In Favilukis, Ludvigson, and Van Nieuwerburgh (2017), "a relaxation of financing constraints leads to a large boom in house prices." In Justiniano, Primiceri, and Tambalotti (2015a), "an increase in credit supply driven by looser *lending*

constraints in the mortgage market can explain ... the unprecedented rise in home prices."

3. Adelino, Schoar, and Severino (2016): "It is beyond the scope of this paper to analyze the drivers of house prices dynamics." Foote, Gerardi, and Willen (2012): "the unanswered question is why this bubble occurred in the 2000s and not some other time. Unfortunately, the study of bubbles is too young to provide much guidance on this point. For now, we have no choice but to plead ignorance."

4. The footnote at the bottom of Table 17 from the Census says: "Previously, householders not responding to this [income] question were excluded from the homeowner calculations for those below/above the median family income level. When compared to previous procedures, this change resulted in an increase in the homeownership rate of 1.9 percentage points for those at or below the median family income and an increase of 0.2 percentage points for those above the median family income level for the fourth quarter 2015."

5. This is a rough but common technique used among practitioners to measure whether a transaction is a purchase for primary residence or an investment purchase.

6. The sample is limited to ZIP codes that have transaction data available from DataQuick for 1998 through 2010 and are in the sample from Mian and Sufi (2009). See the appendix for details.

7. Griffin and Maturana (2016a) show that it was not only the expansion in credit supply that lifted house prices during the housing boom, but also that fraud associated with mortgage originations was an important factor. They show a systematic relation between the presence of mortgage originators who defrauded investors in a ZIP code and house price growth in the ZIP code. The presence of dubious originators is associated with larger house price boom-and-bust cycles.

8. In general, investors were responsible for a large increase in debt. See, e.g., Bhutta (2015) and Haughwout, Lee, Tracy, and Van der Klaauw (2011).

9. There are two reasons that the total amount of delinquent debt may be overstated in Figure 11.8 relative to other measures of aggregate defaults. First, some debt for the individuals in our sample is double-counted because it is joint debt with another individual (a spouse, for example). Second, there may be differences in default rates among individuals in our random sample versus the universe. In either case, we are not aware of any reason that the relative default amounts for low versus high credit–score individuals should be distorted.

Representations and Warranties: Why They Did Not Stop the Crisis

Patricia A. McCoy and Susan Wachter

12.1 INTRODUCTION

Real estate is vulnerable to procyclicality, with real estate booms and busts often leading to financial and economic instability.[1] The Great Recession in the United States was triggered by the collapse of securitized finance, which had spawned a credit-fueled bubble in residential real estate (Levitin and Wachter 2012; McCoy et al. 2009). The bursting of the twin real estate and credit bubbles ultimately crippled the U.S. financial system and the real economy (Levitin, Pavlov, and Wachter 2012; Levitin and Wachter 2012).

In hindsight, we know that securitization was accompanied by a decline in underwriting standards that exacerbated the subsequent economic downturn and that contractual obligations in the form of representations and warranties did not deter this decline. Through securitization, originators pass virtually all mortgage risk to the market. Thus, in order to align the incentives of originators with those of investors in residential mortgage-backed securities (RMBS), originators are subject to put-back risk for violations of representations and warranties. The purpose of these contractual obligations is to assure maintenance of underwriting standards.

This chapter examines why representations and warranties failed to accomplish this key requirement for the integrity and sustainability of the securitization process. These provisions in loan sale agreements for RMBS are paradoxical in nature. Representations and warranties did not stop the wave of bad loans from capsizing the U.S. housing market in 2007 and 2008 and the expectation that they would, arguably, worsened the crisis. Yet more recently, liability for the breach of those representations by originators and other securitization participants, along with loan losses themselves, have been linked to bank lenders' withdrawal from the market and overly tight lending standards, which slowed the recovery process. Post-crisis, lenders' fears over put-back exposure appear to have contributed to a contraction in lending to creditworthy borrowers.[2] This contraction has coincided with the return of thinly capitalized nonbank lenders, who have little capital at risk for future mortgage repurchase claims.

If both are true, then the representations and warranties in securitization documents through 2008 were simultaneously too weak and too harsh, engendering procyclicality.[3] During the run-up to the 2008 financial crisis, these representations gave investors false assurance that mortgage loans were being properly underwritten, contributing to overinvestment in underpriced MBS. Moreover, there was virtually no enforcement of those provisions during the bubble, which exaggerated their cyclical effects. Only later, after the harm was done, did the pendulum swing to excess enforcement and fear of penalties, which encouraged undue restrictiveness in the origination of mortgages and hampered the economic recovery.

Is this paradoxical outcome due to surprise that these agreements would ever be enforced and surprise about how they were enforced; or due to the unforeseen events that made these agreements actionable; or due to misaligned incentives that led agents to knowingly ignore these contractual obligations? Or to some combination of these differing interpretations of ignorance or malfeasance? More critically, going forward, for the integrity of the securitization process, can representations and warranties be reformed to buttress the integrity of the securitization process, or are there intrinsic limitations on the use of contractual terms to assure this outcome?

This chapter proceeds as follows. Part 2 provides an overview, describing the intended role of representations and warranties in deterring loose underwriting and providing compensation for breach, how these contractual provisions failed to halt the deterioration in underwriting during the credit bubble, and the efforts to enforce these provisions following the 2008 crisis. In Part 3, we survey the market responses to put-back litigation, including contraction of credit by bank lenders and the concomitant surge in market share by more lightly regulated nonbank lenders, and propose reforms. In particular, we contend that representations and warranties will not have teeth unless they are accompanied by countercyclical provisioning and capital standards. Part 4 concludes.

12.2 HISTORICAL BACKGROUND AND OVERVIEW OF RECENT MORTGAGE PUT-BACK LIABILITY

The current controversy over mortgage put-backs emanates from the shift of U.S. housing finance from a bank-based system to a capital-markets system over the past 50 years. Fifty years ago, mortgage originators usually held loans in portfolio. But that all changed in the 1970s with the invention of MBS,[4] which gave mortgage lenders the ability to move newly originated mortgages off their balance sheets by bundling those loans into bonds sold to private investors. Over time, securitization became the predominant means of mortgage finance and three securitization channels emerged: Ginnie Mae for FHA-insured and VA mortgages, Fannie Mae and Freddie Mac for other conforming mortgages (also known as agency mortgages), and the private-label (Wall Street) market for nonconforming mortgages (most notably jumbo loans and subprime and Alt-A mortgages).[5] Securitization offers benefits to depository institutions by solving the term-mismatch problem arising because bank liabilities (in the form of demand deposits) are considerably more liquid than their long-term mortgage assets (Diamond 2007).

12.2.A *The Growth of Mortgage Securitization*

The secondary market in the United States, established after the Great Depression, was small, relative to the overall mortgage market until the 1980s. Originators, mostly savings and loan associations (S&Ls), held mortgages in portfolio, other than government-insured Federal Housing Administration (FHA) and Veterans Administration (VA) mortgages. In the aftermath of the S&L crisis, Ginnie Mae and the government-sponsored enterprises (GSEs), Fannie and Freddie, grew rapidly as funding sources (Levitin and Wachter 2013a, 1165–67).

Starting in the late 1990s and accelerating between 2003 and 2007, regulatory shifts (McCoy et al. 2009) and changes to the structure of the mortgage chain led to the onset of a secondary mortgage lending regime dominated by private-label securitization and mediated by Wall Street investment banks (Levitin and Wachter 2012; Wachter 2014). A substantial expansion of credit followed. The number of purchase mortgages originated increased from 4.3 million to 5.7 million and remained above 5.5 million through 2006 (FFIEC 2015). Private-label securities (PLS) had originally funded jumbo mortgages whose size precluded their inclusion in GSE securitizations. The PLS lending of 2003 through 2007 funded nontraditional mortgage (NTM) products and subprime loans. Prior to the PLS boom, most mortgages were conforming, self-amortizing 30-year fixed-rate mortgages (FRMs). However, during the boom, there was a substantial increase in nontraditional mortgages, including non-amortizing (or negative amortization) balloon, interest-only (IO), and option-payment mortgage products, as well as subprime loans and other Alt-A products (which did not require full documentation of income). The market share of NTMs in dollars (including second-lien mortgages) rose from 20 percent in 2003 to 50 percent in 2006 (Figure 12.1). There was a simultaneous change in the types of products sold in the secondary market and a shift to private-label securitization.

While most conforming mortgages were securitized by Fannie Mae and Freddie Mac, most NTMs and subprime loans were securitized in the PLS market. Figures 12.1 and 12.2 (which disaggregate mortgages by type) show the share of PLS and NTM and subprime mortgage issuance peaking during 2006 and almost disappearing after 2008. While the PLS market share rose during the housing boom, the GSE (conventional, conforming) and Ginnie Mae markets shares shrank (Wachter 2014).

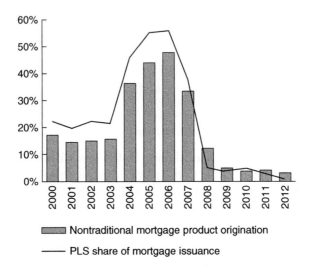

FIGURE 12.1 Market Share in Dollars of Nontraditional Mortgage Products and Private Label Securitization, 2000–2012
Note: Nontraditional mortgage products are subprime, Alt-A, and home equity loans.
Source: Authors' calculations using data from Inside Mortgage Finance 2013 Mortgage Market Statistical Annual; see Levitin and Wachter 2013b, 12.

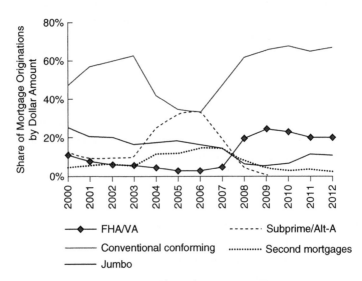

FIGURE 12.2 Origination Shares by Mortgage Type, 2000–2012
Source: Authors' calculations using data from Inside Mortgage Finance 2013 Mortgage Market Statistical Annual; see Levitin and Wachter 2012, 1195.

12.2.B *Principal-Agent Problems in Securitization*

Securitization ushered in new principal-agent problems that the inventors of MBS worked to address. Adverse selection was one issue, consisting of the fear that originators would retain their best loans and securitize the rest. Investors were also concerned about information asymmetries, because lenders know more about the quality of the loans they originate than investors and have incentives to conceal negative information when selling those loans.[6]

Private capital would shun the mortgage finance system absent assurances to investors on both scores. Consequently, securitizers used a host of techniques to address the principal-agent problems in securitization, including disclosures, underwriting standards, quality control, due diligence reviews, and risk retention. Key among those techniques was representations and warranties, the focus of this chapter.

12.2.C *The Use of Representations and Warranties in MBS*

Every mortgage-backed securitization starts out with the sale of a pool of mortgage loans by a seller to a purchaser. The purchaser is generally a GSE, an FHA/VA securitization issuer, or an investment bank that plans to transfer the loans to a special purpose vehicle for bundling into MBS for sale to investors. Often the seller is the originator, but it can also be a large bank that aggregates loans bought from a third-party originator. In the course of the series of transfers that make up a securitization, many of the transferors make representations and warranties to the next transferee down the chain (Murphy 2012).

The central contract governing the loan sale is a *Mortgage Loan Purchase Agreement* between the seller and the purchaser (Miller 2014, 259, 267). This agreement or its equivalents are found in all three major securitization channels, including Ginnie Mae, the GSEs, and private-label securitizations (FHFA 2012, 6, 10–12). The typical agreement contains more than 50 representations, warranties, and covenants by the seller to the purchaser (see, e.g., Master Loan Purchase Agreement 2005, § 5 & Exh. A). The representations and warranties inure to the benefit of the purchaser and sometimes to its assignees, transferees, or designees, including the trustee of the securitization trust (see, e.g., id., § 6).

While these representations and warranties share common subject matters, in PLS transactions their precise language varies (sometimes significantly) across deals (Standard & Poor's 2013b; Tate 2016). In contrast, representations and warranties are standardized for GSE and Ginnie Mae securities. The representations and warranties made to Fannie and Freddie are cheaper to litigate by virtue of their standardization and are also generally stronger than those agreed to in private-label deals (Fleming 2013; Strubel 2011).

Representations and warranties serve dual functions: deterrence and compensation. One reason investors demand those representations is to deter lax loan underwriting by lenders. Investors also require those provisions to assure compensation in the event of breach. For this reason, the enforcement provisions of the Mortgage Loan Purchase Agreement require repurchase of any mortgages that are found to be in breach.

12.2.C.1 The Contractual Representations and Warranties

Some representations and warranties deal with the legal status, bona fides, operating systems, and condition of the seller and related parties (see, e.g., Master Loan Purchase Agreement 2005, § 5(b) & Exh. A), but most involve statements about the legality and quality of the loans being sold. The loan-specific representations and warranties can be grouped into the following subjects (see, e.g., id., Exh. A; Miller 2014, 270–73):

- *Mortgage Loans as Described*: Under this provision, the seller affirms that information relating to the mortgage loans in the pool is complete, true, and correct and the interest rates are those stated in the mortgage notes. A related provision states that all necessary documents have been delivered to the custodian and that the seller possesses the complete, true, and accurate mortgage file.
- *Current Payment Status*: In this representation and warranty, the seller confirms that no loan in the pool is in default or has been delinquent for 30 days or more in the past 12 months. In addition, a warranty provides a safeguard against early payment default by stating that the first three monthly payments shall be made within the month in which each payment is due. In a related, open-ended provision, the seller confirms that it has no knowledge of any circumstances or conditions that would cause any of the mortgage loans to become delinquent.
- *Legality*: Representations and warranties typically provide that each mortgage loan when it was made complied in all material respects with applicable local, state, and federal laws, including, but not limited to, all applicable predatory and abusive lending laws. In addition, the seller warrants that none of the mortgage loans were "high cost" or predatory loans for purposes of federal or state or local anti-predatory lending laws. A companion provision states that the origination, servicing, and collection practices used with respect to the mortgage loans are legal and in accordance with accepted practices.
- *Appraised Value*: Another group of representations and warranties provides that the properties securing the mortgage loans have been appraised

according to the standards specified in the Mortgage Loan Purchase Agreement.

- *No Misrepresentations*: This provision states that no one has engaged in any misrepresentation, negligence, fraud, or similar occurrence with respect to a mortgage loan.
- *Loans Meet Agreed-Upon Underwriting Standards*: In this set of provisions, the seller confirms that the mortgage loans in the pool all meet specified underwriting standards, including maximum loan-to-value ratios and minimum credit scores.
- *Loans Meet Agreed-Upon Loan Features*: In these provisions, the seller agrees that none of the loans in the pool contains prohibited features. This list of prohibited features varies with the loan pool, but sometimes includes balloon terms, negative amortization, shared appreciation, pre-payment penalties, mandatory arbitration clauses, and/or single premium credit insurance terms.
- *Mortgage Loan Fully Marketable and Enforceable*: These representations and warranties provide assurance that the mortgage loans are fully marketable and enforceable and have not been impaired, waived, or modified.
- *No Outstanding Charges*: Here the seller states that all taxes, assessments, insurance premiums, and other charges due under the terms of the mortgages have been paid and are up to date.
- *Underlying Properties Intact and Adequately Insured*: In this representation and warranty, the seller confirms that all of the properties securing the mortgage loans are undamaged and have adequate hazard insurance, including flood insurance where required, as well as title insurance.
- *Conforming Asset Class*: This representation and warranty states that all of the mortgaged properties securing the loan pool belong to the appropriate asset class (e.g., residential properties instead of commercial properties).
- *Owner-Occupied*: The seller affirms that all of the homes securing the loans are owner-occupied.
- *Provisions Regarding the Timing, Amount, and Crediting of Payments*: Several other representations and warranties address the timing, amount, and crediting of payments.

Taken together, these representations and warranties allocate the responsibility for loan quality to the originator or other seller, who can ensure that quality more cheaply than the purchaser (Miller 2014, 263, 286–88, 290).

Despite the wealth of representations and warranties, most put-back requests and disputes turn on a handful of core representations (271–73). These representations include statements that the loans in the pool: (1) are as described (particularly with respect to loan-to-value ratios, credit scores, debt-to-income ratios, owner-occupied status, and the like); (2) have no past delinquencies and will not go delinquent within the first three months after origination; (3) are free from misrepresentations; (4) are legal; and (5) conform with the agreed-upon underwriting standards. In addition, some repurchase requests are prompted by claims of inflated or fraudulent appraisals.

12.2.C.2 Enforcement Provisions for Representations and Warranties

The standard Mortgage Loan Purchase Agreement limits the contractual relief for breach of these representations and warranties to one set of remedies and one set alone[7] (Miller 2014, 274–76). Under the "Repurchase Obligation" provisions in versions of the Agreement before the crisis, if the substance of any representation and warranty was inaccurate and the inaccuracy materially and adversely affected the value of the mortgage loan in question or the interest of the purchaser, then the representation and warranty was breached, even if the seller was unaware and could not have been aware of the inaccuracy when the representation was made (see, e.g., Master Loan Purchase Agreement 2005, § 6). The Agreements go on to state that following prompt written notice of the discovery of such an inaccuracy, the seller shall use its best efforts to promptly cure the breach within 90 days. If the breach cannot be cured, then the seller, at the purchaser's option, shall repurchase the mortgage loan at issue at the purchase price[8] (see, e.g., id., § 6). Effectively, this gives the purchaser a put option for loans that violate representations and warranties.

In theory, this put option is quite strong. This remedy is not technically conditioned on a *realized* loss to the investor; instead, it can apply so long as a breach results in a material paper loss to the mortgage loan in question. As a practical matter, however, operationally relatively "small" errors in representations would not in general lead to exercise of the put option prior to default. In default, such errors become salient. And in the crisis, the decline in real estate prices made such ordinarily ignored errors particularly salient as prices and collateral declined dramatically.

At the same time, the contractual remedy for breach of representations and warranties is only as good as a seller's solvency. For the put option to have bite, a seller must still be operating and have sufficient assets to pay a judgment. This became a particular concern in the case of breaches by nonbank lenders, more than 100 of whom operated with razor-thin margins and capsized after they lost their funding in 2007.[9]

12.2.D The Mortgage Crisis

Had investors given representations and warranties scant credence when they originally bought loans, those provisions might not have mattered. However, investors took representations and warranties seriously. The rating agencies, for instance, touted their review of the representations and warranties for every private-label deal in order to give investors confidence that their ratings had integrity (see, e.g., S&P Global Ratings 2004). After the crisis, the Basel Committee and government investigators concluded that investors had placed undue faith in the efficacy of representations and warranties (Basel Committee on Banking Supervision 2011; Ergungor 2008).

To investors' chagrin, those representations and warranties failed to prevent the spike in mortgage loan defaults that culminated in the 2008 financial crisis. As discussed earlier, by the early 2000s, private-label securitization had outgrown its traditional function of funding jumbo conforming loans to also financing increasing numbers of nontraditional mortgage products. From 2004 through 2007, investors flocked to subprime and Alt-A MBS because of their higher yields (McCoy et al. 2009, 496–97 and fig. 1). Originators met the demand for higher coupon mortgages with risky interest-only and pay-option mortgages with no or negative amortization, which together reached an astonishing 50 percent of all mortgage originations in spring 2005 (id., 497, fig. 1). A series of decisions by federal banking regulators to deregulate residential mortgages also helped pave the way for this unprecedented growth (Engel and McCoy 2011, 151–205).

During the run-up to the crisis, the proliferation of subprime and Alt-A loans was accompanied by a marked deterioration in loan underwriting standards. Between 2002 and 2006, two of the strongest predictors of default rose noticeably: loan-to-value ratios and the proportion of loans with combined loan-to-value ratios of more than 80 percent (Levitin and Wachter 2015). Meanwhile, lenders increasingly layered one risk on top of another, often combining low-equity, no-amortization loans with reduced documentation underwriting (McCoy et al. 2009, 504–05 and fig. 3). Loan fraud also became more prevalent during this period, with private-label securitized mortgages and low-documentation mortgages experiencing particularly high levels of fraud (Mian and Sufi 2015). Loan origination volume shifted to lenders who used private-label securitization with lower and less well-enforced underwriting standards, although there is evidence that there was somewhat of a decline in the GSE underwriting standards as well (Wachter 2014, 2016). Under pressure to maintain market share, other lenders cast aside their reputational concerns and lowered their lending standards in response (Engel and McCoy 2011, 38–40).

As the ensuing disaster unfolded, it soon became apparent that representations and warranties had not prevented the sharp deterioration in underwriting standards during the credit bubble. Increasingly, it became apparent that loan features and performance that were in direct breach of the representations and warranties – including excessive loan-to-value ratios, early payment defaults, and outright fraud – had become commonplace. The first warning signs of higher defaults appeared in subprime and Alt-A adjustable-rate mortgages (ARMs) beginning in mid-2005 and worsened after that (see Table 12.1). As defaults mounted in 2006, the

TABLE 12.1: *Percentage of Subprime and Alt-A Adjustable Rate Mortgages (ARMs) 90 Days or More Past Due or in Foreclosure*

Reporting Period	Subprime ARMs	Alt-A ARMs
July 2005	5.63%	0.43%
July 2006	8.16%	0.74%
July 2007	14.63%	3.06%
December 2007	20%	6%

Source: Board of Governors of the Federal Reserve System, Table Data for Mortgage Delinquency Rates, 2001–07; Board of Governors of the Federal Reserve System, Monetary Report to Congress 6 (2008)

number of mortgage repurchase requests remained modest but started to increase in response[10] (Sabry and Schopflocher 2007). According to Fitch Ratings, early payment defaults were the "root cause" of these early repurchase requests, particularly in loans with layered risks such as lower credit scores, second liens, and stated income underwriting (Fitch 2006).

Through 2006, rising housing values allowed troubled borrowers to refinance their mortgages in order to avoid default. In the first quarter of 2007, however, housing prices began to slide nationwide for the first time since the Great Depression and the foreclosure crisis began in earnest. During this period, the compensatory and deterrent functions of representations and warranties were seriously tested.

12.2.E Repurchase Demands and Actions to Enforce Put-Back Clauses

As falling home prices impeded the ability of distressed borrowers to avoid default by refinancing their loans or selling their homes, mortgage delinquencies skyrocketed and mortgage put-back requests surged (Hartman-Glaser et al. 2014, 28, fig. 3). Data on aggregate recoveries for all put-back demands are hard to come by. But we can get a sense of the magnitude by examining put-back collections by Fannie Mae and Freddie Mac.

The two GSEs sought recourse for bad loans for two lines of business activities. First, Fannie Mae and Freddie Mac lodged repurchase claims against originators or aggregators for defective loans that had been sold to them. While the evidence is incomplete, the percentage of loans subject to Fannie/Freddie buyback claims seems to have been modest (less than 2 percent of balances at origination for GSE 30-year, fixed-rate full-documentation, fully amortizing loans from select deals) (Goodman and Zhu 2013; Goodman et al. 2015, 3–5 and fig. 1). From January 1, 2009 through the third quarter of 2015, as a result of those claims, Fannie and Freddie collected a total of $76.1 billion from more than 3,000 companies for loans repurchased from their mortgage-backed securitization trusts (GSE

Repurchase Activity). This more than doubled the total industry liability that Standard & Poor's had originally estimated for GSE repurchase and securitization claims in 2011 (Murphy 2012). Not all of the GSEs' put-back claims were successful, however, and the two enterprises ultimately withdrew or stopped pursuing another $61.9 billion in repurchase demands (GSE Repurchase Activity). For the put-back claims that settled, the average payment per loan was substantially less than the average purchase price for all of the loans[11] (Siegel and Stein 2015).

In addition, Fannie and Freddie pursued claims for their purchases of private-label MBS during the housing bubble (Hill 2011/2012, 375–81). In January 2016, their regulator and conservator, the Federal Housing Finance Agency (FHFA), reported that it had settled lawsuits against 16 out of 18 financial institutions involving the sale of private-label instruments to Fannie and Freddie. Technically, these were not buyback claims insofar as the actions alleged securities law violations and sometimes fraud in the sale of the PLS. But these claims were also founded on lax mortgages and their financial effect on originators and issuers was similar. Total settlement amounts equaled $18.2 billion as of year-end 2014 (FHFA 2016b).

12.2.E.1 Sources of Put-Back Claims

As this discussion of GSE recoveries suggests, each of the three securitization channels has generated put-back demands and lawsuits (Standard & Poor's 2013a). While these demands share many similarities across channels, there are also differences depending on the channel.

Turning to the private-label channel, many private-label issuances featured long chains of transfers involving mortgage brokers, loan originators, correspondent or wholesale lenders, investment banks, depositors, trustees, and investors. At each link in the securitization chain, representations and warranties were often made. Consequently, put-back demands for any given securitization in the PLS channel usually involved not just one, but a sequence of repurchase requests throughout the chain[12] (Hill 2011/2012, 375; Murphy 2012). Private-label securities were especially prone to buyback claims because they experienced higher average default rates than GSE RMBS (Fitch 2011).

As discussed, the GSE channel also generated repurchase claims. Although the GSEs' issuances performed better on average than their PLS cousins, as noted previously, the representations and warranties made to Fannie and Freddie were stronger in nature and spawned more interpretive case law due to their standardization, making them easier to litigate successfully (Fleming 2013; Strubel 2011).

Finally, defective FHA-insured loans generated their own set of buyback and statutory claims, sometimes by Ginnie Mae and sometimes by the U.S. Department of Justice (DOJ). Some of those claims became turbocharged due to certifications that the originators had to sign when making FHA-insured loans. Under the FHA's direct endorsement program, designated lenders are

allowed to designate mortgages as eligible for FHA insurance. In order to qualify
for this program, lenders must provide annual certifications that their quality
control systems comport with all relevant rules of the Department of Housing
and Urban Development (HUD)[13] (Goodman 2015). Lenders must further
certify that each FHA-insured loan observes all relevant HUD rules[14] (id.).
Before 2015, lenders had to make these affirmations regardless of their knowledge or their ability to detect violations (id.).

The DOJ has taken the position that any lender who knowingly submits loans for
FHA mortgage insurance containing material underwriting defects that disqualify
those loans for FHA mortgage insurance makes a false claim for purposes of the
False Claims Act (U.S. Department of Justice 2016). Under that Act, lenders who
knowingly submit false or fraudulent claims to the federal government for payment
or approval are liable to the government for damages. Justice Department claims
under the False Claims Act pose the highest monetary exposure of any of these types
of claims because violators must pay civil penalties of $5,000 to $11,000 per claim
plus treble damages. In 2011, the United States sued all of the top five mortgage
originators for False Claim Act violations in connection with their certifications for
FHA insurance[15] (Goodman 2015). According to the Justice Department, the federal
government recovered more than $5 billion in these and other claims for housing
and mortgage fraud from January 2009 through October 2015 (U.S. Department of
Justice 2015).

In addition, the DOJ has also pursued Federal Housing Administration claims
under the powerful and flexible civil money penalty provisions in Section 951 of the
Financial Institutions Reform, Recovery and Enforcement Act of 1989 (FIRREA)
(Standard & Poor's 2013a). FIRREA is attractive in many circumstances because it
has a longer limitations period and lower threshold of proof than the False Claims
Act. However, the Second Circuit Court of Appeals cast doubt on the viability of this
theory when it ruled in 2016 that FIRREA precludes recovery for intentional breach
of contractual representations and warranties through the sale of poor-quality mortgages absent evidence that a seller intended to defraud purchasers when the representations and warranties originally were made (United States ex rel. Edward
O'Donnell 2016).

12.2.E.2 Success of Put-Back Claims

As the GSE experience shows, buyback claims have not been invariably successful.
The chances of prevailing on claims for breach of representations and warranties
vary widely according to the type of breach, the passage of time, the litigation
capacity of the plaintiff, and the solvency of the defendant.

To begin with, success may turn on the type of claim. Some breaches of representations and warranties are easily proven because they turn on commonly available evidence using objective standards. Early payment defaults are a good example,

because servicing records normally show whether the borrower was delinquent in the first three months of the loan.

Other breaches are harder to substantiate and subject to dispute. The facts may require further investigation into hard-to-obtain documents outside of the purchaser's possession or the representation in question may be couched in vague or subjective language. Thus, cases alleging false loan-to-value ratios or appraised values require reconstructing the actual appraised value at origination, which is subject to debate and difficult to do. Purchasers who assert other types of fraud or misrepresentation generally must prove those claims based on evidence from the face of the loan or deal documents, which can be daunting (Miller 2014, 300–01). Buyback disputes over loans that supposedly were allowed to depart from underwriting standards due to compensating factors can be particularly messy to litigate.

While it is relatively simple to point to errors in loan documents based on a sample of the contested book of business, the import of those errors will be in question. Were they simple errors (such as whether the borrower was self-employed versus a contractual employee) that would not or should not be counted against the originator? Or is a large share of such errors indicative of sloppy underwriting that should and does matter to outcomes in conjunction with a price decline, even though it is the price decline itself that is a major factor in default and thus in losses?

In addition, the amount of time that has elapsed since the loan sale affects the deterrent role of representations and warranties and the prospects for compensation. Many Mortgage Loan Purchase Agreements predating the crisis contained no hard-and-fast outer time limits on bringing put-back claims. Under those contractual provisions, and absent an otherwise binding statute of limitations, a purchaser could ostensibly demand repurchase at any time upon discovery of a breach of a representation until the loan principal was fully repaid (Hartman-Glaser et al. 2014; Miller 2014, 311; Tate 2016). This is not a hypothetical concern: Hartman-Glaser and colleagues (2014, 2 n. 2) discovered loans from GSE securitizations going back to 1985 that were the subject of repurchase requests between 2011 and 2014. In too many cases, defects did not surface and repurchase claims were not made until those responsible were long gone, eviscerating the deterrent function of representations and warranties.

This timing issue is a double-edged sword for purchasers and sellers. The more time that elapses until a put-back demand is made, the harder it is for the purchaser to prove due to dimming memories, missing witnesses, and lost documentation (Miller 2014, 299–300). At the same time, the specter of open-ended contingent liabilities can erode investors' confidence in a bank or other issuer. For this reason, sellers have aggressively resisted older put-back claims based on lack of reasonably prompt notice[16] or expiration of statutes of limitations (id.).

The litigation capacity of the purchaser also affects the likelihood of successful put-back claims. The vigor with which the GSEs pursued buyback demands reflected their ability to terminate lenders' contractual rights to sell agency loans

(Hill 2011/2012, 371),[17] their greater litigation might combined with that of the federal government, plus the mission of Fannie and Freddie's conservator to maximize the assets in the conservatorship estates in many cases. Similarly, Ginnie Mae's ability to pursue claims through civil actions brought by the Justice Department – together with the threat of treble damages under the False Claims Act – substantially enhanced its power to negotiate favorable settlements.

In contrast, investors found it harder to bring successful put-back claims for private-label securities. One hurdle is that representations and warranties for PLS are less standardized than those for agency MBS (Fleming 2013; Standard & Poor's 2013a, 6). In addition, in order to have standing, at least 25 percent of an issue's shares must first typically vote to demand that the securitization trustee pursue a put-back claim. Only if the trustee fails to take action within a set period of time may investors directly sue. Still, investor groups have managed to surmount this obstacle (Murphy 2012; Standard & Poor's 2013a, 6).

Finally, as noted before, recovery depends on the seller's continued solvency. The largest banks survived years of repurchase claims bruised but intact (Standard & Poor's 2013a, 3, 7–8). However, other mortgage originators failed due in part to high put-back demands (Barr 2007; New Century Bankruptcy Court Examiner 2008, 36, 70–72, 105–06, 405–06), leaving some of those demands unsatisfied.

12.3 MARKET RESPONSES AND POLICY IMPLICATIONS

There have been two major market responses to the post-crisis impact of put-backs. First, citing the need to avoid future put-backs (Lux and Greene 2015, 17, 24), major lenders – particularly well-capitalized lenders who have much to lose in the event of future put-back claims – have either withdrawn from government-insured lending or have imposed on themselves credit overlays that go beyond the requirements of the GSEs, thereby lowering their market share.[18] Second, nonbank lenders have emerged as the major origination channel to fill this gap. The shift is dramatic.

The problems with these market responses are twofold. First, the shift to thinly capitalized entities implies that, in a future crisis, representation and warranty penalties could not be effectively enforced against those entities. This undermines the compensatory value of representations and warranties going forward, as well as deterrence.

Second, lenders who believe they are no longer assured of default insurance through FHA and the GSEs are imposing credit overlays that go beyond the levels required by FHA and the GSEs. These lending constraints go beyond historic levels and beyond the levels historically associated with creditworthy lending, with mortgage market and home lending consequences that are described later.

12.3.A *The Shift to Thinly Capitalized Entities, Growth of Credit Overlays, and Consequences*

Immediately after the crisis, most home mortgages were originated by the major banks that were subject to capital adequacy and repurchase reserve requirements. More recently, however, the market share of mortgage originations by banks and especially the largest banks has fallen substantially (see Figure 12.3).[19] This void has been filled by more thinly capitalized nonbank mortgage originators who are not regulated by prudential banking regulators for solvency (Lux and Greene 2015), renewing concerns about the financial capacity of those lenders to make good on their representations and warranties.

The lack of willingness on the part of established, traditional banks to extend mortgage credit has created an opportunity for a new type of market participant: minimally capitalized nonbank mortgage lenders. These lenders are denoted in

A. Home Purchase

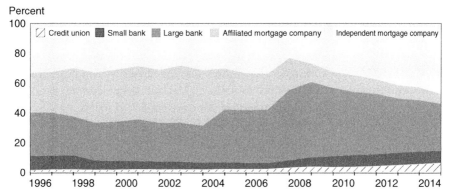

B. Refinance

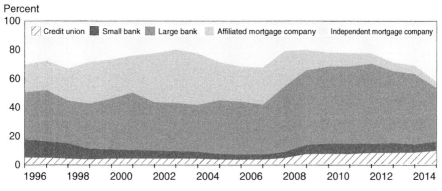

FIGURE 12.3 Market Share by Lender Type, 1995–2014
Source: Board of Governors et al. (2016b), 23 & fig. 10b

Figure 12.3 as independent mortgage companies. In view of the recent history of successful repurchase litigation against banks, nonbank lenders enjoy a distinct competitive advantage because they lack legacy put-back exposure and have scant capital at risk for future repurchase claims. The growth of these institutions (Standard & Poor's 2014) presents unique systemic risk – as these lenders are not subject to traditional capital requirements under prudential bank regulation and are minimally capitalized,[20] their failure can be harmful to the market as a whole (FHFA OIG 2014b, 23–24; FSOC 2015, 10, 114). There is no evidence, moreover, that investors are demanding pricing differentials based on the capital adequacy of individual sellers (Standard & Poor's 2013a).

At the same time, imposition of credit overlays by bank lenders who believe they are no longer assured of default insurance through FHA and the GSEs has resulted in a mortgage market that is notably constrained. This market constraint may be explained in part from regulatory pressures from HUD and DOJ. Although the primary intent of HUD and DOJ enforcement is compliance with HUD rules, it has prompted FHA's largest bank lenders to announce that they are significantly reducing their extension of mortgage credit in response (Goodman 2015). As Goodman states, "lenders have begun to protect themselves the only way available to them: credit overlays, risk-based pricing, or a general pull away from FHA lending" (id.).

As evidence of the role of buyback requests on mortgage underwriting standards, Hartman-Glaser and colleagues (2014) show that the change in the probability of buyback requests on GSE MBS explains tighter mortgage lending standards. Figure 12.4 demonstrates the tightening of standards for FICO scores.

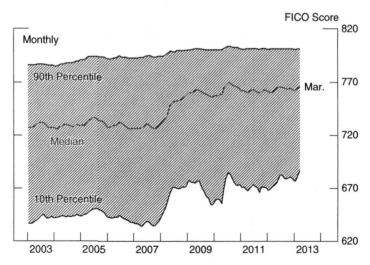

FIGURE 12.4 FICO Credit Scores on New Prime Purchase Mortgages from 2003 to 2013
Source: Duke 2013, fig. 7

The housing market has certainly made a recovery since the financial crisis, with housing starts having doubled since the recession. However, these heightened constraints on mortgage credit continue to suppress demand for housing and home-ownership[21] (Zandi and Parrott 2014). In an analysis of the extent to which con-strained credit has affected the mortgage market, Bai and colleagues (2016) found that 5.2 million more residential mortgages would have been made between 2009 and 2014 if credit standards had been at levels similar to those in 2001.

The tightening of the availability of credit has implications for homeownership. Acolin and colleagues (2016a) estimate the role of the tightening of credit on the aggregate homeownership rate. They find that the homeownership rate in 2010–2013 is predicted to be 5.2 percentage points lower than it would be if borrowing constraints were at the 2004–2007 level and 2.3 percentage points lower than if the constraints were at the 2001 level, before the relaxation of credit took place (Acolin et al. 2016b, 13).

This tightening in lending standards is part of a cycle in lending. During the credit expansion leading up to 2008, representations and warranties contributed to the overheating of the cycle by giving false assurance to investors while failing to deter the race to the bottom in lending standards. Years later, the protracted enforcement of representations and warranties slowed recovery from the crisis by impeding access to mortgages for creditworthy borrowers. This history of under-correction during the bubble and over-correction following the collapse is the hallmark of procyclicality.

This procyclicality has micro- and macro-prudential repercussions as well as serious distributive implications. The after-the-fact use of representations and war-ranties as a means to allocate risk presented solvency threats to individual entities as well as having macro repercussions, by increasing systemic risk and slowing recov-ery. The distributive implications of the unnecessarily tight credit box on low- and moderate-income households and people of color persist.

Accordingly, the goal of reforms to representations and warranties should be to reverse the procyclicality that is inherent in the current system. To achieve this, it will be necessary to right-size the enforcement of these provisions while endowing them with deterrent effect. Doing so will enhance financial stability while expand-ing the credit box in a healthy and sustainable way going forward.

12.3.B Procedural Reforms

One way to increase the efficacy of representations and warranties is to counter the long temporal disconnect between breaches of those representations and enforce-ment. In many cases, the perpetrators of those breaches were long gone by the time repurchase claims were made. Shortening the timespan between the sale of loans and the presentation of put-back claims will enhance deterrence while speeding up recovery.

After the financial crisis, the put-back process was slow to initiate in many cases and arduously protracted afterward, thus prolonging the threat of litigation. In part, this could be blamed on resistance to put-back claims by sellers. However, purchasers contributed to the drawn-out nature of the proceedings by dragging their feet in presenting claims. The GSEs, for instance, did not close out their repurchase claims on loans originated before 2009 until the end of 2013, and only then at the insistence of FHFA's then acting director, Edward DeMarco (Goodman et al. 2015, 7).

The GSEs, FHFA, and other actors eventually instituted a variety of reforms to speed up the put-back process. The GSEs instituted sunset provisions to bring some finality to the put-back process for performing loans.[22] In addition, some court decisions hold that statutes of limitation on buyback claims run from the date of sale, not the date of discovery (Miller 2014, 290, 312), putting the onus on purchasers to make claims more promptly.

Another concern is the vague and open-ended nature of some of the representations and warranties on which sellers are sued. In private-label deals, sellers had latitude to renegotiate the language of the representations and warranties they agreed to, thus potentially undermining their capacity to deter. Their negotiating ability was substantially less in deals with the GSEs and Ginnie Mae.

There will always be tension about the advisability of objective representations versus ones that are more general and ambiguous. Sellers want certainty about compliance and the extent of their exposure; purchasers worry about losses from negligence, fraud, and misconduct that they cannot anticipate in advance. A problem, as discussed further later, is that a breach may be "minor." In the nature of underwriting it may be difficult to avoid such mistakes completely. Then in the aftermath of a crisis, all such mistakes may be grist for put-back claims. But how to tell which claims are important and which are not? While this tension will likely never fully be resolved, the following principles can be used to cabin the open-ended nature of certain representations and warranties:

- First, the industry should adopt improved procedures to expedite the negotiations over put-back claims. Sellers have complained that purchasers insist on repurchase even when loans go delinquent due to life events such as job loss and divorce following origination (Standard & Poor's 2013b). It goes without saying, however, that sellers should not be responsible for events such as these outside of their control unless breach of a representation or warranty exacerbated the loss severity or risk of default. To resolve these and similar repurchase disputes without resort to litigation, sellers and purchasers could agree to send those disputes to neutral third-party arbitration. The GSEs adopted this independent dispute resolution procedure in 2016 (FHFA 2016a; Standard & Poor's 2016) and Ginnie Mae and private-label conduits might follow suit.

- Second, loans that consistently perform for a stated number of years should be exempt from repurchase claims. The GSEs' sunset provisions embody this approach by shielding loans with a 36-month record of on-time payments (12 months in the case of HARP loans) from buyback demands (FHFA OIG 2014a, 15–17; Goodman et al. 2015, 3).
- Third, liability for breach should be excused where the seller was not aware of the problem and could not have discovered it using reasonable investigation. HUD revised its annual certification in this respect in 2015 by adding the language "to the best of my knowledge and after conducting a reasonable investigation" (Goodman 2015).

It would be also advisable to standardize representations and warranties as much as possible in the private-label market. Doing so would promote the growth of arbitral decisions and case law interpreting those standardized terms, which could then provide guidance for faster resolution of similar disputes in the future.

Similarly, it is time to confront the fact that False Claims Act treble damages sanctions are overkill in the absence of knowing fraud. The threat of treble damages is discouraging bank lenders from serving the low- and moderate-income community that FHA loans were designed to serve. Instead, penalties for flaws in FHA loans should be tailored to the FHA's defect taxonomy, according to the seriousness of the violation and the violator's culpability (Goodman 2015; HUD 2014).

In an ideal world, the deterrent effect of representations and warranties could also be strengthened on the front end to curb the proliferation of lax loans during credit booms while obviating the need for enforcement. Suggested reforms have included improved due diligence and internal quality control, stronger data integrity controls for automated underwriting systems, faster post-purchase reviews by investors, and improved, standardized disclosures for put-back obligations (which the Securities and Exchange Commission issued in 2014 (Dodd Frank Act § 943; SEC 2014)).

All of these reforms, in place or contemplated, have a potential flaw, however, which is that they rely on originators' compliance. Standardized disclosures and detailed underwriting guidelines are only as good as the integrity of the underwriting process that generates them. Even if some purchasers carefully monitor loan originations through pre-purchase and post-purchase quality assurance and control as suggested, there is the potential for other purchasers to not do so, thus undermining the quality of underwriting for the system as a whole. Those originators and purchasers who skirt requirements and procedures in the "hustle" for business will rapidly gain market share, even as they lower their costs. The result will be higher prices as loans are made that otherwise would not be made and the higher prices will mask the poor underwriting. The representations and warranties may stop some, but if more aggressive lenders operate in this way, there is an "externality" (Wachter 2014) that results as the quality of the aggregate mortgage book of business deteriorates and risk increases even for more careful lenders. Moreover those lenders who are willing to undermine standards will set the bar lower for other lenders who unless they similarly lower the bar will not be able to attract the marginal borrower (Pavlov and Wachter 2006). And the process is unleashed again.

12.3.C Systemic Reforms

Lenders have called for greater clarity in the representations and warranties that they provide. But better drafting alone is not the answer to deterrence. The events of 2008 showed that lenders ignored even objective representations and warranties such as loan-to-value caps in the rush for greater market share at the height of the credit bubble. The market incentives are for contractual representations and warranties to be procyclically implemented. No one will exercise a put option when prices are rising, but everyone will do so once they have fallen. Besides market forces that lead to sliding standards across firms during the bubble, in the aftermath, there will be competitive tightening: firms will not want to be the lax lender when they fear that representations and warranties will be strictly enforced. While a normal level of "mistakes" is to be expected and not entirely avoidable, such mistakes will become the potential source for put-backs if in the overall market, prices have plummeted due to the aftermath of the unsustainable expansion of credit. And at that point put-backs bite. Accordingly, stronger external measures are needed in order for representations and warranties to have real teeth, to prevent market-wide pressures for deterioration in underwriting. Some of those measures are already in place.

Ability-to-Repay and Qualified Mortgage Provisions: The new ability-to-repay and qualified mortgage rule promulgated by the Consumer Financial Protection Bureau places a federal floor under underwriting practices by prohibiting reduced documentation loans. Because the rule requires documentation and verification of income and assets, it should significantly reduce one of the main sources of put-back claims. In addition, the rule creates a new category of loans with especially risky features such as balloon terms and negative amortization – called *non-qualified mortgages* – and imposes liability for any such loans made in disregard of the borrowers' ability to repay (CFPB 2013; Dodd-Frank Act §§ 1411–1412). The rule is enforced through federal examinations of lenders and through public and private enforcement mechanisms (which apply to poorly underwritten loans and non-qualified mortgages), which should help ensure that the federal floor is observed (Dodd-Frank Act §§ 1024(a)(1)(A), 1025–26, 1042(a), 1413, 1416(b)).

Heightened Solvency Safeguards: Increased solvency supports would give lenders a greater stake in observing representations and warranties *ex ante* in order to avoid liability for breach *ex post*, while providing purchasers with greater assurance of compensation where needed. These supports can take the form of capital requirements, provisioning thresholds, and mandatory risk retention.

To begin with, countercyclical provisioning requirements for representations and warranties would give representations and warranties more teeth while ensuring that the reserves on hand for compensation by lenders are sufficiently deep. Currently, insured depository institutions maintain reserves against their representation and warranty exposures. However, the computation of those reserves is severely procyclical. Because institutions compute these reserves based on losses already incurred, instead of expected future losses (FASB 2016, 1; Standard & Poor's 2013a, 6), they chronically under-reserve for representation and warranty liability during expansions, while struggling to boost those reserves post-crisis once lawsuits spike.

A shift to the countercyclical technique known as dynamic provisioning would reverse this perverse sequence of events. During credit booms, dynamic provisioning triggers a switch in the algorithm for loss reserves that calculates those reserves as if credit were contracting. Later, if an economic downturn strikes, that switch is turned off (Caprio 2009, 22; Ren 2011, 11–19). This model requires lenders to build up their representations and warranties reserves during credit booms, when they have cash, and allows them to spend down those reserves during economic downturns to pay for any legal exposures. To the extent that these added reserves made representations and warranties more effective, any resulting legal liability would be reduced.[23]

While federal regulators have not adopted dynamic provisioning, U.S. accounting standards have made strides toward countercyclical provisioning. In 2016, the Financial Standards Accounting Board adopted a new standard requiring lenders to calculate their loan loss allowances based on expected credit losses, regardless of whether losses have probably been incurred (FASB 2016, 1–2; see Board of Governors et al. 2016a). The provision, which takes effect in 2019, requires lenders to book all projected losses over the lifetime of the loans immediately upon origination. This is not a fully countercyclical approach because some losses for long-term residential mortgages may not become expected until years down the road. Nevertheless, the new provision will require lenders to incorporate forecasts of future conditions in addition to past and current events and record projected losses up front. Importantly, the new FASB provision applies to all bank and nonbank lenders alike.

Minimum capital requirements form another important solvency safeguard. Under Basel III, prudential banking regulators substantially increased the capital adequacy requirements for residential mortgages originated and securitized by federally insured depository institutions.[24] In addition, Basel III imposes a countercyclical capital buffer designed to kick in when credit conditions start to overheat (Department of the Treasury et al. 2013, 62031, 62171). While questions surround the implementation and efficacy of the countercyclical capital buffer if left to regulators' discretion (McCoy 2015, 1204–05 and n. 118), Basel III takes a step in the right direction by increasing the deterrence exerted by representations and warranties during incipient credit bubbles.

In the capital arena, however, regulatory arbitrage remains a serious concern. Federal banking regulators lack jurisdiction to impose minimum capital requirements on independent nonbank lenders (Board of Governors et al. 2016b, 37).[25] Even if they did have jurisdiction, uniform capital standards would be highly unlikely, given federal regulators' conclusion that Basel III is incompatible with the business models of some large nonbank mortgage servicers (id., 37–39). This means that as the nonbank sector grows, it will continue to enjoy arbitrage opportunities and escape the disciplining effect of uniform capital requirements. Not only will this reduce the *in terrorem* effect of representations and warranties, it will perpetuate competitive inequalities among bank and nonbank lenders. Unless Congress empowers federal banking regulators to impose capital adequacy requirements on mortgage lenders regardless of charter, it will be incumbent on the GSEs, Ginnie Mae, and the private-label sector to demand more meaningful safeguards from nonbank originators than they have so far.[26] Whether these investors will impose sufficient capital requirements during a credit boom, when nonbank originators are likely to expand and investors are prone to over-optimism, is questionable. Moreover if investors and private-label securitizers themselves, in a bid to grow market share, fail to demand comparable safeguards from nonbank originators, the game will be on again. We can already see potential warning signs of trouble in the rising numbers of FHA mortgages being made by nonbank lenders to borrowers with FICO scores below 660 (Lux and Greene 2015, 18–25).

12.4 CONCLUSION

During the run-up to the 2008 financial crisis, representations and warranties (contractual statements enforceable through legal action) on lending processes may have given investors false assurance that mortgage loans were being properly underwritten. This assurance in turn may have contributed to overinvestment in MBS in two ways. First, the assumption that legally enforceable penalties associated with representations and warranties would deter lax underwriting may have led to less screening of loans than would otherwise have occurred. In turn, the failure to oversee actual underwriting practices enabled the spread of lax lending practices. The existence of these representations and warranties and the potential penalties associated with them did not deter lax underwriting. Paradoxically, after the fact when the representations and warranties were enforced, this enforcement coincided with a tightening of credit beyond historic norms, with serious distributive implications. Post-crisis, lenders' fears over put-back exposure appear to have caused them to scale back, particularly on government lending to creditworthy borrowers. The representations and warranties as used in mortgage lending in the run-up to the crisis were part of the procyclicality of lending, both in the easing and tightening phases of the lending cycle.

We suggest reforms to add to the deterrent value of representations and warranties. Particularly we suggest a shift to the countercyclical technique known as dynamic provisioning to increase the *in terrorem* effect of representations and warranties. This model requires lenders to build up their representations and warranties reserves during credit booms, when they have cash and when risk is growing, and allows them to spend down those reserves during economic downturns to pay for any legal exposures. To the extent that these added reserves signaled greater risk, they would make self-enforcement of representations and warranties more effective and procyclicality would be reduced. We also propose stricter capital standards.

Nonetheless, such changes would be useless unless they were adopted throughout the lending industry: otherwise, just those entities with risky practices would increase their market share. And next time such entities are more likely to be thinly capitalized, as the lesson of capital exposure to legal risk has been learned, thus further reducing the deterrence effect of representations and warranties, going forward.

AUTHORS' NOTE

Our thanks to Lee Anne Fennell, Benjamin Keys, Karen Pence, and the other participants at the conference sponsored by the Kreisman Initiative on Housing Law and Policy at the University of Chicago in June 2016 for their helpful comments.

REFERENCES

Acolin, Arthur, Jesse Bricker, Paul Calem, and Susan Wachter. 2016a. "Borrowing Constraints and Homeownership." *American Economic Review: Papers and Proceedings.* 106: 625–29.
  2016b. "Borrowing Constraints and Homeownership Over the Recent Cycle." Available from www.ssrn.com, accessed May 4, 2016.
Avery, Robert B., Kenneth P. Brevoort and Glenn B. Canner. 2008. "The 2007 HMDA Data." *Federal Reserve Bulletin.* 94: A107–A146.
Bai, Bing, Laurie Goodman, and Jun Zhu. 2016. "Tight Credit Standards Prevented 5.2 Million Mortgages between 2009 and 2014." *Urban Wire.* The Urban Institute. January 28. Available from www.urban.org/urban-wire/tight-credit-standards-pre vented-52-million-mortgages-between-2009-and-2014, accessed April 28, 2016.
Barr, Alistair. 2007. "Big Banks Control Fate of Subprime Lenders." *MarketWatch.* February 16. Available from www.marketwatch.com/story/big-banks-deciding -the-fates-of-troubled-subprime-lenders/print, accessed May 4, 2016.
Basel Committee on Banking Supervision. July 2011. "Report on Asset Securitization Incentives."
Board of Governors of the Federal Reserve System. Fourth Quarter 2015. "Z.1: Financial Accounts of the United States." Available from www.federalreserve.gov/releases/z1 /20160310/z1.pdf, accessed May 16, 2016.
Board of Governors of the Federal Reserve System, Federal Deposit Insurance Corporation, National Credit Union Administration and Office of the Comptroller of the Currency. 2016a. "Joint Statement on the New Accounting Standard on Financial Instruments – Credit Losses." June 17.

Available from www.federalreserve.gov/newsevents/press/bcreg/bcreg2016
0617b1.pdf, accessed June 17, 2016.

Board of Governors of the Federal Reserve System, Federal Deposit Insurance
Corporation, Office of the Comptroller of the Currency and National
Credit Union Administration. 2016b. "Report to the Congress on the
Effect of Capital Rules on Mortgage Servicing Assets." June. Available
from www.federalreserve.gov/publications/other-reports/files/effect-capital
-rules-mortgage-servicing-assets-201606.pdf, accessed July 6, 2016.

Caprio, Jr., Gerard. 2009. "Safe and Sound Banking: A Role for Countercyclical
Regulatory Requirements?" Paolo Baffi Centre Research Paper No. 2010–76.
Available from www.tcd.ie/iiis/documents/discussion/pdfs/iiisdp311.pdf, accessed
April 28, 2016.

Consumer Financial Protection Bureau. 2013. "Ability-to-Repay and Qualified
Mortgage Standards Under the Truth in Lending Act (Regulation Z)."
Federal Register 78: 6408.

Department of the Treasury et al. 2014. "Credit Risk Retention: Final Rule." *Federal
Register* 79: 77602.

———. 2013. "Regulatory Capital Rules: Regulatory Capital, Implementation of Basel III,
Capital Adequacy, Transition Provisions, Prompt Corrective Action,
Standardized Approach for Risk-Weighted Assets, Market Discipline and
Disclosure Requirements, Advanced Approaches Risk-Based Capital Rule,
and Market Risk Capital Rule: Final Rule." October 11. *Federal Register* 78:
62018.

Diamond, Douglas W. 2007. "Banks and Liquidity Creation: A Simple Exposition of
the Diamond-Dybvig Model." *Federal Reserve Bank of Richmond Economic
Quarterly* 93: 189.

Dodd-Frank Wall Street Reform and Consumer Protection Act. 2010. Pub. L. No.
111–203, 124 Stat. 1376.

Duke, Elizabeth A. 2013. "A View from the Federal Reserve Board: The Mortgage
Market and Housing Conditions." May 9. Available at www.federalreserve.gov
/newsevents/speech/duke20130509a.htm, accessed October 27, 2016.

Dulaney, Chelsey, Emily Glazer, and Joe Light. 2016. "Wells Fargo to Pay
$1.2 Billion over Faulty Mortgages." *Dow Jones Business News*. February 3.
Available from www.nasdaq.com/article/wells-fargo-to-pay-12-billion-over
-faulty-mortgages–3rd-update-20160203–00801, accessed April 28, 2016.

Engel, Kathleen C. and Patricia A. McCoy. 2011. *The Subprime Virus*. Oxford:
Oxford University Press.

Ergungor, O. Emre. 2008. "Covered Bonds: A New Way to Fund Residential
Mortgages." *Economic Commentary*. July. Available from www.clevelandfed.org
/en/newsroom-and-events/publications/economic-commentary/economic-com
mentary-archives/2008-economic-commentaries/ec-20080701-covered-bonds
-a-new-way-to-fund-residential-mortgages.aspx, accessed June 18, 2016.

Fabozzi, Frank J. and Franco Modigliani. 1992. *Mortgage and Mortgage-Backed
Securities Markets*. Cambridge, MA: Harvard Business School Press.

False Claims Act. 31 U.S.C. §§ 3729 – 3733.

Fannie Mae. 2016. A4-2-01: "Net Worth, Liquidity, and Credit Rating Requirements (06/30/2015)." *Selling Guide*. March 29. Available from www.fanniemae.com /content/guide/selling/a4/2/01.html, accessed May 26, 2016.

    2014. "Lender Selling Representations and Warranties Framework Updates." *Selling Guide Announcement SEL-2014–14*. November 20. Available from www.fanniemae.com/content/announcement/sel1414.pdf, accessed May 4, 2016.

    2012. "New Lender Selling Representations and Warranties Framework." *MBS News and Announcements*. September 11. Available from www.fannie mae.com/portal/funding-the-market/mbs/news/2012/announcement-091112.html, accessed May 4, 2016.

Federal Financial Institutions Examination Council (FFIEC). 2015. "Home Mortgage Disclosure Act Data." Available from www.ffiec.gov/hmda/.

Federal Housing Finance Agency (FHFA). 2016a. "FHFA, Fannie Mae and Freddie Mac Announce Independent Dispute Resolution Program." February 2. Available from www.fhfa.gov/Media/PublicAffairs/Pages/FHFA-Fannie-and-Freddie-Announce-IDR-Program.aspx, accessed May 26, 2016.

    2016b. "FHFA's Update on Private Label Securities Actions: 2013 and 2014 Settlements and Remaining Cases." January 4. Available from www.fhfa.gov /Media/PublicAffairs/pages/fhfas-update-on-private-label-securities-actions .aspx, accessed May 4, 2016.

    2012. "Building a New Infrastructure for the Secondary Mortgage Market." Available from www.fhfa.gov/PolicyProgramsResearch/Research/PaperDocuments /FHFA_Securitization_White_Paper_N508L.pdf, accessed May 3, 2016.

Federal Housing Finance Agency, Office of Inspector General (FHFA OIG). 2014a. "FHFA's Representation and Warranty Framework." September 17. Available from http://fhfaoig.gov/Content/Files/AUD-2014–016.pdf, accessed May 4, 2016.

    2014b. "Recent Trends in the Enterprises' Purchases of Mortgages from Smaller Lenders and Nonbank Mortgage Companies." July 17. Available from http:// fhfaoig.gov/Content/Files/EVL-2014–010_0.pdf, accessed June 17, 2016.

Financial Accounting Standards Board. 2016. "Financial Instruments – Credit Losses (Topic 326): Measurement of Credit Losses on Financial Instruments." *Accounting Standards Update No. 2016–13*. Available from www.fasb.org/jsp/FASB/Document_C/DocumentPage?cid=1176168232528& acceptedDisclaimer=true, accessed June 17, 2016.

Financial Crisis Inquiry Commission. 2011. *The Financial Crisis Inquiry Report.* Available from www.gpo.gov/fdsys/pkg/GPO-FCIC/pdf/GPO-FCIC.pdf, accessed May 4, 2016.

Financial Institution Reform, Recovery and Enforcement Act of 1989 (FIRREA). Section 951, codified at 12 *U.S.C.* § 1833a.

Financial Stability Oversight Council (FSOC). 2015. "2014 Annual Report." Available at www.treasury.gov/initiatives/fsoc/Documents/FSOC%202014 %20Annual%20Report.pdf, accessed June 17, 2016.

Fitch. 2011. "U.S. Banks' GSE Mtge Repurchases Weigh on Earnings; Private-Label Remains a Concern." *Business Wire*. February 1.

———. 2006. "U.S. Mortgage Loan Repurchases: Do Early Payment Defaults Spell Trouble Ahead?" *Business Wire*. October 10.

Fleming, Mark. 2013. "The Cost and Uncertainty of No Standards." *CoreLogic Insights Blog*. Available from www.corelogic.com/blog/authors/mark-flem ing/2013/11/the-cost-and-uncertainty-of-no-standards.aspx#.VykMxpD2ZZU, accessed May 3, 2016.

Freddie Mac. 2015. "Subject: Seller/Servicer Eligibility." *Bulletin 2015–8*. May 20. Available from www.freddiemac.com/singlefamily/guide/bulletins/pdf /bll1508.pdf, accessed May 26, 2016.

———. 2012. "Subject: Quality Control and Enforcement Practices." *Industry Letter to Freddie Mac Sellers and Servicers*. October 19. Available from www.freddiemac .com/singlefamily/guide/bulletins/pdf/iltr101912.pdf, accessed May 4, 2016.

Ginnie Mae. 2016. "Ginnie Mae's Role in Housing Finance." Available from www .ginniemae.gov/consumer_education/Pages/ginnie_maes_role_in_housing_fi nance.aspx, accessed March 24, 2016.

———. 2014. "Ginnie Mae Announces Changes in Issuer Requirements at 2014 MBA Annual Convention." October 20.

Glazer, Emily, Aruna Viswanatha, and Joe Light. 2016. "Wells Fargo to Pay $1.2 Billion over Faulty Mortgages." *The Wall Street Journal*. February 3. Available from www.wsj.com/articles/wells-fargo-to-pay-1-2-billion-over-faulty -mortgages-1454506277, accessed May 4, 2016.

Goodman, Laurie. 2016. "A Progress Report on the Private-Label Securities Market." Housing Finance Policy Center, The Urban Institute. March. Available from www.urban.org/sites/default/files/alfresco/publication-pdfs/2000647-A- Progress-Report-on-the-Private-Label-Securities-Market.pdf, accessed May 4, 2016.

———. 2015. "Wielding a Heavy Enforcement Hammer Has Unintended Consequences for the FHA Mortgage Market." Housing Finance Policy Center, The Urban Institute. May. Available from www.urb.org/sites/default/files/alfresco/publica tion-pdfs/2000220-Wielding-a-Heavy-Enforcement-Hammer-Has-Unintended -Consequences-for-the-FHA-Mortgage-Market.pdf, accessed April 28, 2016.

Goodman, Laurie, Jim Parrott, and Jun Zhu. 2015. "The Impact of Early Efforts to Clarify Mortgage Repurchases." Housing Finance Policy Center, The Urban Institute. Available from www.urban.org/sites/default/files/alfresco/publica tion-pdfs/2000142-The-Impact-of-Early-Efforts-to-Clarify-Mortgage-Repurchases .pdf, accessed April 28, 2016.

Goodman, Laurie, Ellen Seidman, and Jun Zhu. 2013. "Sunset Provisions on Reps and Warrants: Can They Be More Flexible While Still Protecting the GSEs?" November 27. Housing Finance Policy Center, The Urban Institute. Available from www.urban.org/research/publication/sunset-provisions-reps-and-war rants-can-they-be-more-flexible-while-still-protecting-gses, accessed May 4, 2016.

Goodman, Laurie S. and Jun Zhu. 2013. "Reps and Warrants: Lessons from the GSEs Experience." Housing Finance Policy Center, Urban Institute. October 24. Available from www.urban.org/sites/default/files/alfresco/publica tion-pdfs/412934-Reps-and-Warrants-Lessons-from-the-GSEs-Experience.PDF, accessed May 5, 2016.

Green, Richard K. and Susan M. Wachter. 2007. "The Housing Finance Revolution." *Proceedings – Economic Policy Symposium – Jackson Hole, Federal Reserve Bank of Kansas City*, 21–67.

GSE Repurchase Activity: Cumulative to Third Quarter 2015. *Inside Mortgage Finance*. Available from www.insidemortgagefinance.com/catalog/datare ports/GSE-Repurchase-Activity-Through-3Q15-1000034878-1.html, accessed April 28, 2016.

Hartman-Glaser, Barney, Richard Stanton, and Nancy Wallace. 2016. "Mortgage Underwriting Standards in the Wake of Quantitative Easing." Available from https://groups.haas.berkeley.edu/realestate/research/2016%20conference%20 papers/mortgagecredit.pdf, accessed April 9, 2017.

Herring, Richard and Susan Wachter. 2003. "Bubbles in Real Estate Markets." In *Asset Price Bubbles: The Implications for Monetary, Regulatory, and International Policies*. William C. Hunter, George G. Kaufman, and Michael Pomerleano, eds., 217–29. Cambridge: MIT Press.

Hill, Julie Anderson. 2011/2012. "Shifting Losses: The Impact of Fannie's and Freddie's Conservatorships on Commercial Banks." *Hamline Law Review* 35: 343–84.

Itzhak, Ben-David. 2011. "Financial Constraints and Inflated Home Prices during the Real-Estate Boom." *American Economics Journal: Applied Economics* 3: 55–87.

Kaul, Karan, and Laurie Goodman. 2016. "Nonbank Servicer Regulation: New Capital and Liquidity Requirements Don't Offer Enough Loss Protection." Housing Finance Policy Center, Urban Institute. February. Available from www.urban.org/sites/default/files/publication/78131/2000633-Nonbank-Servicer -Regulation-New-Capital-and-Liquidity-Requirements-Don%27t-Offer-Enough -Loss-Protection.pdf, accessed April 9, 2017.

Keys, Benjamin, Tanmoy Mukherjee, Amit Seru, and Vikrant Vig. 2010. "Did Securitization Lead to Lax Screening? Evidence from Subprime Loans." *Quarterly Journal of Economics* 125: 307–62.

Levitin, Adam J., Andrey D. Pavlov, and Susan M. Wachter. 2012. "The Dodd-Frank Act and Housing Finance: Can It Restore Private Risk Capital to the Securitization Market?" *Yale Journal on Regulation* 29: 155–80.

Levitin, Adam J. and Susan M. Wachter. 2015. "Second Liens and the Leverage Option." *Vanderbilt Law Review* 68: 1243–94.

   2013a. "The Public Option in Housing Finance." *University of California, Davis Law Review* 46: 1111–74.

   2013b. "Why Housing?" *Housing Policy Debate* 23: 5–27.

2012. "Explaining the Housing Bubble." *Georgetown Law Journal* 100: 1177–1258.

Lewis, Michael. [1989] 1990. *Liar's Poker*. New York: Penguin Group (USA) Inc.

Lux, Marshall and Robert Greene. 2015. "What's Behind the Non-bank Mortgage Boom?" M-RCBG Associate Working Paper Series No. 42. June. Available from www.hks.harvard.edu/centers/mrcbg/publications/awp/awp42, accessed July 6, 2016.

Master Loan Purchase Agreement between Citigroup Mortgage Loan Trust Inc. and Citigroup Global Markets Realty Corp. August 24, 2005.

McCoy, Patricia. 2015. "Countercyclical Regulation and Its Challenges." *Arizona State Law Journal* 48: 1181–1237.

McCoy, Patricia, Andrey Pavlov, and Susan Wachter. 2009. "Systemic Risk Through Securitization: The Result of Deregulation and Regulatory Failure." *Connecticut Law Review* 41: 493–541.

Mian, Atif and Amir Sufi. 2015. "Fraudulent Income Overstatement on Mortgage Applications during the Credit Expansion of 2002 to 2005." NBER Working Paper No. 20947.

2014. *House of Debt: How They (and You) Caused the Great Recession, and How We Can Prevent It from Happening Again.* Chicago: University of Chicago Press.

Miller, Robert. 2014. "The RMBS Put-Back Litigations and the Efficient Allocation of Endogenous Risk over Time." *Review of Banking and Financial Law* 34: 255–315.

Mortgage Bankers Association. 2016. Basel III Treatment of Mortgage Servicing Rights. Available from www.mba.org/issues/residential-issues/basel-iii-treat ment-of-mortgage-servicing-assets, accessed June 17, 2016.

Murphy, James. 2012. "Residential Mortgage-Backed Securities Litigation: Representation & Warranty Lawsuits." Available from www.sifma.org, accessed April 28, 2016.

New Century Bankruptcy Court Examiner. 2008. Final Report of Michael J. Missal Bankruptcy Court Examiner. In re New Century TRS Holdings, Inc., Case No. 07–10416 (KJC) (D. Del.). Available from http://s3.document cloud.org/documents/30572/missal-final-report-on-the-bankruptcy-of-new-century .pdf, accessed May 4, 2016.

Oliner, Stephen D., Edward J. Pinto, and Brian Marein. 2015. "Study Shows Seismic Shift in Lending Away from Large Banks to Nonbanks continued in February." March 31. Available from www.housingrisk.org/study-shows-seismic-shift-in -lending-away-from-large-banks-to-nonbanks-continued-in-february/#more-1651, accessed June 17, 2016.

Parrott, Jim and Mark Zandi. 2013. "Opening the Credit Box." The Urban Institute. September 30. Available from www.urban.org/sites/default/files/alfresco/publi cation-pdfs/412910-Opening-the-Credit-Box.PDF, accessed May 4, 2016.

Pavlov, Andrey and Susan M. Wachter. 2006. "The Inevitability of Marketwide Underpricing of Mortgage Default Risk." *Real Estate Economics* 34(4): 479–96.

Piskorski, Tomasz, Amit Seru, and James Witkin. 2015. "Asset Quality Misrepresentation by Financial Intermediaries: Evidence from RMBS Market." *Journal of Finance* 70: 2635–78.

Reckard, E. Scott. 2006. "Ownit Seeks Bankruptcy Protection." *Los Angeles Times*. December 30. Available from http://articles.latimes.com/2006/dec/30/business /fi-ownit30, accessed April 9, 2017.

Ren, Haocong. 2011. "Countercyclical Financial Regulation." World Bank, Working Paper No. 5823.

S&P Global Ratings. 2004. "RMBS: U.S. Residential Subprime Mortgage Criteria: Legal Criteria for Subprime Mortgage Transactions." September 1.

Sabry, Faten and Thomas Schopflocher. 2007. "The Subprime Meltdown: A Primer." Available from www.nera.com/content/dam/nera/publications /archive1/PUB_SubPrimer_1108.pdf, accessed April 28, 2016.

Securities and Exchange Commission (SEC). 2014. "Asset-Backed Securities Disclosure and Registration Part II: Final Rule." *Federal Register* 79: 57184. September 24.

Siegel, Robert and Philip Stein. 2015. "Mid-2015 Mortgage Crisis Update – The Repurchase Demands Continue." *National Law Review*. June 12. Available from www.financialserviceswatchblog.com/2015/06/mid-2015-mort gage-crisis-update-the-repurchase-demands-continue/, accessed May 4, 2016.

Standard & Poor's. 2016. "Fannie Mae and Freddie Mac Adopt Independent Dispute Resolution Process That Could Shorten R&W Resolution Timelines." February 24. Available from www.researchandmarkets.com/reports/3622615/fan nie-mae-and-freddie-mac-adopt-independent, accessed May 4, 2016.

2014. "New Players in the RMBS Market Could Present Unique Representations and Warranties Risks." Available from www.researchandmarkets.com/reports /2874265/new-players-in-the-rmbs-market-could-present, accessed April 28, 2016.

2013a. "The Largest U.S. Banks Should Be Able to Withstand the Ramifications of Legal Issues." November 25. Available from http://images.politico.com/global /2013/11/26/11–25-13_-_the_largest_us_banks_should_be_able_to_with stand_the_ramifications_of_legal_issues.pdf, accessed May 3, 2016.

2013b. "U.S. RMBS Roundtable: Arrangers and Investors Discuss the Role of Representations and Warranties in U.S. RMBS Transactions." June 28.

Strubel, Ben. 2011. "In Depth Analysis and Valuation of H&R Block (HRB)." *GuruFocus*. Available from www.gurufocus.com/news/124397/in-depth-analy sis-and-valuation-of-hr-block-hrb, accessed May 3, 2016.

Tate, John R. 2008. "Are You Managing Your Loan Repurchase Risk?" Available from www.dwt.com/files/Publication/5ce7cdf1-0180-465d-8641-7dbobf8e315c /Presentation/PublicationAttachment/18db409d-869d-4942-bfff-7ff865cb52b4 /pubs_02-08_LoanRepurchase.pdf, accessed April 9, 2017.

United States ex rel. Edward O'Donnell v. Countrywide Home Loans, Inc., et al., slip op. (2d Cir. May 23, 2016).

U.S. Department of Housing & Urban Development (HUD). 2015. "FHA's Single Family Housing Loan Quality Assessment Methodology (Defect Taxonomy)."

June 18. Available from http://portal.hud.gov/hudportal/documents/huddoc
?id=SFH_LQA_Methodology.pdf, accessed May 4, 2016.

U.S. Department of Justice. 2016. "The False Claims Act & Federal Housing
Administration Lending." Available from www.justice.gov/opa/blog/false
-claims-act-federal-housing-administration-lending, accessed May 3, 2016.

— 2015. "Justice Department Recovers over $3.5 Billion from False Claims Act Cases
in Fiscal Year 2015." Available from www.justice.gov/opa/pr/justice-department-
recovers-over-35-billion-false-claims-act-cases-fiscal-year-2015, accessed May 5,
2016.

Wachter, Susan M. 2016. "Informed Securitization." In *Principles of Housing
Finance Reform.* Susan M. Wachter and Joseph Tracy, eds., 209–21.
Philadelphia: University of Pennsylvania Press.

— 2014. "The Market Structure of Securitisation and the U.S. Housing Bubble."
National Institute Economic Review 230: R34–R44.

— 2010. "The Ongoing Financial Upheaval: Understanding the Sources and Way
Out." *International Real Estate Review* 13(2): 218–37.

Wei Jiang, Ashlyn Aiko Nelson, and Edward Vytlacil. 2014. "Liar's Loan? Effects of
Origination Channel and Information Falsification on Mortgage
Delinquency." *Review of Economics and Statistics* 96: 1–18.

Zandi, Mark and Jim Parrott. 2014. "Zandi: Credit Constraints Threaten Housing
Recovery." *The Washington Post.* January 24.

Notes

1. This relationship between real estate bubbles and busts, financial instability, and
subsequent economic crashes has been observed across countries and over time,
with the severity and frequency of this connection increasing with the integration
of housing finance into global capital markets (Green and Wachter 2007).
2. Critics also assert that the substantial payouts by lenders for breach of representations and warranties – in some cases, contributing to their insolvencies – are proof
that badly underwritten mortgages were not the cause of the 2008 financial crisis
(Miller 2014, 258 & n. 6). This confuses the deterrent function of representations
and warranties with their compensatory function and assumes that those representations were successful in preventing lax underwriting *ex ante.* The evidence
shows, however, that representations did not deter poorly underwritten loans (see
Sections II(d)-II(e) *supra*). Instead, there was a disconnect between lenders' loose
underwriting practices during the credit bubble and their liability, often many
years removed, for the resulting breaches of their representations and warranties.
3. For a general critique of procyclical financial regulation, see McCoy (2015).
4. Ginnie Mae and the government-sponsored enterprises (GSEs) unveiled the first
market innovations between 1970 and 1981. Ginnie Mae pioneered the first
mortgage pass-through security of an FHA-approved lender in 1970 (Ginnie
Mae 2016). Freddie Mac unveiled its first mortgage pass-through certificate in
1971. Fannie Mae introduced its first mortgage pass-through certificate, which it

named a mortgage-backed security, in 1981 (Fabozzi and Modigliani 1992, 21, 23). Meanwhile, Lewis Ranieri is credited as having invented the first private-label mortgage-backed securities while at Salomon Brothers in or around 1979 (Lewis [1989] 1990, 90–102).

5. Jumbo loans are mortgage loans – usually prime mortgages – that exceed Fannie Mae and Freddie Mac dollar limits on the size of conforming loans. Subprime mortgages are mortgages with higher interest rates, designed for borrowers with impaired credit. The meaning of the term "Alt-A mortgages" was more amorphous, but was commonly understood to include loans made with less-than-fully amortizing principal or reduced documentation of income, job, or assets.

6. For discussion of principal-agent problems in securitization, see, e.g., Keys et al. (2010) and Mian and Sufi (2014).

7. Despite this attempt to limit claims against sellers for defective loans, transferees have sued on a wide variety of claims for damages, rescission of entire loan pools, and other types of relief (Murphy 2012).

8. Alternatively, the purchaser at its option may allow the seller to replace the defective mortgage loan with another mortgage loan (see, e.g., Master Loan Purchase Agreement 2005, § 6).

9. One hundred sixty-nine mortgage lenders, most of which were independent nonbank originators, failed in 2007. Avery et al. (2008, A109-10).

10. An early example was subprime lender Ownit Mortgage Solutions, which failed in December 2006 after it was overwhelmed by mortgage repurchase requests (Reckard 2006).

11. Standard & Poor's reported in 2013 that based on settlements publicly disclosed by FHFA at the time, it "seem[ed]" that the settlement amount was 12%-14% of the original unpaid principal balance of securities" (2013a, 7). Professor Julie Hill criticized the repurchase decisions of the GSEs and FHFA as opaque and not always based on the merits of claims for breach, stating:

> [I]n some instances the government allowed the Enterprises to absorb losses even when the losses could be transferred to large banks. Presumably this is part of the government's larger efforts to stabilize systemically important banks. On the other hand, the government allowed the Enterprises to transfer some losses to small banks, even when the losses ultimately resulted in bank failures. The FHFA has likely allowed risk shifting to small banks in part because it determined that even if some small banks fail, the economic impact will not be widespread. (2011/2012, 347).

12. Financial guaranty insurers also lodged claims against insureds for compensation of insurance proceeds paid to investors to cover claims for breach of representations and warranties on the underlying PLS (Murphy 2012).

13. Specifically, the certification states: "The operation is in compliance with all the program's regulations, requirements, and processes."

14. For each loan, the lender must attest that the mortgage "is eligible for HUD mortgage insurance under the Direct Endorsement program" and as to "the integrity of the data supplied by the lender used to determine the quality of the

loan" for loans submitted to automated underwriting. For loans that are manu-
ally underwritten, the lender must state that the underwriter "personally
reviewed the appraisal report (if applicable), credit application and all associated documents and has used due diligence in underwriting the mortgage"
(Goodman 2015, 9 n. 6).

15. Separately, the inspector general of HUD has authority to pursue lenders who
have made false claims under the Program Fraud Civil Remedies Act of 1986.
Under that Act, the IG can seek $5,000 per claim plus double damages, up to
a maximum of $150,000. This relief tends to be used for smaller claims against
smaller lenders that the Justice Department is not interested in pursuing
(Goodman 2015, 9 n. 6).

16. Some private-label Mortgage Loan Purchase Agreements – although not all –
require reasonably prompt notice as a condition of repurchase.

17. In 2012, following a dispute over its put-back requests, Fannie Mae announced
that it would place restrictions on loan sales by Bank of America (Hill 2011/
2012, 374).

18. The private-label market is moribund, thus effectively the GSEs and Ginnie
Mae are the securitization market.

19. Although the relative market share attributable to credit unions (which resemble banks more than nonbank mortgage lenders) has grown, that growth has
been relatively modest. See Figure 12.3.

20. Fannie Mae, Freddie Mac, and Ginnie Mae now require nonbank sellers/
servicers to maintain minimum capital ratios of 6 percent "or their equivalent,"
measured by tangible net worth to total assets (Fannie Mae 2016; Freddie Mac
2015; Ginnie Mae 2014). These capital thresholds are not risk-based and in many
cases, will be substantially lower than the minimum capital expected of insured
banks (Kaul and Goodman 2016).

   In addition, some have attributed Basel III's tighter capital treatment of
mortgage servicing assets (MSAs) to the steady recent migration of mortgage
servicing rights from banks to nonbanks (Mortgage Bankers Association 2016),
although federal regulators have cast doubt on that assertion (Board of
Governors et al. 2016b, 28, 35). Basel III increased the risk weights for MSAs
from 100 percent to 250 percent and also limited the percentage of the common
equity element of tier one capital that can be comprised of MSAs to 10 percent
(id., 17–18). These Basel III requirements apply to banks but not nonbanks (id.).

21. See Dulaney et al. (2016) ("Partly as a result [of False Claim Act claims], over
the past couple years some major banks, such as J.P. Morgan and Bank of
America, have pulled back sharply from the FHA program by imposing their
own more stringent requirements on FHA loans, a move that makes it harder for
less-credit-worthy borrowers to get a mortgage. Wells Fargo, which is still one of
the most prominent FHA lenders, last year said it would raise the minimum
credit score it accepts on certain FHA loans to 640 from 600, reversing a 2014
decision to reduce the required score.").

22. In 2012, the GSEs announced that loans with 36 months of consecutive timely
payments (or 12 months in the case of HARP loans) would thereafter be immune

from repurchase exposure. These sunset provisions only applied to loans sold or delivered on or after January 1, 2013 (Fannie Mae 2012; Freddie Mac 2012; Goodman et al. 2015, 2).

In May 2014, FHFA Director Mel Watt relaxed these sunset requirements to permit loans with no more than two 30-day delinquencies and no 60-day delinquencies during the 36- or 12-month period to qualify for the sunset (FHFA OIG 2014a, 15–17; Goodman et al. 2015, 3).

23. For a review of the literature analyzing the adoption of dynamic provisioning in other countries, see McCoy (2015, 1207).

24. Under the standardized approach, residential mortgages that do not meet specific quality standards or that are nonperforming have risk-weights of 100 percent (Department of the Treasury et al. 2013, 62180–82, 62190–91, 62196–97). In addition, federal banking regulators now require higher capital charges against residential mortgages that are securitized by banks (id., 62116, 62119, 62121, 62194–96, 62253).

25. In contrast, Dodd-Frank's risk retention provisions do apply to non-qualified mortgages made by independent nonbank originators.

26. See note 20 *supra*. Two leading analysts recently concluded that the GSEs' and Ginnie Mae's new capital requirements for nonbank mortgage servicers were "inadequate" (Kaul and Goodman 2016).

13

When the Invisible Hand Isn't a Firm Hand: Disciplining Markets That Won't Discipline Themselves

Raphael W. Bostic and Anthony W. Orlando

The housing crisis of the 2000s exposed fissures in the U.S. financial system. These shortcomings allowed the system to become encumbered with excessive risk and ultimately triggered the worst economic downturn since the Great Depression. In the wake of the deep recession, many academics and researchers wrote post-mortems identifying key causes of the crisis. In 2010, Congress passed the Wall Street Reform and Consumer Protection Act, also known as Dodd-Frank, and President Obama signed it into law. It sought to address many of the identified problems by reforming regulations pertaining to mortgage lending, securities trading, banking, insurance, consumer protection, and corporate governance.

This chapter explores three causes of the crisis that the regulatory reforms have yet to fully address. First, we highlight challenges that prevented credit rating agencies from being a useful source of information for mortgage-backed securities investors to impose effective market discipline on issuers. Second, we show the failure of several institutional arrangements designed to prevent firm owners and managers from looting the institutions over the short run at the expense of shareholders, who are expecting a maximization of profits over the longer term. Finally, we consider markets from the consumer perspective. We note the tension between overcoming market tendencies to ration credit and exposing households with limited resources to risks associated with products that can broaden access to credit by easing borrowing constraints.

In each case, we offer possible strategies for more effectively tackling these problems. Regarding ratings agencies, we propose a new structure where agency-investor conflicts of interest are removed and agencies only assess "ratings eligible" products. Reforms in executive compensation, covenant banking for investment banks, and increased penalties for looting that make criminal liability a real deterrent for firm owners and managers are possible avenues to reduce the likelihood of looting by insiders. Third, we argue that significant investments should be made in financial education to make consumers an additional bulwark – to go with laws and regulations – against abuses and bad outcomes.

To begin, we tell the story of Black Friday, a deep financial crisis that occurred in the mid-nineteenth century. We take this historical approach because Black Friday shares many of the features that brought down the economy during the recent crisis, including the issues that we highlight. Indeed, a punchline of the current analysis is that many of the problems in the recent episode are enduring and inherent to virtually all regulatory structures. This fact should inform what we ask our regulations to address and how we define transparency in financial markets.

13.1 A CAUTIONARY TALE OF UNDISCIPLINED MARKETS

It was Wednesday evening in downtown Manhattan, and Jay Gould had a problem. He had just learned, through a secret letter written from the First Lady to her sister-in-law Virginia Corbin, that the president of the United States was "very much annoyed" by Gould's speculation in the gold market and wanted him to unwind his positions immediately. "I am undone," Gould said to Corbin's husband, Abel, "if that letter gets out" to the public.

The date was September 22, 1869, and Gould had been buying gold since April. By himself, Gould didn't have enough money to move markets, but in this era before securities regulation, he didn't have to work alone. He formed a pool with some of the biggest investors on Wall Street and instructed them to push up the price of gold with their purchases. Meanwhile, he leveraged his position as the president of the Erie Railroad to borrow tens of millions of dollars and multiply his wager. He even paid President Ulysses S. Grant's brother-in-law to lobby the government not to sell its gold reserves.

Now, it seemed, the president had caught on to his scheme.

The next morning, Gould started selling gold at the opening bell, but he didn't tell all of his partners in crime. He feared a fire sale would ensue if everybody tried to exit at the same time, so he got out stealthily and let them keep buying unaware.

It took only a day for the market to figure out what he was up to. Sell orders came in so fast that the telegraph couldn't keep up. "Nearly a thousand individual investors were bankrupted on the day's activity," writes Gould's biographer Edward J. Renehan Jr. "Fourteen brokerage houses went under, along with several banks." Henceforth, September 24, 1869, would be known as Black Friday (Renehan 2005).

We begin our story here because Jay Gould was arguably the first trader to stoke a speculative bubble on Wall Street, followed by a nationwide financial panic, using real estate as collateral. Railroads were the first great real estate companies in American history, gobbling up land to lay tracks across the country and building the biggest corporations the world had ever seen. In their manipulations and innovations, we see many parallels to the housing booms and busts in our own time.

But we also begin our analysis with the tale of Jay Gould because it evokes such a fitting reaction in those who hear it: *This wasn't supposed to happen.* One investor wasn't supposed to have the power to trigger a national wave of bankruptcies. One cabal wasn't supposed to be able to overpower the laws of supply and demand for any asset. One market wasn't supposed to threaten the entire economy.

This is a message of basic economics. Competition forces companies to minimize prices and maximize quality, lest their customers find a better deal elsewhere. We don't need central planners to tell us what to produce or how to invest. And don't worry about bad actors like Jay Gould. The market will discipline them.

We have found this story incomplete – in Gould's day and in our own. The housing bubble, the twin financial and foreclosure crises, and the Great Recession all demonstrated that markets are insufficient safeguards against bad behavior.

Perhaps the most compelling confession of this omission came from the chief regulator himself, former Federal Reserve Chairman Alan Greenspan, when he said, "I made a mistake in presuming that the self-interests in organizations, specifically banks and others, were such as that they were best capable of protecting their own shareholders and their equity in the firms" (Knowlton and Grynbaum 2008).

Market discipline, in other words, was absent. In this chapter, we document the ways in which it was absent, and we propose new forms of discipline to minimize bad behavior in the future. Throughout, we hope you will see that regulation is a necessary component of financial stability, as well as social justice, without which powerful and savvy players like Jay Gould can take advantage of less advantaged individuals and change the very direction of progress in our society.

Jay Gould was not an anomaly. His successful rent-seeking was a creation of undisciplined markets, as evidenced by the many robber barons who played the same predatory game to similar effect. We highlight three levels, though there are others, at which they could have been stopped – investors, board of directors, and customers – and all three had to fail for their ploy to work.

13.2 STEP ONE: FOOL THE INVESTORS

Investors are not stupid. They know that there's a lot they don't know about a firm. There is an information *asymmetry* between what the managers know and what the investors think they know. This is the classic explanation put forth by Myers and Majluf (1984), for example, for why stock prices tend to fall when firms issue new shares. The investors assume that the managers are more likely to issue shares when they think the market is willing to pay more than their assets are really worth, which means the stock price is too high. Managers, anticipating this price fall, will prefer to issue debt instead. So if they issue stock, it means they're really in need of cash, confirming investors' fears. It's in the interest of both the investors and the managers of undervalued firms, therefore, to have better public information to weed out the managers who are trying to get investors to overpay.

The king of getting investors to overpay in this way, of course, was Jay Gould. He issued so much stock during his run of the Erie Railroad that one of his successor's first actions as president was to recall 650,000 shares that he deemed "fraudulent"

(Renehan 2005). But Gould wasn't the only one oversubscribing investors to his cause. By the time Gould left the Erie in 1872, the entire industry was "heavily dependent on capital from Continental European investors," according to economist Scott Mixon. Eventually, it became clear that assets weren't growing as fast as liabilities. Investors started pulling out. Credit spreads widened between high- and low-grade bonds, and equity prices fell for the latter. In September 1873, Jay Cooke & Co., one of the nation's largest and most prestigious banking houses, filed for bankruptcy when it couldn't sell enough bonds to cover the losses on its railroad investments. The stock market lost 25 percent of its value that week, triggering the Panic of 1873 and a six-year recession that came to be known as the "Long Depression" (Mixon 2008). Watching his father lose his fortune in this indiscriminate crash, one young lad resolved to do something someday to help investors sort out those risks – some way to provide the kind of information that might have spared them from being manipulated by insiders like Jay Gould.

That young lad was named John Moody.

Moody's was not the first company to report credit information. As early as 1832, *The American Railroad Journal* was reporting on the state of the industry, extending to financial data such as assets, liabilities, and earnings when Henry Varnum Poor took up the editorship in 1849. The first actual "rating agency," though, was probably the Mercantile Agency, started by Lewis Tappan in 1841. As a merchant in New York, Tappan had accumulated deep knowledge of the major firms' creditworthiness. He figured it would be profitable to share that knowledge with other merchants for a fee. Over time, he built an entire army of information collectors across the United States. By the turn of the century, they were opining on the creditworthiness of more than 1 million businesses every year (Sylla 2001).

Despite this wide reach, the early rating agencies failed to prevent investors like William Moody from buying into the railroad craze that precipitated the Panic of 1873. To John, it was a classic failure of forecasting, a statistical art that was just coming into its own at the turn of the century. Moody's innovation in 1909 was to issue *forward-looking* credit ratings so investors could see the losses coming before it was too late. By 1924, his competitors Standard, Poor's, and Fitch Publishing Company had followed his lead. By 1941, S&P had merged, giving us the "Big Three" as we know them today (Voznyuk 2015).

All this was the market's way of attempting to discipline itself. The strange thing is, it never really seemed to work very well. More than 70 percent of the money invested in bonds that defaulted in the Great Depression had received the stamp of approval from Moody's as "investment grade" (i.e., low risk of default) (Sylla 2001). Despite this mediocre track record, in 1936, regulators prohibited banks from investing in any securities that the rating agencies hadn't designated as investment grade. Essentially, they outsourced their regulatory power to these private agencies. Soon thereafter, state regulators set minimum capital requirements for insurance companies, with higher-rated securities requiring less capital. The Securities and Exchange

Commission took the same approach in 1975 with broker-dealers. They officially defined the Big Three as "nationally recognized statistical rating organizations" (NRSROs) whose ratings were valid for this purpose. In the 1990s, they extended this approach to money market mutual funds (White 2010).

Many critics have pinpointed these regulations as a key cause of the recent housing boom and bust, as they gave financial institutions an incentive to load up on investment-grade securities that weren't as safe as they seemed. The lessons of history point in a different direction. First, we have seen that far more severe booms and busts occurred *before* the rating agencies became powerful arbiters of capital requirements. As Myers and Majluf taught us, high-risk securities issuers have always had an incentive to hide the truth about their assets, and investors have always been willing to take a chance when times were good. Second, the rating agencies have historically performed on par with the markets in predicting default risks (Sylla 2001). The regulators had to use *some* metric to confine institutions, and the rating agencies were the best the market had to offer. It's hard to see how this was worse than the status quo that existed before 1936.

In fact, it turns out that the mistakes the rating agencies made – and investors followed, to their detriment – had virtually nothing to do with regulation. They were, on the contrary, a classic example of undisciplined markets at work.

We can trace their undoing back to 1968, when the world of finance began to change. Ever since the Great Depression, the credit rating business had been a sleepy affair. A generation of Americans had learned its lesson when bonds defaulted, and they were slow to ante up again – partly out of lingering risk aversion, partly due to regulation, and partly because the economy was growing so rapidly that firms and governments could finance their investments with their own earnings. Eventually, those motivations faded. Bonds were back, and they were bigger than ever.

If you need to convince investors to buy a lot of bonds, you need credit ratings. Starting in the late 1960s, bond issuers needed investors – and that meant they needed rating agencies. The agencies were overwhelmed. They couldn't sell enough subscriptions to investors to cover the costs of rating all those bonds. So they changed their business model. Instead of asking the investors to pay, they asked the issuers to pay. It was a simple matter of supply and demand. Bond issuers needed to borrow more than investors needed to lend. The rating agencies went to the highest bidder.

S&P began charging municipalities in 1968. Moody's followed suit in 1970. Later that year, Moody's started charging corporate bond issuers, and S&P joined them four years after that.

As soon as bond issuers started paying rating agencies, investors started complaining about conflict of interest. The issuers wanted high ratings, and the agencies had an incentive to keep their customers happy. Investors could have countered by paying for their own ratings, but they had a coordination problem. Each bond had a lot of investors, but it only had one issuer. There was no mechanism for all those investors to work together to split the cost that it would take to outbid the issuer. It was a classic "free rider" problem.

The "issuer-pays" model has historically underperformed its "subscriber-pays" counterpart. In 2001, Fitch, Moody's, and S&P all failed to downgrade Enron until a few days before it filed for bankruptcy, while the lesser-known Egan-Jones Rating Company, sticking to the old-fashioned subscriber-pays model, was months ahead. The following year, the issuer-pays agencies were late in predicting the defaults of California utilities, WorldCom, Global Crossing, and AT&T Canada (Egan-Jones Rating Company 2002). These failures prompted Johnson (2003) to compare the two models for all their ratings, and he found that Egan-Jones consistently predicted defaults earlier than the issuer-pays agencies since its inception in 1995. Three years later, Beaver, Shakespeare, and Soliman (2006) came to the same conclusion in more exhaustive detail. Even after the SEC designated Egan-Jones as an NSRSO, their superior performance persisted, suggesting that the source of the difference really is their business model and *not* regulation (Bruno, Cornaggia, and Cornaggia 2016).

It shouldn't come as a surprise, then, that the issuer-pays agencies failed to predict the financial crisis in 2008. Fitch, Moody's, and S&P didn't downgrade Bear Stearns until a few days before it collapsed, and they were still rating Lehman Brothers as investment grade on the day it went bankrupt. Egan-Jones was months ahead on both counts. Rapid Ratings, another subscriber-pays agency, had started downgrading homebuilders as early as 2006 (Shorter and Seitzinger 2009).

So far, the research had been telling a David and Goliath story. The subscriber-pays agencies were tiny compared to the Big Three. So, in the wake of the financial crisis, Jiang, Stanford, and Xie (2012) thought it would be more convincing to compare S&P and Moody's between 1971 and 1974, when S&P was still charging investors and Moody's had started charging issuers. They found that Moody's ratings were significantly higher. After 1974, however, when S&P started charging issuers, the difference disappeared. S&P raised its ratings to Moody's level. Finally, economists had clear evidence that undisciplined markets were driving the agencies to inflate ratings and hide risk from investors – precisely the behavior they were created to prevent.

Faced with all this evidence, you might wonder why investors still rely on the Big Three to monitor their investments for them. Why not do the work themselves? The question practically answers itself. Monitoring is hard work. Investors can't afford to spend all day investigating every potential investment. It's more efficient to delegate the job. It would be better if they didn't have to rely on the issuer-pays model, but as we saw earlier, the subscriber-pays model isn't very lucrative. The Big Three can afford to pay large staffs to issue far more ratings, and they have the brand-name recognition to out-market and out-lobby smaller competitors. That's why, eight years after the financial crisis, they're bigger than ever (Martin 2016).

The solution is now obvious. Policy makers must discipline this market by removing the conflict of interest, but they must do so in a way that the agencies can earn enough revenue to rate all large firms and securities on a regularly updated basis. Ideally, an independent government agency would pool investors to overcome the coordination problem, perhaps by charging a fee as a percent of each investment. If this is not feasible, the government should randomly assign a rating agency to each investment with a pre-negotiated fee, so the issuer has less power to shop for the highest rating and reward the most favorable agency with a higher payment.

Unfortunately, this arrangement only benefits investors if the rating agencies have an informational advantage that's worth paying for. In the corporate bond market, the agencies had deep expertise and a long historical record to inform their analyses. When they ventured into structured finance, however, this advantage disappeared. Private-label mortgage-backed securities and collateralized debt obligations were new. They didn't have a track record that rating agencies could use to predict future defaults. They were so innovative that most analysts didn't even understand them completely. Retrospective accounts have discovered, for example, that they didn't account for the correlation between different tranches within the same security (Lewis 2010). Nor did they account for the *timing* of default. The tranches were designed to default one at a time. The "safest" tranche wouldn't default unless all the others had defaulted, basically an economic catastrophe. But this is a very bad time to default – if the economy is in a catastrophe, investors can't afford another loss – so the "safest" tranche wasn't safe at all! It was an "economic catastrophe bond," as Coval, Jurek, and Stafford (2009) named it, and that meant it should have paid investors four to five times more to compensate them for the risk.

The lack of a track record of performance for new financial products and strategies places ratings agencies in a position where their best guess about the risks posed by the new instruments is nothing more than that, a guess. Without past performance, the agencies must rely exclusively on theoretical constructs and analyst intuition. Given that there is no way to create historical data for something that has no history, there is no practical workaround that can result in a high-quality rating. This suggests that the best solution may be for the ratings agencies to simply throw up their hands in those circumstances in which there is no track record and acknowledge that any rating is likely to have much lower precision than a comparable rating for an established product. In the extreme, the ratings agency might limit its analysis only to "ratings eligible" products, where the definition of "ratings eligible" could be established by a government agency or an independent review board. Future research could be helpful for identifying principles and parameters that could be used in defining ratings-eligible thresholds.

Rating agencies are useful. They may even be necessary for a deep, liquid financial market. They are not, however, a panacea for predatory financial behavior for the simple reason that Myers and Majluf elucidated three decades ago: They don't have inside information. The managers who run the firms – and the boards who hire them – will always have better information about the riskiness of the investments they're issuing. That's why the next part of our story is about corporate governance.

13.3 STEP TWO: FOOL THE BOARD OF DIRECTORS

When the new management opened the company's books, they found that Jay Gould had left the Erie Railroad insolvent. They announced that Gould's accounts "were exercises in fiction." The stock price plummeted, making even more money for Gould, who had shorted the stock in anticipation of this discovery. They sued him, but they didn't have the cash to fight a long court battle – and Gould knew it. He made them an offer, and they took it. He got to keep almost his entire loot. A few years later, the Erie filed for bankruptcy (Renehan 2005).

Gould knew that the money he could extract from the Erie Railroad was worth more than the value he could create with it. Put another way, taking out a dollar today was a better bet than investing that dollar in the company and taking it out tomorrow. Akerlof and Romer (1993) crystallized this logic in a now-classic paper. They called it "bankruptcy for profit," or more succinctly, "looting."

Akerlof and Romer had witnessed several "crises" in the 1980s that seemed to defy the Econ 101 story of market discipline. These episodes, we now know, were all warnings for the much bigger global crisis that would strike two decades later. In each case, Akerlof and Romer showed that market participants were acting so recklessly that they couldn't possibly have been trying to make a profit in the long run. They weren't just taking big risks. *They were actively choosing not to do their job.*

Their findings came with a sour whiff of irony. Like characters in an O. Henry story, investors had pursued many of these financial products largely in order to avoid a very similar outcome. Junk bonds and takeovers were solutions to the so-called principal-agent conflict. Shareholders, the *principals*, hire managers, the *agents*, to run the companies they own. Managers, being self-interested, want to maximize their *own* profits. Shareholders must figure out a way to get the managers to maximize the *firm's* profits. In the 1980s, financiers led by Michael Milken at Drexel Burnham Lambert thought they had found one such way. They issued bonds and used the proceeds to take control away from underperforming managers. What investors didn't know, however, was that Milken was pushing up the price of junk bonds with a cabal of fellow bankers, like Jay Gould in the run-up to Black Friday, misleading many of them into firms that couldn't be saved – and that would default in large numbers (Akerlof and Romer 1993; Alcaly 1994).

How was it that, more than a century after the machinations of Jay Gould, investors still hadn't figured out how to discipline these looting bankers?

In Gould's day, they didn't stand a chance. Most corporations were controlled by only a few men. Gould and his cronies, for example, owned the majority of shares in the Erie Railroad. Gould himself was the largest shareholder. It wasn't until his partner in crime, James Fisk, died suddenly that the board of directors was able to wrest control away from him (Renehan 2005). Today, such concentration of ownership is virtually unheard of.

The Erie Railroad wasn't an isolated case. The Vanderbilt family owned the majority of the New York Central Railway. Andrew Carnegie owned the majority of the Carnegie Steel Corporation. The Guggenheims owned the majority of the American Smelting and Refining Company. John D. Rockefeller, along with his brother and brother-in-law, owned exactly half of the Standard Oil Company. Three of his close partners owned another 40 percent. In such an environment, there was no principal-agent conflict. The principal (owner) *was* the agent (manager).

The separation began around the turn of the century. Antitrust policy broke up Standard Oil and other trusts into multiple smaller companies. The big family shareholders sold their majority blocks. According to Becht and DeLong (2005), they wanted to diversify their holdings as a sensible hedge against idiosyncratic risk. The Glass-Steagall Act separated the big banks into independent entities for commercial banking, investment banking, and insurance. By the 1930s, the United States had made the transition from "financial capitalism," with corporations run by a few large investors, to "managerial capitalism," with a professional management class elected by diffuse shareholders.

Adolf Berle and Gardiner Means were the first to warn about the dangers of this separation in their classic book *The Modern Corporation and Private Property*. In the initial decades after its publication in 1932, they needn't have worried. The countervailing forces against executive malfeasance were strong. Regulations limited risky behavior. Labor unions pushed back against outsized profits and bonuses. And even if managers could get away with looting, high tax rates gave them less incentive to seek high rents.

One by one, those protections fell away. The Carter and Reagan administrations initiated sweeping deregulatory reform. The Federal Reserve punished high wage settlements with disinflation and high unemployment. The White House broke the air traffic controllers' union. Congress cut taxes on the rich (Orlando 2013). And for the first time in its history, the New York Stock Exchange, bowing to the same demand for financial capital that was transforming the rating agencies, allowed investment banks to sell shares in their ownership to the public (Morrison and Wilhelm 2008). The principal-agent conflict was back, and it was bigger than ever.

Enter Michael Milken.

Many economists hailed the "junk bond king" for bringing much-needed market discipline to bear on corporate managers. Most famously, Jensen (1986) argued that fixed debt payments forced managers to pay out extra cash, rather than spend it on low-yield projects or other "inefficiencies." More generally, Jensen and Meckling (1976) contended in their classic paper that managers had more incentive to divert profits into their own pockets if they had less of an ownership stake in the firm. This argument was the one that stuck long after the junk bond king went to jail. Starting in the 1980s and continuing to today, firms have increasingly compensated their executives with stock options so that their fortunes were tied to that of their shareholders (Holmström and Kaplan 2001).

What Jensen – and the boards of directors who followed his advice – failed to realize was that *this solution had been tried before*. The robber barons of the nineteenth century owned bigger shares in their companies than today's executives could ever dream of, yet they still managed to walk away with their investors' money. Sure enough, that's exactly what Milken and his cronies did. They borrowed from banks and took deposits from thrifts, they used the money to buy risky companies, they paid themselves handsomely, they hid the initial defaults by issuing more debt, and then when they couldn't hide them anymore, they left all the losses on the doorstep of the banks and the taxpayers who bailed out the thrifts. This was the key insight of Akerlof and Romer: Turning managers into owners didn't necessarily solve the problem – because they still had an incentive to take advantage of creditors and depositors!

The opportunities for looting don't end there. Boyd and Hakenes (2014) show that "owner-managers" (like Jay Gould) and "outside owners" (like the rest of us) are really two different classes of stakeholders, and only the ones on the inside can do the looting. Even an executive who receives all his compensation in stock options has an incentive to exercise them early and leave the other shareholders with the eventual losses. Case in point: In the years before the housing bubble crashed, the top five executives cashed in $1 billion at Lehman Brothers and $1.4 billion at Bear Stearns (Bebchuk, Cohen, and Spamann 2009). Gould would have been proud.

When Lehman and Bear met their grisly end, outside owners were clearly caught unaware. They quickly discovered that every checkpoint that was supposed to protect them – checkpoints that were hidden from their view but they assumed were there – had failed. Executives had built sprawling empires that were too big and complicated to manage (Dash and Creswell 2008). Risk managers had relied on one very imperfect number – known as "Value at Risk," or "VaR" – to measure risks it couldn't possibly predict. Traders had ignored the possibility of unprecedented catastrophic events, known as "black swans" (Nocera 2009). Boards of directors were in a similar disadvantaged outsider position. In order to ferret out the schemes devised by unscrupulous owners and managers, a board would have to conduct ongoing, full-fledged audits of every aspect of these large institutions. Such audits would have to delve into considerable accounting and risk-management minutiae, and would require a large inspection team, not a group of experts only able to devote part-time attention to the company. Such an expectation was (and remains) impractical and never likely to completely eliminate the possibility of looting (Berman 2008).

On balance, the system was practically designed to lose money. And why wouldn't it be? The whole governance arrangement was premised on short-term profits at the expense of long-term solvency. Nocera (2009) got it right when he said, "At the height of the bubble, there was so much money to be made that any firm that pulled back because it was nervous about risk would forsake huge short-term gains and lose out to less cautious rivals. The fact that VaR didn't measure the possibility of an extreme event was a blessing to the executives. It made black swans all the easier to ignore. All the incentives – profits, compensation, glory, even job security – went in the direction of taking on more and more risk, even if you half suspected it would end badly." Is there any doubt that the outcome would have been different if the managing directors couldn't cash out until they retired? Would Chuck Prince and John Theil and Ken Lewis have given free rein to divisions worth tens of billions of dollars if their life savings were on the line? Of course not. They would have been cautious. They would have asked questions. *They would have done their job* – and so would everyone else.

This solution too is now obvious. Bankers need to have a bigger stake in the success *and failure* of their enterprises. Stock options expose them to the upside, but not the downside – and they're too easy to cash out before the market realizes the true value of the stock. That's why Bebchuk (2010) advocates "grant-based limitations" that require executives to hold their equity for a fixed number of years, along with provisions that allow firms to adjust the grants downward if the profits are subsequently wiped out and "anti-hedging requirements" so they can't offset the limitations with side bets.

But these rules only solve the principal-agent conflict. They don't solve the looting problem. To do that, owning equity isn't enough. Owner-managers still have an incentive to extract high salaries and perks in the short run and leave creditors and depositors with the losses in the long run – unless they are personally liable for those losses. The market has proven that it cannot discipline looters. The judicial system must fill the void.

First, investment banks should return to a partnership form – or if that is too restrictive for them to raise sufficient capital, they should adopt "covenant banking" where they agree to be personally liable for part of the bank's debts (Hill and Painter 2015). Second, intentional looting is a crime against society, not just creditors and shareholders. The white-collar crime division at the Department of Justice should be fully funded to make criminal liability a real threat for these banks' willful neglect of their fiduciary responsibility.

For too long, we have left boards of directors and shareholders to govern corporations, but they, like rating agencies, do not have inside information. Even if they do manage to catch looters in the act, it is usually too late – and too costly – to claw back the loot. Undisciplined markets favor the insiders, especially the wealthy ones. That is one reason why it has been so difficult to prosecute alleged fraud in the wake of the recent financial crisis. Making executives liable is an important step, but it still places the burden on the accusers to prove their case. On this turf, outside investors have always struggled to compete with the Jay Goulds of the world.

If we really want to stop looting, we can't simply attempt to punish it after the fact. We have to prevent it before it happens. It is there, in the trenches, that we find the third and final act of our story.

13.4 STEP THREE: FOOL THE CUSTOMERS

It's easy to forget, in all this talk of villains and violations, that there are heroes in finance. The age of Jay Gould was also the age of John Creswell. The age of Mike Milken was also the age of Ron Grzywinski. If you haven't heard these names before, you're not alone. They never became as famous as their wealthier contemporaries. They were on a different mission. Where Gould and Milken chose to exploit their customers, Creswell and Grzywinski sought to empower them.

The market has never done a very good job at providing financial services for everyone. Stiglitz and Weiss (1981) taught us why. Their classic paper showed that banks might not lend to risky borrowers, even if they can earn a higher interest rate. Much like health insurance companies that cherry-pick healthy patients, banks face an "adverse selection" problem. When they can't differentiate between borrowers, they can only charge one interest rate. Safe borrowers won't pay a high rate because they'd have to give away too much of their profit. Only risky borrowers will pay because they're not likely to make a profit anyway, so why not take the gamble? Banks can get rid of some of these risky borrowers by *rationing* credit. They can charge a low rate and only offer enough loans to satisfy a fraction of the borrowers. This way, at least the safe borrowers will balance out the risky ones, whereas a higher rate would have attracted only risky borrowers. If the banks *can* differentiate between borrowers, they will give the loans to the safe borrowers, and the risky borrowers will be shut out completely.

When financial markets first developed, this was exactly what happened. The average American in the nineteenth century didn't have a checking account. They couldn't get a mortgage. "The poor and the middle class ... put their savings under their mattresses," writes Baradaran (2015), "and, should they need credit, were left to the mercy of loan sharks." Banks wouldn't go near them.

Into this void stepped John Creswell.

As postmaster general in 1871, Creswell recognized the U.S. Postal Service was in a unique position to serve the "unbanked." Its post offices reached more communities than any other institution on the continent. He proposed that it open savings banks. For nearly 40 years, the banking lobby beat back repeated proposals in Congress to create postal savings banks. Only in 1910, after multiple financial panics, did President William Howard Taft sign them into law. Within three years, they had attracted $33 million in deposits with "virtually no bank withdrawals" from the private sector. Clearly, there was pent-up demand for banking services.

The market had tried to fill this void on its own. In 1909, Massachusetts created credit unions to pool the resources of the community for local borrowing and lending. Building and loan associations, or "thrifts," had had some success financing homeownership with this model in the nineteenth century. These models overcame the rationing problem by eliminating the information asymmetry. The lenders knew the borrowers personally. They knew who would pay them back, and they could hold them to it. But such a system only worked for small loans and steady deposits, both of which could be monitored and predicted easily, and that meant they couldn't make big profits. Compared to commercial banks, credit unions and thrifts were small but safe.

It was not enough. Without a coordinating authority, cooperative institutions are difficult to forge and doubly difficult to maintain. Most communities couldn't pull it off. Postal savings banks, meanwhile, only accepted deposits. They never lent. And so, the void remained.

Absent better options, many people turned to nontraditional lenders. Loan sharks overcame the rationing problem by eliminating the risk altogether. They didn't care if borrowers eventually defaulted, as long as they could string them along, renewing the loan over and over, collecting more and more fees and interest every time, until the borrower was ruined. Pawnshops played a similar game, but instead of relying on fees and interest, they used collateral. The family treasures the borrower gave them were worth so much more than the loan that they came out ahead either way (Baradaran 2015).

Not all nontraditional lenders were crooks. Many of them honestly believed that borrowers would eventually pay them back if they just kept renewing the loan. Most banks and thrifts, for example, issued short-term loans that weren't amortized – borrowers didn't have to pay off the principal in regular increments throughout the term of the loan – so they were left with a big "balloon payment" at the end that they usually couldn't afford without taking out a new loan. Like the pawnshops, though, the banks and thrifts typically gave loans worth much less than the value of the property. In the case of default, they figured, they could sell the property and still make a profit since the market kept going up (Snowden 2010). That's the trouble with high-risk loans. They're designed to ride the wave, not to weather the tsunami.

Loan failures were at the heart of the Great Depression. Bernanke (1983) famously showed that credit rationing happened as Stiglitz and Weiss had predicted and, crucially, that it had significant negative effects on the real economy. In their wisdom, the architects of the New Deal recognized that this market could not discipline itself. They outlawed nontraditional loans like adjustable-rate mortgages and they subsidized safer features like 30-year terms. They restricted banks from opening branches in multiple states to keep each bank dedicated to its local community. They combined savings banks and thrifts into federal "savings and loans," and they subsidized them along with federal credit unions (Baradaran 2015). In the decades that followed, these new lenders multiplied and spread across the country. The 30-year, fixed-rate mortgage became the dominant product in a uniquely American housing system. Homeownership reached unprecedented heights. And the economy went through a longer stretch than ever before (or since) without a single major banking crisis (Orlando 2013).

Around the time rating agencies changed their business model and anti-looting forces lost their power, these lending protections too began to erode. Credit unions merged and abandoned the community ownership model. Deregulation allowed banks and thrifts to offer risky new products, including adjustable-rate mortgages. Upper- and middle-income white residents moved out of the inner cities, and banks followed them, leaving concentrated pockets of deep poverty with no access to the credit they'd need to escape their misfortune. Banks closed branches in poorer communities and opened more in richer ones. Even postal savings banks closed their doors, ending a successful 56-year experiment.

One of the few bankers who fought back against this onslaught was Ron Grzywinski.

When almost all the banks moved out of the South Side of Chicago, Grzywinski moved in. Along with his colleagues Milton Davis, James Fletcher, and Mary Houghton, Grzywinski purchased the South Shore Bank and invested in community development without concern for immediate profit. It took 10 years for the bank to get out of the red and into the black with its low-income clients and their small bank accounts, but they stuck it out and eventually branched out into low-income communities across the country (Baradaran 2015).

Legislators tried to encourage more banks to act like South Shore. They passed the Community Reinvestment Act (CRA) in 1977 to rate banks on how well they were serving low-income communities, but they stopped short of subsidizing or otherwise providing these services through the government. Regulators could only use the ratings as leverage when approving mergers or other requests. Avery, Bostic, and Canner (2000) analyzed the largest survey ever conducted on CRA activity and found that this threat was effective. A majority of banks issued loans that they would not have otherwise lent. Encouragingly, "the vast majority" were profitable. This isn't surprising. Stiglitz and Weiss taught us that credit rationing shuts many creditworthy borrowers out of the market along with the risky ones. The CRA brought some of them back in. Unfortunately, they were a very, very small fraction of the banks' business.

And so, the void reappeared.

This is where looters thrive. They prey on desperation. "Rather than looking for business partners who will honor their contracts," say Akerlof and Romer, "the looters look for partners who will sign contracts that appear to have high current value if fulfilled but that will not – and could not – be honored." Many of these looters found their way into thrifts in the 1980s and found deals like Mike Milken's that wouldn't be honored in the end. Then, when they failed – with many of them explicitly shut down for fraud – they reopened under a new name as unregulated non-depository lenders issuing subprime mortgages. Two decades later, some of these failed thrift looters were the biggest subprime lenders in the biggest housing bubble in world history. Investigations have revealed how they "brainwashed" salesmen, forged documents, and targeted the most vulnerable, least financially savvy borrowers (Hudson 2010).

These nonbank lenders weren't covered by the CRA. The vast majority of subprime loans issued in the 2000s were outside the CRA's jurisdiction. So it's no surprise that

CRA loans have performed better than comparable non-CRA loans in the wake of the crash (Orlando 2011). Their displacement was at the heart of the bubble.

Some states tried to resist this trend. Illinois, for example, tested a new anti-predatory lending program that required risky borrowers in the City of Chicago to consult with financial counselors certified by the U.S. Department of Housing and Urban Development before agreeing to a loan. The experiment only lasted for a few months, but it had a significant effect. Agarwal, Amromin, Ben-David, Chomsisengphet, and Evanoff (2014) show that fewer risky loans were issued and fewer risky borrowers got loans – and as a result, the loans in these neighborhoods were significantly less likely to default. Similarly, Brown (2016) shows that first-time homebuyers in Tennessee were 42 percent less likely to experience foreclosure if they were required to attend home-buyer education classes. Unfortunately, we don't have many other experiments to learn from. Federal regulators stamped out most state regulations targeting predatory lending (Orlando 2013). One shining exception comes from the Federal Reserve Bank of Philadelphia. It conducted a five-year experiment with first-time homebuyers and found that a two-hour counseling session led to significantly higher credit scores and lower delinquency rates over time (Smith, Hochberg, and Greene 2014).

The design of these programs is crucial. We know from history that blunt instruments like usury laws can wind up pushing borrowers out of the regulated banking system and into riskier nontraditional lending – or simply leave them without access to credit at all. For many borrowers, nontraditional loans may even be beneficial if the terms aren't too onerous and the borrowers understand them. Acolin, Bostic, An, and Wachter (2017) show that nontraditional mort-gages *did* increase the homeownership rate in most communities during the recent housing boom. Unfortunately, these mortgages also exacerbated the bust, but after the dust settled, they still were associated with an increase in home-owners overall. Clearly, there were many creditworthy borrowers who weren't getting loans in the traditional system. Imagine how much more beneficial this infusion of credit could have been if it had gone from reputable lenders to knowledgeable borrowers!

Since the crisis, regulators have restricted these loans. The Dodd-Frank Act created "qualified mortgage" standards, and the Consumer Financial Protection Bureau has been investigating various questionable practices. Still, nontraditional loans have not gone away. Earlier this year, a CNN headline reported, "Unpaid subprime car loans hit [a] 20-year high" (Egan 2016). A few months later, the *Wall Street Journal* and the *Washington Post* reported that homebuyers were increasingly sending mortgage payments directly to the seller, rather than an actual lender, an expensive and shady practice known as "contract for deed." This practice was often used in place of mortgages in the Jim Crow era to prevent blacks from owning their homes (Badger 2016; Hong 2016). Meanwhile, nonbank lenders are making a come-back, taking 20 percent of the market away from commercial banks since the start of the recession (Grind 2016).

Cut off from the regulated banking system, borrowers are once again finding ways to fill the void.

This solution, like the others, is obvious when cast in this light. Credit rationing is real and pervasive. We cannot simply ban the products that caused the most problems in the past. We must also give borrowers access to safe loans, or unscrupulous lenders will find new and innovative ways to skirt the law so borrowers can take a gamble on a better life for themselves and their families.

Anti-predatory programs should not be blunt instruments. They should counsel first-time homebuyers to make sensible decisions, and they should be available throughout the nation. The Department of Housing and Urban Development should be fully funded to take the lead in advising the next generation of homeowners before they sign the deed.

Financial literacy should begin long before families find themselves faced with difficult choices. Many borrowers may be able to avoid payday lenders and other "fringe" banking if they know how to manage their money in the years prior. Many more might be able to find checking accounts that don't cost 10 percent of their income and build a valuable credit history to dig their way out of poverty if they have a stronger economic education. We should encourage our high schools to teach these skills. We should offer classes throughout low-income communities for parents to learn how to pass these lessons on to their children. Critics have argued that financial education is a waste of money – or worse, a distraction from the real problems (see, e.g., Willis 2011) – but history has shown that no amount of regulation can prevent every abuse or anticipate every crisis. A good, fair society must arm its citizens with the knowledge to protect themselves. Not every program has worked, but the ones that have, a few of which we've highlighted here, should inspire us to keep experimenting and educating.

Finally, we should create more lending outlets that serve the unmet needs of our population. We should charter more credit unions and savings banks. We should increase enforcement of the CRA, and we should subsidize banks that lend to creditworthy low-income borrowers. Absent government support, history has shown that community banks cannot achieve the scale necessary to maintain their support of communities in need, a lesson we learned when Ron Grzywinski's great experiment failed in the Great Recession (Yerak 2010). We should reopen postal savings banks, and we should lend to developers who build affordable housing. For too long, we have treated these neighborhoods as wards that need to be protected – or worse, lost causes that are better forgotten – when the best strategy would have been a *positive* one of empowerment and enterprise. Let us invest. Let us innovate. Let us be heroes.

13.5 CONCLUSION

Our favorite story about Jay Gould comes from a youthful trip to New York City – his first adventure, in fact, outside his childhood hometown. His uncle had given him an ornate box to take into the city. Inside the box was a mousetrap that he was supposed to sell at the market. He and his buddy were walking down the street, when a mugger grabbed the box out of his hand and took off. The boys gave chase and caught up with the man, only to realize that he towered over them. They tried to run from the fight, but it was too late. Gould would have gotten away, but his finger got caught in a buttonhole on the man's shirt. The cops found them and took them to the courthouse, where the mugger told the judge that the box belonged to *him* – and Gould and his friend were trying to steal it from him! Gould said if it's really his box, could he tell the judge what's inside it? The mugger guessed wrong, of course, and Gould told the judge it was a mousetrap. When they opened it, the mugger was aghast that he had taken such a great risk for such a cheap reward. The judge sent the man to prison and remarked that surely this was the largest rat ever caught by a mousetrap in New York City (Renehan 2005).

The moral of the story is that looters are taking a dangerous risk, especially if they don't understand what they're trying to loot.

Borrowers, lenders, and investors periodically learn this lesson when a new wave of financial innovation washes onto our shores. Financial innovation is to economic growth as water is to physical growth: necessary, even catalytic, but dangerous if it we get too much too fast. In the latest cycle of innovations, rating agencies didn't know how to rate them, executives didn't know how to manage them, and borrowers didn't know how to use them. The products were untested. The infrastructure was unprepared. Yet we forged ahead as if nothing had changed.

We must learn to adapt better. We will never be able to anticipate every market move before it happens, but we can design public policies that guide the market toward a more sustainable path and correct swiftly when it deviates from the path. We can – and we should – discipline the market.

The chapters in this book are a welcome step in this direction. Matthew Desmond, for example, shows how markets fail to provide high-quality neighborhood amenities in low-income neighborhoods – and raises important questions about how public policy can address this failure. Patricia McCoy and Susan Wachter show how mortgage lenders have exacerbated, rather than tamed, boom-and-bust cycles – and offer solutions to temper their excesses. We hope that this chapter adds to their valuable work in starting a conversation about market failures and policy solutions.

Specifically, we have shown three ways in which markets did not discipline themselves in the run-up to the Great Recession. First, investors put their faith in risky securities and risky firms, and rating agencies blessed their investments as safe and sound by historical standards. Second, executives allowed lenders and traders to make large, risky bets, and boards of directors and shareholders did not question or stop them. Third, nontraditional lenders issued mortgages that weren't accurately priced and couldn't be repaid, and banks followed them over the cliff in the rush to maintain market share. None of these failures are consistent with the story of the "invisible hand" that we tell in Econ 101, where markets coordinate themselves to an efficient equilibrium as if by magic.

Rather, markets fail, and a large literature in financial economics has taught us why. Asymmetric information, principal-agent conflict, looting, and credit rationing all plague our economy. When any of these forces are present, markets will not discipline themselves. When all of them are present at once, the result can be catastrophic.

For all the lessons we have learned from these failures, we still do not know how to deal with the risk of catastrophe. It happens so rarely – and each time in such a different guise – that it is nearly impossible for us to formulate an optimal measure of prevention or response. With each experience, however, we get a little closer. The latest boom-and-bust has pointed to the importance of removing the conflict of interest from rating agencies, giving executives a greater share in the downside risk of their companies, and making safe borrowing options available to all Americans with the requisite education to choose appropriately. Even with these precautions, though, we cannot know what the next wave will bring or what any of these parties should do with the new innovations when they come, let alone the catastrophic risk that they inevitably carry with them.

So we close with humility. John Kenneth Galbraith used to say that memory was a far stronger safeguard than law. Let us hope, then, that the memory of this crisis stays with us long after the next wave has come and gone, for our laws are never perfect, but our innovative spirit perseveres. That is why we have told this story: to keep the memories alive and to learn from them. Someday, someone else will write a new story, and they will pick up where we have left off, and they will judge whether we did indeed learn from the past – or whether we wound up holding a mousetrap that we mistook for a treasure.

REFERENCES

Acolin, Arthur, Xudong An, Raphael W. Bostic, and Susan M. Wachter. 2017. "Homeownership and Nontraditional and Subprime Mortgages." *Housing Policy Debate* 27: 393–418.

Agarwal, Sumit, Gene Amromin, Itzhak Ben-David, Souphala Chomsisengphet, and Douglas D. Evanoff. 2014. "Predatory Lending and the Subprime Crisis." *Journal of Financial Economics* 113(1): 29–52.

Akerlof, George A. and Paul M. Romer. 1993. "Looting: The Economic Underworld of Bankruptcy for Profit." *Brookings Papers on Economic Activity* 24(2): 1–74.

Alcaly, Roger E. 1994. "The Golden Age of Junk." *New York Review of Books*. May 26.

Avery, Robert B., Raphael W. Bostic, and Glenn B. Canner. 2005. "Assessing the Necessity and Efficiency of the Community Reinvestment Act." *Housing Policy Debate* 16(1): 143–72.

2000. "CRA Special Lending." *Federal Reserve Bulletin* 86(November): 711–31.

Badger, Emily. 2016. "Why a Housing Scheme Founded in Racism Is Making a Resurgence Today." *Washington Post.* May 13. www.washingtonpost.com /news/wonk/wp/2016/05/13/why-a-housing-scheme-founded-in-racism-is-mak ing-a-resurgence-today/.

Baradaran, Mehrsa. 2015. *How the Other Half Banks: Exclusion, Exploitation, and the Threat to Democracy.* Cambridge, MA: Harvard University Press.

Beaver, William H., Catherine Shakespeare, and Mark T. Soliman. 2006. "Differential Properties in the Ratings of Certified Versus Non-certified Bond-Rating Agencies." *Journal of Accounting and Economics* 42(3): 303–34.

Bebchuk, Lucian A. 2010. "How to Fix Bankers' Pay." *Daedalus* 139(4): 52–60.

Bebchuk, Lucian A., Alma Cohen, and Holger Spamann. 2009. "The Wages of Failure: Executive Compensation at Bear Stearns and Lehman 2000–2008." *Yale Journal on Regulation* 27(2): 257–82.

Becht, Marco and J. Bradford DeLong. 2005. "Why Has There Been So Little Block Holding in America?" In *A History of Corporate Governance Around the World: Family Business Groups to Professional Managers,* Randall K. Morck, ed. Chicago: University of Chicago Press.

Berman, Dennis K. 2008. "Where Was Lehman's Board?" *Wall Street Journal.* September 15. http://blogs.wsj.com/deals/2008/09/15/where-was-lehmans -board/tab/article/.

Bernanke, Ben S. 1983. "Nonmonetary Effects of the Financial Crisis in the Propagation of the Great Depression." *American Economic Review* 73(3): 257–76.

Boyd, John H. and Hendrik Hakenes. 2014. "Looting and Risk Shifting in Banking Crises." *Journal of Economic Theory* 149: 43–64.

Brown, Scott R. 2016. "The Influence of Homebuyer Education on Default and Foreclosure Risk: A Natural Experiment." *Journal of Policy Analysis and Management* 35(1): 145–72.

Bruno, Valentina, Jess Cornaggia, and Kimberly J. Cornaggia. 2016. "Does Regulatory Certification Affect the Information Content of Credit Ratings?" *Management Science* 62(6): 1578–97.

Coval, Joshua, Jakub W. Jurek, and Erik Stafford. 2009. "Economic Catastrophe Bonds." *American Economic Review* 99(3): 628–66.

Dash, Eric and Julie Creswell. 2008. "Citigroup Saw No Red Flags Even as It Made Bolder Bets." *New York Times.* November 22. www.nytimes.com/2008/11/23 /business/23citi.html.

Egan, Matt. 2016. "Unpaid Subprime Car Loans Hit 20-Year High." *CNN.* March 15. http://money.cnn.com/2016/03/15/investing/subprime-unpaid-auto-loans -oil-crash/.

Egan-Jones Rating Company. 2002. Letter to Jonathan G. Katz, Secretary of the United States Securities and Exchange Commission. www.sec.gov/news/extra /credrate/eganjones2.htm.

Grind, Kirsten. 2016. "Private Lenders Remodel the Mortgage Market." *Wall Street Journal.* May 11. www.wsj.com/articles/private-lenders-remodel-the-mortgage -market-1462984898.

Holmström, Bengt and Steven N. Kaplan. 2001. "Corporate Governance and Merger Activity in the United States: Making Sense of the 1980s and 1990s." *Journal of Economic Perspectives* 15(2): 121–44.

Hudson, Michael W. 2010. *The Monster: How a Gang of Predatory Lenders and Wall Street Bankers Fleeced America – and Spawned a Global Crisis*. New York: Times Books.

Jensen, Michael C. 1986. "Agency Cost of Free Cash Flow, Corporate Finance, and Takeovers." *American Economic Review* 76(2): 323–29.

Jensen, Michael C. and William H. Meckling. 1976. "Theory of the Firm: Managerial Behavior, Agency Costs, and Ownership Structure." *Journal of Financial Economics* 3(4): 305–60.

Jiang, John (Xuefeng), Mary Harris Stanford, and Yuan Xie. 2012. "Does It Matter Who Pays for Bond Ratings? Historical Evidence." *Journal of Financial Economics* 105(3): 607–21.

Johnson, Richard. 2003. "An Examination of Rating Agencies' Actions Around the Investment-Grade Boundary." Federal Reserve Bank of Kansas City, Research Division, RWP 03–01. www.kansascityfed.org/PUBLICAT/RESWKPAP/pdf/rwp03-01.pdf.

Hill, Claire A. and Richard W. Painter. 2015. *Better Bankers, Better Banks: Promoting Good Business Through Contractual Commitment*. Chicago: University of Chicago Press.

Hong, Nicole. 2016. "New York Banking Regulator Investigates 'Seller-Financed' Home Sales." *Wall Street Journal*. May 16. www.wsj.com/articles/new-york-banking-regulator-investigates-seller-financed-home-sales-1463418972.

Knowlton, Brian and Michael M. Grynbaum. 2008. "Greenspan 'Shocked' That Free Markets Are Flawed." *New York Times*. October 23. www.nytimes.com/2008/10/23/business/worldbusiness/23iht-gspan.4.17206624.html.

Lewis, Michael. 2010. *The Big Short: Inside the Doomsday Machine*. New York: W. W. Norton & Company.

Madison, James H. 1974. "The Evolution of Commercial Credit Rating Agencies in Nineteenth-Century America." *Business History Review* 48(2): 164–86.

Martin, Timothy W. 2016. "What Crisis? Big Ratings Firms Stronger Than Ever." *Wall Street Journal*. March 11. www.wsj.com/articles/what-crisis-big-ratings-firms-stronger-than-ever-1457655084.

Mixon, Scott. 2008. "The Crisis of 1873: Perspectives from Multiple Asset Classes." *Journal of Economic History* 68(3): 722–57.

Morrison, Alan D. and William J. Wilhelm, Jr. 2008. "The Demise of Investment Banking Partnerships: Theory and Evidence." *Journal of Finance* 58(1): 311–50.

Myers, Stewart C. and Nicholas S. Majluf. 1984. "Corporate Financing and Investment Decisions When Firms Have Information That Investors Do Not Have." *Journal of Financial Economics* 13(2): 187–221.

Nocera, Joe. 2009. "Risk Management." *New York Times Magazine*. January 2. www.nytimes.com/2009/01/04/magazine/04risk-t.html.

Orlando, Anthony W. 2013. *Letter to the One Percent*. Raleigh, NC: Lulu Press, Inc.

2011. "Don't Repeal the CRA. Expand It." www.anthonyworlando.com/2011/10/14/dont-repeal-the-cra-expand-it/.

Renehan, Jr., Edward J. 2005. *Dark Genius of Wall Street: The Misunderstood Life of Jay Gould, King of the Robber Barons.* New York: Basic Books.

Shorter, Gary and Michael V. Seitzinger. 2009. "Overview of the Credit Rating Agencies and Their Regulation." Congressional Research Service.

Smith, Marvin M., Daniel Hochberg, and William H. Greene. 2014. "The Effectiveness of Pre-purchase Homeownership Counseling and Financial Management Skills." Federal Reserve Bank of Philadelphia. www.philadelphiafed.org/community-development/homeownership-counseling-study.

Snowden, Kenneth A. 2010. "The Anatomy of a Residential Mortgage Crisis: A Look Back to the 1930s." In *The Panic of 2008: Causes, Consequences and Implications for Reform*, Lawrence E. Mitchell and Arthur E. Wilmarth, Jr., eds. Northampton, MA: Edward Elgar.

Stiglitz, Joseph E. and Andrew Weiss. 1981. "Credit Rationing in Markets with Imperfect Information." *American Economic Review* 71(3): 393–410.

Sylla, Richard. 2001. "A Historical Primer on the Business of Credit Ratings." Prepared for conference, The World Bank.

Voznyuk, Lesyk. 2015. "Genesis of the 'Big Three' Credit Rating Agencies." *Financial History* 112(Winter): 32–35.

White, Lawrence J. 2010. "The Credit Rating Agencies." *Journal of Economic Perspectives* 24(2): 211–26.

Willis, Lauren E. 2011. "The Financial Education Fallacy." *American Economic Review* 101(3): 429–34.

Yerak, Becky. 2010. "Chicago's ShoreBank Fails, Is Bought by Investors." *Chicago Tribune.* August 20. http://articles.chicagotribune.com/2010–08-20/business/ct-biz-0821-shorebank-20100820_1_fdic-assets-david-vitale.